RENEWALS: 691-4574

DATE DUE

DEC 11			
FEB 15			
APR 29			
OCT 11			

Demco, Inc. 38-293

TO MOVE
THE WORLD

TO MOVE THE WORLD

*Louis G. Gregory
and the Advancement
of Racial Unity
in America*

by
GAYLE MORRISON

BAHÁ'Í PUBLISHING TRUST
WILMETTE, ILLINOIS

Copyright © 1982 by the
National Spiritual Assembly of the
Bahá'ís of the United States

Library of Congress Cataloging in Publication Data

Morrison, Gayle.
  To move the world.

  Includes bibliographical references and index.
    1. Gregory, Louis G.   2. Bahaism—United States—
Biography.   3. Afro-Americans—Biography.   4. United
States—Race relations.   I. Title.
BP395.G73M67   297'.89'0924 [B]   81-22763
ISBN 0-87743-171-X   AACR2

Design by John Solarz

10   9   8   7   6   5   4   3   2   1

Printed in the United States of America

To Enoch Olinga

in memory of

"his radiant spirit,
his unwavering faith,
his all-embracing love"

Contents

Part 3 / *A Middle Passage*

Part 4 / *The Era of Racial Unity*

Part 5 / *Culminations*

Illustrations

ix

Foreword

The life of Louis Gregory can be understood only in the context of his commitment to the Bahá'í Faith by which his actions in promoting race unity were impelled. As he himself said, the Bahá'í Faith had given him an "entirely new conception" of religion, and "with it," he wrote, "my whole nature seems changed for the better."

At the outset a new religion needs adherents who can champion its claims, whose lives can reflect its transforming power and thus set the pace and tone by which others might be guided. Being one of the earliest Bahá'ís in America, Louis Gregory, the son of slaves, proved to be not only a luminous example in this sense but also, and more important, an instrument of change. His forty years of unremitting labor in promoting race amity was unprecedented in its scope, generated as it was by a universalism incomprehensible even to the most distinguished of the civil rights activists who were his contemporaries. His was a response to a new voice in which he heard the answer to the ringing plea of his downtrodden race for freedom, a plea such as W. E. B. DuBois had raised in his prayer on behalf of black people during the aftermath of the terrible race riot of 1906 in Atlanta. "Tell us the plan," DuBois prayed in part, "give us the sign; whisper—speak—call, great God, for Thy silence is white terror to our hearts! The way, O God, show us the way and point us the Path!"

Louis Gregory heard the voice of Bahá'u'lláh, the Prophet-Founder of the Bahá'í Faith born in mid-nineteenth century Iran, Who proclaimed the purpose of His revelation to be the establishment of the unity of mankind, the prerequisite by which the Christ-promised peace on earth would in this age be realized. Tortured, imprisoned, and exiled for a period of forty years because of His teachings, Bahá'u'lláh stated in a poignant rationale of His sufferings what must have relieved Mr. Gregory's longing for a solution

to racial injustice: "The Ancient Beauty hath consented to be
bound with chains that mankind may be released from its bondage,
and hath accepted to be made a prisoner within this most mighty
Stronghold that the whole world may attain unto true liberty."

Bearing witness to the existence of an "invisible yet rational"
God, Who expresses His progressive will for mankind through the
successive appearances of His Prophets; upholding as the fundamental purpose of religion the promotion of concord and harmony;
asserting that justice is the "best beloved of all things" in God's
sight; proclaiming the equality of the races and of men and women;
calling for the elimination of all forms of prejudice; advocating
compulsory education, Bahá'u'lláh made the oneness of mankind
the pivotal principle and goal of His religion.

The principle implies all that humanity has been taught in the
past about brotherhood and neighborly love but goes beyond those
concepts to make evident the need, as stated in Shoghi Effendi's
words, for "an organic change in the structure of present-day society, a change such as the world has not yet experienced." It calls
for the reconstruction of the social and political life of the planet,
for the establishment of a federated world. This, it suggests, is the
ultimate fulfillment of the process of integration that has been im-
pelling mankind toward world unity since the dawn of history.
Acting as a welding force, this process, which had its beginning
with the family, the smallest unit in human organization, has
evolved through the successive stages of the tribe, the city-state,
and the nation to arrive now at the threshold of the next triumphant
stage, namely, world unity—the hallmark of the maturity of the
human race.

Regarding it as the "greatest of all means for the establishment
of order in the world," Bahá'u'lláh upheld religion as the primary
source of spiritual unity, the cohesive force in all forms of social
experience. Eschewing the man-made, false distinctions that have
erected barriers between the religions of the past, Bahá'u'lláh
boldly stated that all established religions are divine in origin, that
all the Prophets of God "proclaim the same Faith." He thus declared the unity of all religions, explaining that the difference between their Founders is only "in the intensity of their revelation,
and the comparative potency of their light"—a difference made
necessary by the varying capacity and inclinations of the people

among whom They appear and, therefore, not to be construed as any innate incapacity on the part of any of these Founders. In affirming that religious truth is not absolute but relative and that divine revelation is progressive, Bahá'u'lláh presented a comprehensive view of religions as having identical aims, complementary functions, and continuity of purpose. He propounded the concept of progressive revelation. Hence it is contrary to the unifying spirit of the Bahá'í Faith to belittle the importance of any religion, to attempt to distinguish between the ranks of their Founders, to distort their essential teachings, or to ridicule a person's allegiance to any one of them. It is a mistake, however, to regard the Bahá'í Faith as merely comprising eclectic borrowings from the religions that preceded it; it is rather to be viewed as a complete and new revelation that fulfills the expectations of all previous revelations. Equipped with its own body of sacred scriptures, its new code of laws, its unique system of administration, the Bahá'í Faith has come, according to Bahá'u'lláh's explicit proclamations, to establish the kingdom of God on earth.

It is no wonder, then, that Louis Gregory hailed the Bahá'í Faith as having given him an "entirely new conception of Christianity and of all religion." He had undoubtedly found in the Faith a reconciliation of what heretofore must have appeared to him to be irreconcilable poles of consciousness. DuBois, in his essay "Of Our Spiritual Strivings," supplied the language for the problem, describing it as a "double-consciousness" of the American black living in a "world which yields him no true self-consciousness, but only lets him see himself through the revelation of the other world" —that is, the white world. "One ever feels his twoness—an American, a Negro; two souls, two thoughts, two unreconciled strivings. . . ." This psychological dichotomy, it could be reasoned, was an acute example of Bahá'u'lláh's meaning when He lamented that "No two men can be found who may be said to be outwardly and inwardly united" and commented further that "The evidences of discord and malice are apparent everywhere, though all were made for harmony and union." The resolution of these two opposite states of consciousness obviously lay in the latter clause of Bahá'u'lláh's comment, which became the guideline, the motive power for Mr. Gregory's strivings, as his life story amply illustrates. Bahá'u'lláh's statement made it clear that all men were languishing in a state of unconciliated opposites and that nothing short of the acceptance of the Bahá'í revelation would succeed in settling the world's equilibrium.

Released from the limitations of religious and social orthodoxy, given a new framework within which to estimate the value, purpose, and goal of each race in realizing its dream of world unity, Louis Gregory made himself a channel whose purpose at one and the same time absorbed and transcended the immediate need to end racial injustice in America and went beyond the mere objectives of supportive legislation, which, though vital to the realization of civil rights, is sterile and ultimately unsatisfactory in itself, when divorced from the fundamental, animating principle of the oneness of mankind proclaimed by Bahá'u'lláh. Here Mr. Gregory perceived justice to be the servant of love, that suffusive virtue by which every created thing—particularly man, described by Bahá'u'lláh as the "supreme Talisman"—achieves oneness of purpose and affirms its identity with the Creator of the universe in Whom and by Whom all things move.

"O Son of Man!", Bahá'u'lláh, as the Spokesman of God, thus addresses this primary creature, "Veiled in My immemorial being and in the ancient eternity of My essence, I knew My love for thee; therefore I created thee, have engraved on thee Mine image and revealed to thee My beauty." Reconciled by this God-inspired vision with his true identity, man can experience genuine respect, honor, and a vital sense of unity with all other men. In the bright light of this epiphanous awakening is erased any semblance of a "double-consciousness," of that irreconcilable "twoness" which befuddles and arrests the hopes of America's blacks, conducing to their self-condemnation and their sense of inferiority in the presence of the overwhelming arrogance of the white majority.

Louis Gregory belonged to that age and, in thought, to that company of persons—that "talented tenth"—who conceived the Niagara Movement, which eventually was dissolved in the rise of the National Association for the Advancement of Colored People and the National Urban League. He was an unabashed admirer of W. E. B. DuBois, the guiding spirit of the Niagara Movement, whose fierce articulation of the plight and strivings of blacks is immortalized in such of his brilliant essays as appear under the celebrated title *The Souls of Black Folk*. Mr. Gregory was not only fully conversant but deeply sympathetic with the revolt against racial segregation, which this movement represented at the beginning of the century. Yet it was precisely at the time of its dawning, 1909, that he committed himself to the Bahá'í Faith, also referred to then as a "movement," which was understood to have remote connections to Figures and soul-stirring events in the Middle East and, at that particular moment, to 'Abdu'l-Bahá, a religious prisoner in the Holy Land, Who was the current head of the Faith.

In view of Mr. Gregory's previous agnosticism and somewhat radical allegiance to the cause of Negro rights, this act of commitment on his part to an unfamiliar religion was outwardly incongruous. Yet he was instrumental in demonstrating the Faith's relevance to the civil rights movement and in winning the sympathy of the movement's leaders for the new religion he had embraced by unveiling to them its all-encompassing spirit. Mr. DuBois himself knew much about the Bahá'í Faith and was acquainted with its American leaders; in fact, his wife was a member of the Bahá'í community for some time. In the beginning, Bahá'ís lent substantial moral support to the organizations heading the struggle for black rights. For example, they sponsored banquets in honor of the leadership of the N.A.A.C.P. and the Urban League; even more than that, 'Abdu'l-Bahá, released from a lifetime of imprisonment and exile, spoke at the fourth annual convention of the N.A.A.C.P. in Chicago during His epic journey to North America in 1912. The spiritual link between the two "movements" has remained intact, even if each has taken conspicuously different, albeit complementary, paths on the long, tortuous road toward the establishment of the equality of the races.

It does not diminish the importance of the civil rights movement in America to say that Mr. Gregory's beliefs and actions encompassed its stated goals; for the movement reflects the spirit of change that it is the avowed purpose of the Bahá'í Faith to bring about in human affairs. It was not so much that the path he chose was different in purpose from that embarked upon by the civil rights movement initiated at the beginning of the century by Mr. DuBois and others; it was simply that both he and they had different but indispensable components of the same goal to attain. Neither he nor they could ultimately succeed without the other. The fact is, however, that they were not, and even now are not, prepared to play the

part singled out for Louis Gregory and others who embrace the
Bahá'í teachings—a part, which because of its spiritually dynamic powers of integration, cannot in the end be done without.
For even after every civil right has been legally secured for the
black or any other minority, there will yet remain the elusive goal
of uniting that minority spiritually and socially with all other peoples on the planet. In this light, Mr. Gregory's example remains integral to any effort designed to remove racial barriers.

Mr. DuBois declared that "The problem of the twentieth century is the problem of the color line, the relation of the darker races
of men in Asia and Africa, in America and the islands of the seas."
If the color line is a hindrance to the progress of human relations,
so too are the lines drawn between religions, between nations, between classes of people, between systems of governance; all con-
duce immeasurably to the separation of the children of men. The
problems barring the unity of mankind are clearly more numerous
than racial prejudice, admittedly a dominant phenomenon of
American life, and equally intransigent. Racial prejudice may be
the most challenging issue confronting Americans, but it is just
one of a number of vital issues the irresolution of which blocks the
path to world peace.

Nor is it surprising that, on the basis of its claim to be the new-
born force for welding fragmented humanity into a spiritual and
social whole, the Bahá'í Faith would address itself directly to the
racial problems in America, racism being, as it holds, one of the
"false gods" of the age. "Close your eyes to racial differences,
and welcome all with the light of oneness" is Bahá'u'lláh's em-
phatic and repeated instruction. Furthering this emphasis in His ar-
raignment of the basic evils of American society, 'Abdu'l-Bahá,
the son of Bahá'u'lláh and the appointed interpreter of His teachings, warned of the importance of the union of whites and blacks,
"for if it is not realized," He said, "erelong great difficulties will
arise, and harmful results will follow." And again He warned, "If
this matter remaineth without change, enmity will be increased
day by day, and the final result will be hardship and may end in
bloodshed."

It was this same 'Abdu'l-Bahá Who, with full knowledge of the
racial difficulties confronting America, called Louis Gregory to
the service of race unity by saying to him: "I hope that thou mayest

become . . . the means whereby the white and colored people shall close their eyes to racial differences and behold the reality of humanity, and that is the universal unity which is the oneness of the kingdom of the human race, the basic harmony of the world and the appearance of the bounty of the Almighty." Thus 'Abdu'l-Bahá elevated the resolution of racial problems in the United States to the level of universal principle. In fact, in a speech at Howard University on 23 April 1912, He strongly proposed the achievement of unity between black and white Americans as critical to world peace.

If 'Abdu'l-Bahá urged Louis Gregory to perform a signal service, to set a singular example that would effect to a great extent the unity of the races in the United States, He was also preparing the Bahá'ís of this nation to undertake a world mission having as its primary purpose the unity of mankind as a whole. As it turned out, Louis Gregory's work was the initial stage of a divine scheme to cleanse the nation of its virulent racial prejudice and, in so doing, prepare it to become a paramount instrument in Bahá'u'lláh's global plan for world peace. Exhorting the American Bahá'ís, in partnership with their coreligionists in Canada, to spread the teachings of Bahá'u'lláh to all parts of the world, 'Abdu'l-Bahá aroused them to action by solemnly promising that "The moment this Divine Message is carried forward by the American believers from the shores of America and is propagated through the continents of Europe, of Asia, of Africa and of Australasia, and as far as the islands of the Pacific, this community will find itself securely established upon the throne of an everlasting dominion." The response of the American Bahá'ís, white and black, was to engender a spiritual drama reminiscent of the world-shaking, history-making acts of the apostles of old, who braved every difficulty to spread the teachings of Jesus Christ. As a consequence, in less than a century the Bahá'í Faith has been firmly established in more than three hundred countries and dependencies with adherents from every conceivable ethnic, national, religious, and social background—all committed to the goal of uniting the races of mankind.

Propelled by the staggering prospect held out by 'Abdu'l-Bahá, Louis Gregory never failed to see that his work was a preliminary but indispensable phase of a much wider plan in whose world-transforming processes all races must inevitably be involved in asserting their essential oneness. But here in America, black and white, standing in stark physical contrast to one another, must demonstrate this redeeming unity, set the ultimate example of racial equality, or perish with the rest of mankind. This divine plan, operating upon both races equally, invested them with equal challenges and equal blessings. "Love and unity will be fostered between you," 'Abdu'l-Bahá confidently forecast in His Howard University speech, "thereby bringing about the oneness of mankind. For the accomplishment of unity between the colored and whites will be an assurance of the world's peace."

It was not long after 'Abdu'l-Bahá's death in 1921 that Shoghi Effendi, His chosen successor as head of the Bahá'í Faith, was urging black Americans to take the Bahá'í teachings to Africa and other continents, to join with their fellow white believers in creating the circumstances by which America, in the words of 'Abdu'l-Bahá, would become the "distributing center of spiritual enlightenment, and all the world receive this heavenly blessing." In this world-embracing vision of the Bahá'í Faith, black Bahá'ís found an answer to the nagging riddle of the brutal displacement of their slave forebears from the far-off continent of their origin. 'Abdu'l-Bahá's striking assertion of the global outcome of the unity of the two races in America suggested the operation through them of a redemptive power that would not only resolve racial discord at home but even generate a force to move the world. The life of Louis Gregory produced the litmus test of the workability of the Bahá'í teachings in effecting race unity. The successful result of this unprecedented effort would be an example to all peoples for all time. Gayle Morrison's illuminating biography of Louis Gregory certifies the realization and transforming influence of that exalted but practicable hope.

GLENFORD E. MITCHELL

Preface

Four years ago, when I began the research on which this book is based, I knew Louis Gregory as little more than a name. Having been reared in a Bahá'í family, I was familiar with the bare outlines of his role in the early history of the Bahá'í Faith in America. But I had never met him or heard him speak. As far as I knew, there were no direct links between his life and mine. During my earliest years he lived in Maine, far beyond the horizons of my childhood on the other side of the continent. I have no idea when I first heard of him or what I was told by the adult Bahá'ís I knew, who were his contemporaries, except that from them I gained respect for his memory. Louis Gregory remained for me a revered but distant figure. None of the early American Bahá'ís could have seemed more remote from my experience.

In fact, neither my background nor my academic training in Asian history led me to the study of Louis Gregory's life. The project with which I became involved in 1977 was intended to be much less demanding. The Editorial Board of *World Order* magazine—Firuz Kazemzadeh, Glenford E. Mitchell, Betty J. Fisher, Howard Garey, and the late Robert Hayden—had been asked by the National Spiritual Assembly of the Bahá'ís of the United States to publish a special issue on the relations between black and white Bahá'ís in America. An editor and writer with an interest in history was needed to do research and help to put the issue together within a few months' time. I was offered the assignment, and I accepted it as a challenging opportunity.

Although the project entailed a month's absence from my family in Hawaii, with their support the initial obstacles were overcome. I spent October 1977 in Wilmette, Illinois, working mostly among the previously untapped resources of the National Bahá'í Archives, where an abundance of material was steadily being organized by archivist Roger M. Dahl. With his assistance I investigated every available collection that seemed likely to prove useful. At the time there were relatively few: the papers of Louis G. Gregory and his wife Louisa Mathew Gregory; the extensive papers, not completely processed at that time, of Agnes Parsons, the organizer of the first Bahá'í Race Amity Convention in 1921; the Bahá'í Historical Records Cards, compiled in the mid-1930s; the histories of various Bahá'í communities, such as Washington, D.C., and Atlanta, Georgia; the transcripts and other records of Bahai Temple Unity, the first national administrative body elected by the Bahá'ís of North America; and the transcripts of national Bahá'í conventions up to about 1930. In addition, Mr. Dahl located some relevant letters in unprocessed collections, including the papers of Joseph and Pauline Hannen (the Hannen-Knobloch Family Papers), early Bahá'ís of Washington, D.C. Having a limited amount of time to spend in the Archives, I concentrated on simply gathering information, taking notes or making copies whenever I found anything that seemed important.

I left Wilmette with the general outlines of two or three articles in mind. The first would focus on Louis Gregory, who (little as I knew about him then) was clearly the most outstanding black Bahá'í in America in the first half of the twentieth century. The second article would present a general overview of the early efforts of the American Bahá'ís to come to terms with the principle of racial unity as one of the central teachings of the Faith. Finally, the race amity meetings sponsored by the Bahá'ís in the 1920s and 1930s would be covered in some detail in that article or treated as a separate topic.

Soon after starting work on the Louis Gregory article, I realized that these three central themes were inextricably connected. Either as participant or publicist, Louis Gregory was at the heart of every endeavor. His tireless commitment to the oneness of mankind was the thread that ran through forty years of developing appreciation for unity in diversity among the Bahá'ís of North America. Moreover, his efforts extended far beyond the confines of the Bahá'í community. He spoke in large cities and small towns throughout the country, and particularly in the South, where his advocacy of racial unity could easily have cost him his life. He knew and associated with virtually all of the black leaders—educators, clergymen, heads of civil rights organizations—of his day and many leading whites as well. As I studied Louis Gregory's activities, I became convinced of his stature in American cultural history. His leadership role within an interracial religious organization deserves attention in itself, because it was rare for a black to be elected to office by a predominantly white membership. But, aside from administrative recognition, he was well and widely known as a lecturer and writer on racial unity and a variety of other progressive principles.

The three articles I had originally envisioned merged into one long article. The files of material collected in Wilmette, once they had been organized and assessed, proved to contain a wealth of pertinent information. Before twenty pages had been written, the long article had already become a book. By then there was no question of turning back or of meeting the deadline for the initial assignment. The editors of *World Order* graciously acceded to the changing direction and scope of the project. Instead of a single issue, *World Order* eventually published in three consecutive issues articles excerpted from a preliminary draft of the book.*

As the concept grew, it demanded further research. Fortunately, I was able to proceed with this work in local libraries and at home. Early volumes of *Star of the West,* the first national news organ of the American Bahá'ís, were reprinted and made available for purchase in 1978; these proved to be extremely helpful, as did a nearly complete file of *Bahá'í News,* a later publication, that I was able to borrow. A number of individuals who had known Louis Gregory responded generously to requests for specific information and general impressions. Roger Dahl continued to send copies of relevant material from collections he was processing, including the files of various administrative bodies and the papers of Alfred E. Lunt, Joseph and Pauline Hannen, Harlan Ober, and Edith M. Chapman. The letters of Louis Gregory to his friend Edith Chapman, the first Bahá'í of Kansas City, spanned more than thirty years and were invaluable as sources of factual information and of insight.

The first draft of the book was completed in June 1979, but large portions had to be rewritten to incorporate material from the Chap-

---

*Gayle Morrison, "To Move the World: The Early Years of Louis Gregory," *World Order,* 13, no. 4 (Summer 1979), 21–43; Gayle Morrison, "To Move the World—Louis Gregory and 'Abdu'l-Bahá," *World Order,* 14, no. 1 (Fall 1979), 11–30; Gayle Morrison, "To Move the World—Promoting Racial Amity, 1920–1927, *World Order,* 14, no. 2 (Winter 1980), 9–31.

man Papers and other important sources that became available after that time. Writing and research proceeded concurrently even into the final stages of preparation of the manuscript, when I learned that the University of Massachusetts Library had recently made available the W. E. B. DuBois Papers. Because of time limitations I was able to obtain through interlibrary loan only two reels of microfilm from this large collection. These provided several useful letters, however, including a particularly interesting one from Louis Gregory.

Thus the book has evolved through open-ended research—limited, on the one hand, by physical distance from sources, yet, on the other hand, made possible by technology. Without long distance telephone connections, cassette recordings, instant copies, and microfilm, *To Move the World* could not have been written.

Technology has had its limitations, however. I regret not having been able to expand the scope of the book by pursuing various lines of research that seem promising. Louis Gregory's early life, for example, is seen in this work almost solely through his own eyes. Investigation of civil and school records and of the files of black newspapers such as the *Washington Bee* is needed to enlarge the fragmentary view he provides. Newspaper accounts of his activities in later years also remain to be explored. Additional research should be carried out even in the National Bahá'í Archives, where more resources are now available and where some material was probably overlooked in the early stages of inquiry, because its significance was not yet apparent. In the end I have had to be satisfied with simply making a start on a large and complex subject.

The magnitude and complexity of the subject, as I have come to see it, stand in contrast to its neglect. Until now the Bahá'ís have perhaps been too close to Louis Gregory and to their own attempts toward interracial unity; accomplishments and shortcomings tend to be accepted without examination or objectivity. Historians, for their part, seem generally to have overlooked Louis Gregory and the Bahá'í influence on race relations in America. Several black Bahá'ís—such as Alain Locke, Matthew Bullock, and Robert Hayden—appear in historical accounts, but their religious affiliation is almost never mentioned. This disregard for the Bahá'í Faith is undoubtedly a reflection of its relative obscurity during the middle decades of the twentieth century. No longer an intellectual novelty (as it was in its early years), not yet a recognizable force in American life, the Faith has been widely ignored even as it has gained adherents and become widespread. Now that it is emerging from obscurity, its role in race relations, and the unique contributions of Louis Gregory, will become better known as well.

This book seeks to redress the long years of neglect. Louis Gregory lived his life in the forefront of a struggle that is still being waged. The immediacy of his example has the power to inform and to inspire—as I, who knew so little about him, can testify. His voice reaches across barriers of race and class, even of time and distance, to form lasting bonds of affinity. Thirty years after his passing, he is still a living presence, signaling hope for a changing world.

GAYLE MORRISON

Acknowledgments

Without the impetus, financial assistance, and encouragement provided by the Editorial Board of *World Order,* this book would neither have been conceived nor written. My debt to each of the editors—Firuz Kazemzadeh, Betty J. Fisher, Glenford E. Mitchell, Howard Garey, and the late Robert Hayden—extends beyond this project to my association with the magazine from 1969 to 1972. The intellectual stimulation, camaraderie, mutual confidence and respect, flashes of creativity, and appreciation of craftsmanship that I found in their company have influenced the work that I have done in solitary settings since that productive time.

I am grateful to the Editorial Board as a whole for having overseen the publication of three excerpts from the book in the Summer 1979, Fall 1979, and Winter 1980 issues of *World Order.* Several of the editors have, in addition, watched over the development of the book. Glenford Mitchell gave the project its direction and has followed its progress. Firuz Kazemzadeh read both the entire first draft and final version of the book; his editorial comments did much to improve it. Particular thanks are due Betty Fisher, who provided hospitality, a place to work, and moral support during the month I spent doing research in Wilmette, Illinois; to whom I have directed countless requests for help and nearly as many apologies for delays; and who, having edited the excerpts for *World Order,* patiently set out over the same ground as General Editor of the Bahá'í Publishing Trust.

Roger M. Dahl, archivist at the National Bahá'í Archives in Wilmette, was a helpful guide during the initial period of research. His cooperation from the beginning of the project and the excellent work he is doing as archivist are both greatly appreciated.

Extensive use of previously unpublished letters and other archival resources has been made possible by the generous permission of those of the authors or their heirs who could be located: Lauretta N. Moore, as heir of Louis G. and Louisa M. Gregory; Helen Bishop; Bahiyyih R. Winckler, as heir of William H. Randall; Louise B. Matthias, as heir of Ellen Beecher; Betty Lunt Toomes, as heir of Alfred E. Lunt; Sohayl Hannen, as heir of Joseph Hannen; Sylvia Ioas and Anita Ioas Chapman, as heirs of Leroy Ioas; Doris Ebbert, as executor of the estate of Olga Finke; Bernice Williams, as heir of Roy Williams; and Muriel Ives Newhall, as heir of Howard Colby Ives. I thank Katherine Emerson, University of Massachusetts Archivist, and Bernard Jaffee, attorney for the DuBois estate, for facilitating the permission to quote from a letter written by W. E. B. DuBois; it is published with the permission of David DuBois, and its reproduction is not authorized without his consent.

The recollections of individuals who knew Louis Gregory form another important category of resources. Taped or written statements have been obtained from Roy Williams (who plays a leading role in several sections of this work), Bernice Williams, Lydia J. Martin, Sarah Martin Pereira, Albert James, Marzieh Gail, Margaret Kunz Ruhe, Emanuel Reimer, Alice S. Cox, Muriel Miessler, Elena Marsella, Felice Sadgwar, Catharine Nourse, Elaine Snider Eilers, Otto Zmeskal, Elizabeth Hackley, Isabelle Dodge, Ruth Silva, Elta Wheeler, Georgia de Garcie, Gayle Woolson, and David M. Earl. I have also had access to the reminiscences of Walter Blakely, which are located in the Wilmette Archives. Each of these statements has contributed in its own way to the background of the book, although not all have been used directly. To those who shared their memories, I extend sincere thanks, and to the families and close friends of several of the above individuals, who are recently deceased, I offer deeply felt sympathy. I am especially grateful to Mrs. Ruhe and Mr. Reimer for taking on the added trouble of obtaining the reminiscences of others, in addition to recording their own; and to Dr. Pereira, Miss Martin, and Mr. James, who responded at length to specific inquiries. For copyright purposes a number of people have also provided formal permissions to quote from their statements.

Correspondence, clippings, and other materials were shared by Roger White, Alice Cox, Hattie Chamberlin, Doris Ebbert, Voroth K. Degeberg, Craig Quick, and Duane Troxel. Dr. Earl contributed an album of photographs collected by Louis Gregory, some of which are reproduced in this book. The album is now in the National Bahá'í Archives in Wilmette. Additional photographs are reproduced through the courtesy of the National Bahá'í Archives, Sohayl Hannen, Albert James, David Smith, Glenn Egli, and Sally Eiler Cordova.

Several Bahá'í Assemblies and many individuals have given logistical assistance—typing, arranging or conducting taped interviews, responding to various inquiries and requests—or have made constructive comments on portions of the manuscript. Although I cannot name them all here, their help is valued nonetheless.

My acknowledgments, thus far, have reached out to people residing in all sections of the United States and many other parts of the world. To friends and family from the island of Kauai, however, I owe special thanks for having helped me and made allowances for me day by day, in innumerable ways. I am especially grateful to my mother, Corale Borges, for permitting me to use her excellent files of *Bahá'í News* and of annual administrative reports and for shouldering added burdens over the past four years. Duette Rochelle and Dian Miller have spent much time with my children, enriching their experience and giving me many unexpected quiet moments. R. W. and Elaine Reneau have provided access to their home and copying machine at odd hours, day and night. My children, Jennifer Roshan and Kevin Alexander, have grown up with the book. For the most part they have accepted it, without resentment, even when it has conflicted with their interests. I admire their flexibility, and I hope this book will come to mean more to them than the cookies that were never baked and the outings never taken.

Above all, I am indebted to my husband, Gary Morrison. Without his cooperation I would not have undertaken the original project, which was to last a few months, let alone have written a book, which has taken years. His assistance has gone far beyond the extra responsibilities and sacrifices he has accepted and the understanding and reassurance he has consistently given. As both chief editor and sounding board, he has read every version of the manuscript, at every stage, putting aside his own projects whenever I needed his help. He has never wavered in his belief in the importance of the endeavor; indeed, his vision has often sustained me. I could not have had a more capable collaborator or a better friend.

In every century a particular and central theme is,
in accordance with the requirements of that century,
confirmed by God.
In this illumined age that which is confirmed
is the oneness of the world of humanity.
Every soul who serveth this oneness
will undoubtedly be assisted and confirmed.
'ABDU'L-BAHÁ

As to racial prejudice, the corrosion of which,
for well nigh a century, has bitten into the fibre,
and attacked the whole social structure of American society,
it should be regarded as constituting the most vital
and challenging issue confronting the Bahá'í community
at the present stage of its evolution.
The ceaseless exertions which this issue
of paramount importance calls for,
the sacrifices it must impose,
the care and vigilance it demands, the moral courage
and fortitude it requires, the tact and sympathy it necessitates,
invest this problem, which the American believers are still
far from having satisfactorily resolved,
with an urgency and importance that cannot be over-estimated.
White and Negro, high and low, young and old,
whether newly converted to the Faith or not,
all who stand identified with it must participate in,
and lend their assistance, each according to his or her capacity,
experience, and opportunities, to the common task
of fulfilling the instructions, realizing the hopes,
and following the example, of 'Abdu'l-Bahá.
SHOGHI EFFENDI

Part 1/Foundations

1 Standard-Bearer

At the heart of the most challenging issue for the American Bahá'í community—the problem of obliterating racial prejudice—stands Louis George Gregory. A highly regarded teacher, writer, and lecturer throughout the first half of the century, and the first black to serve on the national administrative body of the Bahá'ís of the United States and Canada, Louis Gregory is a major historical figure. Few blacks of his era were ever elected or appointed repeatedly to positions of national leadership in organizations with a white majority. None worked more tirelessly for the removal of racial prejudice. When Shoghi Effendi, the Guardian of the Bahá'í Faith, detailed the "ceaseless exertions," "sacrifices," "care and vigilance," "moral courage and fortitude," "tact and sympathy" that the solution of the racial problem in America requires, he used terms that apply exactly to Louis Gregory's remarkable spirit and actions.[1]

As Shoghi Effendi also indicates, the mainspring of every effort to demonstrate the Bahá'í view of unity is 'Abdu'l-Bahá. Bahá'u'lláh's eldest son and chosen interpreter constantly taught by word and by example the fundamental principle of the oneness of humanity.* He found in Louis Gregory a willing pupil—thoughtful, well-educated, articulate, humble, bridging in his own upbringing the formidable chasm of legal and de facto segregation that separated black and white Americans in his day. Louis Gregory's role cannot be overestimated. Although he was neither the first of his race to become a Bahá'í in America nor the most outstanding black intellectual, he won dual distinction as a leader and

---

*'Abdu'l-Bahá, appointed by Bahá'u'lláh to succeed Him on His passing, served in this capacity from 1892 until 1921. Bahá'u'lláh often referred to His son as "the Master"; this designation has come to be used by Bahá'ís interchangeably with the title 'Abdu'l-Bahá, "Servant of Glory," which He Himself chose.

3

as a spokesman for racial unity.* Wherever he went, with whomever he was, however deeply he was concerned with the universal view, he never allowed anyone to forget his particular commitment to the cause of oneness. Through all the years of waxing and waning enthusiasm for this principle within the young Bahá'í community itself, through all the years of segregation and lynchings and race riots in American society as a whole, he sounded the keynote of "racial amity" with patience, good humor, and unshakable conviction. Both because of his own exceptional personality and because of the awesome achievements 'Abdu'l-Bahá called from him, Louis Gregory deserves to be recognized as the touchstone of the principle of oneness in American Bahá'í history.

By his own account he first "met" 'Abdu'l-Bahá in Washington, D.C., at a Bahá'í meeting he attended "only to humor the fancy of a dear old friend." Although 'Abdu'l-Bahá was still a religious prisoner in Palestine, His presence was reflected in the handful of Bahá'ís gathered together on that "cold, dark, stormy night" late in 1907. The speaker was Lua Getsinger, one of the earliest American Bahá'ís and a member of the first group of Western pilgrims to visit 'Abdu'l-Bahá in the Holy Land in 1898. Pauline Hannen, a white Southerner, was also among those present at the meeting. Along with her husband, Joseph, she was to become Mr. Gregory's friend and teacher. "The light they unfolded," he wrote of his period of study with the Hannens, "was so wonderful that for about a year we sat in dumb amazement, listening to their patient, loving talks, not knowing whether to advance or retreat, yet held by supernal power."[2]

When the Hannens received permission in 1909 to join the

---

*The first black American to accept the Bahá'í Faith was Robert Turner, who was employed by an early believer, Mrs. Phoebe Hearst, and was included in the first group of Western pilgrims to visit 'Abdu'l-Bahá in the Holy Land. The outstanding black intellectual was Alain Leroy Locke. The first Rhodes scholar of his race, he attended Harvard, Oxford, and the University of Berlin, receiving his doctorate in philosophy from Harvard in 1918. Shortly thereafter, while teaching philosophy at Howard University, he became attracted to the Bahá'í teachings. Throughout the 1920s and early 1930s, he assisted Bahá'í racial amity activities, serving on the national amity committee for a number of years. He is best remembered by historians for his major contributions to the emergence and interpretation of the Harlem Renaissance, a flowering of black artistic activity in the 1920s.

rapidly growing stream of pilgrims visiting 'Abdu'l-Bahá, recently freed after nearly a lifetime as a prisoner of the Ottoman government, Mr. Gregory retreated into other concerns. "As they were my sole connection with the Faith," he wrote of this period,

> my interest waned during their absence. A long time afterwards I learned that they had kindly mentioned me to the Master who had instructed them to continue teaching me, assuring them that I would become a believer and an advocate of the teachings. Upon their return they remade the connection. Through the very unusual kindness of these dear friends my mental veils were cleared away and the light of assurance mercifully appeared within when they had taught me . . . how to pray. [3]

Behind the "veils" he found the shining reality of 'Abdu'l-Bahá, the exemplification of Bahá'í ideals, beckoning to him. "At length," he recalled, "as the lesson of humility took effect and every hope vanished save the Will of God, Abdu'l-Baha . . . revealed himself." Thus Louis Gregory became, in his own words, "a confirmed believer" in the Faith of Bahá'u'lláh at the beginning of June 1909. [4]

One of his first actions as a Bahá'í was to confront "the most vital and challenging issue" of racial prejudice as it affected the partially segregated Bahá'í community of Washington, D.C. He found that he had stepped from the radiance of the Hannens' home into a twilight where traditional racial attitudes remained unexamined and where the principles his teachers lived by were as yet imperfectly applied:

> During my early days of investigation I rarely attended a meeting but went to the home of the Hannens where my friends and I were always welcome. As soon as I became a believer and began to teach, however, my colored friends got on my back and began to press me with troublous questions. If this were a New religion which stood for unity, why were its devotees divided? Why did they not meet altogether in one place? Were the Baha'is not full of prejudice like other people? [5]

Lacking any satisfactory answers, he asked the Hannens if he might discuss the problem with them:

If you are not busy on Saturday evening, I want to have a talk with you and have a clear understanding in regard to the attitude of the local assembly toward the colored believers.* It is with sincere regret that I find it necessary to bring this matter up, and only because some impressions are going abroad which I fear will injure our Cause both among white and colored.

I have nothing to complain of that is of a personal nature. But Abdul Baha has said that slight differences now may be great differences hereafter. And for this reason I do not wish the awful responsibility of being the cause or occasion of any schism to rest upon my shoulders.[6]

The Hannens explained that "the matter had never come up" in the community and arranged for him to consult the "Working Committee" or local executive body.[7] There is apparently no record of that meeting, and no immediate steps were taken to begin integrated meetings that year, but the act of consulting with the Working Committee may have strengthened Mr. Gregory's appreciation of the need to work within the community to effect change.

In any case, it neither dampened his enthusiasm nor his desire to share the Bahá'í teachings with others. In July he sent Joseph and Pauline Hannen a note of gratitude for their role in leading him to the Faith:

> It comes to me that I have never taken occasion to thank you specifically for all your kindness and patience, which finally culminated in my acceptance of the great truths of the Bahai Revelation. It has given me an entirely new conception of Christianity and of all religion, and with it my whole nature seems changed for the better. . . . It is a sane and practical religion, which meets all the varying needs of life, and I hope I shall ever regard it as a priceless possession.

In order to share this "priceless possession" with others, he continued, he hoped to arrange a "large scale" Bahá'í meeting, which as many as fifteen hundred people might be expected to attend. It would be held in the fall under the auspices of the Bethel

---

*The term *local assembly* was used at that time to refer to the entire Bahá'í community in a particular city. The elected administrative bodies now known as Local and National Spiritual Assemblies were not established until some years later.

Literary and Historical Association, a Negro organization of which he was president.[8]

Another of Mr. Gregory's first actions as a Bahá'í was to write to 'Abdu'l-Bahá, as was the practice at that time. 'Abdu'l-Bahá's reply, received in November 1909, expressed not only hopes for spiritual development, which were customary in all of His letters, but extraordinary expectations regarding Louis Gregory's singular role in race relations. Without doubt recognizing the qualities of uncompromising forthrightness and tactful leadership that Mr. Gregory had already demonstrated in his first few months of membership, 'Abdu'l-Bahá told him:

> I hope that thou mayest become . . . the means whereby the white and colored people shall close their eyes to racial differences and behold the reality of humanity, and that is the universal unity which is the oneness of the kingdom of the human race, the basic harmony of the world and the appearance of the bounty of the Almighty. In brief, do thou not look upon . . . thy limited capacity; look thou upon the Bounties and Providence of the Lord of the Kingdom, for His Confirmation is great, and His Power unparalleled and incomparable. Rely as much as thou canst upon the True One, and be thou resigned to the Will of God, so that like unto a candle thou mayest be enkindled in the world of humanity and like unto a star thou mayest shine and gleam from the Horizon of Reality and become the cause of the guidance of both races.[9]

For Louis Gregory any hope of 'Abdu'l-Bahá's was to be regarded as an injunction. In 1909, at the age of thirty-five, he turned his back on a secure economic position as a lawyer within the small elite of black professionals, directing increasing degrees of attention to a new unpaid calling. For the rest of his long life he put his Bahá'í activities foremost, finally abandoning his profession altogether to become a "racial amity worker," as he often referred to himself, surviving on a bare subsistence, devoting himself to the self-imposed demands of his work: constant travel, writing, and lecturing in the cause of racial unity.

2 Pain and Promise

Louis Gregory brought to his calling the insight into oppression of a Southern black, born during the era of Reconstruction, coming to maturity as the promise of full citizenship gave way to Jim Crow laws and disfranchisement. But his upbringing also prepared him to build bridges of racial understanding. In his experience, whites were not simply the oppressors; they were also his forebears, playmates, teachers, and friends. He gained as a child both a keen sense of the injustices his people continued to face and an understanding that whites were, in a broader sense, his people too.

He was born in Charleston, South Carolina, on 6 June 1874, during a time of unprecedented hope for supporters of equal civil rights for blacks. South Carolina, one of two states where blacks outnumbered whites, saw blacks achieve their greatest success in exercising the new freedoms of the Reconstruction period. Among all the former Confederate states, only South Carolina had a black majority in the constitutional convention called to reconstruct civil government for all its people. Denounced by white conservatives, the convention nonetheless produced what has been called "the state's first really democratic constitution," a document that continued in force long after the conservatives had regained control of the government.[1] South Carolina was the only state in which blacks predominated in even one of the houses of the legislature. Their majority in the lower house gave them considerable power in the government; they did not control the state, however, since the governor and most of the senate were white. A number of blacks served ably in various high offices. In 1874 South Carolina's state treasurer was Francis L. Cardozo, a free-born native of Charleston, educated at the University of Glasgow and the London School of Theology; he had already served as secretary of state from 1868 to 1872. Six blacks represented the state in the United States House of Representatives.

A beginning at least had been made to involve blacks in the body politic and to provide them with opportunities for education. Their position was strengthened temporarily by the Civil Rights Act of 1875, which prohibited the exclusion of blacks from juries and from public accommodations, such as trains, hotels, and theaters. Yet by denying them land or any other compensation for their years of servitude, Reconstruction failed to put the former slaves on a secure economic footing. Considering their disabilities—economic dependence, lack of education, and fierce opposition by white supremacists—blacks responded amazingly well to the challenges of citizenship. But social justice eluded them. They were blamed for the weaknesses of the Reconstruction governments; especially in South Carolina, opponents attributed every failing to "black rule." Almost no one at that time or for the next half century pointed out that blacks neither ruled nor were responsible for the prevailing conditions that finally destroyed the so-called radical experiment in South Carolina: illiteracy and political ignorance among the population of both races in the state, social and economic dislocation throughout the South, and widespread opportunism and political corruption in the nation as a whole. The easier course was to pronounce Reconstruction a failure and in so doing to discredit racial equality.

During Louis Gregory's early childhood the limited gains made by blacks in the face of pervasive bias and intimidation were being eroded on every side. By 1877 Northern politicians who had supported Reconstruction, without ever committing themselves fully to the transformation of the South, had lost interest or become disillusioned by slow progress and tales of corruption and misrule. The result was the Compromise of 1877: the Republican administration withdrew federal troops, thereby abandoning blacks and radicals to those who had fought to save the old order.

Yet the traditionalist white majority in the South was not uniform in its racism; its views, often reflecting class attitudes, ranged from mild paternalism to implacable bigotry. Nor was it unanimously opposed to some degree of freedom for blacks. C. Vann Woodward has described this period as an "unstable interlude" during which "the old heritage of slavery and the new and insecure heritage of legal equality" coexisted, continuing "to overlap as they had during Reconstruction." Southern cities like Charleston commingled the races, on the one hand, and separated them, on the other. Unlike Northern cities, where ghettos were the rule, urban areas in the South were residentially integrated. At the same time some public facilities remained segregated by custom, as they always had been.[2]

To these paradoxical relations between the races in the South—their intimacy conditioned by the reciprocities of the master/slave relationship that also divided them—had been added a profoundly new element of freedom. Even after 1877 black freedom could not be ignored. "The laws were still on the books," Woodward observes, "and the whites had learned some measure of accommodation. Negroes still voted in large numbers, held numerous elective and appointive offices, and appealed to the courts with hope for redress of grievances." In short, during much of the last quarter of the nineteenth century "alternatives were still open and real choices had to be made."[3]

The inroads against freedom during this period were inexorable nonetheless. Put plainly, the years following the Compromise of 1877 saw "the unimpeded development of a race system that supplanted the old institution of slavery as a mechanism of social control."[4] In 1883 the Supreme Court found the public accommodations provisions of the Civil Rights Act of 1875 to be unconstitutional, thus setting the matter outside the jurisdiction of the federal government. Jim Crow transportation laws gradually spread through a large part of the South. South Carolina, which had held out against Jim Crow for some time, capitulated in 1898; soon both waiting rooms and first- and second-class coaches were segregated. Meanwhile, the movement to disfranchise blacks had also begun. Clearly, whites had made their choice, which they came to regard as immutable: the races were to be rigidly separated, and as far as possible blacks were to be denied the rights of citizenship.

Woodward argues that the adoption of this attitude of "extreme racism" resulted from "a relaxation of the opposition"—consisting of the moderating forces of "Northern liberalism, Southern conservatism, and Southern radicalism"—rather than from any philosophical conversion. In his view:

> All the elements of fear, jealousy, proscription, hatred, and fanaticism had long been present, as they are present in various

degrees of intensity in any society. What enabled them to rise to dominance was not so much cleverness or ingenuity as it was a general weakening and discrediting of the numerous forces that had hitherto kept them in check.[5]

Regardless of the circumstances that allowed racism to become dominant, the result in South Carolina, where blacks had wielded considerable influence for a time, was the same as in states where they had achieved little: human rights were denied to people of color. Extreme racism stood triumphant in the South throughout the rest of Louis Gregory's long life. Segregation laws remained in force for more than half a century, finally beginning to yield to major challenges only after his death.

Louis grew up in the last turbulent decades of the nineteenth century, experiencing a full measure of its pain and its promise. His mother, freed at fourteen, had managed to obtain a little education before marrying and giving birth to two sons. When Louis was small (five, according to one account), his father, Ebenezer George, died of tuberculosis. Louis remembered little of his early life, shadowed first by his father's illness and death, then by poverty and even hunger as his mother struggled to support her family.

Perhaps the sustaining force in this period was Louis' maternal grandmother, a formidable woman who, though virtually illiterate, schooled him in dignity, courage, and the love of laughter. As an adult he told affectionately of his grandmother's "native abilities" and practical knowledge of medicine, gained as a nurse on the plantation, and especially of her "very keen sense of humor." She was, he recalled, "the only person that I have ever known who could make me laugh beyond all control." The amusement his grandmother found even in plantation life helped to make bearable both past and present indignities, the painful memories of slavehood and the harsh realities of emancipation. The sense of humor she nurtured in Louis served to lighten many difficulties in the years ahead. It became a valuable asset in his racial amity work. "If the walls of caste are ever to be shattered," he wrote toward the end of his life, "laughter . . . will be no small power in such a change."[6]

Louis' mother and grandmother had been slaves on the plantation of George Washington Dargan in Darlington, South Carolina.

Their stories of Chancellor Dargan and his family held particular significance because, in Louis' words, "my grandmother, wholly of African blood, was without ceremony his slave wife and my mother his daughter." Dargan had died in 1859, and all connections with the family had ended after Louis' grandmother and mother left the plantation at the end of the war. But their stories gave Louis a certain pride in the Dargan family and a particular regard for one Louise Dargan, whom he identified as the Chancellor's wife, for teaching his mother and grandmother "the kind of religion which involved the mystery of a change of heart and putting of ideals into action."[7]

With characteristic dignity, Louis Gregory rejected bitterness over the manifold wrongs of the past. Instead, he chose from the ambiguities of his descent a birthright of which he could be proud:

> The Dargan family are outstanding and distinguished for their work in the field of religion and education. They accepted the end of slavery cheerfully and stimulated the progress and enlightenment of humanity. I did not choose them as my forebears, but in justice must acknowledge my obligations to them.[8]

Undoubtedly his grandmother's generous spirit helped to shape his attitude toward the white relatives from whom he was separated by insurmountable barriers of caste.

A postscript to the story of Louis Gregory's white forebears illuminates the ironies of the Southern way of life, for both blacks and whites. At the age of seventy-four, when he was no longer able to travel widely and had turned more attention to his literary projects, Mr. Gregory wrote to the postmaster of Darlington, South Carolina, for information on the Dargan family. His letter was referred to a lawyer, George Dargan, the grandson of one of Chancellor Dargan's brothers. On 8 February 1949 Dargan wrote a warm and informative response to the cultivated inquirer from Maine, enclosing a copy of the family tree. George Washington Dargan had been a judge in the South Carolina Court of Equity, his grandnephew wrote. Among his brothers had been a lawyer, three physicians, and an army officer who was killed in the Civil War. The identity of "Louise Dargan" remained something of a mystery, as the Chancellor's wife was named Mary Adeline; quite possibly she was a Louise Wilson, who had married one of the Dargan brothers and been widowed in 1854.[9]

Louis Gregory soon replied, apparently enclosing some material that indicated his views on race, if not his own mixed heritage. He seems to have sparked an adverse reaction. George Dargan's second letter was widely divergent in tone from the first. It was extremely brief, polite, but curt. Dargan began by thanking Mr. Gregory for the enclosures he had received, indicating that he had read them. His own belief, he stated in the second and closing sentence, was that race relations in the South had been damaged by the interference of political rabble-rousers and incendiaries. Clearly, there was for him no more to be said on the subject. A century had passed since Chancellor Dargan formed a liaison with his slave. Walls of illusion continued to shield his descendants and their peers from understanding of themselves and their past. Rather than face the truth, they sought to reinforce the barriers of caste and to deny the indisputable ties between the races, above all the ties of flesh and blood.

In earlier days, however, the strictures of caste were enforced by extreme means. Even the slightest evidences of material success by a black after the Civil War were sometimes seen as an affront to the white man. Among the stories Louis heard from his grandmother was her account of how the Ku Klux Klan had killed his grandfather. A blacksmith who had prospered after the war, he had bought a mule and a horse. Because of this "display of luxury" the Klan rode up one night, called him out of his house, and shot him. Her life hung in the balance while they debated whether to kill her too. Then they rode away. But Louis Gregory's courageous grandmother had refused either to hate or to be put in her place, the two most predictable responses to terrorism. Her final answer to the night riders was to raise a grandson who, like her, could not be intimidated.

The stabilizing influence of his grandmother helped the family through a time of deep poverty and hardship. Louis' prospects were limited, nevertheless, until his mother remarried. "During my early childhood," he wrote of this decisive change in his life, "my mother married George Gregory who became a real father to me so that by his earnest wish I took his name, becoming Louis George Gregory." The close relationship between young Louis and his stepfather continued until George Gregory died in 1929, at the age of eighty-seven. Both the moderate habits that prolonged his life and the spirit that pervaded it impressed his stepson, who observed after his passing that "on the basis of merit and good humor he was highly respected and honored by a large circle of friends among both races."[11]

In addition to emotional security George Gregory provided the family with increased economic well-being and a heritage of freedom that his stepson regarded with pride.

> He was free born and his family were property holders in the days before the civil War. The year-book for 1849 of Charleston shows that free people of color possessed around $400,000 in property and oddly enough, 14 slaves. He was not only not a slave-holder, but [was] a zealous advocate of freedom for all men.[12]

Moreover, during the Civil War he had joined the Union ranks, becoming one of a number of blacks from South Carolina who fought against the Confederacy.

Having been free from birth and educated to some degree, George Gregory helped his wife and children obtain advantages that society would otherwise have denied them. After their marriage, his wife gained, in her son's words, "a taste for good literature and some knowledge of music."[13] The Gregory family was precisely the sort—"a more than ordinarily disciplined and stable family, and . . . one that was literate, as well"—that sociologists claim tended to produce a pioneer generation of black scholars and professionals.[14] George Gregory made sacrificial efforts to provide Louis with the best education possible in Charleston, later assuring that he had a trade by apprenticing him to a tailor and also paying for his first year at college.[15] Thus from his stepfather, as well as from his mother and grandmother, he learned the qualities necessary to overcome a black man's humiliating lot in racism's revanchist era: self-respect, love of learning, assurance, dignity, resourcefulness, and a sense of humor.

Despite the South's problems, Louis Gregory grew up with a deep love for the region. He remembered Charleston in his boyhood as a gracious old city where "courtesy seemed the primal virtue and there was less friction between the races than appeared in many other cities.''[16] Yet the advantages Charleston offered a black child were at least as much the result of changes brought about by the Civil War and Reconstruction as of the city's traditions of cosmopolitanism and culture. Louis' earliest playmates included the children of white Northern troops stationed in the South after the war, and in their company he gained perhaps his first experiences of interracial amity.[17] Throughout his youth, streetcars and some other public facilities were open to everyone; as late as 1898 conservative Charleston newspaper editors argued that Jim Crow laws were unnecessary, and if a separate car were indeed desirable, it would be best used to segregate drunken, white ruffians from respectable people of either color.[18]

Above all, Louis Gregory's generation was the first, black or white, to grow up in South Carolina with the right to a public education. Although whites neither regarded the education of blacks with enthusiasm nor supported it on an equal basis, at least this one essential right was not taken away completely when the white supremacists ''redeemed'' the Southern way of life. In practice, schools were segregated, even during Reconstruction, and black schools were inadequate from the start. ''Without exception the segregated schools were inferior,'' August Meier and Elliott Rudwick have written, ''and failed to give Negroes even the rudiments of an adequate education.''[19] Yet inferior schools were clearly better than none at all.

Louis Gregory's description of his public school years indicates an experience probably better than the norm, but his respect for his white teachers was tempered by awareness of the awkward relationship between them and their pupils:

> My teachers in the Charleston public schools were southern whites. The principal of the Simonton school was an exConfederate soldier. He was a graduate of the College of Charleston, a fine disciplinarian and highly polished gentleman who loved his task and did it well. Likewise efficient were the teachers who served with him and well trained for their tasks. Many expressions of gratitude went out to them from former pupils. . . . Later the time came, none too early, when the colored people were engaged by the Board of Education to man their own schools.[20]

Thus public school was at best a proving ground for a black child; the most one could hope for was to be taught by a staff that was "efficient" and "well trained," guided by a principal who "loved his task and did it well" (the professionalism of these Southern whites apparently triumphing over an ingrained antipathy to the idea of blacks as fully educable beings). The best that could be said was that feelings of ill will were not universal. As Louis Gregory put it:

> I cannot recall a time when at least some whites of the South could not be found who were willing for the colored race to have every right and opportunity, on the basis of merit, which they themselves enjoyed. That minority has grown with the passing years and that it will become a majority ere long is as certain as the sunrise. . . .[21]

Louis passed the test of public education, going on to attend private schools founded and supported by Northern church groups and philanthropists to reach, in his words, " 'the talented tenth' of the Negro race, who might through liberal education become leaders for the masses."* In these schools his teachers were not simply dedicated professionals; rather, they were dedicated humanists who accepted pay far lower than they could have earned in the North because they believed in their ideals. He remembered them as having been deeply affected spiritually by "the great revivals which swept the world around the middle of the last century"—a religious matrix from which came abolitionists, feminists, and champions of the rights of oppressed peoples.[22]

The first private school Louis attended was Avery Institute in Charleston, a black secondary school run by the American Missionary Association. Francis L. Cardozo had been its first principal, and its students were "upper-class and aspiring Charleston children." After graduating in 1891, Louis enrolled at Fisk University, the outstanding institution of higher education established in 1866 in Nashville, Tennessee, by the American Missionary Association. His stepfather supported him financially during his first year at Fisk. Subsequently, he paid his own way, winning scholar-

---

*W. E. B. DuBois coined the phrase *the talented tenth* in an essay by that title that he contributed to the 1903 compilation *The Negro Problem*.

ships and earning extra money, a friend recalled, by "cleaning, pressing and tailoring for the students, and sometimes working as a waiter during the summer vacations." After he received his degree in 1896, he returned to Charleston to teach at Avery Institute.[23]

To have earned a bachelor's degree was in itself an outstanding accomplishment. In 1900, out of a population of about nine million blacks in the United States, only about two thousand—or two hundredths of one percent—had graduated from a college or university. Only about seven hundred black college students were enrolled in that year. Like Louis Gregory, most attended one of the thirty-four "Negro colleges."[24] Relatively few were as fortunate as he in attending schools as good as Avery and Fisk.

Louis Gregory's highest aspirations had not yet been fulfilled, however. When he decided to become a lawyer, the outstanding law school open to substantial numbers of blacks was at Howard University in Washington, D.C. No white schools in the South accepted black graduate students, and very few black colleges offered advanced degrees. A commitment to further study thus required not only exceptional ability and drive but willingness to spend years far from home, to venture from a familiar environment into the unknown.

3   The Path to Reconstruction

Louis Gregory's decision to enter the legal profession entailed leaving the South, not only for a period of study but for the indefinite future. Virtually no openings for black lawyers existed there; as one scholar has observed, "the disfranchisement of the Negro throughout the South and the subsequent denigration of the Negro's stature in public life sharply curtailed opportunities for the entry of Negroes into the legal profession in the section."[1]

Mr. Gregory received his LL.B. degree in March 1902. After being admitted to the bar, he and another young lawyer, James A. Cobb, opened a law office in Washington, D.C. Their partnership ended in 1906, when Mr. Gregory took a position with the U.S. Treasury Department. The men remained close, however. Cobb, who was appointed judge of the District of Columbia municipal court in 1926, wrote after his old friend's death:

> "I knew him as a student, teacher, practicing lawyer, lecturer and friend, and in each capacity he was strong and outstanding. In other words he was a fine student, a lovely character and a person with a great mind which he devoted to the betterment of mankind. . . . those with whom he came in contact were and are better for their association with him. In fact, he was one of those who enriched the life of America."[2]

At the Treasury Department Louis Gregory's ability to form close relationships led to an extraordinary friendship with two colleagues. "There were two fellow clerks, white and very elderly, occupying with me the same room, with my desk between theirs," he wrote many years later. He described them as being "in striking contrast one to the other" in all but age.

One was a Massachusetts Yankee and one-armed veteran of the Civil War. He was not highly educated, but had a keen mind, was efficient in his work and a fine representative of the yeomanry of his state with its traditions of justice and freedom. My other companion was a Marylander, a man of culture, graduate of a New England college, well read in literature, history, and current events, but intensely Southern in his sympathies and outlook on life.[3]

These three disparate individuals—divided by age, race, and background—"frequently relieved the routine by animated discussions." Mr. Gregory admitted to having enjoyed the "pastime" of sparking some of the more lively arguments after he found that "any question about the Civil War, innocently enough asked by me, would bring them into verbal conflict." Despite their differences, however, the three men became close; "they were both to me warm personal friends such as I hope never to forget in time or eternity."[4] Mr. Gregory was particularly impressed at having been invited to the Southern gentleman's home to meet his wife, a courtesy unprecedented in his experience.[5]

For his part Mr. Gregory showed trust in his friends by using them as a sounding board for his ideas. He was at that time, as one might expect, preoccupied with the problems of race relations. As a representative of the "talented tenth" of his race, a graduate of two of the most outstanding institutions of higher education for blacks, a resident in the national capital, and a trained lawyer whose profession made him keenly aware of political movements, Louis Gregory was in a position both to observe the forces affecting his people and to become involved in movements for change.

From the 1890s on, he had seen the steady progress of efforts to disfranchise blacks in the South, accelerated especially after the collapse of the Populist movement, which had briefly demonstrated a potential for uniting blacks and poor whites as political allies. Blacks were denied not only the right to vote but even the protection of the law. From 1884 to 1900 there had been in the United States more than twenty-five hundred lynchings, mostly of blacks and mostly in the South. During the Spanish-American War black soldiers had been abused by Southern whites who regarded a black man with a gun and a uniform as an affront to their social order and a patent danger.

The coming of a new century, which many people believed would bring an end to the bloodshed, simply brought changing patterns of violence. Lynchings continued, to be sure; one hundred blacks were lynched in the first year of the century, eleven hundred by 1914. But terrorism against blacks was also vented in what John Hope Franklin has called an "epidemic of race riots that swept the country early in the century." These riots, unlike those of later years in which blacks took part in the violence, were virtual pogroms. The Atlanta race riot of September 1906 was perhaps the South's most striking example of such "organized brigandage of life and property." The normal life of the city came to a complete halt for days as mobs of whites, their hatred fanned by an election that focused upon the issue of disfranchisement, attacked blacks and destroyed their property. The promise of the new century remained unfulfilled in the North as well. "Rioting in the North," Franklin has observed, "was as vicious and almost as prevalent as in the South."[6] Public outrage over such attacks was undercut by the popularity and respectability of racist theories during the heyday of imperialism and white racial superiority.

The election of Theodore Roosevelt as president in 1900 had initially led blacks to expect some improvements in the racial policies of the federal government. They had hailed Roosevelt as the first president since Lincoln to offer them the hope of equal treatment. Shortly after taking office Roosevelt had invited Booker T. Washington, who had become a prominent and respected figure nationally, to the White House and had dined with him there. This gesture was regarded by blacks as a hand outstretched in friendship and by white racists as a slap in the face. Although even Southern whites generally approved of Washington, it was because they saw his means for Negro progress—vocational training and hard work in the humble trades—as the means for keeping the black man in his place, and that place was obviously not the White House. The President's invitation demonstrated a degree of social equality that not even Booker Washington himself advocated. He was, after all, the same spokesman who had reassured whites at the Atlanta Exposition in 1895 by announcing that "in all things that are purely social we can be as separate as the fingers, yet one as the hand in all things essential to mutual progress."[7]

Roosevelt's break with convention created a sensation that dominated the press for months afterwards. Louis Gregory recalled that

The Roosevelt-Washington dinner, which evoked general comment, had many curious reactions, some of them humorous. A great statesman-editor who filled the public eye, joined in the general chorus of denunciation in a public word. Yet privately he wrote Booker Washington at the time: "Pay no attention to what the newspapers are saying. I am with you!" While Mr. Washington was on a Southern train a Confederate Colonel who was aboard, hearing of his presence sought him out to meet and greet him. The story is that he eulogized the Negro educator as the greatest man in America. Mr. Washington being very modest, demurred to such high praise.

"Who is any greater than you, sir?" demanded his ardent admirer.

"Why of course there is President T. Roosevelt."

"I don't think anything of him sir, since he ate with you, sir!"[8]

By 1906, however, Roosevelt had probably won back the colonel's approval, while losing the confidence of blacks. In response to a riot in Brownsville, Texas, involving three companies of the black Twenty-fifth Regiment, the president dismissed the entire battalion without honor and prohibited its members from future government service, civil or military. One senator called the action an "'executive lynching'" and another worked for years to have Congress establish a court of inquiry to review the case of each discharged soldier.[9] But relatively few white people were outraged by the blatant and pervasive injustice blacks faced throughout the country, which Brownsville typified, and still fewer worked to see justice done. Overreaction against blacks was matched by indifference to white violence. White lynch mobs and rioters—in Atlanta in 1906 as in Springfield, Illinois, in 1908—were never punished for their lawless acts.

In fact the capacity of white society to raise Booker T. Washington to a position of high esteem while closing its eyes to disfranchisement and mob violence helped to create the first major ideological split in the black community in this century. On one side stood Washington, firmly supported by both whites and blacks, distinguished by his own remarkable achievements—the development of Tuskegee Institute, the popularization of a distinctive philosophy of vocational education, the channeling of money from Northern philanthropists into black education in the South, and the carving out of a position of national eminence marked by eloquence and tact. On the other side stood a relatively small number of people who recognized the weaknesses in Washington and his programs, along with the obvious strengths.

Their leader, W. E. B. DuBois, born in Massachusetts and educated at Fisk and Harvard, wrote in 1903: "Easily the most striking thing in the history of the American Negro since 1876 is the ascendancy of Mr. Booker T. Washington." He affirmed that Washington was "certainly the most distinguished Southerner since Jefferson Davis, and the one with the largest personal following." DuBois claimed, however, that criticism among blacks had been stilled by Washington's success as "the leader not of one race but of two,—a compromiser between the South, the North, and the Negro."[10] Even those who disliked compromise had bowed to his extraordinary influence.

DuBois called for criticism to be brought to the surface. He loosed his own forceful attack on Washington's expediency and on his exaltation of "triumphant commercialism," his preoccupation with "a gospel of Work and Money to such an extent as apparently almost completely to overshadow the higher aims of life." He argued that Washington's failure to lend importance to suffrage, civil rights, and liberal higher education for blacks undermined his own goals. Washington advocated that blacks advance by becoming property owners and businessmen; yet "it is utterly impossible, under modern competitive methods," DuBois observed, "for workingmen and property-owners to defend their rights and exist without the right of suffrage." Washington stressed self-respect; but DuBois claimed that "silent submission to civic inferiority . . . is bound to sap the manhood of any race in the long run." Washington emphasized vocational training at the expense of impractical classical education; yet "neither the Negro common-schools, nor Tuskegee itself, could remain open a day were it not for teachers trained in Negro colleges, or trained by their graduates." Thus Washington's program bore the seeds of failure, according to DuBois, and played into the hands of those who expected submission and inferiority to characterize the race indefinitely. Moreover, Washington's doctrine of self-help suggested that success or failure lay solely with blacks themselves, "when in fact the burden belongs to the nation, and the hands of none of us are clean if we bend not our energies to righting these great wrongs."[11]

Disillusioned by Washington's ascendancy and by continuing violence and injustice directed against blacks, DuBois and a like-minded group of young men met at Niagara Falls, Canada, in June 1905 to form a plan of action. The Niagara Movement has been called "the first organized attempt to raise the Negro protest against the great reaction after the Reconstruction."[12] Its demands, considered radical at the time, included manhood suffrage, equal civil rights, equal economic opportunity, free compulsory elementary education and access to high schools and colleges, legal and penal reform to end racial discrimination, fair treatment by both management and labor unions, and abolition of Jim Crow accommodations. Even more radical than the Movement's demands was the anger that charged its rhetoric. DuBois and his fellow members refused to go knocking on white society's back door, hat in hand. The Movement's "Declaration of Principles" was outspoken, forceful, and relentless in its catalog of grievances. A representative paragraph states:

> We repudiate the monstrous doctrine that the oppressor should be the sole authority as to the rights of the oppressed. The Negro race in America stolen, ravished and degraded, struggling up through difficulties and oppression, needs sympathy and receives criticism; needs help and is given hindrance, needs protection and is given mob-violence, needs justice and is given charity, needs leadership and is given cowardice and apology, needs bread and is given a stone. This nation will never stand justified before God until these things are changed.[13]

Nor was there any taint of submissiveness in the 1906 manifesto composed after the Movement's second meeting at Harpers Ferry, West Virginia, which read in part:

> Never before in the modern age has a great and civilized folk threatened to adopt so cowardly a creed in the treatment of its fellow-citizens born and bred on its soil. Stripped of verbiage and subterfuge and in its naked nastiness the new American creed says: Fear to let black men even try to rise lest they be-

come the equals of the white. And this is the land that professes to follow Jesus Christ. The blasphemy of such a course is only matched by its cowardice.[14]

In this same year—1906—Louis Gregory started to work at the Treasury Department and began his discussions with the Yankee and the Southerner who shared his office. Whereas the older men were inclined to rehearse the Civil War, Mr. Gregory tended to outline strategies of black activism that were unquestionably influenced by DuBois and the Niagara Movement. As unlikely as the friendship of these three co-workers may seem to have been, the strength of the bond must have been exceptional for Mr. Gregory to have trusted his friends in this way. His trust was repaid with genuine kindness (the New Englander "used playfully to call himself my grandfather") and openmindedness on their part:

> Mellowed by age, these men were very indulgent to me because of my youth and inexperience. They listened with patience to ideas of mine which were wild-eyed and radical, read articles of mine and others, offered them, without being bored, but seemed to agree upon one thing: That my program of fiery agitation in behalf of a people, whose wrongs only, I could see, would avail nothing in the removal of such wrongs, but would rather move friends and foes to combine against me. Despite my unyielding attitude, their friendship, even affection, for me grew. They lent me books to read, spoke soothingly when my feelings, as not infrequently happened, were ruffled, and through many acts, which showed deep interest and kindness, made an indelible impression upon my life.[15]

Their cautionary words about "fiery agitation" were echoed by many in the black community. Kelly Miller of Howard University, whom DuBois in *The Souls of Black Folk* had numbered among "the thinking classes of American Negroes," responded to the resolutions of the Niagara Movement by describing them as " 'scarcely distinguishable from a wild and frantic shriek.' "[16] Even after the Niagara Movement was assimilated, in 1909–10, by a broader, biracial organization, the National Association for the Advancement of Colored People, conflicts within the black leadership persisted. On the Left, Monroe Trotter, publisher of the *Boston*

Guardian and outspoken critic of Booker T. Washington, refused to join the N.A.A.C.P. because he suspected the motives of the whites involved. To the Right were others equally suspicious of DuBois. In Franklin's words:

> The presence of Dr. DuBois on the staff branded the organization as radical from the beginning. Many feared that it would be a capricious, irresponsible organization that would draw its main inspiration from the dreamings of the Niagara Movement. It was denounced by most of the white philanthropists, and even some Negroes thought it unwise.[17]

But Louis Gregory for one had been deeply influenced by DuBois and the Niagara Movement. Nearly thirty years later, in a review of DuBois' *Black Reconstruction*, he acknowledged the author as the "third of the great national leaders of the American Negro," following Douglass and Washington, and referred to *The Souls of Black Folk* as "his masterpiece." The review is charged with deep admiration for DuBois, despite his recent break with the N.A.A.C.P. and increasing intellectual isolation, and with equally deep regret that this most brilliant and well-educated black leader had turned away from the "simple faith" and "spirituality" evident in *The Souls of Black Folk* and had disregarded the belief in God that is "the major part of his [the black man's] history" and "the major note of his song." Mr. Gregory undoubtedly saw in DuBois a reflection of his own state of mind in the early 1900s, when he had lost interest in religion because, in his words, he "had been seeking, but not finding truth, had given up."[18]

It is doubtful whether anyone, black or white, could have changed the focus of Louis Gregory's "radical" ideas, made an impression on his "unyielding attitude," or renewed his belief in religion, if his "unreconstructed" Southern friend, Thomas H. Gibbs, had not become, as Mr. Gregory described him, "the means of guiding me to the spiritual forces which for many years have directed my life." Gibbs was neither a Bahá'í, nor was he seriously interested in the Bahá'í Faith himself; in fact "he had attended but a few of the meetings and had a very limited understanding of it."[19] What little he knew, however, he liked and wished to share.

Mr. Gregory for his part had no interest in investigating a new religion. Only because his friend "was most urgent and insistent that I attend a meeting, which I had no inclination to do," and because he "thought to do [Gibbs] a favor," did Mr. Gregory finally agree to go to the address the man had given him, "a room in the old Corcoran building, opposite the Treasury Department and long since demolished," to attend a Bahá'í meeting:

> The only occupant of the room when I entered was Mrs.Pauline Hannen. She gave me an unusually cordial welcome, identified me as a friend of Mr. Gibbs and told me that I would hear something very wonderful, though difficult. It would afford me an opportunity similar to that which would have been mine had I lived on earth as a contemporary of Jesus Christ. She urged me to get a full understanding of the message of today, that through it a work would be possible that would bless humanity. She kindly gave me three pieces of Bahá'í literature. . . . Soon thereafter entered another lady, Mrs. Lua M. Getsinger, referred to as "our teacher". A little later came two colored ladies, Miss Millie York and Miss Nellie Gray. So uncomfortable was the night that no one else came.
>
> Mrs. Getsinger gave the message historically, recounting the appearances of the Bab and Baha'u'llah and of the great persecutions and martyrdoms in Persia. Her recital was brief but vivid.[20]

Intrigued by what he had heard, Louis Gregory accepted Pauline Hannen's invitation to another meeting:

> It was held at the home of the two colored friends previously mentioned, among poor people. Mrs. Hannen was the teacher and her loving service was impressive. She then invited me to come to her home where I would meet either herself or her husband for further teaching. Mr. Joseph H. Hannen thus became my teacher, a service in which he was aided by his wife. Over a period of more than eighteen months I went to their home on Sunday evenings, sacrificing time previously given to social life.[21]

Pauline Hannen had warned that the message of Bahá'u'lláh would be challenging, "difficult." Louis Gregory had come upon it inadvertently and attended his first meeting reluctantly. Yet stirred by her assurance that it would make possible "a work . . . that would bless humanity," he began to investigate the Bahá'í Faith. Gradually it proved itself to be the truth he had given up finding. He saw it, moreover, as a remedy for the plight of black Americans, an answer to the "noble . . . prayer" DuBois had raised on behalf of his people after the Atlanta riot of 1906. Widely circulated for many years, the prayer read, as Mr. Gregory once quoted it:

"Bewildered are we and passion tost, mad with the madness of a mobbed and mocked and murdered people; straining at the armposts of Thy Throne, we raise our shackled hands and charge Thee, God, by the bones of our stolen fathers, by the tears of our dead mothers, by the very blood of our crucified Christ: What meaneth this? Tell us the plan; give us the sign; whisper—speak—call, great God, for Thy silence is white terror to our hearts! The way, O God, show us the way and point us the Path!"[22]

DuBois' words had indeed been heard, Mr. Gregory was convinced. "Heaven and earth heard that piercing cry, uttered by one, echoed by millions," he wrote in his review of *Black Reconstruction*. "Earth and Heaven answered."[23] For Louis Gregory the "plan," the "sign," the "way," and the "Path" that DuBois had implored God to reveal was the Bahá'í Faith.

Yet to accept a new "plan" meant to place oneself outside the pale of the "talented tenth," to commit oneself to a seemingly obscure point of view that as yet no other black intellectual shared. If the loneliness of his position worried him, Louis Gregory did not show it. Instead, he labored to establish the credibility of his views. Soon, through his own efforts and those of 'Abdu'l-Bahá, the unfamiliar name *Bahá'í* became widely known among American blacks. During 'Abdu'l-Bahá's visit to America in 1912 He addressed a number of black and interracial audiences, from Howard University to a national convention of the N.A.A.C.P.

DuBois himself met 'Abdu'l-Bahá, lectured one summer at Green Acre, a Bahá'í study camp in Maine, and retained connections with Bahá'ís for many years. His wife, Nina Gomer DuBois, had several close Bahá'í friends with whom she studied the Faith. In 1936 she enrolled as a member of the New York Bahá'í community. On hearing this "joyous" news Louis Gregory expressed the hope that Dr. DuBois, whose allegiance to the Faith he had sought to win since 1912, might also become a Bahá'í.[24] DuBois seems not to have recognized fully the worldwide scope of the Bahá'í movement, however, nor to have grasped its far-reaching implications for social transformation. Instead of drawing closer to the beliefs that his wife had embraced, he became highly critical, ultimately making it impossible for her to remain an active Bahá'í. But other influential black leaders, attracted, like DuBois, to 'Abdu'l-Bahá, eventually became declared believers. Perhaps the best known nationally were Professor Alain Locke of Howard University, who participated as an active Bahá'í in many teaching and racial amity activities in the 1920s and 1930s, and editor Robert S. Abbott, the founder of the *Chicago Defender*, who formally accepted the Faith in 1934.[25]

The response of such leaders vindicated Louis Gregory's decision, years before, to diverge from the path of social activism blazed by DuBois and others. Alain Locke's assertion, in an article published in 1933, that "there is one great spiritual advantage in the tidal series of negative upsets and breakdowns in the contemporary world and that is the ever-accumulative realization of the need for a complete reconstruction of life," and his identification of that reconstruction with "the inspired teachings of 'Abdu'l-Bahá and Bahá'u'lláh," clearly demonstrated that by becoming a Bahá'í Louis Gregory had not abandoned social concern.[26]

His was not the way of religious fanaticism. It may be argued that he became even more unorthodox and radical in a fundamental social sense than he had been in his "wild-eyed" days of commitment to Niagara-inspired activism. He did not put aside his concern for racial equality and social justice in favor of a preoccupation with salvation or spiritual contentment. Nor did he lose touch with individuals and groups working in their own ways for change. Rather, he placed his undiminished concern for the welfare of his people within a universal context: the establishment of a new world order founded, like the great civilizations of the past, on faith in a Supreme Being and on an ennobling vision of human destiny. "This Most Great Reconstruction which the majestic Revelation of Bahá'u'lláh brings to view, is not black or white or yellow or brown or red, yet all of these," he claimed. "It is the power of divine outpouring and endless perfections for mankind.''[27] Indeed, in adopting the Bahá'í point of view Mr. Gregory anticipated by many years DuBois' own inexorable progress toward acceptance of a universal philosophy, a world-encircling path—pan-Africanism and international socialism, in DuBois' case—that would reconcile racial pride with the ideal of human brotherhood.

Thus during the critical years from 1906–09, when black activism was enlarging its scope in America (the Niagara Movement merging into the N.A.A.C.P. and several New York organizations joining forces as the National Urban League), Louis Gregory was also seeking resolution of the problems of his people in a broadly based movement. Unlike the N.A.A.C.P. and the Urban League, however, the Bahá'í Cause was not national but international, not biracial but multiracial, not issue oriented but issue encompassing, not directed toward social change in itself but toward spiritual transformation of both the individual and society. It promised to alter completely the patterns of racial discrimination reinforced by class, caste, and religion in America and throughout the world and ultimately to create a new world civilization in which the characteristics and contributions of all peoples would play a part.

4   Agent of Change

As a Bahá'í in the Faith's early years, Louis Gregory found that he had become of necessity a pathfinder and pioneer. The way toward the "Most Great Reconstruction" had to be made visible and accessible to others. The first major obstacle he encountered was the negative response of many of his friends:

> By far the majority of my friends thought I had become mentally unbalanced. One of my old teachers, a professor of international law and a very affectionate friend, almost wept over my departure from orthodoxy and with others warned me that I was blasting all hopes of a career. The Washington Bee, a well-known colored newspaper, on one occasion gave me two columns of ridicule which remained unanswered. Others, knowing my controversial habits [i.e., habit of engaging in controversy] of the past said, "He must have religion since he does not answer that!"

Nonetheless, he saw even the opposition to his having become a Bahá'í as a partly constructive thing, since "there were always some who were willing to investigate and the opposition seemed to promote inquiry."[1]

The second major obstacle became apparent when his friends began to question the practice of segregation within the Washington Bahá'í community. Bahá'ís in those early years had not achieved unity of conscience with regard to racial equality. Indeed, they were struggling toward a sense of their own identity. They had become Bahá'ís for many reasons, often with very little knowledge or understanding of the full scope of Bahá'u'lláh's teachings or of the implications of His Revelation. They came from every sort of religious, economic, ethnic, and educational background. They were enthusiastic believers; many corresponded with 'Abdu'l-Bahá and were deeply attached to Him. Yet most were still bound by strong ties to churches and clubs, philosophies and intellectual fads that influenced their everyday lives, and all were virtually without access to the untranslated wealth of Bahá'í literature. Having no clergy, which Bahá'u'lláh had expressly excluded from the Bahá'í order, and as yet without a wide selection of sacred literature, the study of which forms the basis of individual spiritual responsibility, and without a functioning administration, the early Bahá'ís in America lacked the means of immediately assuring fundamental unity. They clung to 'Abdu'l-Bahá, to His letters and His very presence in the world; at the same time they remained individualistic, even idiosyncratic, in their communal relationships.

A story told by one of the early pilgrims who visited 'Abdu'l-Bahá illustrates His role in the American community during those years. Anna Watson wrote from 'Akká in 1904 that 'Abdu'l-Bahá had recounted at tea one morning a dream He had about America. In the dream He had been told by a number of His followers that ''there were many earnest believers in America, but that they were far apart and all playing on different musical instruments, so that they did not play in harmony.'' On hearing this, 'Abdu'l-Bahá said He would see what He could do. '' 'Finding one, I told him to stay until I brought others to him, but when I came back with another, the first had gone away piping on his instrument,' '' the Master recounted. '' 'And so it was; I could never get them together.' '' When He awoke from this dream, 'Abdu'l-Bahá added, '' 'I was very tired.' ''[2]

Correspondingly, as Louis Gregory soon found, the fundamental Bahá'í principle of the oneness of mankind elicited varied responses from the Bahá'ís themselves. In fact, as the Hannens told him shortly after he became a Bahá'í in 1909, the practice of separate meetings had never even been discussed by the community members, although 'Abdu'l-Bahá apparently had directed them to hold interracial meetings as early as February of that year.[3] Whites like Lua Getsinger, the Hannens, and Mrs. Hannen's sisters, Alma and Fanny Knobloch, all of whom were well aware of the implications of racial unity in the Bahá'í teachings, were already participating in integrated meetings, both in public places and in private homes. Other white Bahá'ís were not, either because racial mixing was uncustomary or because it was distasteful to them personally. Many who had been attracted to the Faith by one principle or another, or by the Person of 'Abdu'l-Bahá, would have been horror-struck to discover that to be a Bahá'í meant to be a proponent of racial equality. There did not yet exist any administrative means or even any general sense of necessity to bring such unreconstructed whites into conformity with the Bahá'í principle of oneness.

Louis Gregory proved to be an agent of change in the Washington community. He was the first black Bahá'í from the "talented tenth." A cultivated and articulate lawyer, distinguished in appearance and bearing, he was not deterred by any lack of education or social standing from assuming an active role or from challenging the community's racial practices. Under his questioning, the old, unconsidered habits of segregation had to be confronted by the community; and, once the issue had been raised, it could not be dismissed. Louis Gregory began, quietly but uncompromisingly, to lay the groundwork for the changes he knew were inevitable.

Perhaps the most effective challenge to the habit of segregation was brought about by an increase in the number of Bahá'ís or serious students of the Faith from the gifted and influential circle of blacks in which Louis Gregory moved. In July 1909 he had written to the Hannens that he wanted to arrange a presentation of the Bahá'í teachings to a large meeting of the Bethel Literary and Historical Association. The hoped-for meeting turned into a series of meetings, the fourth of which Joseph Hannen assessed in a report to the new national journal, *Bahai News*, the following spring:

> The Bethel Literary and Historical Society, the oldest and leading colored organization in the city, devoted its session of Tuesday, April 5, to the Bahai Revelation, Mr. Hannen and Dr. Fareed speaking on the subject of "The Race Question from the Standpoint of the Bahai Revelation." This Society, of which Mr. Louis G. Gregory is President, has given three previous sessions this season to the Bahai Teachings, and this has exerted a powerful influence in the work among the intelligent circles of this people, whom we are commanded to reach and help as brothers and sisters.

In another report Mr. Hannen mentioned two recent meetings arranged by the wife of a Howard University professor, at which Roy

Wilhelm and Percy F. Woodcock, Bahá'í visitors from the New York area, spoke to interested groups of black intellectuals.[4] Such a ferment of activity, focusing on individuals whose education and professional status made them eminently respectable on every count except color, could not be ignored by the white Bahá'ís. Obviously some action had to be taken to accommodate these people.

The Washington community held its first formal interracial meeting during this period and proudly announced its success in the first issue of *Bahai News:*

> On the evening of March 6th, an important gathering assembled at the home of Mr. and Mrs. Hannen, representing the joining in one meeting of the white and the colored Bahais and friends of this city. Considerable work is being done among the latter, and a regular weekly meeting is held at the home of Mr. and Mrs. Dyer, 1937 13th street, N. W., on Wednesdays. In February of last year, Abdul-Baha commanded that to prove the validity of our Teachings and as a means of removing existing prejudices between the races, a Spiritual Assembly or meeting be held, preferably at the home of one of the white Bahais, in which both races should join. This is the first meeting of that character, and is to be repeated monthly. There were present about 35 persons, one-third of whom were colored, and nearly all believers. It is also planned that every fourth Unity Feast [forerunner of the Nineteen-Day Feast], beginning April 9, should be held in such manner that both races can join. This is a radical step in this section of the country, and is in reality making history.

And on 9 April the Unity Feast was carried out as planned. Joseph Hannen described it in *Bahai News* as "wonderfully blessed and successful" and noted that "several leading men and women of the colored race attended." The hostess for the evening was Fanny Knobloch and the speaker Louis Gregory.[5]

The mixed meetings continued throughout 1910. A large number of people, black and white, attended a meeting at the Dyers' on 15 June at which Hippolyte Dreyfus of Paris spoke, and audiences of one hundred or more filled the hall of the Conservatory of Music for the integrated Unity Feasts of 5 June, 1 August, 16 October, and 12 December, at one of which Mr. Gregory spoke and at another served as host.[6] Yet these integrated meetings were still the exception, and a certain number of whites continued to regard them as an aberration and a liability in their efforts to attract to the Cause the "better sort" of people in Washington, among whom the black intelligentsia obviously was not to be included. Thirty years later Louis Gregory described with remarkable objectivity the conditions that were to continue in the city for many years and at times were to separate completely the different factions:

> One matter that caused much difficulty in adjustment was the wise handling of the American race problem, especially in the Southern atmosphere of such a city as Washington. Some of the friends, reading the command of Baha'u'llah which read: "Close your eyes to racial differences and welcome all with the light of oneness," interpreted it to mean that all barriers of race should be put aside in every meeting that was planned for teaching the Faith. Others knew the principle as wise and just, but felt that the time was not yet ripe for its application. One difficulty was finding places, either private or public, that were willing to welcome all races. In the same family, one or more members being Baha'i and the others not believers, the mixing of races would cause a family disturbance. Even where all the believers were free from prejudices some felt that it would upset inquirers after the truth if they were confronted too soon with signs of racial equality. One of the friends went so far as to state that some of the Baha'i principles would not be operative for a full thousand years! On the other hand, others were [insistent] that such principles should be upheld and applied even though the world should go to smash. As for a thousand years in future, there might be another Manifestation [in Bahá'í terms, the divinely inspired Founder of a major religion] with laws for another day. But the laws of this Manifestation were for this day and must be applied.[7]

Whatever doubts Louis Gregory may have had at first in regard to his role in integrating the Washington Bahá'í community were firmly put aside by 'Abdu'l-Bahá. His first letter to Mr. Gregory in November 1909 expressed the hope that he might become "the means whereby the white and colored people shall close their eyes to racial differences" and "the cause of the guidance of both races." Accordingly, Mr. Gregory began to work in three distinct

LOUIS GEORGE GREGORY

GEORGE GREGORY
Louis Gregory's stepfather,
whose name Louis took by ''his earnest wish''

PAULINE and JOSEPH HANNEN
early Bahá'ís of Washington, D.C.,
who nurtured Louis Gregory's interest in the Bahá'í Faith

though interrelated areas of endeavor upon which he focused his activities for more than four decades.

First, he became a spokesman of the Bahá'í Cause to his own people. In those days of strict segregation in the South and deepening racial animosity in the North, the doors that were closed in the faces of blacks were often closed from the other side to white Bahá'ís seeking to share Bahá'u'lláh's message. As a Southerner residing in Washington, Louis Gregory was uniquely placed both to return to the South to teach and to spread knowledge of the Faith among blacks in the capital and in the large metropolitan areas of the North, which attracted increasing numbers of blacks during and after the First World War. Wherever he went, he was likely to find in the black community friends and acquaintances from Fisk and Howard. In fact, even before becoming a Bahá'í, he had given literature to friends during a 1908 visit to Kansas City, Missouri. One of the recipients, Edith Chapman, eventually became the first Bahá'í there.[8]

In 1910 Louis Gregory made his first teaching trip, stopping in eight Southern cities, including Richmond, Virginia; Durham, North Carolina; Charleston, South Carolina; and Macon, Georgia. "Am just having the time of my life!" he wrote to the Hannens from Charleston. "Have many engagements to speak, in churches and at gatherings, on Bahaism." A subsequent report in *Bahai News* noted that he had spoken directly to about nine hundred people during the trip and that blacks in the South showed promise of being "deeply and vitally interested." Many years afterward he looked back on that first experiment as a traveling Bahá'í teacher with the experience of a seasoned speaker. He recalled that "in every city people were found who accepted the great Message, however crudely and abruptly given, and the spirit was powerful," but communities were not established at the time, because "the system of follow-up work was not then developed."[9]

Later, particularly after 'Abdu'l-Bahá launched a plan for the worldwide expansion of the Faith by the American Bahá'ís, Louis Gregory returned often to the South, traveling for months at a time, meeting friends from previous trips and making countless new ones. A familiar visitor at black colleges and secondary schools in the South, he frequently lectured at Tuskegee Institute (twice at the invitation of Booker T. Washington) and at Fisk. He also maintained close contact with black intellectuals and professionals both North and South and assured that they were well aware of the Bahá'í teachings.

His second area of endeavor was Bahá'í administration. Well suited by his education and legal training to become a leader in the Bahá'í community, he was first elected to office in February 1911, less than two years after he became a Bahá'í, when a special election was called to fill a vacancy on Washington's Working Committee. The election indicated the community's appreciation of his valuable qualities of leadership and of the services he had already rendered in his brief period of membership. It also revealed, as he suggested in the following letter to Joseph Hannen, the determination of the Washington Bahá'ís to do something about the problems of race within their own ranks:

> I have your kind favor of the 4th, advising me of the action of the Working Committee of the Bahai Assembly in electing me to membership. My emotion upon reading it was a commingling of pleasure and [embarrassment]. There is joy, because I know that this action springs from a noble impulse on the part of the committee. It evinces breadth and the Guidance of the Spirit. Who knows how far-reaching the effect will be in advancing the Cause of God in the future?
> The [embarrassment] is due to the fact that what is truly a great honor should be given one so unworthy. I agree to serve temporarily, until some one with a wise head and noble heart may be found, who may thus more fitly represent my race.[10]

From this "temporary" service as the first black on Washington's administrative body Mr. Gregory went on to become the only black elected to the Executive Board of Bahai Temple Unity (as the national Bahá'í organization, formed primarily to oversee construction of the first Bahá'í House of Worship in the West, was known). On 30 April 1912 a tie for the ninth and last place on the Board was broken in his favor by unanimous vote of the delegates to the fourth annual convention.* Later that same day this remark-

---

*The others elected to the Executive Board were Dr. Zia M. Bagdadi, Mrs. Corinne True, Mr. Albert H. Hall, Mr. Roy C. Wilhelm, Mr. Bernard M. Jacobsen, Mr. Willard H. Ashton, Mrs. Annie L. Parmerton, and Mr. Mountfort Mills.

able convention was given lasting historical significance by the arrival of 'Abdu'l-Bahá, Who addressed the final public meeting of the convention.[11]

Louis Gregory again accepted election to the Executive Board in 1918. On other occasions he declined his nomination or election, following a customary practice during the Temple Unity years.[12] In 1921 he and another black, Mabry C. Oglesby of Boston, were appointed to the new National Teaching Committee. In 1922, as the development of Bahá'í administration under the Guardianship of Shoghi Effendi was just beginning, he first became a member of the National Spiritual Assembly of the Bahá'ís of the United States and Canada, which superseded the Executive Board of Bahai Temple Unity. He served on that body a total of fourteen years during three separate periods of membership until ill health curtailed his activities in 1946.* Although other black leaders emerged on the national level during those years, it was not until early in 1946 that a second black, lawyer Elsie Austin, was elected to the National Spiritual Assembly to replace ailing member Roy Wilhelm; her period of membership thus coincided with Louis Gregory's for a few months.

Over the years Mr. Gregory filled a number of unobtrusive but important administrative roles—recording secretary of the National Spiritual Assembly, for example, and member of committees to audit the Temple treasury and to handle legal matters such as drawing up the by-laws of the newly formed National Assembly. He was most in the public eye at the time of the annual national convention, which he often served as speaker, convention secretary, and particularly reporter.

Third, Louis Gregory became a standard-bearer for the cause of racial unity. As a writer, lecturer, and for many years an administrator of a national Bahá'í interracial committee, he advanced that cause both directly and indirectly. Whatever his topic, by the simple act of addressing a largely white gathering, he reaffirmed the principle of racial equality and indirectly raised the consciousness of the audience. His first speaking engagements of national significance occurred in Chicago in 1912, during the Fourth An-

_____
*Louis Gregory served on the National Spiritual Assembly from 1922 to 1924, from 1927 to 1932, and from 1939 to 1946.

nual Convention of Bahai Temple Unity, which he attended as a delegate from Washington. On Saturday, 27 April, he spoke briefly at a special commemoration called the "Feast of Rizwan," organized by the Chicago community and open to the delegates and visitors to the convention. At "a large public meeting" the following morning he gave a featured address on "The Reality of Humanity." Literally overnight, he had established himself as one of the finest Bahá'í speakers of his era. He invariably attracted the attention of the audience, a friend has recalled, with his "musical" tone of voice and his "sweet and personable magnetism," which made one want "to hear his speech regardless of whether you were aware of what he was speaking about."[13]

Thereafter, he spoke regularly during the annual conventions.* In 1913 in New York at the final public session of the convention he "addressed the assemblage in his usual earnest, powerful and effective manner."[14] In 1914 in Chicago he again was a featured speaker, along with Mariam Haney of Washington, D.C., and Edward B. Kinney of New York, at a large public meeting. Alfred Lunt reported to *Star of the West* (as *Bahai News* had come to be called) that

> Mr. Louis G. Gregory then spoke of the object of the Bahai Movement as divine unity of man with God, and the manifestation of this unity in brotherhood, confirming all that is good and true in every religion. That the differences [*sic*] between men, in the final analysis, is a difference of vision, while the difference between the savage and civilized man, in regard to what we call civilization, is entirely a difference of degree. He referred to the great contribution of the state of Illinois to the life of the race, in Abraham Lincoln; how Illinois was to the front of spiritual and practical ideals in granting the franchise to women, one of the Bahai foundations; then read from the *Hidden Words*, "O Children of Men! Do ye know why we have created ye [*sic*] from one clay? That none should glorify himself over the other," etc.[15]

He ranged comfortably over a wide variety of Bahá'í subjects. At

---

*Although the Bahá'í temple (or Mashriqu'l-Adhkár) was being built near Chicago, only about half the Temple Unity conventions were held there. The alternate locations ranged from San Francisco on one coast to Boston on the other.

the 1916 convention in Chicago he gave talks on the "Demonstration of Divinity and Inspiration—the Word" and "The Interdependence of Individuals, Nations and Races." Subsequently, he wrote an account of some of the sessions for *Star of the West*, thus emerging as a regular contributor to Bahá'í publications. In 1917 he spoke at the convention in Boston and again that November in Chicago at the centennial celebration of the birth of Bahá'u'lláh, when his topic was "The New Educational System of Bahá'u'lláh." At the 1918 and 1919 conventions his subjects were "The Underlying Unity of All Religions" and "The Power of the Holy Spirit."[16]

Only in 1920 did he begin to deal repeatedly and directly in his lectures and articles with the theme of racial amity. His misgivings about a direct approach, which some people might see as special pleading for his race, were set aside as 'Abdu'l-Bahá showed mounting concern over racial conflict in America. Mr. Gregory's topic at the convention that year and again in 1921 was "The Oneness of Mankind," and the first volume of the *Bahai Year Book*, later titled *The Bahá'í World*, carried an article called "Racial Amity," based on another public talk given in 1921.[17] When a Racial Amity Committee was formed by the National Spiritual Assembly in 1927, Louis Gregory became its executive secretary; thereafter, he was for years either its secretary or chairman, and he served the committee as speaker on many platforms.

Finally, during all this time he demonstrated in his personal relationships—which he carried on with dignity, common sense, and good-humored disregard for criticism and hostility—his belief that mankind is one family. His circle of white friends and acquaintances among the Bahá'ís widened as he traveled and attended conventions from San Francisco to Boston. Both present-day reminiscences and letters written during his lifetime reveal extraordinary respect and admiration for him. A representative passage appears in a letter from Howard Colby Ives, a former Unitarian minister, who became a distinguished Bahá'í writer and itinerant teacher. "I cannot refrain, dear Louis, from speaking of the great love we both bear towards you," he wrote on behalf of himself and his equally remarkable wife, Mabel Rice-Wray Ives. "Of all the souls in the Cause we know of none whose humble servitude, tranquil power, and selfless teaching is so constant and so unassuming. . . ."[18] The sincere high regard in which these and many other white Bahá'ís held Louis Gregory was itself a force to destroy barriers of prejudice and unthinking discrimination.

5   Pilgrimage

For more than forty years Louis Gregory remained the chief spokesman for racial unity in the American Bahá'í community. His role was partly the result of his own past; it stemmed from his experiences growing up in the South and from his youthful activism in Washington, D.C. But, above all, his dedication to the principle of human oneness was rooted in his close relationship with 'Abdu'l-Bahá, the Exemplar of Bahá'í ideals. From the start 'Abdu'l-Bahá had given Louis Gregory not only the goal but the encouragement he needed in order to achieve it.

Attracted to the Master since his first Bahá'í meeting, when the spirit of the small group of adherents present overcame the chill of a stormy winter night, Mr. Gregory had deepened his acquaintance with 'Abdu'l-Bahá as he investigated the Bahá'í teachings. When he became a Bahá'í in June 1909, he instinctively sought personal contact with the Master, at first through correspondence and later by seeking permission to make a pilgrimage, as his teachers, the Hannens, had done.

After more than fifty years as an exile and a prisoner, 'Abdu'l-Bahá had only recently been freed, along with all the political and religious prisoners of the Ottoman Empire, by the Young Turk Revolution. To the Western Bahá'ís this meant (at least for a time) the end of worry over His safety and the beginning of an increased flow of pilgrims to the Holy Land. When Louis Gregory wrote early in 1910, asking to be allowed to make a pilgrimage, permission was denied, however. "It is at present not in accord with wisdom," 'Abdu'l-Bahá explained. "Postpone this matter to another and more opportune time."[1]

A few months later, exercising His new freedom, 'Abdu'l-Bahá left the Holy Land for the first time in more than forty years to travel to Egypt. It was from Ramleh, near Alexandria, late in 1910, that He sent Louis Gregory an invitation to come "in the spring."[2]

41

Mr. Gregory reserved passage on a ship sailing from New York on 25 March 1911. He was able to plan an extended trip that included stops in Europe as well as in Egypt and Palestine.

Many fellow Bahá'ís in Washington, well aware that Louis Gregory was the first black American to have the privilege and opportunity of pilgrimage at the express invitation of 'Abdu'l-Bahá, shared his excitement.* On 22 March Mr. and Mrs. Andrew J. Dyer's regular Wednesday Bahá'í meeting became a surprise farewell party, attended by more than fifty Bahá'ís and guests. Even though the Wednesday meetings were primarily for blacks, on this occasion a number of white Bahá'ís participated. Joseph Hannen wrote of the evening in *Star of the West*:

> Mr. Gregory was given the seat of honor, at the head of the long table, and his chair was surmounted by a horse-shoe of flowers. While refreshments were being served, speeches were made by a number, including Dr. W. B. Evans, Principal of the Armstrong Manual Training School; Judge Gibbs, former U. S. Consul to Madagascar; Professor W. H. H. Hart, of Howard University; Professor G. W. Cook, of Harvard University; Mr. Edward J. Braithwaite; Mr. Duffield; Miss Murrell, of the faculty of Armstrong Manual Training School; Miss Grace Robarts; Mrs. Claudia S. Coles; Mr. Charles Mason Remey; Professor Stanwood Cobb; Mr. and Mrs. Hannen. Mr. Gregory responded in a feeling manner to the good wishes expressed.[3]

The importance to Louis Gregory of his first overseas voyage cannot be exaggerated. Even as a pleasure trip, it would have been a milestone in his life. He crossed in freedom the ocean that his forebears had traversed in chains. Moreover, he landed on the African continent with a new ethnic awareness. Having been recognized as an American on sight by fellow passengers from other countries, he concluded that blacks had made a unique adaptation to America precisely because their ties with Africa had been so

---

*Robert Turner, the first black American to become a Bahá'í, was also one of the first Westerners to make a pilgrimage to the Bahá'í holy places in Palestine and to meet 'Abdu'l-Bahá; he did so, however, as Mrs. Phoebe Hearst's butler rather than as an independent pilgrim. Louis Gregory described the warm reception he received from 'Abdu'l-Bahá in "Robert Turner," *World Order*, 12, no. 1 (Apr. 1946), 28–29.

ruthlessly cut, and "in fact no other American group . . . is more American."[4] This realization, coupled with a vision of the future development of a cosmopolitan world order, pervaded his racial amity work in the years ahead. It helped him maintain his perspective and confidence during the discouraging years when a world war supposedly fought for democracy was followed in the United States by racial conflict, by the revival of the white supremacist Ku Klux Klan, and by the rise of Marcus Garvey's black separatist back-to-Africa movement. After his voyage Mr. Gregory never doubted that blacks belonged in America and that their rightful presence and full integration in every aspect of society would eventually be recognized even by extremists of both races.

Beyond the sociological insights that the journey provided, Mr. Gregory discovered in the pilgrimage a deeply inspiring and instructive religious experience. 'Abdu'l-Bahá Himself observed that Louis Gregory had been transformed, had become "quite another Gregory."[5] In Palestine the pilgrims visited the shrines of Bahá'u'lláh and of the Báb, His forerunner, and came to know the places where Bahá'u'lláh had lived from His banishment to the penal colony of 'Akká in 1868 until His death in 1892. In both Egypt and Palestine Mr. Gregory met members and close associates of Bahá'u'lláh's family; he was especially impressed with 'Abdu'l-Bahá's young grandson, Shoghi Effendi, who was to become in 1921 the Guardian of the Bahá'í Faith. The other pilgrims also contributed much to Mr. Gregory's experience. An Englishwoman named Louisa Mathew, who was present during his first meeting with the Master, won "admiration" for her "long range of accomplishments and great devotion to the Faith."[6]

But all the aspects of Louis Gregory's journey, even those that were most significant in their own right, were overshadowed by the reality of meeting 'Abdu'l-Bahá. Mr. Gregory had seen many famous people in Washington, D.C. Nonetheless 'Abdu'l-Bahá was unique: "Presidents and senators, cabinet members and ambassadors, justices and kings of commerce and trade, inventors, discoverers, monarchs of other lands, all either singly or together, seem to pale into insignificance when compared with this wonderful man who had spent about forty years in prison!"[7]

Mr. Gregory remembered in detail his first impressions of 'Abdu'l-Bahá:

When . . . I saw him for the first time he was about sixty-seven years of age, about the medium height, with a strong frame and symmetrical features. His face was deeply furrowed and his complexion about the shade of parchment. His carriage was erect and his form strikingly majestic and beautiful. His hands and nails were shapely and pure. His silver hair touched his shoulders. His beard was snow white, with eyes light blue and penetrating, his nose somewhat aquiline. His voice was powerful, but capable of infinite pathos, tenderness and sympathy. His dress was that of the Oriental gentleman of rank, simple and neat, yet very graceful. The color of his apparel was light, the outer robe being made of alpaca. On his head rested a light fez surrounded by a white turban. The meekness of the servant, the majesty of the king, were in that brow and form. [8]

During their interviews the Master dispelled any uncertainty that may have lingered in Mr. Gregory's mind concerning the urgent need for racial unity in America and his particular role in its advancement. 'Abdu'l-Bahá Himself raised the subject of race during their first meeting, when He asked in general terms, " 'What of the conflict between the white and colored races?' " Louis Gregory recalled that

this question made me smile, for I at once felt that my Inquirer, although He had never in person visited America, yet knew more of conditions than I could ever know. I answered that there was much friction between the races. That those who accepted the Bahai teachings had hopes of an amicable settlement of racial differences, while others were despondent. [9]

Later 'Abdu'l-Bahá asked specifically, " 'Are the colored and white believers entirely united?' " Aware as he was of the divisions in the Washington, D.C., community, Mr. Gregory replied tactfully that among the Bahá'ís "there was not entire unity, but that there were earnest souls of both races who desired closer unity and hoped that He would point out to them the means of attaining it." The Master's answer suggested that differences over race among the American Bahá'ís were attributable to a superficial acceptance of the Faith and that real believers would achieve real unity. He said that, in order to attain closer unity, " 'the best means is to accept this Cause. All differences must fade among believers. In the present antagonism there is great danger to both races.'"[10]

'Abdu'l-Bahá also made it clear that the races must become united in the literal sense—through intermarriage. "'Intermarriage is a good way to efface racial differences,'" He told Mr. Gregory. "'It produces strong, beautiful offspring, clever and resourceful.'" 'Abdu'l-Bahá returned to the subject of intermarriage another day, after Mr. Gregory asked whether "in view of the difficulties in the way of inter-racial unity for all meetings, the colored friends should organize separately to observe the nineteen-day unity meetings." The Master replied, "'The colored people must attend all the unity meetings. There must be no distinctions. All are equal. If you have any influence to get the races to intermarry, it will be very valuable.'"[11]

The existence of racial prejudice, even among the Bahá'ís in America, had obviously troubled 'Abdu'l-Bahá. The "expressive and beautiful face," which had "nearly always" seemed "joyful" to Louis Gregory, changed. Suddenly the Master revealed the sorrows of "Him who carries the burden of the world." He paced back and forth in silence, then seated Himself, still remaining silent, and finally retired, explaining that He was "very weary."[12]

After the party of pilgrims returned to Egypt from Haifa and 'Akká, 'Abdu'l-Bahá stressed once again the importance of racial unity. In the presence of a roomful of followers, He addressed to one of the outstanding white Bahá'ís in Washington a letter (or tablet, to use the traditional Bahá'í term, from the Arabic *lawḥ*) regarding racial segregation:

> You have written that there were several meetings of joy and happiness, one for white [and] another for colored people. Praise be to God! As both races are under the protection of the All-Knowing God, therefore the lamps of unity must be lighted in such a manner in these meetings that no distinction be perceived between the white and colored. Colors are phenomenal; but the realities of men are Essence. When there exists unity of the Essence what power has the phenomenal? When the Light of Reality is shining what power has the darkness of the unreal? If it be possible, gather together these two races, black and white, into one assembly and put such love into their hearts that they shall not only unite but even intermarry. Be sure that the result

of this will abolish differences and disputes between black and white. Moreoever by the will of God, may it be so. This is a great service to the world of humanity.

"After dictating this Tablet," Mr. Gregory recalled, " 'Abdu'l Baha took a vessel containing blackberries and gave some of them to each of the friends present."[13]

Undoubtedly, Louis Gregory recognized that 'Abdu'l-Bahá directed His statement not only to the Bahá'ís in Washington but also to those followers who were in His presence that day. Among the latter He then chose to reinforce His words about race by the symbolic sharing of the delicious, black-colored fruit. But, as Louis Gregory and his fellow pilgrim Louisa Mathew were later to realize, the Master's motives were more complicated still. He never explained why He had delayed Mr. Gregory's pilgrimage; but it soon became clear that, whether 'Abdu'l-Bahá had deliberately brought Louis and Louisa together, He had henceforth envisioned for them "a great service to the world of humanity." As a result of His loving encouragement, they soon were to marry, thus becoming the first of many Bahá'í interracial couples to demonstrate the principle of racial unity on the most fundamental level.

When Louis Gregory left Alexandria, however, he had as yet no inkling of the marriage that lay ahead. 'Abdu'l-Bahá had simply restated the personal goal—" 'work for unity and harmony between the races' "—that He had given Mr. Gregory in the first months of his Bahá'í life. During their final visit in Ramleh the Master had suggested the means to achieve this goal. " 'Go forth and speak of the Cause of God,' " He had urged. " 'Visit the friends. Gladden their hearts. You will be the means of Guidance to many souls.' " And, as Mr. Gregory was leaving, one of 'Abdu'l-Bahá's secretaries had brought a parting message of encouragement: " 'This morning 'Abdu'l Baha spoke of you and told me to say to you: "Keep your face turned to the Kingdom and fear nothing!" ' " For the present no greater task seemed possible than the task Louis Gregory had already been given, nor could he have received more soul-stirring encouragement.[14]

At 'Abdu'l-Bahá's request Mr. Gregory visited Germany, Paris, and London on his way home to America. His visit to Germany was particularly significant. The German Bahá'í community had been established only a few years earlier. It had grown largely through the efforts of Miss Alma Knobloch (a sister of Pauline Hannen), who had settled in Stuttgart in 1907. Miss Knobloch assured his welcome in a land where non-European minorities were few and where, scarcely more than twenty years later, racialism, which Shoghi Effendi has termed one of the "chief idols in the desecrated temple of mankind," was to be enshrined by the Nazis in their country's political philosophy.[15]

In a letter to one of the German Bahá'ís, 'Abdu'l-Bahá Himself called attention to Louis Gregory's color: "When he arrived at Stuttgart, although being of black color, yet he shone as a bright light in the meeting of the friends."[16] Thus 'Abdu'l-Bahá shared Louis Gregory, making of him a symbol of racial equality, as He had shared the blackberries among His guests at Ramleh.

The German Bahá'ís, without mentioning color, echoed 'Abdu'l-Bahá's description of Mr. Gregory in the following report of his visit:

In May, 1911, we had the privilege of entertaining Mr. Louis G. Gregory, of Washington, D. C., who came to us from the presence of Abdul-Baha, throbbing with new life and light. A reception in his honor was held at 24 Canzelei Str. To the home of the Stäbler family in Stuttgart; to Mrs. and Miss Kaslin in Esslingen, and to Mr. and Mrs. Schweizer in Zuffenhausen, near Stuttgart, our honored guest came and told the assembled friends much that was interesting.[17]

In letters both to Germany and to America 'Abdu'l-Bahá made absolutely clear the high regard in which He held Louis Gregory and the extent to which the pilgrimage had matured and strengthened him. When one of the Bahá'ís in Stuttgart wrote Him of Mr. Gregory's visit, 'Abdu'l-Bahá replied: "Verily, he has much advanced in this journey. He received another life, and obtained another power. When he returned, Gregory was, quite another Gregory. He had become a new creation. . . . This man shall progress."[18] To one of the Washington Bahá'ís the Master wrote:

Mr. Gregory arrived with the utmost love and spirituality and returned with infinite happiness. He added to his faith and assurance and found firmness and steadfastness. Undoubtedly you shall see these things at the time of his arrival. It is my hope that he may become the cause of increasing the love of the friends.[19]

In still another tablet 'Abdu'l-Bahá suggested the kind of welcome the returning pilgrim should receive in his homeland: " 'Mr. Gregory is at present in great happiness. . . . He will return to America very soon, and you, the white people, should then honor and welcome this shining colored man in such a way that all the people will be astonished.' ' "[20]

6 'Abdu'l-Bahá in America

The extraordinary welcome that 'Abdu'l-Bahá wished for Louis Gregory on his return to America did not take place as the Master had envisioned it. Instead, the white Bahá'ís focused their attention on the arrival of a young Persian Bahá'í, a fellow passenger with Mr. Gregory on the voyage from London to New York. Qudsíyyih Khánum-i-Ashraf (or Ghodsia Ashraf Khanum as she was known in America) was the first woman from her country to seek an education abroad. She arrived in Washington, D.C., in time to attend the First Annual Conference of the Persian-American Educational Society, an association for cultural exchange to which a number of Bahá'ís were firmly committed.[1] The excitement over her arrival overshadowed Louis Gregory's homecoming. Nonetheless, he immediately resumed his Bahá'í activities in Washington. "He has delivered several public lectures since his return," Joseph Hannen reported in *Star of the West*, "and will be more of a power than ever for the Cause. . . ."[2]

That summer Mr. Gregory's teaching efforts took him for the first time to Green Acre, a progressive conference center that had been established in 1894 by Sarah Farmer in Eliot, Maine, and had attracted such notable figures as Vivekananda and Booker T. Washington. Louis Gregory's visit proved to be the beginning of a long and fruitful association with Green Acre.

To his fellow Bahá'ís during the months after his pilgrimage, Louis Gregory often spoke and wrote of his experiences. His recollections of 'Abdu'l-Bahá were charged with the hope that the Master might travel from Egypt to America, as the American Bahá'ís had been longing for Him to do. Mr. Gregory concluded an account of his meeting with 'Abdu'l-Bahá by writing: "Thus the friends of the Cause may catch a glimpse of what is in store for them if he visits America. Nor should we spare any pains or hesitate at any sacrifices to ensure his coming."[3]

'Abdu'l-Bahá had been invited to address the Universal Races Congress in London at the end of July 1911. Although for some time it seemed as if He might actually attend, He finally sent a message to the Congress and decided to travel to Europe later in the summer. He sailed for Marseilles in August. For the next four months He visited Switzerland, England, and France. Then He returned to Egypt to rest for the winter.

'Abdu'l-Bahá's trip to Europe excited still further the hopes of the American Bahá'ís. The dream of having 'Abdu'l-Bahá in their midst seemed incredibly near realization. They showered Him with invitations; they raised money to cover His expenses, only to have it returned. They urged Him to sail on the maiden voyage of the *Titanic*; but when He finally made His travel arrangements, He chose the S.S. *Cedric* instead. The ship sailed from Egypt on 25 March 1912, put in at Naples, and arrived in New York on 11 April. Traveling with 'Abdu'l-Bahá were several Persians— secretaries, an attendant, and a translator—and six Western Bahá'ís, among whom was the Englishwoman Louisa Mathew.[4]

'Abdu'l-Bahá's eight-month-long visit indelibly marked the course of Bahá'í history in America. " 'It is my purpose to set forth in America,' " He was reported to have said on the day of His arrival, " 'the fundamental principles of the revelation and teachings of BAHA 'ULLAH. It will then become the duty of the Bahais of this country to give these principles unfoldment and application in the minds, hearts and lives of the people.' "[5]

In statements to the general public and the press He emphasized that He sought to further the cause of unity and peace. Among the Bahá'ís He stressed that His ultimate purpose was to transform them spiritually, in order that they might help to bring about the oneness of mankind. He told a gathering of Bahá'ís who came to greet Him on that first day:

> As New York has made such progress in material civilization, I hope that it may also advance spiritually . . . so that the friends here may become the cause of the illumination of America; that this city may become the city of love and that the fragrances of God may be spread from this place to all parts of the world. I have come for this. I pray that you may be manifestations of the love of BAHA 'ULLAH; that each one of you may become like a

clear lamp of crystal from which the rays of the bounties of the Blessed Perfection [Bahá'u'lláh] may shine forth to all nations and peoples. This is my highest aspiration.

In this same talk He referred to the effort of the trip as having been both "necessary" and motivated by love: "This long voyage will prove how great is my love for you."[6]
'Abdu'l-Bahá spoke often of unity during those first days in America, in New York and then in Washington, D.C., which He visited later in the month. But it was in the capital on 23 April, with Louis Gregory at His side, that He first confronted—both in public addresses and in a social context—the issue of racial unity. Indeed, the *Washington Bee*, a black newspaper, called attention to the relationship between 'Abdu'l-Bahá and Louis Gregory in an article it published concerning 'Abdu'l-Bahá's visit:

> Abdul Baha Abbas, the leader of the Baha movement for the world-wide religious unity, has been in the city. Through the missionary work of Mrs. Christian D. Helmick (Mrs. A. C. Barney that was), quite a colony of colored Bahaists has been developed in Washington, and these earnest disciples gave their patron saint an especially warm reception. On Tuesday evening the venerable prophet addressed a large audience at Metropolitan A. M. E. Church, in connection with the Bethel Literary Society. At noon Tuesday, the Abdul spoke to the students of Howard University. The principal advocate of the Bahai faith in this city is Mr. Louis C. [*sic*] Gregory, a brilliant young lawyer and government official, whose zeal in the work was so absorbing that he made a comprehensive tour of Egypt and the Holy Land to study at first hand the history and philosophy of this remarkable cult. . . . [7]

Mr. Gregory undoubtedly had been instrumental in arranging for these two major speaking engagements, as he was an alumnus of Howard University's law school, had been for years a leader in the Bethel Literary and Historical Association, and had arranged a number of Bahá'í meetings under its sponsorship. In the Howard speech 'Abdu'l-Bahá stated unequivocally that color is of no importance either before God or in any of the kingdoms of existence—animal, vegetable, or mineral—except as an "adornment," a source of "charm." Only among human beings has it become a cause of discord. He was happy, He declared, to see whites and blacks together in the meeting as a step toward unity, "for the accomplishment of unity between the colored and whites will be an assurance of the world's peace. Then racial prejudice, national prejudice, limited patriotism and religious bias will pass away and remain no longer." [8]

Before the Bethel Literary and Historical Association that evening at the Metropolitan African Methodist Episcopal Church on M Street N.W., He likened the audience to "a beautiful bouquet of violets gathered together in varying colors, dark and light." Then He went on to speak of science as "the most noble" of humanity's many "virtues," all of which should be utilized in "directing our efforts toward the unification of the human race." The result of such efforts will be unity in diversity:

> Then will mankind be as one nation, one race and kind; as waves of one ocean. Although these waves may differ in form and shape, they are waves of the same sea. Flowers may be variegated in colors but they are all flowers of one garden. Trees differ though they grow in the same orchard. All are nourished and quickened into life by the bounty of the same rain; all grow and develop by the heat and light of the one sun; all are refreshed and exhilarated by the same breeze; that they may bring forth varied fruits. This is according to the creative wisdom. If all trees bore the same kind of fruit it would cease to be delicious. In their never-ending variety man finds enjoyment instead of monotony. [9]

Early on that afternoon of 23 April 'Abdu'l-Bahá had sought to demonstrate His teachings on race by challenging the practice of social segregation. After His speech at Howard University, He had been invited by Ali-Kuli Khan, chargé d'affaires of the Persian Legation, and Madame Florence Breed Khan, both of whom were Bahá'ís, to attend a luncheon and a reception in His honor. About nineteen guests were present at the luncheon. Some were "very prominent in the social and political life of Washington," Mr. Gregory recalled, and others were Bahá'í friends of the Khans, individuals such as Agnes Parsons, a Washington socialite, and

Juliet Thompson, a painter from New York, who were comfortable in such circles. [10]

About an hour before the luncheon 'Abdu'l-Bahá had sent word to Louis Gregory to come to the Khans' for an interview. "Louis arrived at the appointed time, and the conference went on and on," a good friend, Harlan Ober, has recounted. " 'Abdu'l-Bahá seemed to want to prolong it." Finally luncheon was announced, and, as 'Abdu'l-Bahá led the invited guests to the dining room, Mr. Gregory waited for the chance to leave the house unobtrusively. "All were seated when suddenly," Mr. Ober continued,

> 'Abdu'l-Bahá stood up, looked all around, and then said to Mírzá Khan, Where is Mr. Gregory? Bring Mr. Gregory! There was nothing for Mírzá Khan to do but find Mr. Gregory. . . . Finally Mr. Gregory came into the room with Mírzá Khan. 'Abdu'l-Bahá, Who was really the Host (as He was wherever He was), had by this time rearranged the place setting and made room for Mr. Gregory, giving him the seat of honor at His right. He stated He was very pleased to have Mr. Gregory there, and then, in the most natural way as if nothing unusual had happened, proceeded to give a talk on the oneness of mankind. [11]

Juliet Thompson's account of the luncheon testifies to the ease with which 'Abdu'l-Bahá defied convention, as if it did not in fact exist. She wrote simply that "a colored man, Lewis [sic] Gregory, was present and the Master gave a wonderful talk on race prejudice." Mr. Gregory himself, although he undoubtedly told the full story of the luncheon to many friends, stated in his formal reminiscences only that "'Abdul Baha' made everyone feel perfectly at ease by his genial humor, wisdom and outpouring of love. . . . He mentioned his address at Howard University which was made at noon that same day and indicated guidance and progress in race relations."[12]

Gently yet unmistakably, 'Abdu'l-Bahá had assaulted the customs of a city that had been scandalized only a decade earlier by President Roosevelt's dinner invitation to Booker T. Washington. Moreover, as a friend who helped Madame Khan with the luncheon recalled, the place setting that 'Abdu'l-Bahá had rearranged so casually had been made according to the strict demands of Washington protocol.[13] Thus, with one stroke 'Abdu'l-Bahá had swept aside both segregation by race and categorization by social rank.

After the luncheon and the Khans' reception, which was attended by such luminaries as Admiral Peary, Alexander Graham Bell, and Yúsuf Díyá Páshá, the Turkish ambassador, 'Abdu'l-Bahá proceeded to another reception at the home of Mrs. Parsons. Once again Juliet Thompson was there. She pictured 'Abdu'l-Bahá, Who had been a prisoner and exile throughout most of His life, far removed even from the refinements of His early childhood in Iran, as being perfectly at ease among the trappings of wealth and prominence in Western society. Yet, rather than fitting in, He transcended His surroundings.

> Into this room of conventional elegance, packed with conventional people, imagine the Master striding with His free step, walking first to one of the many windows and, while He looked out into the light, talking with His matchless ease to the people. Turning from the window, striding back and forth with a step so vibrant it *shook* you.[14]

It was without doubt this commanding presence, this charisma, that enabled 'Abdu'l-Bahá to do and say astonishing things without creating a storm of controversy.

The following evening He lent His support to the Dyers' Wednesday night meeting, regularly attended by black Bahá'ís and their friends. He compared the racially mixed audience that night to "a beautiful cluster of precious jewels,—pearls, rubies, diamonds, sapphires." He spoke on existence and nonexistence, life and death, finally likening fellowship to life and discord to death. "In the clustered jewels of the races, may the colored people be as sapphires and rubies, and the whites as diamonds and pearls. The composite beauty of humanity will be witnessed in their unity and blending." And once again, as He had at Howard, He linked the unity of black and white in America to the cause of world peace. "When the racial elements of the American nation unite in actual fellowship and accord, the lights of the oneness of humanity will shine. . . ."[15]

In Chicago, the next city He visited, 'Abdu'l-Bahá returned to the theme of racial unity in three major speeches given on 30 April.

Addressing the public meeting that concluded the annual convention of Bahai Temple Unity, 'Abdu'l-Bahá stated that "the ages of darkness have passed away and the century of light has come. Ignorant prejudices are being dispelled and the light of unity is shining."[16]

To a mixed audience of several hundred at Jane Addams' Hull House, He spoke of points of agreement and points of difference between the races in America, arguing that "in physical bodies, in the law of growth, sense endowment, intelligence, patriotism, language, citizenship, civilization and religion you are one and the same. A single point of distinction exists; that of racial color." And He asked, "Shall this, the least of all distinctions be allowed to separate you as races and individuals?"[17]

Another important talk that day was addressed to the closing session of the Fourth Annual Convention of the National Association for the Advancement of Colored People. In its journal, *The Crisis*, W. E. B. DuBois, who was serving as editor, printed both his version of the text of the Master's talk, which appears also to include passages from the Hull House talk, and a general account of the convention. DuBois mentioned "the calm sweet universalism of Abdul Baha" and the large audience at that session, when "a thousand disappointed people were unable to get even standing room in the hall."[18]

'Abdu'l-Bahá's theme on that occasion was that the Old Testament teaching that God made man in His image gives us the standard by which we are to be judged. This standard, He said, has nothing to do with wealth, fame, or color—qualities that are "accidental." "Man is not to be pronounced man simply because of bodily attributes. Man is to be judged according to his intelligence and to his spirit." The standard is thus the "Divine Virtues" within man: human spirit and human intelligence.[19]

'Abdu'l-Bahá's addresses to large gatherings of influential blacks in Washington, D.C., and Chicago, two of the nation's most racially mixed cities, permanently established the Bahá'í Faith in the consciousness of black America. The new religion had been almost unknown among blacks until Louis Gregory became a Bahá'í. Through his efforts, it was by 1912 no longer completely obscure. Yet, within just one week, 23–30 April, 'Abdu'l-Bahá had greatly extended the process of acquainting black Americans with the teachings of Bahá'u'lláh. N.A.A.C.P. members, university students and teachers, and others who had heard 'Abdu'l-Bahá subsequently scattered throughout the country; their favorable impressions of the Master opened many doors for Louis Gregory and other Bahá'ís in the years ahead. If the Faith was not yet widely or well known, at least a significant minority of blacks had heard of it and was willing to hear more.

From Chicago 'Abdu'l-Bahá returned to New York, stopping briefly in Washington but giving no major addresses. In the months ahead He traveled extensively throughout the country. Louis Gregory, having gone to Chicago for the Bahá'í convention, would have remained gladly at the Master's side. Instead, his responsibilities took him back to Washington, where he followed the news of 'Abdu'l-Bahá's journeys and occasionally received messages of encouragement from the Master.

Finally, in the late fall, 'Abdu'l-Bahá returned to Washington, D.C. From 6 to 10 November He gave a number of talks. One of the highlights of His last visit to the capital was a Bahá'í banquet held on 9 November at Rauscher's Hall. A history submitted by the Washington Bahá'ís to the Historical Religious Survey of the Works Progress Administration singled out the event for special mention: "A large dinner and meeting, exclusively for Baha'is, was held at Rauscher's on Connecticut Ave.—an interracial gathering of great spiritual and historic interest for it was the first time that the white and colored friends met together at such a function and in such a place."[20] 'Abdu'l-Bahá said to the gathering:

> May you view mankind as the sheep of God and know for a certainty that he is the real shepherd. . . . Verily this shepherd makes no distinctions whatsoever; to all the sheep he is equally kind. Therefore we must follow the example of God and strive in pathways of good-will toward all humanity.[21]

The following day, His last in Washington, He spoke to a "beautiful" racially mixed audience in the home of the Hannens about Bahá'u'lláh's black attendant, Isfandíyár. To 'Abdu'l-Bahá, the "Servant of Glory," servitude was not demeaning; it was, rather, the best of human conditions. Of Isfandíyár He said, "Truly he was a point of light." When Bahá'u'lláh was first imprisoned in 1852, Isfandíyár had refused to flee to safety. He had paid the debts of the Holy Family after all their possessions were confiscated. "If a perfect man could be found in the world," 'Abdu'l-Bahá asserted, "that man was Isfandyar." In closing He referred again to the racial diversity of the audience, stressing the need for even greater diversity.

I hope you will continue in unity and fellowship. How beautiful to see colored and white together! I hope, God willing, the day may come when I shall see the red men, the Indians with you, also Japanese and others. Then there will be white roses, yellow roses, red roses and a very wonderful rose-garden will appear in the world.[22]

Louis Gregory listened carefully, as he always had, absorbing not only 'Abdu'l-Bahá's words but His rapport with the audience. "By studying the public addresses of Abdul Baha," he wrote to Joseph Hannen some years later, "one marvels at the Divine Wisdom and Insight—which knew the difficulties as well as hopes of each gathering He addressed." From 'Abdu'l-Bahá's example, Mr. Gregory learned to become familiar with the goals and concerns of each audience he addressed, to find "the point of contact."[23]

He also learned that to find the point of contact one did not have to tell an audience what it wanted to hear or to commiserate over its problems. Indeed, 'Abdu'l-Bahá's addresses both to blacks and to Jews in America never dwelled on their misfortunes. Although He, too, had known suffering at the hands of the unjust during more than half a century of imprisonment and exile, in His public talks to minority groups He did not go over the common ground of persecution. That He did not do so, despite His demonstrated concern and compassion in personal and private situations, indicates a conscious motive.

That motive, it seems, was to promote a particular psychological reorientation of the minority's attitude toward the majority and toward itself. Rather than intensify a natural preoccupation with oppression, 'Abdu'l-Bahá sought to foster confidence in the power to effect change. For blacks, whose color He described with approbation, this meant, on the one hand, development of a sense of one's own beauty and worth, and, on the other hand, reinforcement of the good qualities of whites through praise and appreciation. It also meant taking a larger view, broadening one's perspectives both historically and internationally; 'Abdu'l-Bahá noted in two of His speeches to largely black audiences that black Americans did not realize fully their good fortune in being Americans, in being free to strive toward "equal attainments with the white race," even in being able to hold such interracial meetings. Nor, He implied, did they appreciate fully the international consequences of the struggles of whites in their behalf.[24]

From the vantage point of late-twentieth-century skepticism, such remarks might well be misunderstood. But they must be placed within the context of the times—with regard to the political and social position of blacks everywhere and to the particular hopes of black Americans—and judged by the numerous examples of 'Abdu'l-Bahá's understanding of the gravity and complexity of America's racial problems.

However difficult their lot, black Americans in the early 1900s were among the few nonwhite groups anywhere in the world to enjoy even rudimentary freedom under a democratic form of government. Most of the world's people—regardless of color—were not free in any sense of the word. Most blacks at the time lived under colonial rule with little or no access to the kind of education that would pave the way toward equality. The status of black Americans was far more encouraging if seen in global rather than national terms. As Louis Gregory once put it:

> We have our problems to solve in this country, but let us not become despondent over them, realizing that today the whole world is having its problems and difficulties. There is no country in the world today that has not difficulties equaling, if not surpassing, our own. I do not say this with the suggestion that misery loves company, but in order that we may not be despondent and think that these difficulties are hindrances.[25]

'Abdu'l-Bahá addressed Himself to the hopes for the future shared by His black audiences, rather than to their fears. He knew that in general blacks still held to the American dream and to a faith that whites would share that dream with people of color. He was also well aware that pervasive injustice threatened to undermine both the optimism of blacks and the American dream itself. For if blacks were to lose the will to achieve equality and were to give in to hopelessness and anger, that dream would become a hollow shibboleth.[26] Indeed, if optimism were to die because of continued humiliation, exploitation, antagonism, and betrayal by whites, the result would be a widening nightmare of violence.

'Abdu'l-Bahá repeatedly warned of the disastrous consequences of continued prejudice and injustice toward blacks. Early pilgrims to Haifa recalled His saying, " *'The blacks hate the whites and the whites distrust the blacks. You must overcome this by showing that you make no distinction. The end will be very unfortunate for both if the differences are not removed.'* "[27] In 1912 He predicted, in a letter to a Chicago Bahá'í, that, if racial attitudes in America did not change, "enmity will be increased day by day and the final result will be hardship and may end in bloodshed." Then violence would engulf blacks and whites alike, for "until these prejudices are entirely removed from the people of the world, the realm of humanity will not find rest. Nay, rather, discord and bloodshed will be increased day by day, and the foundation of the prosperity of the world of man will be destroyed."[28] Several years later, in a letter to Roy Williams, one of the most active black Bahá'í teachers at the time, 'Abdu'l-Bahá referred to racist attitudes as a "wound" and a "disease" and again warned that, if not checked, "the antagonism between the Coloured and the White, in America, will give rise to great calamities."[29]

Moreover, in 1920 'Abdu'l-Bahá reportedly cautioned that even the existence of America was at stake. " 'When I was in America, I told the white and colored people that it was incumbent upon them to be united or else there would be the shedding of blood,' " He affirmed to Dr. Zia Bagdadi, whom He had sent from the Holy Land a decade earlier to help establish the Bahá'í Cause in the West. " 'I did not say more than this so that they might not be saddened. But, indeed, there is a greater danger than only the shedding of blood. It is the destruction of America.' " And 'Abdu'l-Bahá added: " 'Now is the time for the Americans to take up this matter and unite both the white and colored races. Otherwise, hasten ye towards destruction! Hasten ye toward devastation!' "[30]

The Master's warnings also formed the basis of a powerful statement on race in America made by Shoghi Effendi many years later. In 1954 the Guardian declared that the United States was passing through a grave and "dangerously underestimated" crisis, threatened externally by the Cold War and the buildup of armaments and internally by deteriorating moral standards, "rampant materialism," and—a factor of equal importance—"ingrained racial prejudice":

> No less serious is the stress and strain imposed on the fabric of American society through the fundamental and persistent neglect, by the governed and governors alike, of the supreme, the inescapable and urgent duty—so repeatedly and graphically represented and stressed by 'Abdu'l-Bahá in His arraignment of the basic weaknesses in the social fabric of the nation—of remedying, while there is yet time, through a revolutionary change in the concept and attitude of the average white American toward his Negro fellow citizen, a situation which, if allowed to drift, will, in the words of 'Abdu'l-Bahá, cause the streets of American cities to run with blood. . . .[31]

But in His public talks in America 'Abdu'l-Bahá never touched on the prospect of such catastrophic racial violence. He preferred, as He Himself explained, not to "sadden" His audiences. He did not dwell on the deficiencies of the present order. Instead, He encouraged His listeners, pointing out "the oases rather than the deserts of their environments," as Louis Gregory once observed. " 'Abdu'l-Bahá envisioned a new sociology for the world in general and America in particular."[32]

His public themes did not spring, therefore, from unfamiliarity with or disregard for the terrible obstacles blacks faced in their efforts to achieve equality in America. Rather, He sought to nurture the positive attitudes among blacks that would stave off desperation, hopelessness, growing hatred, and the ultimate disaster of racial warfare so violent that it would "cause the streets of American cities to run with blood."

Louis Gregory heard both the encouragement to constructive action in 'Abdu'l-Bahá's speeches and His private warnings about racial violence. He readily understood the personal implications of 'Abdu'l-Bahá's assertion that brotherhood "is not possible without will and effort on the part of each" of the races.[33] For whites, the quest for brotherhood entailed putting aside ingrained attitudes and habits of superiority. For blacks, it demanded building a basis for trust. Mr. Gregory believed that the teachings of Bahá'u'lláh had stripped away all traces of anger and hatred from his own heart. He knew that these emotions, however well justified, simply intensify oppression, whereas positive attitudes erode its foundations. As he once told an audience,

It is only by co-operation, mutual appreciation, and good will that we can get anywhere in the solution of these problems that vex us. If this room were filled with darkness we could not remove that darkness by intensifying the darkness, nor can we remove discord from the face of the earth by increasing discord.[34]

Yet a hopeful attitude did not come easily even to Louis Gregory, although he turned invariably toward the standard set by 'Abdu'l-Bahá. In 1919, for example, he wrote to his friend Joseph Hannen:

The Bahai teacher must maintain a state of happiness if he is to do his work effectively. And this seems possible only by constant prayer and as far as one can, ceaseless activity. Otherwise, the well-authenticated reports of cruel injustices and crimes against defenceless peoples would entirely absorb the powers of concentration.

He added that he had to agree with a friend who had said, " *'If the devil aint [sic] loose now, he has a devil of a long rope!'* "[35]

If the world did at times seem to be an infernal place, Louis Gregory clung nonetheless to a heavenly vision. Hell itself could not withstand 'Abdu'l-Bahá and the regenerative power of the divine will for humankind that He proclaimed. "He is able to make all places fruitful," Mr. Gregory remarked. "His is a wonderful culture of hearts and minds."[36]

During 'Abdu'l-Bahá's visit to America, and particularly during the eventful last week in April 1912, Louis Gregory witnessed 'Abdu'l-Bahá's concerted efforts to cultivate the soil of racial unity. At the same time Mr. Gregory received incomparable support for his own efforts to carry out the task the Master had given him, that of working "for unity and harmony between the races." In both public and private meetings 'Abdu'l-Bahá stated clearly and repeatedly that color was simply incidental in nature, that it had absolutely no validity as a measure of the worth of any human being, and that it should be regarded as a source of attraction, just as a variety of colors within a flower garden is more interesting than a monotonous repetition of red or blue or white alone. In His own conduct, in His treatment of Louis Gregory and other black Bahá'ís, and in His obvious pleasure in interracial gatherings, 'Abdu'l-Bahá demonstrated not only His beliefs but His freedom from social constraints.

To these proofs of the Bahá'í stand on race He added one final, unarguable testimony: He brought Louis Gregory and Louisa Mathew together in marriage. Their union served as a perpetual reminder of the Bahá'í position on the oneness of humankind.

LOUISA MATHEW
who met Louis Gregory in the presence of 'Abdu'l-Bahá

LOUIS G. GREGORY
encouraged by 'Abdu'l-Bahá to
'' 'work for unity and harmony between the races' ''

LOUIS G. GREGORY
"How luminous is the face of this person!" —*'Abdu'l-Bahá*

LOUISA MATHEW GREGORY
whose "long range of accomplishments and
great devotion to the [Bahá'í] Faith" won Louis Gregory's admiration

LOUIS G. and LOUISA MATHEW GREGORY
'Abdu'l-Bahá described their marriage as ''an introduction to the accomplishment''
of good fellowship between blacks and whites

7 Marriage

After her pilgrimage Louisa Mathew (or Louise, as she was called by those close to her) had returned to Europe, apparently intending to follow the Master's suggestion that she travel to America. But 'Abdu'l-Bahá Himself soon arrived in France, giving her a reason to linger there. Her own health, always frail and particularly poor at that time, contributed to further delay. Indeed, during her pilgrimage the Master had prescribed for her a restorative diet of chicken and fish. He later told her, " 'I found you almost dying in Egypt. . . .' " He added that, if she had not followed His counsel, she would have been "worse" than another English Bahá'í and fellow pilgrim "who was very ill from consumption & who died 4 months after Abdul Baha said this to me." [1] Finally, 'Abdu'l-Bahá offered her the opportunity to travel to America with Him, and all obstacles disappeared. Teasing her about her sudden enthusiasm for the trip, the Master said, " 'Just now you said it was too far but as soon as you hear of my going it gives you strength to go.' " [2]

Miss Mathew was not a young woman. Born in 1866 of wealthy parents in southern England, she had studied economics and languages at Cambridge University and voice both at Cambridge and in France, where she had become a Bahá'í. Despite her background and her considerable accomplishments, she was unassuming—"shy and modest," as a friend described her. [3] Physically plain and preoccupied with her frailty, she hardly expected that with the trip to America she would begin a full new life.

But the Master had plans for her and a larger purpose than she could have anticipated. "My marriage as you know," she wrote a friend some years later, "was entirely brought about by Abdul Baha. I had no thought of marriage when I came to this country." Her future husband was equally unsuspecting. Shortly before their

marriage he wrote to Pauline Hannen, "Last year we visited Abdul
Baha at Ramleh and the Holy Tomb at Akka and although greatly
attracted to each other not even dimly realized its future bearing."[4]
Even if they had recognized the potential in their relationship from
the start, without 'Abdu'l-Bahá's explicit encouragement they undoubtedly would have considered race too great an impediment to
overcome.

During their pilgrimage, when 'Abdu'l-Bahá stated that black
and white Bahá'ís should not only be in unity but should intermarry, He addressed the sexual myths and fears at the heart of
American racism. The result of intermarriage, He emphasized,
would be to "abolish differences and disputes between black and
white."[5] But to the Bahá'ís of Washington, D.C.—many of
whom hesitated to hold interracial meetings, especially in white
homes, out of concern for what people would say—intermarriage
was virtually unthinkable. In the West "scientific" theories of racial inferiority and superiority and of the harmful effects of racial
admixture abounded. Intermarriage in America thus defied not
only social convention but popular science. Moreover, it was actually a criminal offense in many states. Under the circumstances
even the mention of intermarriage was a challenge to the precon-
ceptions of many whites.

Controversy over intermarriage raged in the Washington Bahá'í
community for years, despite 'Abdu'l-Bahá's frequent public and
private statements of the principle of oneness and His innumerable
demonstrations of freedom from prejudice and conventionality. In
1914 Agnes Parsons, who had become a leader in the community
by virtue of her highly respected social position and her deep devotion to 'Abdu'l-Bahá, wrote Alfred Lunt, a Boston lawyer and
leading figure in the Bahá'í administrative order, for information
on the legal aspects of intermarriage. She was obviously worried
that the Bahá'ís were being encouraged to form marital unions that
were socially unacceptable and often illegal. Mr. Lunt's long letter
of reply reported the results of his research into the statutes of the
various states. He discovered that, out of the forty-eight states and
the District of Columbia, a majority of twenty-five governments
prohibited or did not recognize interracial marriage. The
twenty-five prohibiting states included all those in the Southern

and border regions, the Western states of California, Idaho, Nevada, Oregon, and Utah, and all of the Southwest except New Mexico.

Mr. Lunt also addressed Mrs. Parsons' fears by sharing his own reasoned views. His comments reveal much about the confusion of the American Bahá'ís with regard to race in those early years.

> I have felt that the marriage side of the question is in danger of over emphasis, and that the uncertainty and doubt regarding it has tended to dishearten the believers on the broad question of Oneness of the races, and the spiritual teachings of Unity. . . . *But* the heralding forth of the principle of the oneness of humanity, and the *fundamental spiritual union* of all races, "living in one land, and walking with the same feet etc" will scatter the present false basis of judgment on this question. The superstitious and limited biological ideas taught today will vanish before the flame of the Love of God, and the problem [intermarriage], simplified, will become merely what it should be, an individual problem of selection. But this cannot be unless we bravely and unfalteringly herald the *Principle*. In Washington, as you know, some of the souls are in an attitude of apology and distortion toward the great principle elucidated by Abdul Baha [the oneness of mankind]—seeking to please and attract the believers in superstition on this subject. Had the Manifestations Themselves adopted this policy of concealment and compromise, they might have preserved thereby their lives and possessions, but the Divine Civilization would never be realized. Baha'o'llah said that the Divine Laws are revealed strictly according to the *capacity* of the people at the time of Appearance. The unanswerable corollary must be that had the people of the world not been capable today of living according to the law of *oneness* it would not have been decreed.[6]

To those Bahá'ís—in Washington and elsewhere—who eluded the principle of the oneness of mankind with "an attitude of apology and distortion," 'Abdu'l-Bahá not only announced the goal of intermarriage but demonstrated it with a fait accompli: the marriage of Louis and Louise Gregory. Aside from race, they were as unremarkable a couple as could be imagined. Both were well-educated and cultured, both mature—indeed, middle-aged. Their economic positions were balanced; although she came from a wealthy background, she lived on a modest income, and he had risen from poverty into the professional class. Yet because of race they constantly faced disapproval and the threat of violence. Their marriage was regarded by many as an eccentricity at best, even within the Bahá'í community. To strangers it was an affront or, quite literally, a crime. In a country where sexual relationships between black men and white women were grounds for lynching, her age, plain appearance, and English nationality helped to protect them from extremes of hostility. However, the possibility of violent attack remained with them always. Indeed, the fact that they did not provoke attack was perhaps more unexpected than a violent incident would have been. "Louise and I have been in a great many different places together," Mr. Gregory once observed, ". . . but no one has ever molested us."[7]

Considering the formidable obstacles to their union, their readiness to accept 'Abdu'l-Bahá's encouragement of their relationship is astounding. They had no idea of flouting the mores of a prejudiced society. They did not see themselves as a cause, except insofar as 'Abdu'l-Bahá had made an example of them; and, happy as they were to give encouragement to the cause of racial unity, they did not relish the attention their marriage focused upon them. Beyond superficial differences of color and background, they saw themselves simply as fellow believers, as friends who had, through the good offices of 'Abdu'l-Bahá, become loving partners in life.

On the *Cedric* in Naples, as Louise told the story in a letter to Agnes Parsons years later, 'Abdu'l-Bahá had asked her to join Him for a walk on deck, if she wished, with only His secretary Maḥmúd present.

> Then He turned round & said "I said what I did because I saw a seed in your heart." Then almost immediately added "Now is the watering time." I could not understand what He meant—I only thought it must be something of a spiritual nature. A moment later He turned round again & said "I saw one seed in your heart, I wish it to produce many seeds."
> In this country Abdul Baha first revealed to me symbolically, through a white flower which He told me to give Mr. Gregory & by looking at me in a peculiar way conveyed his meaning to me, that He wished me to marry Mr. Gregory. Curiously enough

after this love began to grow in my heart & the desire for the marriage whereas before I only liked Mr. Gregory as a friend. Later Abdul Baha said before Dr. Getsinger, Fareed & others in the train to Chicago to me "How are you & Mr. Gregory getting along?" Startled I answered "What do you mean, we are good friends?" To which He replied emphatically & with His face wreathed in mischievous smiles "You must be *very* good friends."

Before He left Chicago I asked Abdul Baha plainly one morning early if I had understood aright that He wished Mr. Gregory & myself to marry. He said "yes." He did wish it. "I wish the white & the colored people to marry" He added.

Then on my intimating that as a woman I could do nothing to bring it about He asked "Do you love him, would you marry him if he asked you?" & I replied "yes." Then He said "if he loves you he will ask you." Later in the morning as I learnt some time afterwards, He told Louis it would give Him much pleasure if he & I would marry, which came as an utter surprise to Louis who had no thoughts of marriage. Abdul Baha said "What is the matter? Don't you love her?" "Yes as a friend" Louis said. "Well think of it" said Abdul Baha, "& let me know; . . . marriage is not an ordinance & need not be obeyed, but it would give me much pleasure if you & Miss Mathew were to marry."[8]

Within a few months they were married. A week before the ceremony Louis Gregory confirmed to Pauline Hannen that the wedding was to take place at noon on Friday, 27 September. "But please do not mention this except with the utmost discretion," he cautioned, "as we do not wish any sensational newspaper articles written at the time and are exerting ourselves to avoid such things."[9]

Because the Bahá'ís in America were not then empowered legally to conduct marriages—indeed, the first such civil recognition was achieved nearly thirty years later in Chicago—the couple sought a sympathetic minister and a favorable location.[10] As a result, the wedding was held in the parsonage of an Episcopal church in New York City. In order to assure that the ceremony took place quietly and without incident, only a few people were asked to attend.

Mr. Gregory added in his letter to Pauline Hannen that he was

sorry that the Hannens would not be there. But their encouragement—like that of 'Abdu'l-Bahá, who spent that day on
a train headed westward from Denver—contributed to the Bahá'í
atmosphere of the wedding. Three days after the marriage he wrote
Mrs. Hannen again, describing the ceremony in some detail:

> Some weeks ago, Abdul Baha, who has watched over Louise
> and me with the tender solicitude of a loving father, sent me a
> Message directing me to use the utmost judgment in order to
> avoid criticism in regard to our approaching Marriage. With me
> "the utmost judgment" was prayer for Divine Guidance, in
> which Louise heartily joined me. Our prayers have been heard
> and answered and we are very happy. Every matter connected
> with the event went off without friction, although some things
> were quite difficult.
>
> On last Friday at noon, at the residence of Rev. Everard W.
> Daniel, just nine persons were present, including the minister
> and his wife, the bride and groom. After the ceremony of the
> Church of England was completed, the groom said, "Verily we
> are content with the Will of God." And the bride responded,
> "Verily we are satisfied with the Desire of God" [the Bahá'í
> marriage vows, as they were then translated]. Then Mr. Mac-
> Nutt read the Tablet of Abdul Baha on marriage. Mr. Braith-
> waite followed, reading a Tablet revealed to the groom three
> years ago of which the following is an extract: "I hope that thou
> mayest become the herald of the Kingdom, become the means
> by which the white and colored people shall close their eyes to
> racial differences, and behold the reality of humanity." Mrs.
> Botay closed with the Tablet of Baha'o'llah, *Protection*. Then
> the wedding party repaired to the wedding breakfast. In this
> small company were represented Christian and Jew, Bahais and
> non-Bahais, the white and colored races, England and America,
> and the three Bahai assemblies of New York, Philadelphia
> and Washington.
>
> During the ceremony there was a light rainfall. This, Mrs.
> Nourse says, was a Bahai sign, the Bounty of God. After the
> ceremony the skies cleared, the sun shone and everything and
> everybody seemed to be happy. The same afternoon we arrived
> here [in Atlantic City] on our honeymoon. We find ourselves
> very harmonious and very happy.[11]

Their honeymoon in Atlantic City not only served to give them time for each other but for Bahá'í activities as well. Louis Gregory wrote with evident appreciation of the community's freedom from racial tension:

> There are some believers here in Atlantic City who are very much alive. Some years ago Mrs. [Elizabeth B.] Nourse lived in Washington and belonged to the wealthy and fashionable set there as she does here. It appears that she moved here about four years ago, and during her stay has done a most effective work in spreading the teachings. She is known for deeds of philanthropy and at the weekly Bahai meetings held in her home welcomes alike white and colored people, and is very much loved. We shall have more than one meeting here this week, for the friends of Abdul Baha like to put each other to work for the Cause.[12]

One can well imagine that it was a happy time—to have been carrying out 'Abdu'l-Bahá's wishes, knowing that He would soon be returning to the East Coast and enfolding them in the warmth of His acceptance.

Beyond both the initial difficulties and the unexpected happiness of the marriage there emerged in time a sense of its significance. Louise Gregory told Mrs. Parsons how she had eventually come to understand the Master's words to her in Naples:

> Some two years after our marriage I suddenly realized what Abdul Baha had meant when He said "I saw a seed in your heart etc." The seed I realized was the attraction between Louis & myself, the watering time the ripening of this feeling into love leading to marriage its fruit, the "one seed producing many seeds" the attraction of the hearts of the white & colored races to be produced by our love & marriage.
>
> Our marriage therefore is important as Abdul Baha has indicated. He said I heard later that the importance of our marriage was not understood at that time but would be understood later. It was the first inter-racial marriage between these two races among the Bahais you know & known to be brought about by Abdul Baha Himself thus encouraging inter-racial marriage & letting the Bahais know that He encouraged it. Since then I suppose you know there have been two of these marriages among Bahais neither of which I think would have taken place without the example of our marriage.[13]

The "seed" of their marriage thrived despite manifold obstacles. It was difficult for the Gregorys to travel together, difficult simply to find a place to live. Told of their problems, 'Abdu'l-Bahá reportedly "replied emphatically that at Haifa they would be received with open arms."[14] But in America such acceptance was rare. With one exception, they were never together in the Southern region upon which Mr. Gregory concentrated so much effort as an itinerant racial amity worker. That exception was a summer spent together in Maryland, where intermarriage was considered, as he expressed it, "an infamous crime."[15]

In Washington, D.C., their home for a number of years, their union was legal but ill-received. Even the Bahá'ís—black as well as white—found it difficult to accept the marriage or to imagine its survival in a segregated society. "The vile reproaches of people of both races descended upon me for a step which I have never regretted," he recalled. Even for such an amiable person as Louis Gregory, friends were "none too many." He never forgot those few individuals or ceased to be grateful to them. Years later, for example, he told a friend that the Ali-Kuli Khans, whose own marriage bridged the gulf between East and West, had demonstrated "such real Baha'i love and understanding as I hope never to forget in time or eternity."[16]

Outside the small circle of their friends, the Gregorys' actions were subjected continually to scrutiny and criticism. Once, when the Bahai Temple Unity moved to send Louis on a teaching trip through the South, Agnes Parsons worried so over the prospect of Louise's accompanying him that she wrote to William H. Randall of the Temple Unity: "Mr. Gregory has had much to meet in Washington from members of his own race because of his marriage and in the farther south the marriage will be taken even more seriously. I cannot see how he will reach either white or colored there—if his wife be with him."[17] Mrs. Parsons was neither malicious nor insincere, but her overcautious intervention illustrates the extent to which even well-meaning speculation and interference intruded upon their lives.

Yet when Louise, having been effectively prevented by circumstances and discretion from traveling with her husband, decided in the 1920s to follow her own independent course and teach the Bahá'í Faith in Europe, gossip and conjecture only intensified.

LOUISA MATHEW GREGORY
known to her friends as Louise

LOUIS G. GREGORY
"During the years we have had but one spirit, one purpose
and one purse." –Louis Gregory

LOUISE GREGORY

The Gregory home near Green Acre Bahá'í School, Eliot, Maine.
"It is really very pleasant to be home once more and Louise, my wife,
is doing all in her power to make me comfortable." –Louis Gregory

Once she even contemplated returning ahead of schedule to the United States in order to attend a major Bahá'í event with Louis, "to set at rest the reports which are going around among the colored people, so Louis told me, that we had separated." As she explained to Mrs. Parsons, with whom she eventually established a congenial relationship:

> This report about our separation bothered him somewhat & he was even ready to think we had made a mistake in my coming as he is very desirous of convincing the colored people that the Bahai Movement makes all things possible even inter-racial marriages & he knows Abdul Baha had said there was a special purpose in our marriage & he did not wish them to think I had gone to Europe because I found conditions in America on account of my marriage unbearable which is what the colored people had been expecting ever since our marriage & now they seemed ready to say to each other *"I told you so."* [18]

The difficulties and frustrations the Gregorys experienced as an interracial couple were never unbearable, however, because their unity fortified them. They enjoyed each other's companionship. Each found encouragement in the other's accomplishments and in a common purpose, even when their fields of endeavor were on separate continents. "I was greatly blessed," Louis Gregory wrote Edith Chapman after a quiet summer in Portsmouth, New Hampshire, near Green Acre,

> by . . . the presence of my angel wife, Louise, who had a four months' "furlough" from her teaching campaign in Bulgaria. That Balkan region is where the world war started & it is still a seething caldron of unrest. Hence the importance of the Great Message reaching it[s] varied peoples so full of racial & religious & national hatreds, all of which spell tragedy these days. We were supremely happy together in our quaint old home near the sea.

As the years passed, their shared goals in life continued to bind the Gregorys together. Louis observed in 1950 that Louise's "fine cooperation in teaching service has been a tower of strength to me." [19]

Above all, whether they faced the challenges of living together as an interracial couple in a deeply prejudiced society or of living apart to fulfill their individual destinies, Louis and Louise Gregory found constant strength in their relationship with 'Abdu'l-Bahá. He had brought them together, and He never failed to assure them of His support. "Continually do I remember you," He once wrote them. "I beg of God that through you good fellow-ship may be obtained between the white and the black for you are an introduction to the accomplishment."[20]

8   A Divided Community

During the Gregorys' early years together in Washington, the interracial fellowship that 'Abdu'l-Bahá envisioned for the Bahá'ís seemed elusive, if not unattainable. The Master's visit, rather than having ended the patterns of racial discrimination in the community, had brought matters to a head. The Washington Bahá'ís became increasingly divided on the issue of race. A small faction of whites, steeped in the prejudiced attitudes of the time, clung to their views despite 'Abdu'l-Bahá's clear statements and demonstrations of belief. Another faction, both white and black, was emboldened by 'Abdu'l-Bahá's example to demand that evidences of discrimination be eliminated from the community. A large number of whites found themselves on uncertain ground, hesitant about full integration, fearing to challenge the unyielding attitudes of society or even to scrutinize their own. By 1914 even the pretense of unity had broken down, and the Bahá'ís of Washington began to separate into several groups. The Gregorys found themselves having to act, as Louise put it, "the difficult part of peacemaker, explaining the difficulties of the white people to the colored & the point of view of the colored people to the white."[1]

The crisis was precipitated in part by the community's decision to give up its rented center at Studio Hall, 1219 Connecticut Avenue, where integrated meetings had been held. For some time a monthly interracial meeting also had been held in a white home. The "nineteen day unity feasts," as they were then often called, had been open to blacks periodically, once every four feasts, until 'Abdu'l-Bahá sent clear instructions that all Bahá'ís should be free to attend.[2] But meetings for inquirers—both "firesides," as smaller gatherings have since come to be known, and public talks—presented problems. Even when held in a public hall identified as a Bahá'í Center and open to both races, such meetings were not particularly comfortable for those who were accustomed to social separation of the races.

By early 1914 the controversy had divided the community into separate camps. One group, claiming that "mixed meetings were the one serious obstacle to the growth of the Cause in this locality," agitated for rental of a public hall where blacks would not be welcome—a prestigious sort of place, in other words, that would be considered proper by whites of conventional values. Others, including the Gregorys, believed that such a policy was "against Abdul-Baha's wishes & commands," even if the purpose was ostensibly to attract more white inquirers and gradually to teach them the principle of oneness. [3]

A third position was that a center was unnecessary. Louise Boyle, a white Bahá'í, expressed this opinion in a letter to Mrs. Parsons. A center "should stand for Oneness," she felt, if only because it had become a symbol in the eyes of most Bahá'ís, rather than simply a place to hold meetings; but she saw no particular need for a center. In her view all kinds of good results flowed from the decision to give up Studio Hall:

> Nothing ever happened so happily for Washington as the freeing of individuals through the abandonment of the Centre. . . . I am finding wonderful opportunities as I wrote you, and *know* conditions are limbering up. Group meetings are held everywhere, the friends attract strangers to them just to the extent of their spiritual power. [4]

For her the issues of the center and of integrated meetings were beside the point. The key to successful teaching was the quality of the individual Bahá'í's life: "Neither the centre nor the color question retards our activity and the growth of the Cause. We *have not become* the 'Essence of essences'. We have to reach the world as the Beloved reaches it, through suffering with its pain and ministering to it, reflecting clearly some divine *Light* to the *ready* people in the world." [5]

Mrs. Boyle's analysis was accurate, up to a point. Among real believers, 'Abdu'l-Bahá had observed years earlier to Louis Gregory, racial differences would inevitably fade. Thus incomplete commitment among the American Bahá'ís was the fundamental reason for their lack of growth, and the issues of "the Center" and of "the color question" were simply manifestations of that problem. Despite the claims of some Bahá'ís, a center with integrated meetings certainly had not retarded "the growth of the Cause." It was true that racial integration was a barrier to many whites; as Mrs. Boyle put it, "in having the color element in meetings of strangers, to the evolved Bahai it is the sign of Truth, to the stranger it is an unintelligible sign."[6] But, for blacks attracted by the Bahá'í principle of oneness, segregated meetings were as much "an unintelligible sign" as integrated ones were for whites. The "spiritual power" of the Bahá'ís to which Mrs. Boyle referred was the only force capable of creating a new perspective among those afflicted by prejudice.

The way that the Bahá'ís faced the "color question," however, ultimately determined their "spiritual power." "An attitude of apology and distortion," such as Alfred Lunt once described, failed to win even those whites to whose bias some Bahá'ís catered—at the risk of driving away the black believers, dividing the community, and losing the good pleasure of 'Abdu'l-Bahá. The issue of the center and of the kind of people who could be invited there was far more important, therefore, than Mrs. Boyle at first realized.

"The freeing of individuals through the abandonment of the Center" did not lead to the regeneration of the community that Mrs. Boyle had predicted. Instead, it created favorable conditions for the seeds of disunity already present among the Bahá'ís in Washington. The controversy grew and deepened. 'Abdu'l-Bahá's advice was sought; but, as Mrs. Parsons later recalled, He "remained silent for a long time, undoubtedly in order that we might work out a solution of the trouble." On the first of May 1914 one of the Washington Bahá'ís finally received a tablet on the subject that 'Abdu'l-Bahá had Himself written in Arabic. In it He said:

I know about everything that is happening in Washington. The sad, sombre news is the difference between the white and the colored people. I have written to Mr. Hannen requesting him, if possible, to arrange a special place of meeting for the white people only, and also a special place of meeting for the colored people, and also one for both the white and the colored, so that all may be free. Those who prefer to do so can go to the white meeting. And those who prefer can go to the colored meeting, and those who do not wish to bind themselves either way, they are free, let them go to the meetings of the white and the colored people in one place. I can see no better solution to this question.[7]

Clearly, 'Abdu'l-Bahá was grieved by the racial division in Washington. Moreover, He had delayed giving any opinion on the subject, according to Mrs. Parsons, and had finally done so with obvious reluctance, allowing separate meetings only because "no better solution" could be found. However, those who favored segregation took 'Abdu'l-Bahá's words as an affirmation of their views. They believed that He was withdrawing His earlier insistence that functions for Bahá'ís should be open to all, regardless of race. Indeed, most Bahá'ís in Washington immediately assumed that by "meetings" 'Abdu'l-Bahá meant all activities and that in effect He was permitting three autonomous Bahá'í "assemblies" in the city. As incredible as this may seem to present-day Bahá'ís, with their experience of a unified administrative structure, it was some time before anyone thought to question whether the Master had been referring only to gatherings primarily for inquirers. By then it was too late to ask for a clarification; the outbreak of war had cut communications with the Holy Land. Thus the Washington Bahá'ís were left on their own to solve the difficulties they had created.

Even before the arrival of 'Abdu'l-Bahá's letter in May 1914, the community had divided into three groups. A white meeting had been organized at the Pythian Temple on Sundays, a "colored" meeting at the Washington Conservatory of Music on Wednesdays, and a mixed meeting in the home of a white Bahá'í on Fridays. Almost immediately, the three meetings became four. Although the Pythian Temple meeting drew large crowds, it was infected by the blatantly racist views of at least one member whose agitations eventually led to a lengthy estrangement from the Bahá'í community. This hardly seemed to be what 'Abdu'l-Bahá had in mind when He asked Joseph Hannen, whose freedom from prejudice was well known, to arrange a meeting for whites. Therefore, Mr. Hannen started a second meeting at Lewis Hall. The meeting at the Conservatory of Music, which continued the tradition of Wednesday night gatherings at the Dyer home, had to be discontinued; it had been integrated, like the Wednesday meetings of previous years, but because it was labeled a "colored" meeting, blacks stopped attending. Instead, a meeting had been organized on T Street. The so-called mixed meeting on Fridays fared no better. Louise Gregory observed at the end of the year that the hostess, concerned about potential problems with her neighbors and the management of her apartment building, had not really wanted large numbers of blacks and had not allowed them to figure prominently in the meetings; few had attended in any case.[8]

Finally on 1 October 1914 representatives of each of the four meetings met to try to resolve some of their differences. Mr. Hannen had stated that he and his wife would be happy to attend the Pythian Temple meeting if it would repudiate the racist views, sometimes in the form of anonymous letters, that had been circulating in Washington and in other parts of the country as well, creating the impression that its members did not accept the principle of the oneness of mankind. Everyone present repudiated the letters, and the Pythian Temple representatives stated that they had not known about them before they were distributed, did not agree with them, and had simply made allowances for the writer. The representatives reaffirmed the essential purpose of holding separate meetings, which was to provide a place for those who could not (because of family or other pressures) or would not (because they were inquirers or very recent Bahá'ís from prejudiced backgrounds) attend fully integrated gatherings. Later in the month, on 25 October, the Pythian Temple group passed a resolution denying any prejudice and declaring its meetings to be educational and expedient.[9]

Still the dissension continued. On 21 December 1914, Louise Gregory wrote of the situation to Mrs. Parsons: "I know that you are very anxious to establish harmony among the believers here in Washington & are troubled at the unfortunate state of affairs here that is bringing the Cause into disrepute to the outside world as well as troubling the believers, colored & otherwise." She went on to explain that she had come to believe that 'Abdu'l-Bahá's instruction to Mr. Hannen to arrange a meeting for whites had been misunderstood, that what had been meant was a meeting in a private home where the colored Bahá'ís would not go anyway, arranged as a private rather than assembly matter. With such an arrangement there would be a place to take whites who did not yet recognize the principle of oneness; yet public, official meetings would remain open to all. As for the suggestion offered some time earlier by one of the Bahá'ís, that a public hall be rented and one white-only meeting held there, Louise responded: "Both my husband & myself were exceedingly troubled at the suggestion as we foresaw the disastrous consequences to the teaching [of] the Cause to the colored people, in fact we foresaw all that has happened now—for the work here is practically at a standstill among the colored people & many who were believers or on the brink of becoming so will have nothing to do with us."[10]

Apparently the situation changed little the following year. In October 1915 Mrs. Parsons, in her role as advisor to the Washington community, wrote a general letter on the problem. In it she laid much of the blame on those who had failed to wait for 'Abdu'l-Bahá's decision and on those who subsequently undermined the separate meetings, even though 'Abdu'l-Bahá had permitted them:

> we hear such murmurs as the following: "Although Abdul Baha allows this, it is well understood what He really wishes." "Although the Pythian Temple Meeting for white people alone is established, it will surely exist but for a short time, when it will be changed into a mixed meeting." In this way the undercurrent of dissatisfaction continues, causing the members of that meeting to feel unsure of their ground. Also, those who are not in sympathy with it are restless, hoping for a change. Dear Friends! I hope you will try to develop a sympathy for every kind of meeting which is for the spread of the Cause, for Abdul Baha has called such meetings "good."
>
> A Universal Teaching must have a message for all. Those who object to mixed meetings must find a prepared way to receive the Message in the manner they are willing to take it. It is for us to provide the means.
>
> Undoubtedly there is an important work to be done by the believers whose special field is the Pythian Temple. They should work spiritually and quietly, making every effort to overcome the prejudices of the inquirers. If this work be done wisely, be-

fore the minds of the opposers are fully awakened to the fact that belief in the Oneness of Mankind is spreading among the people, it will have had the necessary time to become so rooted in the hearts that nothing can dislodge it. This belief is a new and tender flower of this Blessed Day, and if we should force it into the strong winds of opposition, too soon, its precious growth will be retarded. However, we should know that the ideal Bahai meeting is the mixed meeting, and all should unite in giving to it the love and sympathy essential to success.
I approve of trying a Hall again. . . .[11]

Mrs. Parsons' attempt to be fair and moderate failed, however, to consider Louise Gregory's assertion nearly a year earlier that 'Abdu'l-Bahá may well have meant a private fireside in a white home rather than any official community activity. Neither did Mrs. Parsons even allude to the racist views that had been circulated, contributing to a climate of suspicion (an "undercurrent of dissatisfaction," as she put it) about the motives of the Pythian Temple group. Nor did she recognize the extent to which the "important work" of the Pythian Temple group might be an escape from the real challenge of racial unity. As long as the Temple meeting continued, doubt and dissension would remain.

Finally, two years after it had begun, the Pythian Temple meeting was discontinued. As Dr. Edward C. Getsinger wrote of it to Mrs. Parsons, who was summering in New Hampshire, "The Temple meeting agreed unanimously to *dissolve* for the sake of unity." He encouraged them, he said, to begin an inquirers' meeting, if they should wish to do so in the future, with no mention of excluding anyone, and to arrange it "in a better spirit to begin with, than before."[12] A group had plans afoot, he reported, to rent a hall to be used as a center. He advised waiting until the fall.

By then, however, the terrible lack of communication with 'Abdu'l-Bahá had been temporarily breached. Five of a series of letters to the American Bahá'ís called the Tablets of the Divine Plan had reached America and been published in the 8 September 1916 issue of *Star of the West*. Addressing the Bahá'ís of Canada and of the Northeastern, Southern, Central, and Western states, 'Abdu'l-Bahá had called for teachers to go to the many cities and states where the Bahá'í message had never been heard. The editors of *Star of the West* called these tablets "a trumpet call to action."[13]

Through renewed connection with 'Abdu'l-Bahá the American Bahá'ís were given a renewed sense of direction and purpose.

Suddenly occupied with fresh concerns and reinvigorated by contact with 'Abdu'l-Bahá, the Washington community settled on an approach to the problems that had divided it for so many years. As Louis Gregory put it:

> the decision was reached that meetings for teaching which were publicly advertized through the press should welcome and teach any who responded, regardless of race. On the other hand those holding private meetings for contacting and teaching their friends might use their own discretion about bringing the races together where such a step seemed premature. As simple as all this now seems its final adjustment was brought about only after a number of years which were a sore trial to many of the friends.[14]

Separation from 'Abdu'l-Bahá had played no small part in that difficult period. Upon Turkey's entry into the First World War late in 1914, the conflict spread to the Middle East. It was not until British forces entered Haifa in September 1918 that a steady flow of letters and visitors between Haifa and the rest of the world could begin to be reestablished. Yet 'Abdu'l-Bahá had carefully prepared the American Bahá'ís for separation during His long stay among them. As Shoghi Effendi has written,

> An inscrutable Wisdom, we can well imagine Him remark to His disciples on the eve of His departure, has, in His infinite bounty singled out your native land for the execution of a mighty purpose. . . . A winter of unprecedented severity will soon be upon you. Its storm-clouds are fast gathering on the horizon. Tempestuous winds will assail you from every side. The Light of the Covenant will be obscured through my departure. These mighty blasts, this wintry desolation, shall however pass away. The dormant seed will burst into fresh activity. It shall put forth its buds, shall reveal, in mighty institutions, its leaves and blossoms. The vernal showers which the tender mercies of my heavenly Father will cause to descend upon you will enable this tender plant to spread out its branches to regions far beyond the confines of your native land.[15]

During the years when the ''Light of the Covenant'' was ''obscured,'' the infant American community gained a new degree of maturity. It had always depended on 'Abdu'l-Bahá. When communication was cut, the community was held together and guided by its vivid memories of Him, by the records of His visit, and by His correspondence over the past twenty years. As problems arose, instead of turning to 'Abdu'l-Bahá, the Bahá'ís had to search for solutions in the accumulated heritage of His wisdom.

Viewed in this light, the racial problems in Washington, D.C., from 1914 to 1916 cannot be seen simply as an example of a religious community failing to live up to its ideals. Rather, these early Bahá'ís are revealed as having been immature, deprived of their accustomed leadership, on their own and groping toward the light of understanding. The decision to follow either the Bahá'í way or the way of the world was theirs to make, without even a further word of prompting from 'Abdu'l-Bahá. Thus—however many unresolved feelings may have remained on both sides for many years to come—the 1916 resolution to end the white-only meeting and demonstrably reunite their efforts proved the sincerity of their commitment to a changing order.

9 A New Calling

As an interracial couple Louis and Louise Gregory felt the full impact of the disintegration of the Washington Bahá'í community. They had been brought together by 'Abdu'l-Bahá as a living demonstration of a new conception of human oneness that erases the racial and national barriers dividing one soul from another. But from 1913 to 1916 they found themselves in virtual isolation on that plane of unity, separated from most of the other Washington Bahá'ís by a profound gap in understanding.

Their isolation, however, did not lead to estrangement from other Bahá'ís or from the Faith itself. Rather than dissociate themselves from their fellow believers in Washington, they sought to be peacemakers, as a result often landing in the middle of the fray. When the community ceased to function as a unit, the Gregorys assumed responsibility, administratively and to some extent financially, for charitable work that had been undertaken by the assembly before it fell into disunity. Louise in particular seems to have become the social conscience of the splintered community. She corresponded with Agnes Parsons regularly during these years about assistance to certain needy individuals. Mrs. Parsons, for her part, remained a principal benefactress of such charities.

Like many other Western Bahá'ís, the Gregorys also took an interest in providing scholarships for the education of poor children in Bahá'í schools in Iran. Mr. Gregory's name appeared in a list of scholarship sponsors published late in 1913. Until 1917, when the demands of the Temple fund and of Mr. Gregory's travels took precedence, the couple contributed to the organization called the Orient-Occident Unity, which directed the scholarship program.[1] 'Abdu'l-Bahá commended them for their contributions to this body and for their other charitable efforts. "Continually do I remember you," He wrote them shortly before the outbreak of the First World War. "I am most pleased with your philanthropic activities, especially your contribution toward the final payment of the debt of the Orient-Occident Unity. I know also that your thought and mention by day and by night is the guidance of the *souls*—white and black. Therefore be ye most happy, because you are confirmed in this great matter.''²

The national prominence that Mr. Gregory had achieved by 1912, when he was first elected to serve on the Executive Board of Bahai Temple Unity, was not diminished by Washington's racial troubles. Although he was not reelected to the Board for several years, he continued to attend the annual conventions, as he had since 1911, and to give featured talks. In 1914 he was appointed to a committee to audit the accounts of the Temple Unity treasury.

He also made another trip to the South as a Bahá'í lecturer, visiting Nashville and Atlanta during the autumn of 1915. Five years earlier he had toured the South with fresh enthusiasm but limited knowledge of the Bahá'í teachings. He returned as a seasoned speaker, well-versed and mature, deepened by close association with 'Abdu'l-Bahá.

In Nashville he met Professor George W. Henderson, head of the Business Department of Roger Williams University, who became deeply interested in the Bahá'í Faith and later played an important role in establishing a community in Memphis, Tennessee. In Atlanta Fred Mortensen, a young man from Minneapolis, who is well known in Bahá'í history for having "ridden the rods" to see 'Abdu'l-Bahá in New England in 1912, was engaged in spreading the Bahá'í teachings. He lived in Atlanta from 1914 to 1916. During this time he was instrumental in introducing the Faith to two prominent black clergymen, Bishop Flipper and Dr. Ponton, both of whom became outspoken champions of the Faith.³

The first white Georgian to accept the Bahá'í Faith, James Elmore Hays, also shared his beliefs with individuals of both races. During Mr. Gregory's week-long visit to Atlanta in 1915, Hays became his close companion. " 'We went everywhere together,' " Mr. Gregory is reported to have said, " 'eating at the colored Y.M.C.A. He said he was badly scared when he received news of my coming but afterward revived his courage.' " Mr. Gregory spoke at Atlanta University, Morehouse College, Morris Brown University, Clark University, Gammon Theological Seminary, Spelman College, and the First Congregational Church. The youthful Hays accompanied him to all of his talks.[4] This companionable effort between two Southern men, black and white, clearly showed the potential of the Bahá'í teachings for fostering unity in the region.

A year later the first five segments of 'Abdu'l-Bahá's Divine Plan reached America. Addressing the Southern states, 'Abdu'l-Bahá indicated particular concern because so few Bahá'ís resided in the region. He called for teachers to arise to establish the Faith there, assuring them that they would be "assisted and confirmed." Each of them would be "like unto a farmer who scatters pure seeds in the rich soil." "Appreciate ye the value of this time," 'Abdu'l-Bahá encouraged His followers, "and be ye engaged in the sowing of the seeds. . . ."[5] Louis Gregory responded immediately, turning his attention naturally toward that part of the country where he had discerned such promise and still had so many ties, and where, as 'Abdu'l-Bahá had indicated, the need was so great and the soil so rich.

The Bahai Temple Unity made plans at once to carry out 'Abdu'l-Bahá's instructions. Shortly after receiving them, William H. Randall of the Executive Board sent Agnes Parsons copies of the tablets and told her that the Board was planning to send Louis Gregory, among others, to the Southern states. "He feels that his pilgrimage should be in the South," Mr. Randall explained in a subsequent letter, noting that a departure date of "about November 1st" had already been set.[6]

Mr. Gregory left even earlier than planned. By 31 October, when he wrote to Joseph Hannen from Tallahassee, Florida, he had spoken to "nearly 5000 souls, representing many communities," with "practically no opposition." At Florida A. & M. College he reported that "the professors & three hundred students here received three of the principles, the Message, & the reading of the Word, with hearty appreciation last night, and two addresses are scheduled for today. The president has read some of the literature." He added that in Jacksonville he had given six addresses, in schools, churches, and the Y.M.C.A.[7] For the next six weeks or so he traveled extensively in the South, ultimately reaching "probably more than fifteen thousand" people, "most of them students."[8]

"Abdul Baha has made it all possible," Louis Gregory

claimed, and he avowed that the Master's assurance of assistance and confirmation had animated him from the beginning. ''I do not now recall whether or not I told you a dream I had during the days of preparation for this journey,'' he wrote Joseph Hannen from Tulsa late in November.

Abdul-Baha was standing before an audience in the attitude of teaching. By his direction I was serving as a waiter, passing to the people bread from a tray. When the wafers reached the people, they were transformed into tablets and upon them they were to indicate how many of them accepted the teachings and became Bahais. An overwhelming number of those who received the tablets thus signified by writing their acceptance. I awoke feeling very happy.

By the way the doors are opened to deliver the Message and the happiness manifested among those who give ear, this dream becomes a glorious reality. . . .

Tonight there is an audience of five hundred in a Methodist church. The pastor has given the right of way. The Bahai address will take the place of the sermon.[9]

He returned to Washington eager to resume his travels for the Faith. The long hours in dirty Jim Crow railway cars, with poor food and omnipresent coal dust, did not daunt him.

I . . . am very happy over the journey, which gave wonderful opportunities and privileges for service. . . .

I hope, God willing, that in the future my affairs can be so arranged as to give more time to service of this kind (the opportunities seem limitless). The number of institutions in the south that cannot be reached must be very small.[10]

His way of arranging his affairs to devote more time to Bahá'í work in the South was—with Louise's wholehearted concurrence—simply to relinquish them. Many years later a close friend of the Gregorys' explained that the decision had entailed closing his law practice and a real estate firm he had just established and later turning down an offered position on the law faculty at Howard University. The sale of their home provided the funds necessary for his travels, as he confided to Alfred Lunt in September 1917.

I am grateful to God that through Divine Favor the way is opened to this unworthy servant. My dear little wife, the Flame of whose spiritual love is aglow, suggested the sale of our home that a fund might be raised for the spread of the teachings. Negotiations for this are now in progress with signs of success. As a result, I expect, God willing, to be able to spend the best part of a year in the field. Am very happy over the prospect.[11]

Both Louis and Louise Gregory unerringly sensed the urgency of the Master's summons, although they had not yet received 'Abdu'l-Bahá's second tablet to the Southern states with its strong plea for sacrificial effort: ''We must not sit inactive for one moment; we must sever ourselves from composure, rest, tranquillity, goods, property, life and attachment to material things.''[12]

''Mr. Louis G. Gregory is planning to leave for an extended teaching tour,'' Pauline Hannen wrote in an October 1917 issue of *Star of the West*, ''having closed his home and given up his business for that purpose. . . .''[13] The ''extended teaching tour'' lasted without interruption for fifteen years. It became a series of tours, punctuated by periods of administrative and organizational activity, throughout which Mr. Gregory devoted his time wholly to the Faith.

In his travels he followed the example set by 'Abdu'l-Bahá, rising early for prayers at dawn, filling his daily schedule, often giving several major talks in addition to informal meetings and interviews. From Louisville, Kentucky, in 1919, he reported that he had given two lectures at the New Thought Center, six in one Methodist church, one each in a Congregational, a Baptist, and two other Methodist churches, one at the State University, one at each of two women's clubs, one before a Socialist group, two in a socialist church, and ''almost numberless meetings with individuals and small groups and the end is not yet.''[14]

Like 'Abdu'l-Bahá, he found in the experience of teaching the strength to continue the pace for months at a time. ''It is really most heartening and inspiring to see the happiness of people when they hear the Glad Tidings of the Kingdom,'' he exclaimed to Joseph Hannen. ''And the compliments they pay the teacher would be enough to give any one 'the big head' who was not well disciplined by Mrs. Hannen to avoid conceit. So when complimented after an address I often find myself saying to Abdul Baha 'This praise is all Thine!' "[15] The satisfaction of finding receptive listeners made the difficulties and hardships of his travels seem insignificant.

His sense of humor was another source of strength and balance. Just as it dampened any thought of self-importance, it cast a glow of real enjoyment over the variety of his experiences. Pleasure in the unexpected was an antidote to the monotony of long periods of travel. It allowed him to approach each encounter with a fresh spirit. After his first visit to an integrated evangelical church, for example, he wrote Joseph Hannen: "In this meeting for the first time, I saw 'white folks' shout and Hallelujah! and cry 'Glory to God!' at the top of their voices as 'culled folks' are wont to do in camp meetings. I thought I knew you 'white folks' but now I see I am not on to all your ways."[16]

He viewed the individuals he met with the same gentle sense of humor. "Do you know our Bahai sister, Mrs. Emma B. Stott?" he inquired after a month-long visit to Louisville, Kentucky. "If not, can you imagine the late Teddy Roosevelt a Bahai and wearing skirts? This will give you an idea of the moral enthusiasm, tireless energy and fearlessness of Emma Stott, who is withal entirely feminine. I left the arrangement for meetings largely to her."[17]

During his early years on the road Louis Gregory profited from countless opportunities to develop his talents as a public speaker —to find the "point of contact," as 'Abdu'l-Bahá had done, with audiences large or small, predominantly white or predominantly black, conservative or progressive, educated or unlettered, Methodist, Baptist, socialist, or Bahá'í. His active concern for the advancement of black people, dating back to the time before he encountered the Bahá'í Faith, and his special interest in unity between blacks and whites, the mission given him by 'Abdu'l-Bahá, never narrowed his vision or limited his audiences. Rather, oneness served as a key to his understanding all the various elements of a new world order and to his genuine concern for all oppressed people.

A 1917 talk he gave in Boston on "The Equality of Men and Women" illustrates the scope of his views:

The Day of God is the day of freedom for all the varied elements of humanity. It accords with divine justice that each and all may develop their powers without hindrance from their fellows. Hand in hand with the oneness of humanity is the other principle, the equality of men and women. Humanity "cannot exist half-slave and half-free." Women must be free in order that men may be free. Considering the physical, mental and spiritual effects: thralldom rests as heavily upon the oppressor as upon the oppressed.[18]

These were strong words at a time when women were still fighting for suffrage in America. For Louis Gregory, however, the civil rights aspirations of women and of blacks were not in competition with one another, as some people perceive them to be even today. Instead, he saw that both movements must proceed "hand in hand."

In his efforts to eradicate prejudice of all kinds he found encouragement in small victories. A dinner invitation from white Bahá'ís in Louisville, or a request for books from a receptive Catholic priest, was never overlooked in his reports. Some of the incidents he recorded might be seen as simply normal, civilized behavior. But Louis Gregory never took human behavior for granted. Particularly in the South, efforts to overcome prevailing racial attitudes made by any white person—Bahá'í or non-Bahá'í—were worthy of mention. Recognizing the pressures of tradition and socialization, he noted with appreciation each sign that their negative effects were on the wane.

Louis' letters to Louise related the news of his travels—happily, for the most part, and with equanimity in times of hardship. A typical letter, addressed to Louise from Cleveland, where he had stopped to speak in November 1917 on his way to Chicago for the centennial celebration of the birth of Bahá'u'lláh, reads:

My Darling:
. . . The unity feast will be held tonight. A hall has been engaged for tomorrow night and altho' it is election night we expect a good attendance of both races. There is great harmony between the white and colored people here. I believe it would make Abdul Baha very happy to see the white and colored children attending the same public schools and playing peacefully together in the yards at time of recess. It looks like the varigated [sic] flowers in a garden, of which He so beautifully speaks.

The Bahais are every where wonderfully kind to me. Their love and kindness are a reflection of the Divine Love.[19]

Despite the positive tone of his letters to Louise, it is evident that the months and years they spent apart were difficult for them. Even if Louise's health and temperament had permitted her to adapt to his life on the road, his commitment to the South effectively prevented their traveling together. There is no indication that they ever considered doing so. Even in the North their life was trying, particularly after the sale of their home forced them to rent a succession of temporary lodgings; in the South it would have been impossibly dangerous. During their long separations, Louise lived alone, in Washington or in the Northeast for the first several years, and later in Europe, where her background and knowledge of languages equipped her well for extended periods of Bahá'í activity.

Perhaps because he was sure that Louise knew his feelings, or because he hesitated to intensify her own loneliness, Louis Gregory's letters to his wife seldom touch on their separation. But to his friend Edith Chapman he clearly revealed a sense of personal deprivation, no less painful because it was consciously chosen. "My wife is on a teaching trip in Europe and will not return until spring," he told Mrs. Chapman in 1932. "She is meeting with success in giving the message. Tho' I miss her greatly, the defense against lonliness [sic] is keeping busy." And on another occasion he confided, "It is our hope that our enforced separation along the line of service to the Divine Cause will mercifully bring to us eternal reunion in the worlds of God."[20]

Even in loneliness and hardship it did not occur to them to abandon their endeavors. They accepted the difficulties their way of life entailed, viewing them as corollaries of their parallel paths of service. "Abdul Baha saved my life," Louise once wrote, "therefore it belongs to Him to use for the Cause." In their letters to each other and to friends the Gregorys never expressed even a hint of regret about giving up their home and their settled life together. They had made the decision in full agreement, and neither one ever looked back. "During the years," he observed two decades later, "we have had but one spirit, one purpose and one purse."[21]

Implicit in their sense of purpose was the desire to fulfill the special destiny that 'Abdu'l-Bahá had set before Louis Gregory. From the beginning Louise did all she could to make his work possible. Her concern was to work out the incidentals of their life, to assure that her husband was eating properly, getting sufficient rest, not worrying about money. During their long separations her letters dealt with the same practical matters. Whether she wrote from Washington, D.C., New England, or Eastern Europe, she made suggestions about his diet, for example, or in later years discussed repairs to a little house they had bought in New Hampshire. Yet, despite her practicality, Louise's letters do not indicate any lack of attachment. She wrote as a woman deeply in love, intent on the well-being of her husband, and acutely conscious of the miles between them. In 1934, about to leave Bulgaria for Yugoslavia, she expressed her awareness of distance in poignant terms: "I do wonder how you are getting on & where you are my sweet boy. I shall be a bit nearer you at Belgrade but it will take at first longer even to get your letters as they will come here first."[22]

Her protectiveness was not rooted in any desire to bind him to her or to change the fundamental pattern of his activities. 'Abdu'l-Bahá had asked them to "sever" themselves from personal comfort, even from "rest" and "tranquillity." Yet Louise realized that the Master did not expect His followers to ruin their physical and mental health, or their marriages, in the path of service. She sought simply to moderate the effects of the punishing pace of her husband's life.

The process of adjustment, during which Louis Gregory pushed himself almost beyond endurance and Louise worried about keeping both her husband and her marriage healthy, seems to have lasted several years. In January 1921, after four years at the disposal of the Temple Unity and two years of almost continual travel, Mr. Gregory was on the road, as usual, tentatively planning to return to Washington, D.C., the following month. Although they had given up their home in Washington years before, Louise was living in the city temporarily, settled in an apartment on P Street N.W. that she had managed to obtain until spring. The prospect of being able to spend some time with her husband in relative comfort and privacy spurred her to turn to Mrs. Parsons for help, even at the risk of getting "into trouble with Louis." She asked Mrs. Parsons to use her influence, if possible, to arrange for his work to bring him back to Washington for a few months.[23]

During the previous two years, since the formal launching of the Divine Plan in April 1919, they had never spent even as long as four weeks together at any one time, she explained. Moreover, when they did have a few weeks together, the reunion was often marred by trying conditions. Once, after a separation of seven months, they had been together again for three weeks, living in a small and noisy furnished room. "After such a long absence adjustment under these circumstances was very difficult," she confided, "& never became entirely effected." Ten days spent happily at Green Acre the following summer had helped to restore their relationship, but again not in a home environment. Now that he was about to return, although he wrote that "he never felt in better health," she was not reassured; he had told her the same once before, convinced that it was true, but had returned from his travels unable to relax and "so nervous & irritable[,] so unlike himself that I was in despair." Thus she appealed to Mrs. Parsons:

> For the first time in 2 years we have a place where we can live a real home life, have our meals together in our own home & I do not know when this will happen again as we have to give this up in April. . . . If Louis could be found work to do in & around Washington for a time while we have this flat with visits to not far distant cities it seems to me it would be well both for his sake & my sake & perhaps his future usefulness for the Cause as he is not strong enough to keep up that strain constantly year after year without longer & more frequent periods of rest & relaxation & our relations & their importance to the Cause would seem to me to make it necessary that we should be more together.[24]

Eventually the Gregorys established a workable routine, returning from their respective travels to spend most summers together in New England. During these relatively quiet summers with Louise, he regained his strength and prepared for the relentless pressure of travel and administrative work that began again without fail each autumn. At last he seemed to have realized his limits, as Louise had earlier, and to have accepted his need for her protective care. "Arrived here toward the end of May," he wrote Edith Chapman from Portsmouth, New Hampshire, in 1930,

> so very tired out that I fear something would have snapped had I continued a week more. Have been doing but little work save

routine since coming and with sleep, regularity of habits and a wise selection of foods seem to be nearly back to normalcy, as the late President Harding was wont to say. It is really very pleasant to be at home once more and Louise, my wife, is doing all in her power to make me comfortable. She is truly one of the jewels of Baha'u'llah, so full of the spirit of sacrifice and service and so self-forgetful. [25]

In addition to giving up a settled home life, the Gregorys readily put aside their "goods, property, . . . and attachments to material things." They took to heart the words that 'Abdu'l-Bahá had directed to the Bahá'í teachers who were to be sent, regardless of personal sacrifice, to the South: " 'If God guide, through thee, one soul, it is better for thee than all the riches!' " [26] In the early years they supported Mr. Gregory's travels, as far as possible, from their own resources. By the fall of 1918, their savings had been used up. Then Louise "unexpectedly" received a thousand dollars, which she sacrificed in order to support his work for another year. [27] Her small income from family investments in England covered her own expenses and helped to maintain a simple home for them when they could be together for a few weeks or months. She later financed her travels to Europe in the 1920s and 1930s. But, as his original commitment to travel for a time in behalf of the Faith gradually extended from 1917 into the indefinite future, they found that they did not have the accumulated savings to finance his travel expenses.

Rather than give up his new calling, Louis Gregory agreed to accept financial assistance. "It is a matter of deep regret to me that with the exhaustion of my own resources in the year of teaching Oct. 1917 to Oct. 1918, it now becomes necessary to accept financial help from others," he confided to Harlan Ober in September 1919. His initial reluctance had been overcome only by 'Abdu'l-Bahá. "My belief is that the teacher should not ask for funds, but only accept for his necessities what comes freely and voluntarily from severed souls," he explained to Joseph Hannen. "I did not see even this latter possibility until it appeared in the Instructions of Abdul Baha." [28] Written in 1917 but not disseminated in America until the spring of 1919, the statement to which Mr. Gregory referred made it clear that, although 'Abdu'l-Bahá had always refused offers of money, even though "on certain occasions we were in most straitened circumstances," others might accept such assistance. He advised that, "if a soul for the sake of God, voluntarily and out of his pure desire, wishes to offer a contribution (toward the expenses of a teacher) in order to make the contributor happy, the teacher may accept a small sum, but must live with the utmost contentment."[29]

Louis Gregory had already, in his first two years on the road, become adept at carrying on his work with only "a small sum." His average expenses in 1919—including transportation, donations given in churches and other places where they were expected, and Bahá'í literature—were about one hundred dollars a month. He felt that this was adequate, although he sometimes wished for an additional ten or fifteen dollars because "there have been times when I felt my work might have been more effective, had there been more to spend for literature." When a friend—such as Roy Wilhelm, who had recently given him nineteen dollars—wanted to contribute toward his efforts, he applied the sum to his budget for books and pamphlets. His only stipulation was that the contributor be a committed Bahá'í: "Contributions offered in churches and by other outside people are not infrequent and are uniformly refused."[30]

Difficult as it was to accept money, at least among Bahá'ís he could be sure that the nature of his work was understood; and, although financial dependence troubled him, he sought "consolation," as he explained to Harlan Ober, "in the thought of Abdul Baha, that there is the closest connection among the friends, both upon the material and spiritual planes."[31] Holding on to this view of the interconnectedness of the Bahá'ís, Louis Gregory attempted to set aside nagging doubts and discomfiture about his subsidization.

The details of the financial assistance that he received, particularly in this early period before the establishment of the National Spiritual Assembly, may never be fully known; official records are scant, and personal contributions were seldom recorded. But 'Abdu'l-Bahá apparently gave unqualified approval of Louis Gregory's role as a full-time worker for the Faith. Years later Mr. Gregory recalled that " 'Abdu'l Baha, in making the arrangement, told Harry [William H.] Randall that my work for the cause would be such as would prevent me from earning a living."[32]

Having come to terms with subsidization, he accepted financial help in the spirit in which it was offered, regarding it as a contribution to the Bahá'í Cause and as an offering of means that frequently involved hardship for the giver. "As a rule the friends are not overburdened with cash," he observed to Joseph Hannen, "and those in Boston and elsewhere who are contributing are making a most noble and glorious sacrifice." Help from wealthy Bahá'ís was accepted in the same dignified manner, quietly and without apparent embarrassment. According to Walter Blakely, who worked for Florence Morton, a prominent Massachusetts Bahá'í, Louis Gregory regularly received assistance from Mrs. Morton. The total amount he received, from general Bahá'í funds and from individuals was barely enough, however, to provide subsistence.[33]

Although his poverty was real, he did not advertise it. On the contrary, he paid careful attention to his appearance. "Mr Gregory wore his clothes very well indeed," Walter Blakely has recalled. "When he stepped out he looked like a Fashion plate." He was conscious of his role as a representative of the Bahá'í Faith and of the importance of looking his best, according to the standards of the time. His training as a tailor enabled him to maintain his well-groomed appearance even during long months of travel. Roy Williams, a friend and associate for many years, has observed that by careful brushing and pressing Louis Gregory made the most of even one suit; he always looked distinguished and created a favorable impression. He was well aware that for most Americans, white or black, a life of sacrifice holds very little appeal. As he once wrote Joseph Hannen, with regard to an old friend he had met, who had become wealthy: "He is quite amazed that I don't take money for lecturing and mentions this to every body. I fear if he knew my poverty it would be a great veil to him as he would probably think it meant the Nth degree of insanity."[34]

Yet the Gregorys not only endured financial hardship but accepted it cheerfully. "I have learned to be happy and rejoice over my poverty, which is almost as great as when I started [out in] life twenty three years ago," he explained to Harlan Ober in 1919. At an age when most people become concerned about their material security, the Gregorys gave it little thought. The economic uncertainties of the postwar years, culminating in the Great Depression, intensified their feeling that the world was in the throes of transformation; thus they devoted themselves to building a new world order rather than to salvaging any temporary security from the old one. The path they had chosen was for them the greatest source of well-being. "I might have made money," Mr. Gregory suggested, reminding Edith Chapman that he had once considered, before becoming a Bahá'í, the idea of establishing a law practice in Kansas City, "but probably would have lost the opportunity which came a little later, to get a fuller understanding of the Baha'i Cause and to do my present work which has been fraught with the greatest happiness despite its difficulties."[35]

After 1916 his increased commitment of time to Bahá'í pursuits gave rise to greater and wider-ranging responsibilities as an administrator and writer. He emerged as a leader of great capacity in connection with the national Bahá'í conventions. His first reports of the annual meetings, published in *Star of the West,* were so well received that he continued to serve as convention reporter for many years. In 1917 and 1918 he was chosen to serve as permanent secretary of the Ninth and Tenth Annual Conventions. In 1918 he was elected to the Executive Board, tied with Alfred Lunt for fourth place in number of votes cast.[36] These early activities on the national level prepared the way for his long years of membership on the National Spiritual Assembly of the Bahá'ís of the United States and Canada during the first formative decades of its history.

Yet Louis Gregory always preferred the role of teacher to that of administrator. Speaking about the Bahá'í Faith to individuals or to groups of any size was for him the "most divinely emphasized" and "the most confirmed" of all activities.[37] When he turned to other tasks, his love of teaching imbued them with a special spirit. He administered for the sake of teaching, to further "the promulgation of the Universal Peace and the proclamation of the oneness of the world of humanity." 'Abdu'l-Bahá had declared to the Bahá'ís of America, *"This is the work!"* —and Louis Gregory had taken it as his own.[38]

10   The Divine Plan

Receipt of the first portion of the Tablets of the Divine Plan immediately created change in the American Bahá'í community, as it had in Washington, D.C., and in the lives of the Gregorys and others who responded to 'Abdu'l-Bahá's call to action. The time of separation from 'Abdu'l-Bahá had not yet ended, however. The war continued for another two terrible years, during which the Master remained in serious danger and isolation. The direction and impetus that He had given their teaching efforts in 1916 helped to guide the American Bahá'ís through this difficult time, but in the administration of their affairs they remained on unsure ground. Progress toward the construction of the Chicago Temple slowed, and in 1918 the Executive Board of Bahai Temple Unity found itself seriously divided over a problem involving a Chicago group that claimed to be Bahá'í but diverged from the teachings. Without 'Abdu'l-Bahá to turn to, some Bahá'ís felt they did not have the authority to disassociate themselves from the offending group and urged a permissive attitude; others felt equally strongly that they had no choice but to protect the Faith from the tampering of individuals bent on their own interpretation.

Yet the immediate response of the Bahá'ís to the part of the Divine Plan that they had received proved that they were worthy of the Master's trust and of the full range of national and international responsibilities that was to become evident when the entire plan was received. Before 'Abdu'l-Bahá wrote the last of the tablets early in 1917, teachers had been sent into all of the regions of America that He had singled out. At the annual convention that year an attempt was made to set in motion an appropriate teaching program.[1]

The enthusiasm of the Bahá'ís for the Divine Plan brought new life even to long-established centers. A December 1916 issue of *Star of the West* reported that hundreds of people were attending meetings in St. Louis; that in New England new communities had been formed in Springfield, Hartford, and New Haven; and that the Bahá'ís of Boston had "trebled in numbers in the last six months." By April 1918 teaching in Harlem had been so successful that the "assembly" there sent a message to the annual convention in Chicago, listing the names of more than twenty people, and forwarded a special contribution of $30.50 to the Temple fund. Among the members of the "Harlem Branch of the New York Assembly" was Roy Williams, who was soon to become closely associated with Louis Gregory as a traveling teacher. [2]

Thus during the final years of the First World War the energies of the American Bahá'ís were focused upon national growth and development. By the spring of 1919, when all fourteen Tablets of the Divine Plan (eight written in March and April 1916, including the five that reached America that year, and six additional tablets composed in February and March 1917) were presented in New York at the annual convention—the "Convention of the Covenant," as 'Abdu'l-Bahá called it—much had already been done on the homefront to prepare the way for the assumption of increased international responsibilities after the war. [3] In one of the first of His general tablets to the Bahá'ís of the United States and Canada, written in 1916 but received in 1919, 'Abdu'l-Bahá stated:

> The range of your future achievements still remains undisclosed. I fervently hope that in the near future the whole earth may be stirred and shaken by the results of your achievements. The hope which 'Abdu'l-Bahá cherishes for you is that the same success which has attended your efforts in America may crown your endeavors in other parts of the world, that through you the fame of the Cause of God may be diffused throughout the East and the West and the advent of the Kingdom of the Lord of Hosts be proclaimed in all the five continents of the globe. [4]

Three general tablets written in 1916 and one concluding message dated 8 March 1917 detailed the new worldwide mission with which 'Abdu'l-Bahá had entrusted the American Bahá'ís. He mentioned more than 120 specific countries, territories, regions, and islands or island groups, focusing particular attention on Central and South America and the West Indies but also including such far-flung spots as the Orkney Islands and New Caledonia.

He reinforced His initial statements to the various regions of the United States and Canada with an additional series of five tablets. In His second message to the Southern states He observed that the region's moderate climate and its beauty are factors most conducive to human development; therefore, its spiritual development must be outstanding. In strongly worded passages 'Abdu'l-Bahá stressed the need for action and dedication on the part of the Bahá'ís:

> At this time and at this period we must avail ourselves of this most great opportunity. We must not sit inactive for one moment; we must sever ourselves from composure, rest, tranquillity, goods, property, life and attachment to material things. We must sacrifice everything to His Highness, the Possessor of existence, so that the powers of the Kingdom may show greater penetration and the brilliant effulgence in this New Cycle may illumine the worlds of minds and ideals.
>
> It is about twenty-three years that the fragrances of God [i.e., the teachings of Bahá'u'lláh] have been diffused in America, but no adequate and befitting motion has been realized, and no great acclamation and acceleration has been witnessed. [5]

He went on to point out how the efforts of one lone disciple of Christ had illumined Armenia. Then, alluding to the racial problems of the South, 'Abdu'l-Bahá called for the same kind of sacrificial effort in behalf of the oneness of mankind:

> Therefore . . . become ye sanctified above and purified from this world and the inhabitants thereof; suffer your intention to become for the good of all; cut your attachment to the earth and like unto the essence of the spirit become ye light and delicate. Then with a firm resolution, a pure heart, a rejoiced spirit, and an eloquent tongue, engage your time in the promulgation of the divine principles so that the oneness of the world of humanity may pitch her canopy in the apex of America and all the nations of the world may follow the divine policy. This is certain, that the divine policy is justice and kindness toward all mankind. . . . And every moment we must render a hundred thousand thanksgivings that . . . we are freed from all the ignorant prejudices, are kind to all the sheep of God, and our utmost hope is to serve each and all, and . . . educate every one. [6]

After the years of separation from 'Abdu'l-Bahá, the unveiling at the eleventh annual convention of His Tablets of the Divine Plan—"not only in single messages," as Joseph Hannen expressed it, "but literally in a volume of general Tablets and advices, explanations and exhortations"—lent extraordinary significance to the occasion. It was better attended than any previous convention. Perhaps six hundred Bahá'ís and guests filled the banquet hall of the McAlpin Hotel for the opening "Feast of Rizwan"; hundreds more could not be accommodated.[7]

All of the sessions of the convention were imbued with a heightened sense of purpose. A cataclysmic war had just ended. The world awaited the results of the Paris Peace Conference, which was at that time wrestling with the challenge of creating a new world order. 'Abdu'l-Bahá's summons to universal peace had never seemed more timely. "It is within the ready recollection of many of us, that the Bahai teachings were called 'ahead of the times' and termed a dream philosophy, perhaps adapted to some future age of the world," Mr. Hannen asserted. "And now, how rapidly 'the times' have caught up with The Message, so that today men talk the world over in terms of internationalism and world unity, strange to their minds and tongues, but familiar to the Bahais."[8]

For Joseph Hannen, Louis Gregory, and the hundreds of other Bahá'ís who gathered together that April in New York, it seemed clear that their convention offered a greater assurance of peace than any political conference. The Tablets of the Divine Plan—"the Charter of the New Age," as Mr. Hannen called them—served to "outline in no uncertain terms the part America is to play in the spiritualization of the world." Whatever the statesmen decided in Paris, however much "doubt and uncertainty . . . the epoch of reconstruction" might bring to those who lacked "the hope of the age," in the years ahead the American Bahá'ís could at least be sure of their responsibilities.[9]

Soon after the Convention of the Covenant several dedicated individuals made plans to assume their part of the assignment. Martha Root, a journalist who was to become the outstanding international Bahá'í teacher of the period, took on the lion's share. She sailed in July 1919 on a lengthy tour of South America, the first of many voyages for the Faith.[10] In the next few years others joined her and the handful of Americans who had been disseminating the Bahá'í teachings abroad even earlier in the century. Among them was Fanny Knobloch, Pauline Hannen's sister, who went to South Africa in 1921.

Within the United States and Canada fresh recruits arose to assist those who, like Louis Gregory, had already been engaged in bringing the Bahá'í message to new areas. At this time Roy Williams first traveled to the South, spending many months on the road during the summer and fall of 1919. His successful teaching efforts there in the early years ranked second only to those of Louis Gregory himself.

In a sense the Divine Plan assured Louis Gregory a unique place in American Bahá'í history. It focused his energies, formed his calling as a traveling speaker, elicited ever greater degrees of personal sacrifice, and confirmed him as a leader in the national Bahá'í community. Just as he had been among the first to respond to the initial phase of the Divine Plan in 1916, once again he was in the front ranks in 1919. The launching of the full plan provided an impetus to continued effort; he could not stop, even though the few years that he had thought of devoting to full-time teaching work might become a lifetime. "We must not sit inactive for one moment," 'Abdu'l-Bahá had urged, "we must sever ourselves from composure, rest, tranquillity, goods, property, life and attachment to material things." Louis Gregory accepted the Master's words without hesitation, as he always had, and proceeded to obey them as if they were a personal instruction—indeed, as if (in 'Abdu'l-Bahá's words) they were "pictures engraved on stone," to be made "permanent and ineffaceable in the tablets of the hearts."[11]

11   The Sowing of Seeds

In 1916 'Abdu'l-Bahá observed in His first tablet to the Southern states that the Bahá'ís there were few. By 1919, through the efforts of Louis Gregory and others, progress had been made, but, as 'Abdu'l-Bahá expressed it in His second tablet to the South, "no great acclamation and acceleration . . . [had] been witnessed."[1] Thus a systematic program for spreading the Bahá'í teachings in the region was launched after the Convention of the Covenant.

In June 1919 *Star of the West* published an outline of this comprehensive plan and a news bulletin on activities in the South, both written by Joseph Hannen. Under the new system—devised with the help of Aḥmad Sohráb, a former secretary of 'Abdu'l-Bahá, who had brought from the Holy Land the letters that comprised the Divine Plan—regular reports were to be made to and records maintained by a "Central Bureau for the South" in Washington, D.C. The bureau was to serve as a clearinghouse for information vital to the propagation of the Bahá'í Faith in the region, such as the names and addresses of individuals and groups who would be willing to have a speaker, an up-to-date card file of Bahá'ís residing in the South, and the names of newspapers that would be willing to publish articles submitted to them. Moreover, reports by traveling teachers would form the basis of a follow-up system, to assure that places that had been visited would be put on the itineraries of subsequent travelers.[2] Although the staffing of the Central Bureau was not discussed in *Star of the West,* Joseph Hannen was clearly at the heart of the project. During the months ahead, he continued to serve, as he had for so many years, as the leading publicist and administrator of Bahá'í teaching efforts in the Southern states.

Impelled by 'Abdu'l-Bahá's call to action, Louis Gregory set out for the South once again immediately after the Convention of the Covenant with the goal of visiting all sixteen states mentioned in 'Abdu'l-Bahá's tablets to the South.[3] He spent nearly a year in the region, interrupting his travels only to attend the annual Bahá'í convention in New York in the spring of 1920. Roy Williams joined him in the field; and by June 1919, when the first regional bulletin was published, the two were already generating news. They were "sending in lists of those interested, showing splendid results, and . . . [were] most happy in the work," Mr. Hannen reported.[4]

They traveled together for some time enroute to the Deep South; then they separated, striking out in different directions at some points and occasionally doubling back upon a common path. "I have not yet covered much of the ground over which he worked," Mr. Gregory remarked in one of his regular reports to Joseph Hannen, "but good reports have come about him. . . ." In Austin, Texas, for example, he found it easy to arrange speaking engagements at Sam Houston College and Tillotson College because of the favorable impression that Roy Williams had made earlier that year.[5]

Although Roy Williams had planned to rejoin Mr. Gregory in Texas at the end of the year he apparently found it necessary to interrupt his journey because he lacked the money to continue. "He has been under the difficulty of insufficient funds during a good part of the time, and this is a real difficulty to one in the field," Mr. Gregory observed. "It seems little short of a miracle, any how, that he started with practically nothing and stayed in the field for about nine or ten months." In another letter, written in Oklahoma City, Louis Gregory deplored the loss of his coworker's assistance: "He has rendered a very valuable service to the Cause and I hope and pray that the Hope of Abdul Baha for him will be fully realized. With a certain amount of money that he can rely upon, he will in future, I hope, accomplish even larger results."[6]

Subsequently, Roy Williams returned to the field and traveled widely in the South. His achievements were extensive, yet he regarded them as a reflection of Louis Gregory's, for in most cases he either followed in Mr. Gregory's footsteps or used his network of contacts. "In a way that network just was like a great fishing net that could be thrown over all these states," Mr. Williams recalled half a century after their joint teaching ventures, "and the lines [were] crisscrossed by . . . travel on the railroads, which were the only ways we had to travel.'' As he traversed those lines, he was acutely aware of his connection with Louis Gregory. 'Abdu'l-Bahá's reference to him as Mr. Gregory's ''fellow-traveler'' became, according to the Atlanta Bahá'ís, ''a title and honor he highly prized.'' He followed closely Louis Gregory's indefatigable example. In Atlanta alone he spoke at several black colleges and in more than twenty-five churches. On one occasion he addressed over a hundred ministers, and their bishop commanded them to open their pulpits to him. On another occasion, after referring to Bahá'u'lláh and Christ in terms of equality, he was literally ordered off the speaker's platform by the white president of Clark University, only to be invited by the faculty to finish his talk that evening in a nearby church. [7]

Louis Gregory's own efforts met, as usual, with a favorable response. Opposition was rare: ''No one in Dallas raised objection except the pastor of the Holiness Church, but this only after he had permitted the Glad Tidings to be given to five hundred souls. The seed was sown and the work done before his demurrer was entered.'' [8]

The lack of advance preparation for his visits—both with regard to obtaining accommodations and scheduling meetings—was at times the only real obstacle. It was counterbalanced by Mr. Gregory's resourcefulness and flexibility. Where there were no Bahá'ís, as was most often the case on a first visit, he relied upon friends and acquaintances from his school days or on individuals whose names he had been given by mutual friends. Usually he found a way to make each stopover a success, as his account of a visit to Corsicana, Texas, illustrates:

Next it was a question about going to Corsicana, as the Bahai friend to whom a letter was written made no reply. (It afterwards was found that she had left two years ago.) I decided [to go] without knowing this and not knowing where to find a room for the night. Arriving at 3 p.m. it took just about four hours to get lodging and to find a friend who was so situated that she could and was willing to have her house used for a meeting. The fuel shortage has sometimes made things difficult. About ten persons, perhaps, were reached over the 'phone and six responded and came. At the end of the meeting one of them said, *''You have six converts.''* . . . It was also reported to me, on leaving the next morning, that they intended to get a supply of literature and form a study class.[9]

Yet he never took success for granted. " 'This city was entered without my previous acquaintance with a living soul,' " he reported of a visit to Helena, Arkansas. " 'Consider then how mighty are the Confirmations of the Covenant that old established churches open their pulpits to a perfect stranger to proclaim the New Day of God.' " [10]

As impressive as were these accomplishments in the South in the early days of the Divine Plan, with large numbers of talks given and of individuals addressed, no one had fewer illusions about their impact than Louis Gregory. "At most, even in a long journey," he told Joseph Hannen, "when the millions of people are considered, we are only touching the surface of things at strategic points." [11] But such was the nature of the task 'Abdu'l-Bahá had assigned His followers: "Appreciate ye the value of this time and be ye engaged in the sowing of the seeds. . . ." [12]

Nonetheless, by 1920 or so, Bahá'ís traveling to the South were increasingly likely to find " 'many scattered believers,' " as Louis Gregory put it in *Star of the West*, " 'and vastly more who sympathize with the Cause as far as they understand it.' " One strategic point of activity was Memphis, where George Henderson had moved shortly after becoming a Bahá'í and had established a successful black business college. The Faith was well-received there, and many students and teachers embraced its principles. In September 1917 Louis Gregory reported that the Memphis Bahá'í community consisted of sixty people: "3 white [and] 57 colored." "Henderson is the 'teachingest' busy man I ever saw," he wrote to Joseph Hannen during a visit to Memphis two years later. "He seems to take some time to mention the Cause to every one he meets. In this way he has interested a number of whites whom he meets in a business way, some of whom have attended the meetings. With all the eight teachers in his school Bahai, the students find the atmosphere full of it." A short time later "the entire faculty and student body" addressed a letter to 'Abdu'l-Bahá. [13]

Development into a functioning Bahá'í community was slow, however. Distant from the mainstream of Bahá'í activity, the group depended heavily on George Henderson, who had many other interests and responsibilities competing for his time. More-over, for many years Louis Gregory provided the group's only contact with other Bahá'ís. In 1929, after a long period during which neither he nor any other Bahá'í visited the college, Mr. Greg-ory returned to find that Henderson was away and that the group had become relatively inactive in its isolation. Yet old ties were soon reestablished, and "many opportunities to speak to groups, schools, churches and individuals" were soon presented to him. Informed of his old friend's arrival, George Henderson returned quickly to Memphis. The close relationship between them was so completely reconfirmed that Mr. Gregory wrote a friend of his de-sire to go on pilgrimage to the Holy Land with George Hender-son.[14] Meanwhile, the Bahá'ís at the college addressed their sec-ond letter to Haifa, this time to Shoghi Effendi.[15]

Mr. Gregory's efforts over a period of more than twenty years finally culminated in the formation of the first Spiritual Assem-bly of the Bahá'ís of Memphis, of which George Henderson was elected a member, in April 1941. After Mr. Henderson's death in 1944 Louis Gregory published a tribute to him in *The Bahá'í World,* describing him as a loved and respected public figure whose professional concerns dominated his life yet were always related to his beliefs as a Bahá'í.[16]

George Henderson's enthusiastic adherence to the Faith is par-ticularly noteworthy because so few black Bahá'í teachers resided in the region in these early years. Louis Gregory singled out only three in a 1920 summary of the development of the Bahá'í Faith in the South: Caroline W. Harris, who taught in a summer colony at Harper's Ferry, West Virginia; Harriet Gibbs Marshall of Arkan-sas, who had become a Bahá'í in Washington, D.C.; and George Henderson himself.[17] The efforts of these three, along with those of a handful of black traveling teachers, were so successful, how-ever, that relatively large numbers of people—blacks and some whites, as well—were becoming aware of the Bahá'í Faith.

By 1920 more white than black Bahá'í teachers either lived or wintered in the South. Yet their teaching work, when it focused on whites, produced mixed results. A case in point is Louisville, Kentucky, where Louis Gregory spent a highly successful month during the summer of 1920. " 'I did not feel adequate to the work here, so complex is the situation,' " he admitted at the end of his stay. " 'Kentucky is known historically as "dark and bloody ground" on account of the feuds.' " He had in fact hoped to have an experienced white teacher like Mason Remey or Albert Vail, a former clergyman and well-known Bahá'í lecturer and writer, go there instead. " 'But the people have all been wonderfully kind and courteous, and outside of some of the clergy, there has been little opposition.' " " 'Spiritual confirmations' " abounded: " 'one . . . might say that miracles have happened.' " A wealthy white Bahá'í had even opened her home for " 'a semi-weekly meeting attended mainly by people in her set.' " She had, according to Emma Stott, another Louisville Bahá'í, " 'invited all her close friends to hear Mr. Gregory, and left nothing undone or unsaid to bring the Glad-tidings to her friends, and even had a Feast.' " On the last Sunday of his visit the Bahá'ís and their friends had joined together in a Unity Feast— " 'a real Feast—just like we have had among Bahais everywhere: a mixed Assembly, and both a material and spiritual feast,' " Mrs. Stott enthused. " 'Mr. Gregory was so happy to have this perfect Bahai meeting, both colors.' "[18]

But when a seasoned white Bahá'í, Mrs. Ellen ("Mother") Beecher, went to Louisville the following winter with the hope of establishing an assembly, she found more obstacles than miracles. "It has been a hard place to work," she wrote to Alfred Lunt in 1921, "because of the bitter prejudices of the races—however we have sown much seed, & given the message over & over both in public places, from the platform, & individually. The harvest is with God."[19]

Mother Beecher had worked closely with a black couple, Dr. and Mrs. Moses L. Murphy, who had become Bahá'ís during Louis Gregory's visit. Dr. Murphy had been seriously ill with tuberculosis when Mrs. Stott arranged for Mr. Gregory to visit them, and " 'that visit was the grandest thing,' " she recalled, " 'a genuine life line.' " Both of the Murphys had accepted the Faith immediately and had invited Mr. Gregory to stay with them for the rest of his visit. Dr. Murphy's health had begun to improve rapidly, so that before Mr. Gregory left he was already driving his car again and visiting some of his patients. Mrs. Stott remarked that " 'I felt if I had never done any good in this world, here was something;—linking hearts who will work together absent or present.' "[20] During Mother Beecher's stay the Murphy home had been open for many meetings, and all of the feasts had been held there. A small number of inquirers had become confirmed Bahá'ís. The formation of a local administrative unit, which Mother Beecher had hoped to achieve and which Mr. Gregory had encouraged in a letter to the Murphys, posed insuperable problems, however. The wealthy white woman who had opened her home to Mr. Gregory apparently found it impossible to continue such efforts toward interracial unity on a regular basis. A new Bahá'í, "she considered it would be fatal to the Cause to bring the two races together, and again, it would ruin her reputation & influence in this City—she would simply be ostracized."[21]

Since Mother Beecher had no intention of assisting with the formation of a racially segregated assembly, she reported the situation to Alfred Lunt of the Executive Board of Bahai Temple Unity and then, rather than forcing the issue, she let the matter rest, hoping that attitudes would change in a year or two. That summer Dr. Murphy died, depriving the group of one of its most active members.[22] The opportunity for Louisville to become a focal point for early Bahá'í expansion in the South was irretrievably lost. It was twenty-two years before a Local Spiritual Assembly was formed in Louisville. When a picture of the community members appeared in the November 1943 issue of *Bahá'í News*, no blacks were among them.[23] Although neither Louis Gregory nor Mother Beecher would have considered their work wasted, the history of the Louisville Bahá'í community reveals how sincere, patient, successful endeavors in the South could be virtually effaced because prejudice had not been fully overcome among the Bahá'ís themselves.

Louis Gregory was undoubtedly saddened when the attitudes of white Southerners who became Bahá'ís in the South, and of the white majority of believers in America as a whole, set back the progress of the Faith. But he felt that the answer was more effort among whites, not less.

They [white Southerners] are perhaps more orthodox [than blacks] and will not so readily open their established institutions, but there is a vast work for teachers among them. Abdul-Baha, speaking of teaching in the South, says: "Become ye firmly rooted in this great aim. Send ye teachers to all directions and become ye not apprehensive should ye meet strong opposition."[24]

Many of the white Bahá'ís did indeed demonstrate real courage in the face of opposition. In those days a simple encounter between black and white Bahá'ís was often fraught with danger. To blacks, who had no actual security under the law or in the eyes of society, this meant a difference in the degree of danger that they regularly faced. As for whites, who were normally immune from such danger, the commitment to a Bahá'í life placed them upon a lonely and perilous road. To their great credit, individuals such as James Elmore Hays of Atlanta conquered their fears and carried on their work. Roy Williams wrote of Hays:

> 'This Bahá'í was like a shining sun—strong of physique and equally strong of spirit. He was entirely devoid of any racial prejudice. He was my and Louis Gregory's closest companion whenever we were in the city. Mr. Hayes [*sic*] worked for the Atlanta Constitution as a mailing clerk. The amusing albeit very dangerous methods he employed to spend an hour or two with me will always live in my memory. Under cover of darkness walking across the city sometimes very late at night, he would come to our house at 2 Beckwith Street, and sit, eat and talk for hours—just a happy intimate fellowship.'[25]

Equally courageous, according to Roy Williams' account, was Dr. James Charles Oakshette, an Englishman who had become attracted to the Bahá'í Faith while he was studying medicine at the University of Illinois. In the spring of 1917 an inquiry from Dr. Oakshette about the Bahá'ís of Atlanta had been forwarded to Louis Gregory, who suggested in a letter to Joseph Hannen that the man be referred "to Mr. J. Elmore Hays[,] an employe [*sic*] of the 'Atlanta Constitution,' who is a wonderful soul, very active, and will put Mr. O in touch with other believers there." Two years later, when Mr. Williams went to Atlanta after the Convention of the Covenant, he found Dr. Oakshette to be a strong, exemplary Bahá'í:

> 'During my first teaching trip I met Dr. Oakshette by arrangement with him in his office in the Hurt Building. This had to be

done very secretly but he never showed any fear and we spent many happy hours discussing ways and means and contacts he knew among colored people. I have never met a more charming and lovable character—doing all that he possibly could almost alone under the harsh conditions then existing in Atlanta . . . he told me of his many persistent contacts with persons in all walks of life in Atlanta—whether black or white—Jew or Christian—Protestant or Catholic. No doubt these seeds have or will bear fruit as he was without doubt a true and selfless Baha'i. Of all the Southern or Northern Baha'is I have met all over the country I can truthfully say that . . . Dr. Oakshette personified the best of the ideals of the Cause under all conditions—even the worst that existed in Atlanta around 1919–1920–1921.'[26]

Great obstacles to the functioning of an integrated Bahá'í community persisted for many years in the South, with believers of both races facing the threat of danger and harassment. As late as 1940 a brief visit by Louis Gregory to a private school in Atlanta run by two white Bahá'ís, Olga Finke and Doris Ebbert, caused the disruption of lives and livelihoods; ". . . a few minutes after you stepped out of the door,'' Miss Finke wrote him a number of years later, ''we were told by the landlord who lived in the house, that we had to move.''[27] But the bond between white and black Bahá'ís that brought them such difficulties also testified to the depth and firmness of their convictions. Louis Gregory valued each experience of interracial unity as a confirmation of the transforming power of Bahá'u'lláh's teachings of oneness.

In a report to Joseph Hannen he recounted one such experience. A friend had written to tell him that a white Bahá'í, Anna Reinke, resided in Austin, Texas, where he planned to visit. On his arrival there, he contacted her. ''We had a pleasant conversation over the 'phone,'' he reported,

and she invited me to visit her, which was impracticable. But the next morning she came through the heavy rain to a meeting at the colored high school. Her radiant smiling face made a deep impression there and was a demonstration to those present of the Power of the Covenant, which thus brought two races together in a city where the race problem is acute. . . .[28]

He was convinced of the positive effects of such demonstrations of interracial unity and regarded them as a vital part of the process of seed sowing in which he was engaged.

While the systematic approach to implementing the Divine Plan in the South was still in its beginning stages, however, it suffered an irreparable loss that was shared by Louis Gregory and by the cause of interracial unity as well. On 27 January 1920 Joseph Hannen died after having been struck by a car in Washington. Even his death was bound up with the work to which he had devoted himself. The accident occurred just after he had stopped at the post office to pick up mail to be forwarded to Louis Gregory and Roy Williams. The letters were found"stained and bespattered" with his blood, Charles Mason Remey wrote in *Star of the West,* "a symbolic testimony of his last service to the friends." Indeed, the last letter that Mr. Gregory addressed to his "Brother Joseph" mentions that he looked forward "to find[ing] mail" waiting when he reached Shreveport, Louisiana.[29]

On his arrival he discovered, instead, that his friend had been killed. His sense of loss was acute, for Joseph Hannen had played a singular role in his life. Both of the Hannens were responsible for his having pursued inquiry into the teachings of Bahá'u'lláh after the first meeting he attended in 1907. He believed that, were it not for them, the Bahá'í Faith might well have receded into the back of his mind, a subject of mild interest but of little relevance to the dominant concerns in his life. "I shall always remember with deepest gratitude," he wrote his "beloved Bro. Joseph" in 1916, "the zeal, enthusiasm, love, attraction & wisdom of my spiritual parents when they guided me gently to the Path of El Abha [Bahá'u'lláh]."[30]

Working together as they did after 1909 on Bahá'í community activities in Washington, on articles for Bahá'í publications, and on Southern teaching projects, Joseph Hannen and Louis Gregory were bound ever closer in mutual admiration and respect. Mr. Hannen demonstrated repeatedly the personal characteristics that had compelled Louis Gregory to return to the Hannen home week after week to study their Faith. Joseph Hannen "was the standby in the Washington assembly—the one upon whom every one depended," Charles Mason Remey observed in an obituary published in *Star of the West.*

He was always in the meetings and gatherings of the friends, and when anyone wanted anything done quickly and without delay he was the one to whom they turned, knowing that on him they could depend with certainty. Moreover, Brother Joseph was always cheerful and happy in his service, and his firmness in the Covenant was a fortress and protection to all who knew him. He made great sacrifices in the path of Abdul-Baha, the fruits of which many of the friends have already witnessed, while those who knew him are convinced that in time the far-reaching effects of his Bahai work will become more generally and widely recognized and acknowledged than it is at present.[31]

Barriers of skin color had no place in his life, as Louis Gregory had realized from the beginning of their relationship. Joseph Hannen was consistent in his efforts for racial unity. When the community stood divided over race, he was one of the handful of white Bahá'ís who never wavered in his support of the principle of oneness. When the expansion of the Bahá'í Faith among blacks was going well, the contributions made by the Hannens were equally evident. "I am very happy over the way the work is progressing, especially among the colored people," Louis Gregory once exclaimed to Pauline Hannen. "You can see the amazing results of the seed-planting of yourself and Mr. Hannen."[32] An exemplary stand on race was in fact one of the components of the admirable life described in Joseph Hannen's obituary. He "served alike the white and the colored friends." Even his funeral was a testament to his values. "At the request of his family both colored and white united in carrying his remains to the grave. He was ever striving to create unity and good fellowship between the two races."[33]

As deeply shocked and personally grief-stricken as he was by the death of his "spiritual parent," Mr. Gregory's immediate concern for Mrs. Hannen and the rest of the family overshadowed his own feelings of "separation" from the friend who had "occupied so large a place in my life." He addressed a loving letter of condolence to Pauline Hannen. In it sadness was balanced by firm belief in life after death. "I know he is infinitely happy and would not for worlds return. But no doubt it is his earnest desire and prayer for the dear loved ones left behind to be comforted." Seeking to offer such comfort, he described the death as the culmination of a life of sacrifice:

In thinking, thinking, thinking, as so often I do about him, I have recalled that you once related to me how Abdul Baha had told him during the pilgrimage, that he would be a martyr in the Cause. He was without doubt as much a martyr as those precious souls whose blood dyed the soil of Persia in the early days of the Cause. His labor was ceaseless, his service to the friends of God and all humanity universal in its nature and his forgetfulness of self characteristic of the martyrs. . . . Now and in the years to come the circle of the influence of his life will widen.[34]

For the present, however, the Bahá'í teaching effort in the South could ill afford the loss of Joseph Hannen as its champion. Administratively he had been Louis Gregory's counterpart during the early years of Bahá'í expansion in the South. After his death the work continued, but the systematic mobilization of resources by a Central Bureau for the South seems to have died with him.

Louis Gregory carried on with his planned itinerary for the remainder of the winter and early spring of 1920. In April he attended the national convention in New York, where the delegates unanimously adopted a resolution in memory of Joseph Hannen. By summer he was back in the South once again, traveling through the border states. "Mr. Louis G. Gregory has been in Maryland and Kentucky the past month," *Star of the West* noted, "particularly good reports come from Louisville where he has been staying for over two weeks." The article went on to quote Mr. Gregory's own summary of teaching activities by both white and black Bahá'ís, and friends of the Faith, in the South up to that time. Although he referred to over thirty individuals and did not mention his own work, his role in the region is implicit in the report itself. No one else could have compiled it. His firsthand knowledge of the Southern states was unmatched in Bahá'í circles, particularly after Joseph Hannen's death.[35]

Although he must have longed at times for others to take on the burdens and to share in his absorbing interest in the South, Louis Gregory never gave in to impatience over slow progress toward the goals of the Divine Plan. "The work of seed-sowing goes forward thru Divine Favor," he wrote a friend in 1922. "Am now once more in the South and find great interest. . . ." Content with the time of seed sowing, he traveled as widely as possible, nurturing individuals and groups that showed the promise of growth. "His radiant enthusiasm and spiritual zealousness, his comprehensive presentation of the Bahai Message and teachings of this new Day of God, are attracting wide attention wherever he goes in the Southland," the Teaching Committee reported in *Star of the West*. "He is meeting with great success and not antagonism."[36] He had no doubt that the harvest time would come.

12   Time of Transition

Progress by the American Bahá'ís toward achievement of the goals of the Divine Plan suffered a major interruption in November 1921, when a cablegram from Haifa broke the shocking announcement: "His Holiness Abdul-Baha ascended to Abha Kingdom."* The blow to the American Bahá'ís, the community that He had raised up and nurtured with lavish attention, was profound. Nearly two months passed before Bahíyyih Khánum, 'Abdu'l-Bahá's sister, cabled the news that Shoghi Effendi had been appointed Guardian of the Cause in the Master's Will and Testament. Shortly thereafter Shoghi Effendi sent his first message to America, a brief cablegram that commented on the "Americans' unswerving loyalty and noble resolve" and asked them to "accept my loving co-operation." Several months elapsed before his first letter to America, published in the 21 March 1922 issue of *Star of the West,* finally gave some indication of the exceptional qualities of leadership that the Bahá'ís would find in their youthful Guardian.[1]

The loss of 'Abdu'l-Bahá's living presence was thus compounded by uncertainty about the future. Knowledge of the provisions for succession of authority filtered gradually through the American Bahá'í community. A March 1922 letter to Alfred Lunt from Louis Gregory, who was traveling in the West, indicates how information was received, little by little, during those first months after 'Abdu'l-Bahá's passing:

Many thanks for yours of the 24th ult. transmitting enclosures of the wonderfully solemn and impressive Tablet ['Abdu'l-Bahá's last] to America and the letter of Shoughi Rabbani, whose hands may God uphold. Greatly appreciated is your

---

*The Kingdom of Glory (in Bahá'í usage, the afterlife).

kind thoughtfulness in sending them. If a copy of the Will is available, shall look forward with eager interest to its perusal.[2]

A translation by Shoghi Effendi of the Will and Testament had indeed been received late in February. It was some time, however, before the document could be published and made generally available.

Moreover, Shoghi Effendi's leadership had not yet been firmly established in the consciousness of the community when it was subjected to its first severe challenge. In Haifa the Guardian was assailed not only by a small group of people who had always regarded themselves as opponents of 'Abdu'l-Bahá but also by followers who now refused to accept His appointed successor. The shock of such opposition, added to the burdens of leadership that had weighed heavily even upon 'Abdu'l-Bahá, was so great that Shoghi Effendi withdrew from the Holy Land for a perod of months in 1922, 1923, and again in 1924 in order to regain his strength and confidence. During these months he left the affairs of the Cause in the capable hands of his great-aunt, Bahíyyih Khánum, but at the time no one could be sure of the outcome of this troubled passage in Bahá'í history.

In America the ability of the Bahá'ís to transfer the focus of their highly personal loyalty from 'Abdu'l-Bahá to Shoghi Effendi was tested by a number of agitators. Under the circumstances the energies of the active Bahá'ís were spent on maintaining unity and optimism more than on expansion. Louis Gregory was among the few who addressed both needs. He continued to travel extensively, teaching the Faith to new people as always and providing invaluable encouragement to the Bahá'ís themselves. The secretary of the Bahá'í Assembly of Denver, for example, reported that

"Mr. Gregory reached Denver just two days after we received the staggering news of our Beloved's Ascension. All were cheered and comforted by this dear brother, through whom the heavenly confirmations seem to flow uninterruptedly. The believers tried, in their deep sorrow, to appreciate more fully Abdul Baha's Words concerning the time when He would be no longer with us upon this earth. The hearts are filled with greatest longing to 'rejoice His heart, satisfy His cravings, comply with His request and fulfill His anticipations', and the arrival of Mr.

Gregory provided a blessed opportunity for service, in which privilege all have shared most beautifully. What Mercy and Bounty has He bestowed on us, enabling us at this time of grief to prove our love for Him in active service! But the real service has been, by His Grace, through Mr. Gregory's loving and tireless efforts."[3]

Louis Gregory's success was in part a reflection of his fundamental confidence in the new period that the Bahá'í Faith had entered. His attitude toward the Guardian revealed from the beginning the quality that Bahá'ís term firmness in the Covenant of Bahá'u'lláh, a loyalty to the central figures and institutions of the Faith so unshakable that it prevents disunity and eventual schism. Moreover, Louis Gregory had seen the promise in the Master's eldest grandson years before, while on pilgrimage. In general it was true that, as Ugo Giachery has written, "in the early 1920's the Guardian had been, at least to the Western Bahá'ís, an almost intangible figure, the symbol of an institution functioning on an extra-human plane," but Louis Gregory was among the few who, having met Shoghi Effendi, easily superimposed the aura of leadership on the well-remembered youth.[4]

Thus, although he had been strongly attached to 'Abdu'l-Bahá, he had no difficulty in accepting the authority of Shoghi Effendi, no trepidation about the future progress of the Cause, and no doubt about the importance of continuing the work that 'Abdu'l-Bahá had given him. The latter point was cited by the National Teaching Committee as having been "first and foremost" in Mr. Gregory's success. The second element pointed out by the committee was his whole-hearted devotion and "absolute attention" to 'Abdu'l-Bahá, and the third was Mr. Gregory's humility as a teacher.[5]

Furthermore, wherever he went, he looked for indications of growth and development, and when he found them, he called them to the attention of others. Referring to his reports of his travels during the fall, winter, and spring of 1921–22, the National Teaching Committee Bulletin observed, "As the encouraging news literally poured into this 'office' from day to day, we were lifted high above the world and its concerns, and truly experienced how life-imparting is the constructive work of Teaching; and understood more fully from day to day why the Beloved Master invariably very promptly replied to the letters containing good news of the spread of the Cause."[6] In the summer of 1924, for example, Louis Gregory informed Alfred Lunt of his recent experiences in typically positive terms: "Have been in Worcester, Montreal and Toronto since I last saw you. In all these centers new faces appear among the friends, indicating the onward march of the Cause." Then he added a comment that reveals both his good humor and his habit of understating the problems he found among the Bahá'ís. "The friends, too, are in great love and understanding among themselves," he remarked, *"a sign of life, indeed!"*[7]

Louis Gregory's activities during the early years of the Guardianship were in themselves a sign of life in the American Bahá'í community. At the annual convention in 1922, the first after the loss of 'Abdu'l-Bahá, the National Teaching Committee described Mr. Gregory's travels during the previous months not only as one of the highlights of the year but as a milestone in the history of the Bahá'í Faith in America. "Every one, I think, appreciates to the fullest extent the work accomplished in this country from coast to coast the last year by Mr. Gregory," Mariam Haney, secretary of the committee, told the delegates.

> I do not think we have had anything that approached it in any way in the 24 years or since 1895 when the Cause first started in this country. Now there are many reasons why I think this was a very extraordinary work from a spiritual standpoint, because it is the first time that any teacher so marvelously illumined as Mr. Gregory has been able to reach thousand[s] and thousands of people, colored and white. This is why we consider it a very remarkable spiritual work. . . . Abdul Baha said more than once that he [Mr. Gregory] would be the cause of the guidance of both races. He was received warmly in every direction, and had very wonderful opportunities for service through the doors that were opened to him.[8]

During the early fall of 1921, following a summer's respite at Green Acre, Louis Gregory set out on the journey that he was to call, toward the end of his life, "the longest in point of time of all my teaching tours." Enroute from Boston to the Midwest he visited Oberlin and Cleveland, Ohio, and Chicago and its nearby suburbs. Although he often visited Chicago, this time the visit was "particularly fruitful," according to the National Teaching Committee. "An average of a meeting a day, sometimes more, was the order. Hundreds were given the Message at these meetings, and the signs of confirmations were seen in the number of new faces at the Bahai meetings."[9] From Chicago Mr. Gregory headed northwestward into unfamiliar territory. In many places he was the first Bahá'í to visit since the Western tour of Mírzá Asadu'lláh, Fáḍil-i-Mázindarání, a scholar from Iran, who had been sent to America by 'Abdu'l-Bahá in 1920. In Minneapolis and St. Paul, Minnesota, a large number of meetings were arranged, especially in the black community. Mr. Gregory singled out the efforts of Dr. Orrol Woolson of St. Paul for particular praise, and she in turn wrote that " 'the Spirit of Abdul Baha has been in our midst.' " A Minneapolis Bahá'í called attention to the twofold effect of Louis Gregory's presence; on the one hand, the Bahá'ís had become " 'more united,' " and on the other, they sensed an unprecedented public response, indicated by the fact that they had " 'never had such meetings and so much interest shown.' " From Duluth, Minnesota, Mr. Gregory reported that " 'the Bahai Teachings have now reached practically all the colored and many thousands of white people.' "[10]

Successful meetings were arranged in both Lincoln and Omaha, Nebraska. Mr. Gregory was especially impressed with the Omaha Bahá'ís: " 'It is quite amazing how quickly the Western people act. They do not stand on any ceremony, but see what is to be done, and go right after it. Small wonder that Jenabe Fazel [Fáḍil-i-Mázindarání] admired them.' " In Lincoln Louis Gregory addressed the local chapter of the N.A.A.C.P., as he had in Duluth and Omaha, and was yet to do in many other cities.[11]

During his stay in Denver, the grief of the Bahá'ís over the sudden loss of 'Abdu'l-Bahá did not prevent them from taking every opportunity to use Louis Gregory's services as a lecturer. In two weeks he spoke at twenty-two meetings, reaching " 'all classes' " in a variety of churches and organizations. Interest was so marked that "many of the seekers followed our eloquent teacher from meeting to meeting, just as they followed Jenabe Fazel when he spoke in Denver last year."[12]

Next Mr. Gregory felt impelled to go to Pueblo, Colorado, although no Bahá'ís resided there to help with arrangements. He found a man who worked " 'like a veteran in service' " to schedule talks under the auspices of a number of black churches and organizations. Mr. Gregory also spoke to two white audiences on the subject of interracial amity. The highlight of the visit to Pueblo was a talk on the Bahá'í Faith to eight hundred students at the Central High School: " 'You know that youngsters are not inclined to restraint when happy. I have seen nothing like the ovation they accorded since visiting Tuskegee Institute some years ago. The Superintendent of Schools, Principal [and] fifty-two teachers, joined in the enthusiasm, and extended a cordial invitation to return.' " [13]

In Salt Lake City, where as in Pueblo there were no resident Bahá'ís, Louis Gregory was welcomed as a speaker by the Theosophists, two black churches, and a women's organization. "He mingled freely in this City with the Mormons," the Teaching Committee noted, "attended their church and was politely and cordially welcomed, but he did not feel guided to give them the Message." [14]

From Utah Louis Gregory traveled north to Montana, stopping in Butte and Helena. In both cities he met a full speaking schedule. Fred Mortensen, who had contributed much to the establishment of the first Bahá'í group in Atlanta, had moved to Helena. Having worked with Mr. Gregory in the South, he was well aware of the range of " 'Brother Gregory's' " teaching abilities. " 'From the moment of his arrival he found Helena no place for rest,' " Mr. Mortensen reported. " 'Every lecture (of which we had eight in six days) was well attended and all the comments I heard were simply those of extreme contentment and satisfaction.' " Louis Gregory's talents as a writer were also put to use in Helena. " 'The lecturing was but one part of the work here,' " Fred Mortensen added, " 'for I kept Mr. Gregory so busy writing articles for the newspapers that he must have remained up and at work most nights.' " As a newspaperman himself, Mr. Mortensen was committed to furthering the interests of the Bahá'í Faith through the medium of the press. " 'Fred Mortensen, young, strong, devoted—led me such a pace that temporarily the use of my right arm was lost through writing so much and so fast,' " Louis Gregory recalled with affection.

" 'Truly he is "Frederick the Great." ' " As a result of their combined efforts, articles on the Faith were circulated through much of the state. [15]

The intense pace of his journey was maintained in the state of Washington, where he gave thirteen meetings in nine days in Spokane and twenty-four meetings in eight days in Seattle. On a single Sunday in Seattle he addressed five gatherings—one of the Bahá'ís, two at churches, one at the black Y.W.C.A., and a banquet attended by nearly fifty people. Among the " 'unusually intelligent and progressive' " black community of Seattle he found several individuals who he felt might become teachers of the Faith. " 'Words cannot express what Mr. Gregory's visit in Seattle has meant—not only to the Bahais, but to the whole community,' " the Local Assembly wrote in gratitude. " 'The spirit of unity and harmony manifested was unusual. Our dear brother is such a wonderfully illumined soul; we just kept him going at "top-notch speed," sending out his bright rays to at least two audiences a day and sometimes as many as four. . . . He was always so willing and gracious about everything, that we just felt we wanted him to stay in Seattle all the time.' " [16]

Vancouver, British Columbia, had only recently been virgin territory for the Bahá'ís. A year after the launching of the Divine Plan, Marion Jack, a staunch Canadian believer who had at one time taught English to 'Abdu'l-Bahá's grandchildren in 'Akká, went to live in Vancouver for several months. By the winter of 1922 the city had a small, active community that arranged five meetings during Mr. Gregory's visit. Shortly thereafter the Vancouver Bahá'ís formed the first Assembly in western Canada. [17]

Portland, Oregon, which already had a well-established Bahá'í community before 'Abdu'l-Bahá came to America, echoed Seattle's desire for an extended stay by Mr. Gregory: " 'The only thing that ever should be changed in an event of this kind is the shortness of the visit.' " In little more than a week he addressed fourteen diverse gatherings. He lectured on the "Unity of Religions" to the congregation of the First Divine Science Church, on "The Seven Valleys" to the Psychology Club, on "Interracial Amity" to the Oregon Social Workers, and on "The Harmony between Religion and Science" at the Metaphysical Library. A " 'beautiful response' " greeted his talk on "The Equality between Men and

Women" to a club meeting at the black Y.W.C.A. He also spoke
on "Universal Peace" and "The Abandonment of Prejudice" at
two black churches. Aside from these formal meetings he attended
smaller social gatherings, such as one hosted by Beatrice
Cannady-Franklin, the editor of the local black newspaper, who
was to remain an active Bahá'í for many years to come. Even when
he was not engaged, Mr. Gregory remained busy. " 'Throughout
the week during his spare moments,' " George Latimer of the
Portland Assembly observed, " 'he called on sick friends and
Bahais who could not get out to hear his admirable talks.' "[18]

In a visit to the San Francisco Bay Area—described by Ella
Cooper, one of the first Bahá'ís of the West, as " 'all too
brief' "—Louis Gregory spoke at a number of meetings in black
churches, public halls, and private homes. The meeting he " 'enjoyed most' " was held at the University of California at Berkeley
" 'under the joint auspices of the Cosmopolitan and Chinese Student's Clubs.' " Like 'Abdu'l-Bahá, Louis Gregory loved interracial and international assemblages, and this particular meeting was
distinguished by unusual variety for its day: " 'Chinese, Hindoos,
Americans—white and colored—made a picturesque and radiant
gathering.' "[19]

" 'No one who has ever been here, can ever forget the Golden
West,' " he wrote from Los Angeles, where he spent about twelve
days and was impressed by the " 'heavenly harmony' " of the
Bahá'ís. He headed east once again by way of Phoenix, Arizona,
and Oklahoma City. In Tulsa he found that his experience contrasted sharply with the city's record of racial violence. " 'You
may recall that last summer this City was shaken by a terrible riot in
which there was great loss of life on both sides, and nearly the entire "colored section" was destroyed by incendiary fires,' " he
reminded the Teaching Committee in his report. Nonetheless,
" 'nearly all' " of his talks—in churches, public schools, to various organizations, and even to prisoners at the city jail—were
given before integrated audiences. " 'I am as safe here as anywhere else in creation, for, after all, the only Safety is the Power of
the Covenant, which is unlimited.' "[20]

From Oklahoma Mr. Gregory proceeded to Topeka, Kansas;
Kansas City and St. Louis, Missouri; and Springfield and Urbana,
Illinois. By the end of April he had returned to Chicago once

again.[21] The final stages of the trip were crowded, like the rest, with speaking engagements that may have seemed at the time neither more nor less noteworthy than the hundreds that had gone before. One lecture in Kansas City gained unusual significance retroactively, however. "It will be thrilling to you to know, as was the discovery to me, that President Truman was in that meeting of the Literary Digest Psychology club, which you arranged for me to address," he wrote Edith Chapman in 1949. The president "remembers it well," he added, although he did not give the source of his information.[22] Convinced as he was that the Bahá'í principles of oneness have a vitality and power of their own, regardless of the effectiveness of the speaker or the apparent receptivity of the hearer, he was particularly gratified to think that the president who led his country into the United Nations had been exposed to Bahá'í thought a quarter of a century earlier. One never knew upon what fertile ground the seed of world-embracing ideals might fall.

Louis Gregory's long journey from coast to coast, which the National Teaching Committee in its March 1922 bulletin called "one of the most brilliant Bahai Teaching Tours we have ever been privileged to have in this country," concluded with his attendance at the annual Bahá'í convention in Chicago. Although he constantly repeated his view that " 'it is all the Will and Power of Abdul Baha which brought success,' " he had clearly emerged as one of the outstanding Bahá'ís of America, as effective in the West as he had been for years in those sections where he was a frequent visitor.[23] He was elected to the National Spiritual Assembly that April and continued to serve for two consecutive years until April 1924.

Although his membership on the National Assembly precluded long tours such as the one he had undertaken in 1921–22, he continued to travel constantly for the Faith. After the convention he managed to take a "short trip into the South," visiting several cities in Virginia before the next Assembly meeting in New York in the latter part of June. He spent the summer and early fall in New England with Louise. "Mr. Louis G. Gregory visited Washington for several days after leaving Green Acre, and gave two public addresses while here: one on 'The Underlying Unity of All Religions'; and the second on 'Proofs of Immortality of the Soul,' " the *Teaching Bulletin* reported. "He is at present serving in and around Boston where he will remain until Mrs. Gregory sails for England later in the month. A teaching tour through the South will be Mr. Gregory's program for the coming months."[24] However, he was apparently unable to carry out his intention to go south. He spent much of the winter in Washington, D.C., instead, and also made a tour of the Northeast, the primary purpose of which was to meet with the Bahá'í Assemblies in the region to inspire them to contribute financially to the building of the Wilmette Temple.

When he was finally able to return to the South after the 1923 convention, the necessity of planning his itinerary around a scheduled National Assembly meeting in New York at the end of June prevented him once again from extending his stay. He traveled as far south as Atlanta, stopping enroute in Nashville and Chattanooga, Tennessee. During the summer he spent some time in the peaceful environment of Green Acre. The fall and winter seasons, like those of the previous year, were taken up with extended visits to major Bahá'í centers in the East—Washington, D.C., New York, Boston, Worcester—where intensive teaching efforts did not interfere with his responsibilities as a member of the National Spiritual Assembly.

When he was not reelected to the Assembly in 1924, he immediately returned to his pattern of spending long periods of time on the road. That summer he traveled among cities and resort areas in the North. In the fall he headed south, stopping in North Carolina, Virginia, South Carolina, Alabama, and Tennessee. In his home city of Charleston he gave thirteen talks in eight days. One of the high points of the journey was a return visit to Tuskegee Institute, where he had been warmly received in the past. This time, in addition to addressing the entire student body, he discussed the Bahá'í teachings with George Washington Carver and the widow of Booker T. Washington. At Fisk, however, the atmosphere that he had described as joyful in the spring of 1923 had been transformed. The school was, in his words, "about torn to pieces" as a result of student protests against an administration that they perceived to be highly conservative.[25] Yet he took this changing mood in stride. Having known his share of righteous anger during the early 1900s, he remained both undismayed and undeterred in his effort to spread a healing message of goodwill and hope.

At the 1925 national convention, which was held at Green Acre in July, Louise Boyle, who had been asked to present a report on the development of the Faith in the South, produced "a little card catalogue of the believers" there. She had made a superficial "survey," as she put it, that focused on the centers of activity in each state. Her assessment differed little from Mr. Gregory's own five years earlier: that there were "many scattered believers" and "vastly more" who were friends of the Faith. Both categories had grown without as yet producing the "acclamation and acceleration" for which 'Abdu'l-Bahá had called under the Divine Plan. Mrs. Boyle's survey showed that in many cities, and even in some states, the Bahá'í Faith was represented by no more than one or two individuals.[26]

Yet a number of these people carried on with remarkable disregard for their isolation. Mrs. Boyle told the story of a man in Charleston, South Carolina, whose name had somehow come to Louis Gregory. Mr. Gregory had written a letter and sent the man a little booklet on the Faith. On his next visit to Charleston, he went to the address to which he had written and "asked if any Bahais lived there, and a voice responded, 'Yes, I got the letter, and I am a Bahai.' " The man had been so inspired that he had begun to preach on street corners, had been jailed several times, and had only stopped because his activities were causing his children to be ridiculed and because Mr. Gregory "advised him not [to] work in that way." Through the efforts of such dedicated individuals, Bahá'ís in the South could increasingly be found clustered in groups, although, as Mrs. Boyle pointed out, none of these was as yet large enough to form a Spiritual Assembly.[27]

Louise Boyle's report reflected an increasing awareness of the need to consolidate thirty years of Bahá'í development in America by forming administrative bodies in at least the major cities of each region. In response to this clear need, Louis Gregory made plans to return to the South in the fall of 1925. After a brief reunion with Louise, who had been in Europe during the previous year, he was on his way southward by October. He focused his attention on Florida, where there were seven Bahá'í groups, according to Mrs. Boyle's report. Successful meetings were held in Jacksonville, St. Augustine, and Miami. In the latter city a new Spiritual Assembly was formed with the assistance of white Bahá'í settlers and traveling teachers of both races from the North.[28] It was a victory for all who had worked there and above all for Louis Gregory, whose efforts at Louisville, Atlanta, and other cities had not yet resulted in the formal establishment of Spiritual Assemblies.

The movement toward consolidation was indicative of the substantial change that had occurred in the American Bahá'í community since 'Abdu'l-Bahá's first messages about the Divine Plan were received in 1916. A period of preoccupation with expansion—in terms of both an increased number of adherents and a wider geographic distribution—had been interrupted after five years by the passing of 'Abdu'l-Bahá. Thereafter, in the first five years of the Guardian's ministry, the community had responded to a different challenge, that of accepting a new focus of authority. Although few may have recognized the extent of change at the time, it now seems clear that, as Louis Gregory and others journeyed to San Francisco to attend the Eighteenth Annual Convention in April 1926, a profound transformation had already occurred in the American Bahá'í community.

Indeed, the convention itself symbolized a break with the past. The number of delegates and visitors from the old established centers in the eastern and midwestern states was much lower than in previous years, but the total attendance was greater than ever; the halls were filled with new faces from the West. Another important change was that, in accord with the principle of proportional representation prescribed by Shoghi Effendi in 1923 and first applied in 1925, the delegates had been for the first time apportioned by the National Assembly itself on the basis of membership rolls.[29]

It seems especially fitting that the secretary of the Southern Regional Teaching Committee, Louise Boyle, presented to the convention an evaluation of Louis Gregory's work up to that time that implied the end of a period of initial seed-sowing and the beginning of a new stage of growth. Her statement of high praise, made at only the midpoint of Mr. Gregory's career as an itinerant teacher, seems even more remarkable in the light of all of the years of effort yet to come: "The value of the services of dear Louis Gregory in the South during past years cannot be estimated; they have paved the way for much of the later accomplishment, and his spiritual influence is plainly felt by all those following in the path of this severed servant of the Cause."[30]

Part 2/The Era of Racial Amity

13 A Program for Racial Amity

The extension of teaching efforts after the Convention of the Covenant in 1919 occurred during the most turbulent period of racial animosity that America had ever experienced. 'Abdu'l-Bahá had expressed deep concern about the possibility of such an outbreak for many years. In conversations and in correspondence with many American Bahá'ís He had warned repeatedly of the dangers of continued racial division and discrimination. ''Until these prejudices are entirely removed from the people of the world,'' He wrote a Chicago Bahá'í in 1912, ''the realm of humanity will not find rest. Nay, rather, discord and bloodshed will be increased day by day, and the foundation of the prosperity of the world of man will be destroyed.''[1]

His predictions of worsening race relations were amply borne out. Deepening animosity toward blacks, both in the North and the South, was vented in unprovoked attacks on them and their property. Race riots occurred even during the First World War years, despite wartime preoccupations and concern for national solidarity. After the war the racial conflict intensified. Black soldiers, returning victorious from battles in Europe fought in the name of democracy, were subjected to a wave of violence that spread over the whole country. The Ku Klux Klan, which had reestablished itself in the South in 1915, grew rapidly and spread north and west. Lynchings were frequent; some of the victims were soldiers still in uniform. Eleven blacks were burned alive.[2] In the cities blacks and whites vied for jobs as industry readjusted to peacetime production and millions of rapidly demobilized servicemen sought employment. Riots broke out in record numbers.

John Hope Franklin has written of this time, ''It was the summer of 1919, called by James Weldon Johnson 'The Red Summer,' that ushered in the greatest period of interracial strife the nation had ever witnessed. From June to the end of the year approximately 25 race riots were held in American urban centers." As in earlier years these riots were instigated by whites, as "the lawless element of the population undertook to terrorize the Negroes into submission." But increasing numbers of blacks fought back:

> In the post-war racial strife the Negro's willingness to fight and to die in his own defense injected a new factor into America's most perplexing social problem. It was no longer a case of one race intimidating another into submission. Now it was war in the full sense of the word, and Negroes were as determined to win it as they had been in Europe.[3]

Tne bloodshed that 'Abdu'l-Bahá had predicted stained even the large cities of the North and touched either directly or indirectly the Bahá'í communities there. In July a riot in Washington, D.C., began with the familiar pattern: inflamed white mobs, in this case consisting mainly of white servicemen, attacked blacks. The riot turned to race warfare when white gangs attempted to burn the black district and its residents arose to defend themselves and their property. Later that month in Chicago, Bahá'ís were caught up in the worst race riot the nation had ever experienced. One Bahá'í home was bombed, and two members of a Bahá'í family were jailed briefly before the charges against them were dropped. Dr. Zia M. Bagdadi, a Persian physician in Chicago, was, as a fellow Bahá'í recalled, the one white man who went into the black sections during the riot and brought food to the hungry.[4]

The events of the "Red Summer" of 1919 awakened in the American Bahá'ís a heightened sense of responsibility. On 13 August 1919, shortly after the Chicago and Washington riots, Louis Gregory was asked to meet with the Executive Board of Bahai Temple Unity. He and Dr. Bagdadi, a member of the Board at that time, discussed the riots with the Board, laying much of the blame on "the greed and schemes of certain white landlords in both cities" who stood to gain by driving blacks from their neighborhoods into the ghetto. The minutes of the meeting recorded that Alfred Lunt "spoke of the race question and its significance and cause and the responsibility of the Bahai bodies to proclaim the true principle which alone would alleviate race prejudice and urged a greater realization of our responsibility."[5]

During that eventful summer, and on into the fall and winter, Louis Gregory and Roy Williams, undeterred by the tide of violence, traveled throughout the South, trying—in Mr. Gregory's words—to bring "the Glorious Message of the Kingdom to the oppressed and broken-hearted."[6] On Mr. Williams' first visit to Jacksonville he found the people in a "state of terror"; but, returning after spending some time in southern Florida, he was able to arrange many speaking engagements, and a number of people accepted the Faith. Mr. Gregory arrived in Helena, Arkansas, shortly after a race riot occurred there. He gave six public talks on the Bahá'í Faith amidst "people who have been in a state of grim pessimism and despair." In such an atmosphere any outsider, black or white, tended to arouse suspicion. But, as Roy Williams reported, presentation of the Bahá'í teachings dispelled mistrust, even among whites in authority, thereby serving to protect the teacher: " 'the Message of the Covenant is the safest thing for this part of the country and is the cause of both the surety of mind and the surety of limb.' "[7]

At its September meeting the Board once again discussed "the problem of the oneness of humanity and its antagonist, race prejudice, and the best means to promote this great principle of oneness." The minutes continued:

> Letters were read from Brother Joseph Hannen, Brother Zia Bagdadi and Brother Louis G. Gregory on this subject. It was realized on the part of all the members that the problem at this time called for a definite spiritual attitude on the part of the Bahais and a more careful examination of the elements and causes of the recent outbreaks of race prejudice, and greater attention to the duty on the part of the Board as to the best means of promulgating and promoting this principle of human unity.[8]

At this time Harlan Ober, as a concerned individual, also suggested in a circular letter that the Bahá'ís sponsor consultative meetings on race relations. In response Louis Gregory told his friend that he approved the idea as a means "of doing something helpful and constructive in the matter of racial adjustment and the removal of friction between the races.'' He also proposed that, in addition to holding such meetings of "the thinking people of both races" in various cities, "mass meetings" of the "rank and file" be organized to reach those among whom there tended to be "the greatest friction and animosity."[9] However, neither proposal seems to have gone any further, although the Executive Board did approve, as one sign of its increased awareness, public talks on "The Oneness of Mankind" by Mr. Gregory at both the 1920 and 1921 annual conventions.

While the Executive Board and other concerned Bahá'ís were still discussing "the best means of promulgating and promoting this principle of human unity," 'Abdu'l-Bahá Himself took the issue outside the consultative meetings of the national Bahá'í administration and made it a matter of public commitment. Several months after the "Red Summer" He initiated a major response by the Bahá'ís to deteriorating race relations in America. In Louis Gregory's words, He "set in motion a plan that was to bring the races together, attract the attention of the country, enlist the aid of famous and influential people and have a far-reaching effect upon the destiny of the nation itself."[10]

This plan was the initiation of a series of large, well-publicized interracial meetings, conducted not to protest any specific grievance or to seek improvement of the lot of American blacks in some particular way, but to proclaim the oneness of mankind and to promote "racial amity" between black and white Americans. In a period when segregation was still the law of much of the land and when few organizations of any kind, including churches and religious groups, stood for equality, such conferences or conventions for racial amity were literally unprecedented.

They addressed the need of many Americans, black and white, to find some ray of hope in the relations between the races. The events of the "Red Summer" had startled many whites who had never before given much thought to the racial problem. They shared the liberal minority's dismay over the unbridled animosity that white rioters had unleashed upon blacks and particularly upon veterans of the war. Many blacks were equally concerned about the mood of their own communities. "Unrest and disappointment seized a considerable portion of the Negro population," Franklin has observed. The tide of bitterness over the failure of democracy touched even those organizations that were working through Congress and the courts to effect change. The limitations of such organizations, soon readily apparent, contributed to the undercurrent of dissatisfaction. The Commission on Interracial Cooperation, for example, formed in 1919 " 'to quench, if possible, the fires of racial antagonism which were flaming at that time with such deadly menace,' " sought to educate whites and stressed the importance of civil rights for blacks and of improved race relations.[11] But the Commission never attacked segregation, which was central to the problem. Furthermore, neither the Commission nor the National Association for the Advancement of Colored People nor the Urban League reached the masses of black Americans.

The general black populace was influenced to a greater degree in this period by Marcus Garvey's militant separatism. On the one hand, he spoke to their real need to feel pride in their heritage and in their color. On the other hand, he aggravated their bitterness toward white society and toward the more privileged socioeconomic classes of their own race. As many militants were to do in the 1960s, Garvey linked racial pride to an abandonment of belief in America, its professed ideals, and its prospects for becoming a truly democratic, multiracial society. "In his newspaper, *The Negro World,*" Franklin has written, "he told Negroes that racial prejudice was so much a part of the civilization of the white man that it was futile to appeal to his sense of justice and his high-sounding democratic principles."[12] Instead, Garvey urged that American blacks return to Africa to establish their own nation. His followers, mostly uneducated and recently urbanized, numbered at least a half million by the early 1920s. Their enthusiasm for Garvey's point of view and his rhetoric represented, however, more an outlet for frustration than a serious will to leave America. Thus, although the movement flourished, it failed to achieve its goals. At the same time it did nothing to enhance the efforts of the N.A.A.C.P., which Garvey rejected, or of the Pan-African congresses that W.E.B. DuBois had organized to further the interests of blacks on an international level.

The message of the Bahá'í amity conventions was strikingly different in content and scope from anything else that was being said at the time. It spoke of pride in the context of human diversity and placed the principle of equality within the framework of a new world order. As Louis Gregory proclaimed at the first amity convention in 1921:

> The divine springtime has appeared and the great enlightened principles, which are the light and progress of the whole world of humanity, are set in motion. These relate to the great peace, the universality of truth, to the great law that humanity is one, even as God is one, to the elevation of the station of woman, who must no longer be confined to a limited life but be everywhere recognized as the equal and helpmeet of man. These pertain to the universality of education, to the oneness of language, to the solution of this economic problem which has vexed the greatest minds of the world and its noblest hearts, and to that supreme dynamic power, the Holy Spirit of God, whose outpouring upon the whole world of flesh will make this a world of light, of joy, and of triumph.[13]

Whites were accustomed to thinking of the "race problem" in the narrowest of terms. The broad Bahá'í perspective not only challenged them to enlarge their thinking but served to reaffirm belief in modern ideals, which had been shaken by the war. The Bahá'í approach also worked to expand the points of view of blacks. It stressed, in addition to racial equality, the importance and interrelationship of the equality of religion, nationality, and gender. The Bahá'í view upheld "the oneness and wholeness of the human race," as Shoghi Effendi later put it, "as the hall-mark of Bahá'u'lláh's Revelation and the pivot of His teachings," and conferred upon the realization of human oneness the guarantee of divine inevitability.[14]

'Abdu'l-Bahá's plan for racial amity conventions was all the more remarkable because His instructions were first implemented by Agnes Parsons, a wealthy white socialite. Mrs. Parsons was generally regarded as the "mother" of the Washington, D.C., Bahá'í community—not because she was one of its earliest members, for she had become a confirmed believer in the Faith only in 1910, when there were already a number of Bahá'ís there, but because of the respect she inspired. 'Abdu'l-Bahá praised her highly; she had entertained Him on many occasions at her elegant home in

Washington and at her summer estate in Dublin, New Hampshire. A gracious and philanthropic person, she regularly assisted many people, Bahá'ís and non-Bahá'ís alike. Mrs. Parsons accepted—intellectually—the principle of the oneness of mankind. When the Washington Bahá'ís divided over race, she sought the middle ground, rejecting the extreme positions of the Pythian Temple group. But she also found their attitude of racial exclusiveness more understandable than the demand for immediate integration of all meetings. Shaped as her thinking was by the narrow confines of high society, she had difficulty with such practical demonstrations of oneness as intermarriage and social equality. Yet her sense of social responsibility and her flowering Bahá'í conscience led her into a network of relationships with interracial implications. She worked closely with Louis Gregory in Bahá'í administrative and teaching projects, for example, and at times contributed financially to his endeavors; she also formed a cordial relationship with his wife, Louise. The man who was in 1919 the president of Fisk University was, according to Mr. Gregory, "a spiritual protegé [sic]" of Mrs. Parsons.[15] Nonetheless, she was temperamentally and philosophically unsuited to direct involvement in racial amity work. Only her devotion to 'Abdu'l-Bahá and her profound desire to conform to the principles that He had taught her explain how her name came to be linked forever with the development of Bahá'í racial amity activities in America.

Indeed, Louis Gregory at first played a relatively minor role in a field in which he was later to work closely with Mrs. Parsons and which was finally to bear his stamp. Until 1927, when he was asked by the National Spiritual Assembly to assume major responsibility for the racial amity work, he deferred to Mrs. Parsons. He preferred to devote most of his attention to itinerant teaching, particularly in the South. In his view 'Abdu'l-Bahá had made a perfect choice in asking Agnes Parsons, "a white Baha'i of wealth and social prominence," to arrange the first amity convention. "No one could question the motives of such a soul," he wrote Edith Chapman some years later, "when you consider both her spiritual illumination, devotion etc., added to her worldly station."[16]

The new direction in Mrs. Parsons' activities began early in 1920 during her second pilgrimage to the Bahá'í holy places in Haifa and 'Akká, Palestine. Mariam Haney, for many years a member of the Washington community and a colleague in Mrs. Parsons' amity work, has described how this American aristocrat—who, until she became a Bahá'í in her middle years, "had never known nor associated with any one outside of her own immediate circle"—became the improbable instrument of a new activism:

> During this second visit she received from 'Abdu'l-Bahá a remarkable instruction—a command—which, carried into execution, placed her in the ranks of those who rendered pioneer services to the Cause. "The blessings that come to one are greater than those one seeks," said 'Abdu'l-Bahá. This instruction was not sought by Mrs. Parsons; it came to her from the heaven of the Master's Divine Will, and was in truth and in fact a great and overwhelming surprise to Mrs. Parsons herself. [17]

A few years later Mrs. Parsons described how 'Abdu'l-Bahá had placed this new responsibility upon her shoulders:

> One evening at supper time when there were about twenty, twenty-two or twenty-four people at the table Abdul Baha suddenly turned to me, quite out of the blue, . . . and said: "I want you to arrange a convention in Washington for amity between the colored and the white." I thought I would like to go through the floor, because I did not feel I could do it. He said: "You must have people to help you." I waited for more instructions and he said nothing more. I then made an appeal. I said "Mr. and Mrs. So and So will also help me." This man was in official life and I thought they could help me, at that moment. He said[:] "He is interested in his own people, but she might help you." Well, then a very extraordinary thing happened. I felt suddenly the power of his creative words. . . . I was really getting the confidence that of course was necessary, and Abdul Baha said absolutely nothing more to me. I was hoping every day that I would have some more instructions, but he did not give it [sic] to me. [18]

Agnes Parsons returned to the United States with newfound confidence but little idea of how to proceed. She had never organized a major event, although she had been involved in administrative activities as a member of the Executive Board of

AGNES S. PARSONS and her son JEFFREY
Wealthy and prominent in Washington, D.C., she was the instrument
chosen by 'Abdu'l-Bahá to organize the first Bahá'í amity convention
for blacks and whites in America in 1921

*The second Bahá'í race amity convention in America,
held in the auditorium of Central High School, Springfield, Massachusetts, 5–6 December 1921*

Bahai Temple Unity and of the Washington community. Furthermore, having overcome much in herself to achieve even a nonactivist stand on racial unity, she found it difficult immediately to assume a new role. Finally, "many of her most influential friends were heedless and indifferent."[19]

"The summer passed," she recalled, "and I had the convention very much on my heart, but nothing seemed to be developing until Mrs. [Louise] Boyle arranged that I should see ex-Senator [Moses B.] Clapp [of Nebraska], who had always been a great friend of the colored people. We had a talk for about two hours, in Mrs. Boyle's apartment, and he was undoubtedly the instrument whom Abdul Baha used to give me the plan." The plan that the senator suggested was to get a group of women to help organize the convention, and, in order not to alienate conservatives, to adopt a "conventional" approach, by which he meant to avoid creating an impression of political extremism or polarization, which had made enemies for many liberal reformers. He urged that protest be avoided and a positive note struck. Indeed, his advice became Mrs. Parsons' byword: " 'Do not make a protest about anything. Lift the whole matter up into the spiritual realm and work for the creation of sentiment.' "[20]

This thought appealed to Mrs. Parsons' strong instinct to avoid too combative or controversial an approach to the subject. It was even echoed—for different reasons—by Louis Gregory when she turned to him for advice. He was not in any way reluctant to be bold, but he was tired of empty rhetoric. "Nothing short of a change of hearts will do," he wrote her. "Unless the speakers are able to make the power of love felt, the occasion will lose its chief value." He saw the purely social or economic interracial conferences, such as those held under the auspices of the Commission on Interracial Cooperation, as having been largely unproductive. Interracial committees, formed throughout the South on the local and state level, were carrying out educational activities designed to improve race relations. But the Commission, which received public support from many white leaders and officials in the South, was limited in both its scope and its purpose: it reached only the relatively enlightened minority, and it sought simply to reduce the excesses of racial discrimination, rather than to promote unity and integration. Mr. Gregory felt that people of goodwill met and talked at Commission functions but that nothing more was accomplished because a spiritual remedy was lacking:

> There are many, many souls throughout the South today who are working and longing for a better day. But without the Light of Abha [Bahá'u'lláh] their efforts seem infantile and helpless. Even some members of the state inter-racial committee, earnest, thoughtful, hard-working men, have voiced to me despair. If the Washington inter-racial congress is along these conventional lines I fear it will like the others, be fruitless. But if it be aflame with the Fire of the Divine Love, the hearts will be powerfully influenced and the effect will be great in all the years to come.[21]

The convention that Louis Gregory envisioned was in no way conventional. He urged the adoption of a fairly direct Bahá'í program. Moreover, he stressed that the convention "be held very soon, as the situation seems to be getting more critical day by day, this despite the fact that many earnest and sincere souls of both races are striving for harmony and understanding." Adding to a sense of urgency, as he reminded Mrs. Parsons, were 'Abdu'l-Bahá's recent words to Dr. Bagdadi: " 'Now is the time for the Americans to take up this matter and unite both the white and the colored races. Otherwise, hasten ye towards destruction! Hasten ye toward devastation!' "[22]

When Mrs. Parsons sought people to help her plan the convention, as 'Abdu'l-Bahá had suggested, "she took as consultants the local Spiritual Assembly and a few personal friends, gradually widening the circle," Louis Gregory recalled. Mariam Haney described the committee that was finally formed as having been "helpful, active and earnest." Its members were Mrs. Parsons, Mrs. Haney, Mrs. Boyle, Gabrielle Pelham, and Martha Root. The committee scheduled the convention for 19–21 May 1921 at Washington's First Congregational Church. It was to be "the first convention for amity between the white and colored races in America," Mr. Gregory claimed, "and so far as we know, the world."[23]

Confronted with the task of arranging and publicizing a major interracial meeting in the nation's capital, which less than two years earlier had been torn apart by one of the "Red Summer's"

worst riots, the convention organizers met an unexpectedly positive response. "The workers had unusual experiences," Mr. Gregory reported, "and the spirit of reconciliation seemed to sweep
the city." Help came from many sources. Following Senator
Clapp's suggestion, Mrs. Parsons turned to the women of her elite
circle for assistance. "Nineteen ladies from the social life of the
city," wrote Louis Gregory, "gave the prestige of their names as
patrons." A senator and two congressmen agreed to speak at the
convention, and a commanding general of the United States Army
sent a message to be read. President Warren Harding knew about
the convention, according to Mr. Gregory, and unofficially supported it. Howard University, where 'Abdu'l-Bahá had spoken in
1912, provided valuable assistance, responding "in a way that
showed the fruitage of seed sown by the Master nine years before."[24]

The extensive newspaper publicity for the convention was
handled by Martha Root. Nineteen thousand programs were circulated in churches, schools, hotels, stores, and other public
places. The program straightforwardly announced the purpose of
the convention and was thought-provoking in itself:

Half a century ago in America slavery was abolished.
Now there has arisen need for another great effort in order
that prejudice may be overcome.
Correction of the present wrong requires no army, for the
field of action is the hearts of our citizens. The instrument to be
used is kindness, the ammunition—understanding. The actors
in this engagement for right are all the inhabitants of these United States.
The great work we have to do and for which this convention
is called is the establishment of amity between the white and
colored people of our land.
When we have put our own house in order, then we may be
trusted to carry the message of universal peace to all mankind.[25]

The problem that Louis Gregory had raised—whether to have
the Bahá'í perspective dominate the program—was solved by a
compromise. Bahá'ís were asked to serve as chairmen of the session or to give addresses. They included distinguished whites such
as William H. Randall and Mountfort Mills of the Executive

Board; Albert Vail, an unusually gifted speaker; and Howard Mac-Nutt, a staunch worker for the Faith from New York; and blacks such as Louis Gregory; Coralie F. Cook, whose husband was a professor at Howard University; and Alexander H. Martin, a Cleveland attorney, who was one of the first blacks elected to Phi Beta Kappa in the nineteenth century. The organizers undoubtedly hoped that the Bahá'í participants would help to create a harmonious atmosphere. Additionally, Mrs. Parsons talked with each of the non-Bahá'í speakers: "To the men in public life who spoke I always said: 'Don't make it a question of putting anything through, any personal thought, but just speak in a very general way.' Then I used to quote Senator Clapp's words: 'Lift the whole matter up into the spiritual realm and work for the creation of sentiment.' "[26] Still there could be no prior assurance that the meetings would not degenerate into the sort that Louis Gregory had found to be fruitless, where people talked about and despaired over improvements that they could not hope to achieve without effecting a "change of hearts."

The first sign of success was the large audience that gathered for the opening session on Thursday evening, 19 May. About two thousand people waited expectantly for Mr. Randall to begin the meeting. Then, as Mrs. Parsons described it, his remarks were so appropriate that they infected even his fellow speakers with a spirit of unity:

> At each session of the convention there was a Bahai Chairman and the chairman invariably gave the keynote for the whole evening. One of these senators the first night turned to Mr. Randall and said: "I was going to make a political speech, but would it be better for me to try to follow what you have said in a harmonious way?" Mr. Randall said: "I think it would be a very good plan." So the man changed his speech. Each night that happened. The men probably came with the idea of giving their own personal ideas about this wrong, and that wrong, but they invariably spoke along the line that the chairman had indicated.[27]

The spirit established at that first meeting pervaded subsequent sessions, two in the daytime, which were well attended, and two more on the evenings of the 20th and 21st, which also drew crowds of fifteen hundred or more. Interest was maintained by a wide variety of musical presentations, from traditional spirituals to works by a black composer, performed by the Howard University chorus, to a violin solo by Joseph Douglass, a grandson of Frederick Douglass. The talks were equally varied. One featured the works of black poets, foreshadowing the Negro or Harlem Renaissance, the surge of black literary activity later in the 1920s. The man who was to become the ''acknowledged dean'' and ''liaison officer'' of the Renaissance, Howard philosophy professor and first black Rhodes scholar Alain Locke, chaired an evening session.[28]

For the Bahá'ís the significance of the convention was made irrefutable by a special message from 'Abdu'l-Bahá, related by Mountfort Mills, who had just returned from a pilgrimage to Haifa:

> ''Say to this convention that never since the beginning of time has one more important been held. This convention stands for the oneness of humanity; it will become the cause of the enlightenment of America. It will, if wisely managed and continued, check the deadly struggle between these races which otherwise will inevitably break out.''[29]

Louis Gregory's highest hopes for the gathering had been realized. Many non-Bahá'í speakers had been involved, yet all had conformed to his idea that ''there should be the real love of mankind for the sake of God among those who take part.''[30] He had told Mrs. Parsons that numbers present mattered far less than the spirit of the convention; in fact, both excellent attendance and extraordinary spirit were achieved. Besides the thousands of people who attended, many thousands more were reached by the printed program with its unequivocal statements on the abolition of racial prejudice.

The convention represented a great victory for the Washington Bahá'ís, who had for so many years failed to confront the corrosive effects of prejudice within their own community. Neither Mrs. Parsons nor most of the other white Bahá'ís were by nature liberal reformers committed to the cause of civil rights for blacks. Rather, their belief in Bahá'u'lláh superimposed new values on the natural inclinations of their background and training and created growing commitment to a wide range of social causes—such as the equality of men and women, economic reform, disarmament and world peace, and the adoption of a universal auxiliary language—within a framework of individual spiritual rejuvenation.

The Washington amity convention was also important historically because it was the first of its kind, the first conference on race to focus on interracial accord and to reach beyond the confines of the liberal reform movement. It clearly established to large numbers of people, both black and white, the Bahá'í principles of unity. It also inspired other groups to action. "An interesting after effect of the first amity convention," Louis Gregory observed, "was the stimulus it gave to orthodox people [that is, members of the established churches and religious groups], who started the organization of interracial committees very soon thereafter."[31]

In His statements concerning the race issue 'Abdu'l-Bahá always emphasized the importance of intangible results within the realm of ideas and of social change made meaningful by a change of heart and a new spirit. "It is this spirit of oneness," He wrote to Mrs. Parsons shortly before the first convention, "which imparts new life to the hearts of the people of the world." He described the effect of "this spirit of oneness" on Mrs. Parsons herself. "Really thou art a true Bahai," He told her, "and the fire of the love of God is in fervor in thy heart. Therefore thou art the cause of the promulgation of the Teachings of God and strivest after harmony between the white and the colored." Thus she was impelled toward a course of action of far-reaching importance for her and for race relations in America. "The formation of the Congress for the colored and the white is productive of eternal glory for thee," 'Abdu'l-Bahá assured her, "and is conducive to the comfort and ease of the continent of America, because if the colored and the white do not acquire harmony between them, there will appear great difficulties in the future."[32]

In the months following the convention 'Abdu'l-Bahá wrote several letters to Mrs. Parsons in which He praised both the convention and her efforts and assured her of good results. In July He exclaimed, "Praise be to God that the Race Convention was carried through in utmost perfection." And in October:

> The Convention of the colored and the white was in reality a
> great work. Because if the question of the colored and the white

should not be solved, it would be productive of great dangers in future for America. Therefore . . . confirmation . . . shall constantly reach any person who strives after the conciliation of the colored and the white. Thank thou God that thou art the first person who established a Race Convention.[33]

In another letter 'Abdu'l-Bahá referred to the Washington convention as having been the first of many to come. Such meetings would be held in other places as well, He said, although Washington would always be an important location "because in that city there is great animosity between the white and the colored" and because there "Abdul Baha himself laid the foundation of this unity and harmony in the assemblies, churches and universities of the colored and white; and thou certainly rememberest the speeches which were delivered." Ultimately, however, the Washington, D.C., convention and Agnes Parsons as its unlikely organizer achieved special significance simply by having been first:

The Convention, comprising the white and the colored, which thou hadst organized, was like the Mother, from which in near future many other meetings shall be born. But thou wert the founder of this Convention. The importance of every principle is at the beginning, and the first person to raise the banner of the unity of the white and the colored, wert thou. It is certain that it shall bear great results.[34]

14   The Work Continues

The first offspring of Washington's mother convention was in a sense a stepchild, as it neither answered any specific request of 'Abdu'l-Bahá nor involved Agnes Parsons directly. It was born, however, in an abundance of enthusiasm, received 'Abdu'l-Bahá's special permission, and gained its own measure of success. At the 1922 national Bahá'í convention, five months after the passing of 'Abdu'l-Bahá, Roy Williams was asked to explain how this next amity convention came to be held. "Last fall," he told the delegates,

> I received a call from Springfield, Massachusetts. . . . I went there with the intention of simply holding a few group meetings, but to my intense astonishment, when I got there I was informed someone who had journeyed to the Washington convention had so interested the people in Springfield, including several ministers, in the possibility of organizing a similar race convention that they had taken up the idea with the intention of promoting it at once when I arrived. . . .[1]

The Bahá'í community of Springfield at that time consisted of only two people, Olive Kretz and Grace Decker. Even with Mr. Williams' help, lack of manpower posed an initial problem. A second obstacle emerged when Mr. Williams explained that 'Abdu'l-Bahá had recently instructed Mrs. Parsons to organize the next amity convention in New York or, if a majority of Bahá'ís preferred, San Francisco.[2] The group decided to see whether there would be sufficient public support to warrant holding a convention in Springfield. When they had ascertained that there was, they sent a cablegram to 'Abdu'l-Bahá on 8 November 1921, requesting permission to hold the convention. Three days later their doubts about the appropriateness of their plans were resolved by a return cable from the Master. His message constituted, as Mr. Williams put it, probably "his last words affirming a public service by the Bahais of America." It read: " 'Approved; God confirms.' "[3] 'Abdu'l-Bahá passed away on 28 November, and the convention was held as scheduled on 5 and 6 December, in the first bleak days following the loss of 'Abdu'l-Bahá and before the announcement that He had appointed Shoghi Effendi as His successor. Thus, inadvertently, the Springfield amity convention was the first major demonstration of the resolve of the American Bahá'ís to carry out 'Abdu'l-Bahá's plans for them after His passing.

The mayor of Springfield helped secure, free of charge, the auditorium of the Central High School, the second largest hall in the city. The mayor, a rabbi, a military officer, and three ministers agreed to speak, as well as four Bahá'ís: Roy Williams, Alfred Lunt, William H. Randall, and Dr. Zia Bagdadi, who had given a well-received address at Howard University that year. Several clergymen and concerned citizens assisted with preparations.

The encouraging show of support could not guarantee a large attendance, however. Roy Williams recalled that even Mr. Randall, who had witnessed the success of the Washington convention, had his doubts before the first session:

> Mr. Randall told me when he came to Springfield, "You will not be able to get a very large number of people there. Springfield is a very conservative city." I said, "Mr. Randall, here is the cablegram from Abdul Baha. God confirms. Let us go to the hall and see what God confirms." Mr. Randall told me himself . . . he did not expect to see nearly a thousand people in front of him, representative of all races and colors, and all creeds. He said, "This is indeed the confirmation of God". . . .[4]

The large audience of about equal numbers of blacks and whites grew even larger the second night.

Remarkably, a tiny Bahá'í group had been able to organize interracial meetings that reached thousands of people, directly or indirectly. The success of the endeavor demonstrated the potential of the program that 'Abdu'l-Bahá had fostered. Roy Williams urged the assembled delegates at the Fourteenth Annual Convention to lend their support:

I hope that the friends will think and pray that more of these conventions may really be put forth quickly because the need is great, and the good that is done through one of these meetings is immense and immeasurable, even as a means of giving the [Bahá'í] message to a large number of people, of different classes. It is the most successful way I have ever seen of getting people together, and the way in which people answer the call for these conventions and come out en masse is something unusual.[5]

Despite the glowing reports from Washington and Springfield, it was nearly two years before the next amity convention was held. Partial explanation lies in the difficult transition from the "Heroic Age" of Bahá'í history, as Shoghi Effendi has called the period from 1844 to the passing of 'Abdu'l-Bahá, to its "Formative Age." Ugo Giachery, a close associate of Shoghi Effendi, has observed that in these years of uncertainty

the old believers, in East and West, were slowly recovering from the extremely severe loss of their beloved 'Abdu'l-Bahá and from the shock of what appeared to them to be an irreparable vacuum in the affairs of the Cause. The newer believers were trying with difficulty to become part of the as yet dimly understood administrative pattern.[6]

When the third amity convention was finally held, however, it built upon the achievements of those that had been carried out with 'Abdu'l-Bahá's express approval. It was held in New York, as 'Abdu'l-Bahá had recommended, on 28–30 March 1924. The Washington and Springfield conventions had received valuable assistance from churches and public officials. New York went a step further by inviting a number of civic groups to join in the planning. These included, according to Louis Gregory, the National Association for the Advancement of Colored People, the National Urban League, and the Committee on International Cooperation of the League of Women Voters. Emphasis was placed not only on black-white race relations but on other races and ethnic minorities as well. The impressive list of speakers included James Weldon Johnson, secretary of the N.A.A.C.P.; Jane Addams; Alain Locke; John Herman Randall of the Community Church; Rabbi Stephen S. Wise; Franz Boas, Professor of Anthropology at Columbia University; and Mountfort Mills, representing the Bahá'ís.[7]

The talk by Dr. Boas was undoubtedly one of the high points of the convention. For the first time in any of the race amity meetings, a scientific argument against racism was added to the moral and philosophical themes. The significance and controversial nature of such an approach must be seen in the light of the times, when physical evolution was hotly denied by many religious leaders and was excluded from the curriculum of many schools, when racial bias clearly influenced the setting of U.S. immigration quotas, and when racialist theories still flourished, even in academic circles. The stature of Dr. Boas, who is considered one of the founders of the discipline of anthropology, assured that advanced scientific thought was well represented at the convention. Indeed, no one was better qualified to challenge the myth of white racial superiority. Boas' work, later vilified by the Nazis, was helpful to those who opposed America's discriminatory immigration quotas in the 1920s and also to civil rights workers seeking to establish equality for blacks in the 1950s.

Thus the New York convention was even more successful in some respects than the mother convention in Washington, which 'Abdu'l-Bahá had described as a "great work." "This praiseworthy effort," Louis Gregory observed, "showed the possibilities of the work and led to a brilliant succession of similar conferences, interracial dinners and fellowship meetings. . . ."[8] It helped to put the New York Bahá'í community, which had already been teaching actively in Harlem, into the forefront of racial amity activities for many years to come. It also seems to have spurred the appointment of an Amity Convention Committee by the National Spiritual Assembly of the Bahá'ís of the United States and Canada. On 19 May 1924 a letter from Horace Holley, secretary of the National Assembly, was sent to all Local Spiritual Assemblies, announcing the formation of the committee and the appointment of Agnes Parsons, Elizabeth Greenleaf, Mariam Haney, Alain Locke, Mabel Ives, Louise Waite, Louise Boyle, Roy Williams, Philip R. Seville, and Mrs. Atwater as members.[9]

A fourth convention was held several months later in Philadelphia. Once again, as in Springfield, Roy Williams played a key role in the convention. The secretary of the Philadelphia Spiritual Assembly, Jessie Revell, reported that it was "our brother Roy Williams, member of the National Amity Committee, who first planted the seed of the Amity Convention in this City and worked in conjunction with the Phila. Amity Committee and were it not for his earnestness and enthusiasm, we probably would not have held it at this time."[10]

Although Louis Gregory was not a member of the national committee, he too became involved in preparations for the convention, which was scheduled for 22–23 October 1924. He arrived in Philadelphia several weeks beforehand on his return east from a successful teaching venture in a black summer colony in Northern Michigan and a subsequent visit to Columbus, Ohio. "Mr. Gregory," Jessie Revell wrote, ". . . spent about a month with us and worked faithfully writing articles for newspapers, spoke in many meetings telling of the coming Amity Convention and served in innumerable other ways." She added that "the Philadelphia Tribune, a . . . weekly paper of the colored population, published very fine articles both before and after the meetings, written up by Mr. Gregory."[11]

Because the Philadelphia convention was held solely under Bahá'í auspices, and the number of Bahá'ís in the city was small, outside assistance proved to be essential. In addition to Mr. Williams and Mr. Gregory, several Bahá'ís from Washington, D.C., helped: Mrs. Parsons, who came to Philadelphia to discuss general planning; Mason Remey, who made signs and distributed programs; and Louise Boyle, who worked on publicity. The National Spiritual Assembly supported the convention with funds.

The printed program clearly announced the convention's Bahá'í sponsorship and provided a brief history of the series of "Interracial Congresses" that had preceded it. It featured a quotation from Jesus ("These things I command you, that ye love one another.") and six passages from the writings of Bahá'u'lláh and 'Abdu'l-Bahá. Copies were sent to the clergymen of Philadelphia together with a cover letter from Miss Revell, asking that the convention be announced to their congregations and seeking their support. She later reported that "several ministers distributed programs to their congregation the Sunday prior to the Convention."[12]

About six hundred people attended the first session of the convention, chaired by Horace Holley of New York, to hear lectures by Agnes L. Tierney, a member of the Society of Friends; Leslie

Pinckney Hill, the black principal of a teacher training school; and Albert Vail. Excellent press notices the following day helped to boost attendance at the second session to nine hundred. Particularly noteworthy was "a very long article" in the newspaper *Jewish World,* which urged people to attend. [13] The chairman for the second session was Dr. Bagdadi. The speakers were Alain Locke, who discussed "Negro Art and Culture"; Judge John M. Patterson of Philadelphia; Louis Gregory; and Hooper Harris, a Bahá'í from New York.

The following day, 24 October, the Bahá'ís supported a Conference on Inter-racial Justice organized by the Friends. Louis Gregory spoke at the conference's dinner meeting. "It had so happened," he later recalled, "that the Bahá'ís and the Society of Friends at the same time, as moved by one Spirit, had planned interracial conferences. As the dates selected were contiguous but not conflicting, each agreed to boost the spiritual enterprise of the other as well as its own. The result was phenomenal success for both." [14] Follow-up meetings, at which both Albert Vail and Louis Gregory spoke, were also held by the Bahá'ís on 25 and 26 October.

The Philadelphia amity convention, like those that preceded it, cannot be evaluated simply in terms of measurable results. Unlike an antilynching crusade, or some other campaign directed toward a specific problem or grievance, the amity convention attempted to promote fundamental attitudinal change about human rights and the universality of human dignity. Progress in such an endeavor can scarcely be perceived, let alone evaluated. Indeed, even the most concrete forces shaping the movement for black equality in the twentieth century, as C. Vann Woodward emphasizes in *The Strange Career of Jim Crow,* are difficult to assess:

> It will long be a matter of debate as to the relative importance played by the agitators, foreign and domestic propaganda, the courts, the White House, party politics, two or three wars, postwar prosperity, the seemingly interminable Cold War, or the dubious influence of nationalism and oppressive conformity working in a new direction. It would be foolhardy to attempt, with no more than the foreshortened and distorting perspective we now have, to arrive at anything more than a very tentative

assessment of the bewilderingly complex forces involved and the relative importance of the part each has played.
The evaluation of ideas and their agitation is most difficult because of the impossibility of measuring the results.[15]

Yet it was in this realm of "ideas and their agitation" that 'Abdu'l-Bahá's program for racial amity was to have its greatest impact. Woodward goes on to point out some of the major forces leading toward a modern reconstruction in race relations. Striking links between the Bahá'í Faith and several of these forces—the N.A.A.C.P., the Harlem Renaissance, and changing "religious sentiment"—testify to the success of 'Abdu'l-Bahá's efforts to put Bahá'í thought into the forefront of the movement for social change.[16]

'Abdu'l-Bahá Himself contributed much to the friendly relations between His followers and the leadership of the N.A.A.C.P. His talk at the organization's 1912 convention seems to have created a lasting impression among the thousands who heard or read it. In fact, either through 'Abdu'l-Bahá's addresses in 1912 or through the series of amity activities He initiated in 1920, the Bahá'í message of unity reached beyond the N.A.A.C.P. to virtually all of the leaders concerned with the struggle for racial equality in America: W. E. B. DuBois, James Weldon Johnson, Walter F. White, Arthur B. Spingarn, John Hope, Mary White Ovington, Jane Addams, Stephen S. Wise, Franz Boas, and Robert S. Abbott, to name a few. Representatives of both the N.A.A.C.P. and the Urban League participated in numerous Bahá'í interracial activities in the 1920s and 1930s and contributed much to their success. In 1932 the friendly relations between these organizations and the Bahá'ís reached perhaps their highest point: a banquet in New York City in honor of the N.A.A.C.P. and the Urban League, sponsored by the national Bahá'í interracial committee. On this occasion Walter F. White, then secretary of the N.A.A.C.P., praised "the Bahai movement," according to an account in the *Chicago Defender,* calling it "one of the great forces of human understanding."[17]

The Harlem Renaissance, another of the elements that changed race relations, according to Woodward, succeeded "in arousing the sympathy and stimulating the support of white intellectuals and

philanthropists.'' The central figure in this upsurge of black literary activity in the 1920s was Alain Locke, whose major contributions to the Renaissance coincided with the intensification of his
interest in the Bahá'í teachings. He had been attracted to the Faith
even before he participated in the first amity convention in 1921. In
1925, as his anthology *The New Negro* was being published, he
made a Bahá'í lecture tour to the South and also addressed the annual Bahá'í convention. Later in the decade he became an active
member of the national Bahá'í interracial amity committee and
visited the international headquarters of the Faith in Haifa, where
he met Shoghi Effendi and visited the shrines of the Central Figures of the Faith. ''Haifa makes pilgrims of all who visit her,'' he
stated in his ''Impressions of Haifa.'' ''The place itself makes
mystics of us all, for it shuts out the world of materiality with its
own characteristic atmosphere and one instantly feels one's self in
a simple and restful cloistral calm. But it is not the characteristic
calm of the monastic cloister; it is not so much a shutting out of the
world as an opening up of new vistas.'' He was deeply impressed
by sepulchres filled with light, which took away ''the melancholy
and gruesomeness of death'' and replaced them with ''poetry'' and
with ''the thought of memory, responsibility and reverence''; by
gardens that ''dramatize the emotion of the place and quicken the
soul even through the senses''; by Shoghi Effendi, ''a master of
detail as well as of principle, of executive foresight as well as of
projective vision''; and by the ultimate, ''irrepressible'' destiny of
the Faith—''There is a New Light in the world: there must needs
come a New Day.''[18]

Finally, in the area that Woodward terms ''religious sentiment,'' the Bahá'í Faith actively promoted change; it was not only
the first religion to initiate racial amity activities in America but the
first to elicit interfaith support. From the beginning, help was
sought from other religious groups. The Washington convention,
for example, was held in a Congregational church, was promoted
from many pulpits, and was begun with an invocation by a Christian minister. Later, when other groups such as the Friends began
to hold similar conferences, the Bahá'ís lent their support. The effort to gain the backing of religious leaders and to interest their
congregations in the idea of racial amity helped to create a new
climate of opinion about race in religious circles.

The four amity conventions held between May 1921 and October 1924 represented an historic achievement by the American Bahá'ís. Yet at the time few besides Louis Gregory saw them as they were: barely the beginning of an attempt to raze the barrier of racial prejudice. Conflict continued in many cities; the Washington, D.C., convention, however worthwhile it was in itself, could not prevent the fires of hatred from breaking out in Tulsa a few months later. But for Louis Gregory and others, the violence was not a source of discouragement. It pointed clearly to the need for redoubled effort and commitment.

15 Setback

After the Philadelphia convention, race amity activities lost momentum once again, as they had in 1921. Louis Gregory was particularly concerned about the neglect of amity work in Washington, D.C., where the Bahá'ís had been so deeply affected by dissension over race and where so much had been overcome in order to hold the first race amity convention in 1921. Although the Gregorys had moved from Washington to Somerville, Massachusetts, he returned often to the city on his way to and from teaching tours in the South. It was during such a visit late in 1924 that he wrote to Horace Holley, as secretary of the National Spiritual Assembly, of his frustration with the lethargy of Washington Bahá'ís in the face of a racial situation that had deteriorated rather than improved since 'Abdu'l-Bahá had warned of its dangers. Motivated by his own intense concern over the social climate of the city and over the disregard of the Bahá'ís for 'Abdu'l-Bahá's warnings, Mr. Gregory confided that

it is hoped that an Amity Convention may be held here next spring. It is *greatly needed*. It is now to see all the members of this assembly who are seeable to urge closer unity and cooperation. Would this particular job were yours rather than mine! Yet there is hope ahead. So many thoughts revolve around small things, as what this or that person has said or done. It is the hope that by concentrating upon something big, something to relieve humanity, like the holding of an Amity Convention or the organizing of an inter-racial committee, thoughts may be removed from personal realms and harmony established.[1]

He enclosed with this letter a copy of a proposal he had written, entitled "An Inter-racial Committee: Its Great Need, and How It Can Serve Washington, the Nation, and the World." In it he claimed that "there is no more vital need today . . . than a Com-

mittee on Race Relations and Good Will in the national capital.''
Sketching the "dark background" of the racial situation, he observed:

> The stranger to American institutions, the visitor who comes
> from foreign lands, finds conditions here that are passing
> strange. Impressed in his own country by reports from America,
> (and often the only news about this country that reaches foreign
> lands is that of inter-racial clashes, so often resulting in blood-
> shed) the visitor would find upon his arrival here that the hopes,
> ideals, convictions and accomplishments of the hundred thou-
> sand colored people who reside in the District of Columbia are
> as vague and unknown to the greater number of their white
> neighbors as if the colored people were citizens of another land.
> The two races little understand each other. Apprehensions, imag-
> inations, prejudices, resentments, fears, hatreds destroy con-
> fidence in each other's good intentions and create a wall of sepa-
> ration which is generally thought impassable.
>   The danger of the situation is extremely grave. This city
> which is a nation's pride has already been disgraced by rioting
> and lawlessness on the part of mobs, during which shots were
> fired even within a block of the White House, and scenes of like
> [nature] are continually threatened. The feelings of many
> people are bitter and intense. Such feelings are the augury of no
> good. Wherever in the world today there is hatred of class for
> class, nation for nation, race for race, tragedy lurks. Its outbreak
> may be delayed, but unless sentiments are changed it cannot be
> prevented.[2]

Mr. Gregory went on to note the signs of positive change in
Washington and elsewhere. "The spirit of cooperation grows in
the world," he reflected. "The ideal of brotherhood grows, even
though men attain it after untold disaster, suffering and ruin." In
Washington itself people were "nobly interested in the welfare of
humanity in foreign lands." He asked, "Should they not be
equally interested in the solution of a problem which daily con-
fronts them in their own environment?" Because of Washington's
importance as the nation's capital, its achievements would have
wide-ranging consequences: "Should Washington set a high
example in the solution of her own domestic problem on a basis of
justice, [kindliness] and altruism, the result will be felt throughout

the nation and the earth.'' The city had considerable resources, moreover, upon which to draw in organizing racial amity work: a handful of integrated civic organizations, some concerned religious groups, and a relatively well-to-do black population with the nation's greatest concentration of black professionals, business people, and public servants. The only requirements remaining were the will, the vision, and the dedication to undertake the task. And the Bahá'ís, he added in a subsequent letter, could easily take the initiative: ''Efforts of the clergy to conduct such a committee here have utterly failed, so the Baha'is have an open field, if guided to use it.''[3]

But Washington did not form an interracial committee for a number of years, nor did it hold an amity convention in the spring, as Mr. Gregory had hoped. Neither did any other Bahá'í community. Although the conventions in 1924 had been as successful as their predecessors and a National Amity Convention Committee had been appointed to assure continuity, the Philadelphia convention was the last to be held until a burst of amity activity animated the American Bahá'í community in 1927.

The committee continued to function and make plans. In a letter to Mrs. Parsons dated 3 December 1924 Louis Gregory alluded to the existence of plans for race amity conventions, which were to be presented to the National Spiritual Assembly: ''This will meet the desires of Shoghi Effendi that all such matters should be passed by the N.S.A.'' At least one convention was formally scheduled for April 1925 but postponed; Louise Gregory referred to it in a letter to Mrs. Parsons, mentioning that she had been planning to return from Europe in order to attend the convention with her husband. In March of that year Mr. Gregory wrote Mrs. Parsons about a man he had met in his travels, suggesting that he might be enlisted to help with the amity work. Thus, although no conference was held, a certain level of expectation was maintained.[4]

The National Spiritual Assembly reappointed the committee with essentially the same membership for the period 1925–26, and plans went forward for another major amity convention in Washington, D.C., in April 1926. On learning of the National Assembly's approval of the plans, Louis Gregory was enthusiastic: ''This is good news indeed in view of the critical nature of the local situation which it may go a long way toward helping. I hope that it will be possible with this new effort to do wise and systematic follow-up work."[5] But once again the convention was cancelled, and, when committee appointments were made for the year 1926–27, a new World Unity Conferences Committee was among them and the Amity Committee was not.

The failure to hold amity conventions in 1925 and 1926 was at least partly attributable to lack of enthusiasm in Washington, D.C., where the committee was centered. Despite Louis Gregory's patient efforts, the Bahá'ís there were still far from being wholly united on the racial issue, and Mrs. Parsons was still immobile in the role of leadership she had been given. Several years later Mariam Haney, having been asked to tell of Washington's interracial activities at a national convention, observed that the community had begun at last to realize that it had to do more than talk about unity:

Now, we may get up and speak gloriously of the oneness of mankind, speak marvelously of the creative effect of the Holy Utterances of today, but until we really demonstrate that the creative effect of this word has taken effect in our own lives, so that we are willing to go forward with this in a sincere and honest way and demonstrate that to the nth degree, we are not going to get very far on the subject of interracial amity.[6]

The inability to generate support for a race amity convention in Washington was a direct result of discontinuity between professed belief and the ''creative effect'' of the ''word'' in the lives of the believers.

Another factor in the loss of momentum in 1925–26 was the ambiguous connection between Louis Gregory's periods of service on the National Spiritual Assembly and the pace of amity activity. He had been elected during the 1922 convention, in the aftermath of the Washington and Springfield amity meetings. Indeed, as he explained to Alfred Lunt in 1923, race had influenced his own decision to accept the results of the election; he had concluded that the vote signalled a willingness to work toward racial harmony. In view of 'Abdu'l-Bahá's emphasis on racial amity in the last few years of His life, Louis Gregory found that he could not obstruct the delegates' fragile commitment to an active stand on race by refusing to serve. Moreover, his own feelings of "unworthiness" had to be "subordinated" to more pressing concerns: protecting the Cause at a crucial juncture in its development, and promoting "the most vital principle of the oneness of humanity, the last in view of the serious and menacing nature of the race problem in America." Because he knew where he stood on those two issues, he realized that he had an important role to play as a member of the National Spiritual Assembly.[7]

He did not wish, however, to prolong the responsibility. "Personally I feel that my work on the Board is almost ended and shall feel a sense of relief when the end comes," he continued in his letter to Alfred Lunt.[8] The relief that he had foreseen, when it finally came more than a year later, was at first unmixed by any misgivings. In the fall of 1924 he returned to the work he loved, traveling for the Faith in the South, and racial amity activity flourished in New York City and Philadelphia. But with time it began to seem as if the tide of enthusiasm for racial amity that had swept him into office had receded, and his not having been re-elected was an indication of that receding tide. Without his presence on the National Assembly the will to implement 'Abdu'l-Bahá's program for racial amity faltered, and, as interest dwindled in the general community of believers, the effort was in effect set aside.

Financial difficulties also seem to have played a part in the decision not to hold amity conventions in 1925 and 1926. The diversion of National Assembly funds to the Philadelphia convention in October 1924 provided an ostensible excuse for the postponement of another in Washington the following spring. Chicago was considered as a possible site for a convention, but plans faltered when its Assembly asked for national support such as Philadelphia, a much smaller community, had received. In February 1925, Horace Holley, as secretary of the National Spiritual Assembly, wrote to Mrs. Parsons of the Amity Committee:

I am very sorry to learn from you that the Chicago Assembly is only willing to hold an Amity Convention this spring if the National Fund meets the expenses. This does not strike me as showing a very strong spiritual longing to help the Cause of Racial Understanding and Peace! On the other hand the moment we set the precedent of helping the Philadelphia friends we really opened the door for just such an attitude on the part of other assemblies. I agree with you that we should not accept their proposition.[9]

The serious lack of funds hampering the affairs of the American Bahá'í community, combined with a general stagnation in growth, led to the inauguration early in 1926 of a national "Plan of Unified Action," the goals of which were "to revitalize the local assemblies and groups while at the same time producing a fund sufficient to build the first permanent unit" of the Temple.[10] Delayed by the war and postwar economic dislocations, construction had begun in 1920 with the building of a circular basement on the Bahá'ís' Sheridan Road property in Wilmette, a suburb north of Chicago. But by the mid-1920s the structure remained unsightly and unusable and the large grounds overlooking Lake Michigan completely unimproved. The goal of the Plan of Unified Action was to raise the $400,000 necessary to complete the first story of the Temple and meanwhile to create a foundation hall suitable for meetings and to begin minimal improvements to the grounds.

Yet, even though the Plan was endorsed by Shoghi Effendi, who personally pledged ninety-five dollars a month at its inception, it did not create an immediate outpouring of funds. Shoghi Effendi wrote on 23 March 1927, "It is a matter of deep concern to me that the response of the believers to the call embodied in the Plan of Unified Action has been so feeble and uncertain." By January 1928 contributions—which, as a matter of principle, were accepted from Bahá'ís only—were meeting the National Assembly's operating expenses but were not creating a growing building fund; in fact the treasurer, Carl Scheffler, explained that "at the present rate of income it would take about nine years to accumulate the amount aimed at by the Plan, even provided every activity of the Cause that involved an expenditure were stopped."[11]

The lack of progress on the Temple not only symbolized the frustrated hopes of the American Bahá'ís but had become a source of embarrassment. The *Baha'i News Letter* observed in March 1925:

> Not until the Foundation Hall and grounds have been made dignified and beautiful; not until they have been placed in con-

dition such as not merely to remove all source of criticism on the part of non-Baha'is, but to become the object of admiring and friendly interest among the thoughtful people of this country—will the Cause in America progress one single step *in any direction.*

And in January 1928 Shoghi Effendi directed an "earnest plea to all the believers to make a supreme and self-sacrificing effort to raise the necessary sum before the end of this year, as otherwise the prestige of the Cause will be gravely affected."[12]

The financial crisis both reflected the lack of growth in numbers of adherents that characterized the community in this period and contributed to it by limiting expansion activities. In launching the Plan of Unified Action the National Spiritual Assembly observed, "It would seem that the average Assembly some time ago reach[ed] a certain point of growth and that it is difficult to leave this point behind." Searching for the means to stimulate growth, the National Spiritual Assembly adopted a teaching plan with world unity conferences as its central feature and appointed a committee consisting of Florence Morton, Mary Movius, and Horace Holley to coordinate the program. Mrs. Morton, who had been for two years treasurer of the National Spiritual Assembly, resigned her office to serve as secretary of the committee.[13]

The conferences were patterned on successful efforts that had taken place in San Francisco in 1925 and in Worcester, Massachusetts, in March 1926. Their purpose was to provide a forum for Bahá'ís and others interested in the varied aspects of a world-embracing spirit of unity. The national committee organized a world unity conference at Green Acre on 7–8 August 1926, and the entire month was devoted to a "Green Acre Summer School of World Unity." Conferences in Cleveland and Boston in November and December featured talks by clergymen and university professors, usually with a Bahá'í chairman. A four-day conference was held in Dayton, Ohio, in January 1927. Later in the month a conference in Chicago—held at the Morrison Hotel, "the only centrally located hotel free from racial exclusiveness"— offered a prestigious roster of non-Bahá'í speakers, including the dean of the Divinity School and the president of the University of Chicago. A world unity conference was also scheduled in conjunction with the Nineteenth Annual Convention of the Bahá'ís of the United States and Canada in Montreal in April 1927. Many other conferences were held during the year in major cities of the East. [14]

Louis Gregory spoke at the Worcester Conference and served, along with Albert Vail and Howard MacNutt, as a co-director of the Green Acre Summer School of World Unity. But in practice the emphasis on world unity tended to subsume and subordinate the topic of racial unity unless special efforts were made to focus upon it. This was done only once, at the Dayton Conference, which devoted its first session to the subject of racial unity. The chairman of that session was Horace Holley. It featured addresses by Louis Gregory and Albert Vail and music by the Glee Club of Wilberforce University, one of the oldest black colleges in the country.

In first announcing the world unity activities the National Spiritual Assembly had stated:

> This action was based upon the conviction that the present phase of the Cause in this country, considered in connection with the general trend of affairs throughout the world, demands at least one effort of a continuous character to uphold publicly the ideal of world unity—the ideal inherent in the teachings—upon a basis capable of demonstrating the universality of the Cause. The intention is to establish the Cause publicly in terms of this inherent ideal, raised far above the traditional conceptions of an exclusive or dogmatic religious movement, and thus bring to the various local Assemblies a greatly increased opportunity to extend their membership. . . .
>
> Surely the decisive hour has come when the Baha'is should no longer be content to stand passive while other movements are arising to serve the noble ideal of unity with purity of motive and energy of execution. . . . The general condition is such that unless the believers prepare themselves for large undertakings of the character of the World Unity Conferences, the initiative and influence will pass to others, for the longing for unity has become a passion. . . .[15]

Yet, though no Bahá'í could quarrel with the ideal of unity, and though at least some of the conferences were extremely successful, added to the prestige of the Cause, particularly in intellectual circles, and created a favorable opinion among liberal-minded people, the conferences did not necessarily stress that world unity was a Bahá'í theme, nor did they attract large numbers of seekers to become Bahá'ís. In fact, they became increasingly indirect in their relationship to the Bahá'í Faith. This tendency disturbed many Bahá'ís, who favored more direct teaching efforts.

Moreover, at a time when financial concerns severely troubled the American Bahá'í community, the expense of the conferences could not be overlooked. During the fiscal year 1 April 1926 to 31 March 1927, a total of $5,816.85 was spent on the conferences, more than the total for *Star of the West* and all Bahá'í publications for the year. Approximately half the amount was spent on non-Bahá'í speakers. Later the National Assembly explained that "all funds supporting these activities, with very few exceptions, have been special contributions, although paid through the National Fund."[16] But, considering the limited resources of the Bahá'ís, many concluded that there was an obvious connection between the large expenditures for the world unity conferences, which were becoming increasingly peripheral to the concerns of the average member, and the lack of funds for activities that presented the Faith to the public in a more direct manner.

Throughout the period of enthusiasm for world unity conferences, letters from Louis Gregory and others who were deeply committed to racial amity work indicate a degree of frustration and dismay. They had, of course, no objection to upholding the ideal of world unity as an overarching concept. But 'Abdu'l-Bahá had called for conventions on racial amity as such and had stressed the vital relationship of racial amity to the health and even to the continued existence of America. Since that time only four conventions had been held, and none at all since 1924. According to one concerned observer, Sadie Oglesby of Boston, the Bahá'ís were neither attracting new black believers nor holding on to those who had once been interested. "A few years ago," she stated at the 1927 national convention, "we could go around and see sixteen or seventeen at a meeting [in Boston]; today, my husband and myself, only, attend."[17]

Inevitably, the world unity conferences, however well-intentioned and important in themselves, diverted attention from racial amity work to a concern both less specific and less controversial. Although the National Assembly had noted that "the longing for unity" had become "a passion," at least in some circles, the same could hardly have been said about racial amity. The world unity conferences thus offered any individual or Bahá'í community not fully committed to racial amity yet another opportunity to turn aside from the hard realities of racial adjustment.

As it became apparent that 'Abdu'l-Bahá's plan for public programs on racial amity was in danger of being forgotten, Louis Gregory intensified his effort to keep the idea alive. "It is clearly my duty," he wrote Mrs. Parsons, "to keep this matter before the attention of the people as far as possible and without causing inharmony." His method, he continued, was to encourage them to hold world unity conferences, if they wished, but to continue to urge commitment to racial amity as well:

> the Washington friends, like many others, are now planning a world unity convention. It is my hope and prayer that each and all give hearty support to this. The title is picturesque and appealing. . . . Perhaps these friends, if supported now by those who prefer an Amity Convention, will later respond and assist what to some of us seems the more vital need. [18]

He also sought to spur Mrs. Parsons herself to action in behalf of race amity. When he asked her to remind the National Spiritual Assembly of the Master's instructions to her with regard to the amity conventions, his words of caution were obviously intended for her as well: "It appears that there is considerable misunderstanding about the grave and transcendent importance of this matter and the vital need of quick action. It may soon be too late, I fear." [19]

Meanwhile, he put his concern directly to the National Spiritual Assembly:

> During two and a half centuries America attempted to settle the problem of races by a series of compromises. All of these failed and made inevitable the great issue of war out of the suffering of which there came a revolution in the organic law decreeing justice for all men. Present difficulties are due to lax enforcement of such laws, the spirit of which does not reach the masses. This never will be effective until aided and directed by the Spirit of God. Unless the teachings of the Universal [Educator,]

Baha'u'llah[,] are presented and accepted, there is nothing but chaos ahead. How great therefore is the responsibility of those who have the only remedy that will heal.[20]

In the same statement, written in December 1926, he summed up the position on race that he had reached in his first days as a Bahá'í in Washington and that he was to hold for the rest of his life:

I do not wish to dwell too much upon these matters, as there is always danger that one's individual work may absorb the point of view. One of the Baha'i ideals is an unfailing sense of proportion, which relates each activity to the general advancement of the Cause. Yet on the other hand, the tremendous emphasis given the subject of inter-racial understanding by the Master Himself would seem to command all forces of mind and heart among all the friends. It cannot be a side issue. It is always to the fore whether one wants it or not.[21]

16 The Challenge to Action

The abandonment of amity work in 1925 and 1926, as discouraging as it was to those Bahá'ís who believed in its importance, proved to be only a temporary setback. It had not been deliberate, nor had it reflected outright opposition. The National Spiritual Assembly had indeed emphasized world unity in its approach to the public, without assuring that the format included racial unity as well. Encouragement to hold race amity conventions had certainly diminished. Yet inattention cannot be equated with intentional neglect. Although the National Assembly had never expressed the enthusiasm for the theme of race amity that it had for world unity, it seems to have maintained a general sense of responsibility to do something about a program that had been of undeniable importance to 'Abdu'l-Bahá.

Stirred by this underlying concern, or perhaps more directly by the promptings of those who were especially committed to race amity, in the latter part of 1926 the National Assembly took a first step toward establishing a consistent policy of support for interracial activities. In November it invited a group of black and white Bahá'ís to a special consultation on race. Each of the consultants—Louis Gregory, Agnes Parsons, Louise Boyle, Alain Locke, Leslie Pinckney Hill, Roy Williams, Zia Bagdadi, Mariam Haney, and Coralie F. Cook—had been involved in at least one of the four amity conventions as a speaker or organizer. But in asking for their assistance the National Assembly apparently envisioned a program more ambitious than the occasional amity conventions in which they had participated up to that time:

> In view of the overwhelming importance of the racial amity problem in this country, and desiring to assist in any constructive plans that might be advanced by those of the friends who have given this subject deepest thought, the National Spiritual

Assembly has voted to invite you to attend a special conference on the subject of racial amity to be held in Washington, D.C. on January 9th. The hope is that it will be possible for you to spend perhaps a day as a committee in drawing up some constructive plan of promoting racial amity and present this to the National Assembly at a joint meeting the evening of the same day. [1]

Since Louis Gregory had already agreed to assist with preparations for the World Unity Conference in Dayton, scheduled for 13–16 January, he was unable to attend the special consultation. He seems to have had no qualms about missing it, however. "The workers mentioned in your letter will all be able to tell much that is healing, constructive and heartening," he assured the National Assembly. "Prof. Locke and Mrs. Boyle who are particularly well informed with regard to the inter-racial work in the Southern states will doubtless be able to bring forth much that is illuminating and helpful." For his part, motivated by concern over the National Spiritual Assembly's support for world unity conferences at the expense of racial amity, Louis Gregory suggested only that race might at least be included in the format. "If there are three sessions to consider world unity," he proposed, "devote one to international unity, another to religious unity and the third to inter-racial unity. These are the three greatest needs of the world of humanity." [2] Undoubtedly his thinking helped to shape the Dayton conference, the first session of which was devoted to race.

When the special committee met in Washington, seven of those invited—all but Mr. Gregory and Professor Hill—were present. The group's recommendations to the National Assembly were that a National Amity Committee be created and that Local Spiritual Assemblies be encouraged to engage in interracial work and to cooperate with the national committee; that a national program "to stimulate racial activity by the local Assemblies" be formulated; that opportunities to publicize Bahá'í views and activities be utilized and that a concerted effort be made to inform " 'the wise men of the nation' " of the Bahá'í teachings on interracial harmony. At the bottom of the work copy of these recommendations someone had written, "We realize that the plans suggested cannot bring forth the desired results until every believer purifies his heart from any trace of race prejudice." [3]

The National Spiritual Assembly responded by immediately appointing a National Bahá'í Committee on Racial Amity, with its functions based upon the Washington recommendations. Mrs. Parsons was appointed chairman and Mr. Gregory executive secretary. The other members were Mrs. Boyle, Mrs. Haney, Mrs. Cook, Dr. Bagdadi, and Dr. Locke. The new committee was directed to concentrate on three areas of activity: preparing a compilation on race amity for general distribution; holding race amity conferences in cooperation with Local Assemblies; and bringing the Bahá'í teachings to the attention of other groups working for unity. The National Assembly voiced the hope ''that the Racial Amity Committee will stand in the forefront of the Baha'i teaching effort in this country.'' In March the announcement of the new committee in the *Baha'i News Letter* noted that ''the importance of this work cannot be overestimated by the American believers.'' 'Abdu'l-Bahá's remarks concerning the first amity convention were quoted, and the committee's objectives were listed. Finally, the National Assembly stressed the role of the individual, for ''the success of efforts by Bahá'is to heal this spiritual sickness afflicting the body of humanity depends upon each worker purifying his own heart from all trace of racial prejudice.''[4]

The first potential obstacle the committee faced was related to its organization. Louis Gregory had been ''unanimously'' chosen by the National Assembly as the committee's executive secretary. ''We feel,'' the National Assembly's letter of appointment stated, ''that this field of service will by no means limit Mr. Gregory's capacity as a Baha'i teacher, but, on the contrary, greatly increase the results of his service by a better organization of his time and effort.'' He had some serious reservations, however. He had always preferred teaching to the administration of Bahá'í activities. Long committed to traveling in behalf of the Faith, he had been on the road when the decision to appoint the committee was made, and another trip had prevented him from attending the special consultation in Washington. Moreover, his wife had just gone to Europe to help establish the Bahá'í Faith there, and he had anticipated spending his time during her absence on similar efforts on the homefront. His plans seemed incompatible with the duties of an executive secretary. He wrote Louise Boyle that, as she put it, ''he did not know why 'a roving secretary' had been appointed," but, willing as always to serve, he "hoped for success."[5]

In his correspondence with the National Spiritual Assembly and with committee members he left a stronger objection unstated, feeling perhaps that it would be misunderstood or that total candor would be unproductive. Years later, when he was no longer a member of the committee, he told another black Bahá'í that he had been reluctant to accept a position for which he felt a white would have been better suited. "As 'Abdu'l-Baha himself instructed for the first racial amity conference, he wisely, I think, put that matter in the hands of Mrs. Parsons, a white Baha'i of wealth and social prominence." Her motives could not be questioned by other whites, or at least she could not be seen as acting for personal gain, he felt. But his own intentions might be suspect. "To have a colored man always clamoring for colored people's rights," he confided, "savors somewhat of politics and agitation, rather than of a Cause whose dynamics is Spirituality. It is far better for a white person to do this in the Cause and for the colored to lend their consultation and support. We must all do what we can to aid such work. . . ."[6]

Nonetheless, Mr. Gregory attended the organizational meeting of the committee late in February. Shortly thereafter the National Spiritual Assembly moved to clarify its intentions in appointing him executive secretary of the committee. Horace Holley wrote that he and the chairman of the Assembly, Allen McDaniel, had decided that it would be better for Mr. Gregory to stay in Washington and to place "the work of this new committee on a firm foundation" than to travel as he had planned.[7] Accordingly, he set aside his reservations, and the work of the committee got under way. For the next eight years—with the exception of one, during which race amity was placed under the National Teaching Committee— Louis Gregory was to serve either as secretary or chairman of the committee.

The second obstacle to be faced as the committee began its work was the disparity of attitude and experience between the committee's chairman, Mrs. Parsons, and the other members. Having come to race amity work through the wishes of the Master, rather than through any personal inclination, she found herself stunned by the committee's ambitions. On 2 February 1927 she confided her misgivings in a letter to Horace Holley, to be shared with the National Assembly "if advisable":

> It is borne in upon me to tell you how seriously I am looking upon the elaborate program which our Amity Com. desires to launch! This is the most difficult matter we have to handle and if we attempt to learn by doing in this line of activity the result might be disastrous. My attitude of caution may seem annoying. You can't imagine how much easier it would be for a person of my temperament to keep hands off, and I want you to know that it is only, what I like to call "holy boldness" that makes me speak! I find in the spirit of Abdul Baha's instructions the idea that we should enter into this work little by little. He said that later the Amity Conventions would be given in other cities. But these conventions are only a small part of our ambitious program. I hope someone in the N.S.A. preferably *you* will become an expert in this work, making a study of what others have done, knowing their successes & failures etc. before we, as Bahais, plunge into experiments. I wish I might go into the subject with you with excerpts from Abdul Baha's Tablets in hand. . . .[8]

Mr. Holley's reply of 8 February, noncommittal about his personal views, stated that the National Spiritual Assembly could not do anything until the committee met; then, if a difference of opinion persisted, it could be reported to the National Assembly and steps to establish unity would be taken.[9]

At about the same time another committee member, Louise Boyle, also turned to Mr. Holley for advice about the committee. After bringing up the problem of the " 'roving secretary,' " Mrs. Boyle focused on the thorny issue of Mrs. Parsons' admitted "attitude of caution."

> Apart from this is a matter about which I hesitate to write, yet it is so basic, no hope for progress can be held until it is met: Mrs. P's conservatism in the Race question. How we can work for this principle on a paternalistic policy I cannot see, yet that is the way Mrs. P's feels we should & she is of course the only one of the Com. who has such idea. I have told her today, when she sought to have me join in with her thought, that we should have a frank clarifying of our convictions *in the Com.* & determine a

policy in advance of all work. I told her the Quakers & others now active today in this work all believe in cultural intercourse, which she feels is "social equality" & it is—and in my judgment any Bahai work undertaken in the field, of a more conservative nature, would be confusing to say the least. Mrs. P. & I are very harmonious and I have always avoided meeting this issue with her. . . .

Will you kindly tell me, Horace, just for my enlightenment, do *you* see any other element of caution in the Cause to put with hers? Has she *any* ground which one might, in justice to the Cause, join her upon? You know in her home the Master seated Louis G. on his right at table,* yet He was so tender in all His work with her—suggesting Amity "as a remedy" etc., that she deeply feels it is all because she must *protect* the rest of us on this point. You see? I feel we have a real problem here, and I frankly need help in trying to meet it.[10]

Mrs. Parsons' attitude came as no surprise to Horace Holley, for he had once confronted it himself. In 1925, when Mrs. Parsons was chairman of the ill-starred amity convention committee, he had written to her with a suggestion motivated by concern for the continued and prevalent pattern of lynching in the South. "The news about another lynching in Missouri in yesterday's paper filled me with anguish," he told her, "and I realized our great spiritual responsibility to overcome this terrible injustice." He suggested that the committee might publish a statement in the *Baha'i News Letter* requesting each Local Assembly to respond to reports of lynchings and other racial incidents by writing to the newspaper in that city or town "expressing the sorrow of the Baha'is and their hope that the best citizens will combine and prevent such terrible happenings in future." As secretary of the National Assembly, he wrote, he could also send general statements to the mayor and town officials, the governor, senators, black organizations and newspapers. "Will you, as chairman, draft the statement for the News Letter? Or if you prefer, I will do it and print it over your name."[11]

Mrs. Parsons answered a few days later that at first she had been enthusiastic about his suggestion concerning "a protest . . . against lynching" but had been unable to write immediately.

---

*The incident to which Mrs. Boyle refers actually occurred at the home of Ali-Kuli and Florence Khan and is described in chapter six.

Meanwhile, she had begun to think that such "a widespread protest" might stir up "an antagonism toward us by the enemies of the colored people" which would possibly hinder or deter the amity convention work specifically commanded by 'Abdu'l-Bahá. "Booker T. Washington," she averred, "could never have accomplished what he did had his method not been a purely constructive one."[12]

Mr. Holley's next letter, unlike the first, was typewritten and formal:

August 19, 1925.

Mrs. Agnes S. Parsons,
Dublin, New Hampshire.

My dear Mrs. Parsons:

I have read your letter most carefully and quite agree with you that anything which would interfere with the great work of the Amity Conventions would be most undesirable. However, it was not part of my idea that the local Assemblies should write letters of such a nature as to create any feelings of antagonism against the Cause, but rather that their letters should express such a universal spirit that they would penetrate at least a little light into the gloom of racial hatred.

I believe that this matter is something which you should take up with your committee as soon as possible and report back your conclusions to the N.S.A. As you know, the racial situation is rapidly approaching a climax and we should do all in our power to bring healing to this mortal wound. I question whether one or two Conventions a year, no matter how well conducted and how spiritual in character, are sufficient alone to turn back the flood.

I know that you will consider this in the most sympathetic way and as a means of assisting the Conventions and not interfering with them.

Faithfully yours,
Horace Holley
Secretary[13]

The matter went back and forth for at least another month. After learning from her that she had presented the suggestion to Mrs. Boyle, Mrs. Haney, and Mr. Gregory, and none thought such action "advisable," although she did not elaborate further, Horace Holley backed off somewhat and apologized for pressing the point. But he continued to defend the action as a positive approach, rather than a protest, and as a legitimate course for the Bahá'ís.[14] In the end it was not so much his suggestion he was defending as a point of view, a willingness to be forthright on the issue and to enlarge the scope of the Bahá'í community's interracial activities.

The conflicting views raised by Mrs. Parsons and Mrs. Boyle in the early days of the committee's existence did not precipitate a crisis requiring National Assembly intervention, however. When the committee met, Louis Gregory's determination to achieve "an unfailing sense of proportion" undoubtedly helped Mrs. Parsons to go along with the expanded scope of the new committee's activities. Moreover, he was perhaps even more willing than Mariam Haney and Louise Boyle to regard Mrs. Parsons with a sense of proportion, to recognize her devotion and generosity, and to understand her slowness in coming to terms with the full significance of the work 'Abdu'l-Bahá had given her—to see, in Mrs. Boyle's words, that "it is just her own dear way of seeing it because of her background."[15]

Mr. Gregory's attitude toward Agnes Parsons had always been unfailingly kind and understanding. In 1915, while the Washington community to which she stood in the role of mother was disunited and ineffective, he assured her of his high regard for her: "Again I beg to thank you for your whole-hearted devotion to the Cause of God, which makes obedience on the part of your spiritual children both an honor and a joy." Even when they had disagreed over the handling of Washington's racial problems, he had hastened to avoid any breach with her. "I hope you will not construe my words, in our conversation this afternoon," he wrote on 10 June 1915, "as indicating any lack of appreciation or cooperation with you in your noble efforts to serve the cause and promote harmony." After reiterating his view that "differences based on human limitations [would] give way," he agreed to cooperate (even if, he implied, some degree of segregation was allowed to continue): "Meantime, I strive to be at least reconciled to any plan which the friends may adopt. . . ." Without surrendering his principles, he reaffirmed his pride in the community and his admiration for her:

The Washington Assembly is advanced, despite its difficulties and is greatly beloved by Abdul Baha. No one can doubt your earnestness and sincerity. Your position in the assembly must be also extremely difficult and trying, because of the many complaints and criticisms that are brought to you. But the Power of the Covenant overcomes all. I pray for you and yours, and hope you will always count me among your loyal supporters.[16]

Ten years later, asked by Mrs. Parsons for advice on the handling of a personal matter, he replied humbly that it seemed presumptuous of him to make suggestions, not because of any worldly differences between them, but because of the special position conferred on her by the Master: " 'Abdu'l Baha once told you that you would attain to the Abha Kingdom, giving you absolute assurance. For this servant and others he has gone no further than to express hope.'' That assurance of illumined immortality (attainment to the Abhá Kingdom) seemed obviously to be the result of her unusual qualities of spirit—her "spiritual illumination," in Mr. Gregory's words—which one had no choice but to recognize, whatever her limitations. "I believe the friends everywhere have full faith in your nobility of purpose, universal kindness and devotion to the Cause,'' he told her in 1927. "Such is my own view.''[17]

Louis Gregory's moderating influence also pervaded the statement of purpose that the committee agreed to compose as its first major task. Addressed to the National Spiritual Assembly and all Local Assemblies in the United States and Canada, the letter stressed 'Abdu'l-Bahá's consistent "promotion of inter-racial unity and accord,'' His concern for "the welfare and happiness of the colored people,'' and His conviction that "the nation itself would rise or fall as determined by the way it would settle this matter.'' "The National Spiritual Assembly, mindful of its great responsibility, has now taken action,'' the letter continued, by appointing an amity committee "to stimulate action among the friends, and to execute the plans revealed and directed by 'Abdu'l-Baha, now and evermore supported by Shoghi Effendi.'' Having established its credentials, the committee went on to remind the Bahá'ís of the importance of amity conventions and to suggest additional activities, such as cooperation with interracial committees already in existence in some cities. A forthcoming compilation of the Bahá'í teachings on race relations, entitled *The Oneness of Mankind*, was announced, with the recommendation that it be read and circulated. [18]

Another unifying factor as the committee began its work was that plans were immediately begun for a race amity convention in Washington, a project which Mrs. Parsons might seek to delay but to which she could hardly object, since it was, in her view, the one activity that had been clearly mandated by 'Abdu'l-Bahá. The amity committee's continued existence was ultimately assured less by its own initial achievements, however, than by Shoghi Effendi's direct intervention. As Guardian of the Bahá'í Cause, he corresponded regularly with the National Spiritual Assembly, and he had received a copy of the amity committee's letter of 23 February. At about the same time he had met Sadie Oglesby, the first black woman from America to make a pilgrimage to the Bahá'í holy places in Palestine, and had discussed the racial situation in America with her. His response to the enterprising new committee was immediate. On 12 April Shoghi Effendi sent the National Assembly a major message on the subject of interracial amity. This letter, in Louis Gregory's words, mentioned "with approval the activities of the newly appointed National Racial Amity Committee."[19] In fact, Shoghi Effendi's praise of the committee's letter of 23 February far exceeded mere "approval":

> I have . . . received and read with the keenest interest and appreciation a copy of that splendid document formulated by the National Committee on inter-racial amity. . . . This moving appeal, so admirable in its conception, so sound and sober in its language, has struck a responsive chord in my heart. Sent forth at a highly opportune moment in the evolution of our sacred Faith, it has served as a potent reminder of these challenging issues which still confront in a peculiar manner the American believers.[20]

Then, as Louis Gregory described it, the Guardian went on to provide "a powerful portrayal of the needs of the work." Shoghi Effendi stated clearly that the success of the Bahá'í Faith in America was closely linked to the actions of the Bahá'ís with regard to race:

the future growth and prestige of the Cause are bound to be influenced to a very considerable degree by the manner in which the adherents of the Bahá'í Faith carry out, first among themselves and in their relations with their fellow-men, those high standards of inter-racial amity so widely proclaimed and so fearlessly exemplified to the American people by our Master 'Abdu'l-Bahá.[21]

Shoghi Effendi appealed directly to the individual as a committed Bahá'í and as a "conscientious upholder of the universal principles of Bahá'u'lláh." He placed upon such active workers, the backbone of the American Bahá'í community, the full responsibility for success—not only in meeting the challenge of abolishing racial prejudice but in firmly establishing the Faith itself. "I cannot believe," he wrote, "that those whose hearts have been touched by the regenerating influence of God's creative Faith in His day will find it difficult to cleanse their souls from every lingering trace of racial animosity so subversive of the Faith they profess." In Shoghi Effendi's view, the task of such devoted Bahá'ís was "twofold": first, a "conscious effort" toward personal transformation by the individual Bahá'í, then an attempt to influence society.[22]

The Guardian made it clear that he was not deceived by superficial adherence to the principle of human oneness, as revealed in "the mere exchange of cold and empty formalities often connected with the organizing of banquets, receptions, consultative assemblies, and lecture-halls." Rather, Bahá'ís of both races must exercise their freedom from prejudice in "close and intimate social intercourse" beyond the confines of the official activities of the community:

In their homes, in their hours of relaxation and leisure, in the daily contact of business transactions, in the association of their children, . . . in short under all possible circumstances, however insignificant they appear, the community of the followers of Bahá'u'lláh should satisfy themselves that in the eyes of the world at large and in the sight of their vigilant Master they are the living witnesses of those truths which He fondly cherished and tirelessly championed to the very end of His days. If we relax in our purpose, if we falter in our faith, if we neglect the varied opportunities given us from time to time by an all-wise and gracious Master, we are not merely failing in what is our most vital and conspicuous obligation, but are thereby insensibly retarding the flow of those quickening energies which can alone insure the vigorous and speedy development of God's struggling Faith.[23]

Shoghi Effendi especially exhorted the National Spiritual Assembly "to reaffirm by word and deed the spirit and character" of 'Abdu'l-Bahá's "insistent admonitions" with regard to race. He stressed the importance of the Bahá'í summer study camp at Green Acre in Maine as a means "to further this noble end" of racial unity. Then, lest anyone misunderstand him, he summarized his expectations of the American Bahá'ís as individuals and as members of elected Assemblies:

Not by merely imitating the excesses and laxity of the extravagant age they live in; not by the idle neglect of the sacred responsibilities it is their privilege to shoulder; not by the silent compromise of the principles dearly cherished by 'Abdu'l-Bahá; not by their fear of unpopularity or their dread of censure can they hope to rouse society from its spiritual lethargy, and serve as a model to a civilization the foundations of which the corrosion of prejudice has well-nigh undermined. By the sublimity of their principles, the warmth of their love, the spotless purity of their character, and the depth of their devoutness and piety, let them demonstrate to their fellow-countrymen the ennobling reality of a power that shall weld a disrupted world.

We can prove ourselves worthy of our Cause only if in our individual conduct and corporate life we sedulously imitate the example of our beloved Master, whom the terrors of tyranny, the storms of incessant abuse, the oppressiveness of humiliation, never caused to deviate a hair's breadth from the revealed Law of Bahá'u'lláh.

Such is the path of servitude, such is the way of holiness He chose to tread to the very end of His life. Nothing short of the strictest adherence to His glorious example can safely steer our course amid the pitfalls of this perilous age, and lead us on to fulfill our high destiny.[24]

Never since the days of the Master had the Bahá'í principles of interracial equality been stated in such terms. Indeed, Shoghi Effendi's 1927 message on race is perhaps his most urgent and forceful assessment of any specific problem confronting the American Bahá'ís up to that time. He drew upon their major strength, unbounded personal devotion to 'Abdu'l-Bahá, to combat their gravest weakness, failure to come to terms with racial prejudice. He cited 'Abdu'l-Bahá not only as an example of ideal conduct but as a living presence, fully aware of the strengths and shortcomings of His followers, from the members of the National Spiritual Assembly, "the Trustees of God's sacred Faith," to the humblest individual believer.[25]

The small band of Bahá'ís dedicated to racial unity were, in Louis Gregory's words as secretary of the amity committee, "fired with new zeal by the stirring letters of Shoghi Effendi and the news of his deep and abiding interest in this work."[26] As long as Shoghi Effendi's words remained fresh in the minds of the American Bahá'ís, there could be no doubt concerning their racial policy: active promotion of racial unity was consistent with the Bahá'í principles and concordant with the expressed wishes of the Guardian. The new race committee thus received immeasurable support both for its efforts and for its very existence. Those who had questioned the need for such a committee or had failed to support its activities could scarcely ignore Shoghi Effendi's condemnation of "the mere exchange of cold and empty formalities" among the Bahá'ís and his abhorrence of "the silent compromise of the principles dearly cherished by 'Abdu'l-Bahá." Those, like Mrs. Parsons, who had upheld racial amity on principle without truly accepting the full range of social and personal transformations it required were compelled to reexamine their views.

In the light of Shoghi Effendi's statement Mrs. Parsons, as a loyal and devoted Bahá'í, could no longer defend a commitment to spiritual equality while denying social equality, nor could she withdraw in good conscience from the field of service to which 'Abdu'l-Bahá had directed her. To her great credit, she remained in the forefront of racial amity work and grew with it. In 1928 Louis Gregory wrote her that "Shoghi Effendi appears greatly pleased with the work of a committee of which you are chairman" and thanked her for "your splendid cooperation at all times and your deep and sacrificial interest in this particular line of service." There is evidence that she continued to favor an "indirect" format for the amity conventions, like that of the first convention in Washington in 1921. She even contemplated sponsoring such a conference outside the purview of the Bahá'í Faith, along the lines of the world unity conferences of previous years, because the amity committee was interested only in a more directly Bahá'í approach. But she also became a spokesman for a more enlightened attitude toward race among the white Bahá'ís. In 1929, writing to her about the annual report of the committee, Louis Gregory observed:

> One of the thoughts that I am incorporating in it is yours, that people of one race should avoid approaching those of other races in a spirit of patronage and condescension. Perhaps this wording will prevent it from being unpalatable to any one. Such a suggestion coming from a Baha'i like yourself who is prominent socially will, I think, make it easier for others to appreciate its value.[27]

No one was more encouraged by Shoghi Effendi's strong statement on race than Louis Gregory himself. His contention that the principle of racial unity was central to the Bahá'í teachings—that it must always be "to the fore whether one wants it or not"—had been fully vindicated. He had entered a new period of his life, a time of intense involvement in amity activities and of close interaction with the Guardian of the Bahá'í Cause in shaping a new racial consciousness in America. The reciprocity of their labors was recognized by Shoghi Effendi from the start. In 1928, a year and a half after Mr. Gregory assumed the administrative responsibilities of the new race committee, he received a letter of appreciation from Shoghi Effendi. At the end, in a postscript written in his own hand, the Guardian conveyed not only his personal regard for a devoted follower but a sense of Louis Gregory's historic role in the development of a new world order:

> My very dear & precious co-worker:
> Your letter has infused strength & joy in my heart. . . . I have nothing but admiration & gratitude for the heroic constancy, mature wisdom, tireless energy, and shining love with which you are conducting your ever-expanding work of service to the Cause of Bahá'u'lláh. You hardly realize what a help you are to me in my arduous work. Your grateful brother,
> Shoghi[28]

17 Apogee

The year 1927 marked the beginning of a new stage of progress toward racial unity by the American Bahá'í community. Race was discussed at length and with unprecedented frankness at the Nineteenth Annual Convention held that April in Montreal. As secretary of the amity committee, Louis Gregory presented a history of the race amity meetings. Then a pilgrim recently returned from the Holy Land, Edwina Powell, spoke on the subject of race, as the Guardian had asked her to do. She reported that Shoghi Effendi had stressed that it was no longer enough to have meetings in public halls that were open to all races, for the homes of the Bahá'ís must be open as well: "It is our duty to recognize social equality as well as spiritual equality. . . ." Shoghi Effendi's message, as she sought to convey it, was that the elimination of racial prejudice was "of supreme importance at this time."[1]

Sadie Oglesby made the same point when she took the floor to share with the assembled delegates and visitors the substance of her conversations with Shoghi Effendi during her recent stay in Haifa. She said that he had come back to the subject of race again and again. When another pilgrim would try to change the course of conversation at the dinner table, for example, the Guardian "would say: 'That is not vital', and then he would go back to this subject." He was concerned over the small numbers of black Bahá'ís in the various communities of North America. Asked if this was because they were not made to feel welcome, Mrs. Oglesby replied tactfully that black Americans " 'approach the Cause looking for trouble; we are looking to find flaws—that seems natural, because all the churches stand for universal brotherhood . . . and yet, the colored group has knocked at so many doors to try and find the spirit of universal brotherhood.' " She admitted that she and her husband became and remained Bahá'ís only because they could find no flaw in their "spiritual teachers," Harlan and Grace Ober:

> if it had been that I found them off duty once, we would have turned our faces in another direction; we were guilty of looking for shortcomings, but we have never seen them off duty with us, or with anybody else, at any time. If they had not remained in Boston until my husband and myself were strong enough to turn our eyes towards God, I assure you, dear souls, we still would have been looking in the dark.

She spoke of the Obers to Shoghi Effendi—"I could not help it, because they were my salvation"—and he assured her, " 'When our Baha'is can hold up a light like that, that will draw souls from darkness, against their wills, then, that is the Bahai light.' "[2]

Shoghi Effendi stressed that the obstacles that were preventing blacks from becoming Bahá'ís in greater numbers must be removed—" 'not for the sake of the Colored Group, but, for the sake of the whole well being and harmony and safety of the world, and for the sake of establishing the Kingdom of God on earth.' " Race prejudice was "America's vital problem," but it was not simply a matter of national concern: "Shoghi Effendi says that the tranquility of all the peoples of the earth depends on this one thing, the coming together of the White and the Black." The Bahá'ís must play a pivotal role in the solution of this problem, he told her. In order to begin to assume this role " 'the Negro [must] be represented, that he might express his viewpoint, that you might understand his position; that we might reach across this chasm. . . .' " Therefore, every Bahá'í committee should have at least one black member, he emphasized, even if the same individual had to be appointed " 'over and over again.' " Above all, every effort should be made to open the door for large numbers of black people to enter the Cause.[3]

"Don't think of the words, or my inadequacy," Mrs. Oglesby asked in closing, "but just turn your heart and see that great centre of love that is yearning, yearning that you and I shall become like one body. . . ." The assembled Bahá'ís recognized in her, rather than any inadequacy, a candid directness balanced by an eloquence that not only conveyed but inspired deep feeling. She had been able to say things that few Bahá'ís at that time (or at any time, perhaps) would have chanced to say publicly—for example, "I looked around today, knowing that this group represents all the Bahai Centres over the United States and Canada, and I see just about one drop of Negro blood—and if I asked you who that Black Woman was, you could hardly place her. . . ." Yet, because she spoke to their real longing to free themselves from the impediments to unity, the delegates responded by voting unanimously that a transcript of her talk and Mrs. Powell's be sent to each Spiritual Assembly.[4]

The account of the convention in the *Baha'i News Letter,* written by Lucy Marshall (a white Bahá'í from San Francisco) and Louis Gregory, summarized the two talks. It also included a subsequent reading by Dr. Zia Bagdadi of a recent letter he had received from Shoghi Effendi:

> "I desire you to redouble your efforts in connecton with the promotion of inter-racial amity and understanding. *Urge* the believers to show more affection, confidence, fellowship and loving kindness to the colored believers. No trace of mistrust, no sense of superiority, no mark of discord and aloofness should characterize the relations of the white and colored believers. They should openly, bravely and sincerely follow the example of our Beloved and banish prejudice from their hearts. May He reinforce and bless your efforts in such an important field of work."

Dr. Bagdadi went on to repeat the warning that 'Abdu'l-Bahá had given to him in Haifa in 1920, that America would be caught in a widening stream of violence because of its failure to resolve the racial problem.[5]

The resurgence of concern about racial unity in the early months of 1927 impelled Louis Gregory once again into the forefront of national leadership. Even before the consultation on race, he had been elected secretary of the convention and then returned to the National Spiritual Assembly for the first time in three years.[6] As a member of that body for the next five years, he undoubtedly helped to maintain the momentum of interracial effort that had begun in 1927 with the appointment of a new national committee, the hold-

ing of the first amity conferences in years, and the receipt of strong
encouragement from Shoghi Effendi in his first message on race in
America. The National Assembly's commitment to racial unity in
this period clearly demonstrates the point that the Guardian had
asked Mrs. Oglesby to make on his behalf: that blacks must be
represented in every facet of the Bahá'í administrative order, for
their participation helps to assure " 'that we might reach across this
chasm.' "

In 1927 the American Bahá'ís began to make a strong and persistent effort to close the chasm between the races. A decade later
Louis Gregory looked back on 1927 as "that memorable year for
amity congresses.' '[7] It began with the session devoted to racial
unity at the Dayton World Unity Conference in January. The new
amity committee's first scheduled event—the first race amity convention to be held since 1924—took place in Washington, D.C.,
early in April. Although it was carried out with less than two
months of planning, the convention attracted several prominent
non-Bahá'í speakers: Dr. Pezavia O'Connell, dean of Morgan
College in Baltimore; Dr. Samuel C. Mitchell, a history professor
at Richmond University, who had met 'Abdu'l-Bahá at the Lake
Mohonk Peace Conference in 1912; and Rabbi Abram Simon,
chairman of the Synagogue Council of America, who had also met
'Abdu'l-Bahá. Albert Vail, Mountfort Mills, Horace Holley, and
Allen McDaniel represented the Bahá'í Faith.[8] The effort was so
successful that the Washington, D.C., Bahá'í community approved
having another convention that same year.

The frequency of interracial meetings increased as the year pro-
gressed. Green Acre was the site that summer of the first of a series
of annual race amity conferences. During the fall and winter the
Northeast saw successful efforts in New York state—at Geneva,
Rochester, and New York City—and in Portsmouth, New Hampshire. On 27 November black poet William Stanley Braithwaite addressed an amity meeting in Boston. It was the first in a series of
monthly amity meetings that attracted speakers as notable as newspaper publisher and union organizer A. Philip Randolph.[9]

Washington's second convention in 1927 was held on 10–11
November in the same meeting places used in April, the Mt. Pleasant Congregational Church and the Auditorium of the Playhouse.

Coralie F. Cook presided at the opening session, during which addresses were given by Albert Vail and Dr. Mordecai W. Johnson of Howard University. The following day's meeting was chaired by Mr. Vail. The speakers were Professor Leslie Pinckney Hill of Cheyney Institute and Siegfried Schopflocher, a Bahá'í from Montreal. The convention received considerable attention in Washington, as had the one in April. Both helped to put the Bahá'ís "on public record," as Louis Gregory phrased it, "as standing for such enlightened principles in action."[10] Subsequently, several Washington Bahá'ís attempted to give substance to their favorable publicity by organizing an interracial discussion group to which were invited not only black intellectuals and artists, many of whom were acquainted with Coralie Cook, a mainstay of the group, but also Asians who worked in the capital. The discussion meetings, which continued for a number of years, took on only a fraction of the work that Louis Gregory had envisioned in his 1924 proposal for an interracial committee in Washington; but they did succeed in moving from "the mere exchange of cold and empty formalities" lamented by Shoghi Effendi toward the goal of "a close and intimate social intercourse."

The combination of resurgent activity and heightened enthusiasm for racial amity among the Bahá'ís had generated so much news that the amity committee—which then consisted of Mrs. Parsons, Mr. Gregory, Dr. Bagdadi, Dr. Locke, and Mrs. Hannen—prepared a progress report on interracial work to December 1927. Yet the committee clearly felt that what had been achieved was simply a beginning:

> "The workers in the field of inter-racial amity have been fired with new zeal by the stirring letters of Shoghi Effendi and the news of his deep and abiding interest in this work. We are happy to report inquiries, many responses and increasing signs of activity in reply to our previous letter. It is far from our purpose to convey to anyone feelings of coercion or constraint. But it is our earnest wish to see realized the aim of the Master, 'Abdu'l Bahá, for the gradual spread of the spirit of amity and accord throughout America. The convention for amity has been found to be a specific remedy for many present ills, an objective for heavenly bounties and a magnet for attracting souls to . . . [Bahá'-u'lláh]."[11]

Louis Gregory was particularly delighted by the new spirit he perceived among the Bahá'ís. He wrote enthusiastically to Mrs. Parsons that "the different amity efforts over the country . . . have quickened the friends with new spiritual life." In another letter he observed: "The amity work seems everywhere greatly confirmed and blessed and is helping the assemblies to get together and solve other difficult problems. As the invitation for this work came from Abdu'l-Baha Himself we should expect fine results in trying to move in the direction of His Will."[12]

Meanwhile, on 23 October, the National Spiritual Assembly had voted to sever its "official connection" with the world unity conferences. It reaffirmed the existence of "the strongest spiritual bond between the World Unity Conference Committee and this body" and claimed "a full understanding . . . of the nature and scope of the work undertaken by the said committee, who have as their aim the only (teaching) approach now possible to many people of capacity, and to awaken gradually within them a desire for the teachings and message of Bahá'u'lláh." Soon thereafter an independent World Unity Foundation, chartered by the State of New York, was established. Its trustees were individuals already deeply involved in the work: John Herman Randall of the Community Church of New York, who had become a major force behind the conferences, had been praised by Shoghi Effendi for his work, yet had never formally affiliated himself with the Bahá'í Faith; Alfred W. Martin of the Ethical Culture Society; Melbert B. Cary; Mountfort Mills; and the original members of the Bahá'í committee, Florence Morton, Horace Holley, and Mary Movius.[13] Thus, within less than a year, the preoccupation with world unity conferences had given way to—and perhaps to some extent prepared the way for—a greatly expanded program of conferences and activities on the theme of racial unity.

The pace established in 1927 continued into the following year. Chicago held its first amity conference on 22 January 1928; 450 people attended, one-third of whom were black. Albert Vail chaired the meeting; the speakers were A. Eustace Haydon, a professor of comparative religions at the University of Chicago, Rabbi Louis Mann, and Louis Gregory, who called the event "a great credit to the Chicago amity workers."[14] Mr. Gregory also spoke at a conference in Montreal on 11–12 February and in Urbana, on the

University of Illinois campus, on 6 May. Green Acre was once again the site of a race amity conference from 24 to 26 August.

Activities on a smaller scale also achieved success. The Philadelphia Bahá'ís organized an Amity Night meeting as part of Friendship Week, a project of a Unitarian church. The New York Bahá'í Assembly appointed an amity committee that started a series of public lectures. In Seattle amity dinner meetings "engendered a new spirit of unity among the colored and white who attended."[15]

Later in the year the national committee published another statement in the *Baha'i News Letter*. In view of the growing preoccupation of the American Bahá'ís with their reponsibility for Temple construction under the Plan of Unified Action, Mr. Gregory, on behalf of the committee, reported that a talk on the unific aspect of the Bahá'í Temple had been included in the Green Acre amity conference, with Albert Vail as speaker, and through the generosity of individuals the budget allotted to the Amity Committee had been returned to the National Treasurer. As for the future, financial restrictions should not prevent the continuation of amity activities:

> It is now humbly submitted, in view of the state of the world and the powerful words and examples of 'Abdu'l Bahá and our Guardian, that there be no halt in the brilliant activities of the past year which have covered a wide area. On the contrary, such services should be renewed and intensified. If because of the sacrifices and concentration needed for the Temple, the planning of large affairs be now deferred to wisdom, let us not forget that Amity Conferences between individuals, groups, and races can at any time be inexpensively arranged in a small way in homes and other places and that wherever there is sincerity of intention our Glorious Lord bestows his guidance and approval. It is most significant that interracial Amity work has hitherto been uniformly successful. 'Abdu'l-Bahá has indicated to us that when efforts lag the confirmations cease. Please inspire us with reports of your noble services.[16]

After a slow period during the latter part of 1928, amity efforts flourished once again in 1929. Several amity conferences—in Detroit, Dayton, Columbus, Buffalo, and Rochester—were held in the early months of the year. All were on a smaller scale than in the past, but, as the amity committee had observed, small meetings

could have their own measure of success. The Rochester conference attracted one hundred people, two-thirds of whom were black.
Although the attendance was small, compared with the thousands
who had attended earlier meetings, the community reported that it
was the most successful event they had ever held. In April Louis
Gregory, having served as a speaker at the recent series of meetings, commented about them to Mrs. Parsons:

> The teaching-amity work is going very well indeed and dur
> ing all the years I have never before found such capacity in souls
> for the direct message [of Bahá'u'lláh]. This applies to many
> classes in many cities. The efficiency of the friends in arranging
> amity conferences at short notice, no doubt reflects the profi
> ciency of Shoghi Effendi. Every such effort succeeds. . . .[17]

Thus, despite his initial reluctance about taking on the responsibility of amity work, he had discovered great satisfaction in it. At
first his time had been largely taken up by administrative tasks, and
his travels were curtailed. "I am being kept very busy both night
and day," he wrote Edith Chapman from New York in December
1927. "Am also tied up with committees, which somewhat limit
the geographical range of my activities. . . ."[18] Throughout 1927
and the first half of 1928 his journeys were made mostly in connection with the amity work in the Northeast and the northern Midwest. After the 1928 annual convention in Wilmette, for example,
he assisted with an amity conference in Urbana and gave eleven
talks on race relations to sociology classes at the University of Illinois. Enroute to his home base in New England, he maintained as
full an itinerary as he ever had on his long tours in earlier years.
That summer he both lectured at public meetings and taught classes
at Green Acre, and he helped to organize the second annual race
amity conference there.[19] But no other work, however satisfying,
could replace his determination to travel in the South.
    In September 1928 he began a four-month-long double circuit
through the mid-Atlantic seaboard region, planned around a late
fall meeting of the National Spiritual Assembly in New York City.
His destination on the first part of the trip was North Carolina, with
stops in New York City, Pennsylvania, New Jersey, and Washington, D.C. In Durham, North Carolina, he gave a number of address

es in schools and churches. Perhaps the most noteworthy was a talk on "The Meaning of Bahá'i (Light)" attended by 540 high school students. On the second leg of his journey, after the National Assembly meeting, he traveled through Maryland and Virginia, with another stopover in Washington.[20]

Following a similar schedule after the 1929 convention, Mr. Gregory visited Milwaukee, Kansas City, Memphis, Nashville, and Louisville. Although Louise had just returned from a stay in Europe and a pilgrimage to Haifa, his trip prevented him from joining her immediately. But by June the couple was reunited in their New England home, which Mr. Gregory described in a letter to Edith Chapman as a refuge for both from the demands of their work: "And now with my dear wife . . . I am united once more after nearly a year of separation and we are happy in our little nook in the heart of the woods. The Green Acre activities proper will not start until next month, so that meantime we are getting some rest."[21]

That fall he made an unexpected trip to the South when he was called to Charleston on the death of his stepfather, George Gregory, who was struck by a car at the age of eighty-seven. Although he had never become a Bahá'í, the elder Gregory "always took a deep interest in the Cause, distributed the literature and was quite active in arranging meetings even when he was feeble because of his advanced years." Louis Gregory read Bahá'í prayers at the funeral, and he realized after his father's death how truly close to the Bahá'í spirit the man had come in his last years. A sense of his spiritual development was implicit in the tributes that were paid to him at the service, which was attended by about a thousand people of both races.[22]

In a year of scaled-down amity activities George Gregory's funeral proved to be a major occasion for proclaiming the Bahá'í stand on the oneness of mankind. The period from April 1929 to April 1930 brought even more severe financial limitations than the year before, when the National Teaching and Inter-Racial Amity Committees were affiliated for a time as an economy measure. In its annual budget the National Assembly alloted five hundred dollars to the amity committee. It was suggested that two hundred be used for the annual conference at Green Acre, which had cost four hundred the year before, when it was supported by private donations. Under such an austerity program the committee no longer had the means to support local activities. But when Louis Gregory wrote to the members of the committee in June, he expressed the hope that the lack of funds would not preclude creative efforts, since the previous year had shown that many effective activities required little money. And he noted that "it is clearly the wish of our Guardian to have no abatement of this vital activity even during the extraordinary effort for Temple construction." Yet by the fall a large amount of money—over $77,000—was still needed to complete the Plan of Unified Action goal of raising $400,000 by 1 January 1930. That the full amount was raised—in cash—by March 1930, despite the onset of the Great Depression in October 1929, with its immediate effects on the disposable incomes of people of all classes, is a measure of the attention that the American Bahá'ís gave to this extraordinary effort.[23] Inevitably amity activities during this period were limited further still, if not actually suspended.

The Interracial Amity Committee that year conducted nearly all of its consultation by correspondence. Its annual report, published in April 1930, concentrated on successful local meetings held in Milwaukee; Portsmouth, New Hampshire; Chicago and Wilmette; Boston; Cleveland; Akron; and Montreal. Probably the most ambitious conference of the year was held in Philadelphia, where Albert Vail and Louis Gregory each spoke at three sessions. The most unusual efforts were perhaps those of the New York Bahá'í youth group, which organized an interracial and international evening of music, drama, and verse at a home in Harlem, then followed it with an interracial concert at the Bahá'í Center on another evening. In addition to providing moral support for these activities, the committee arranged for the third annual conference at Green Acre.[24]

In another line of endeavor, the committee, at the request of the National Assembly, drafted a letter to President Hoover's wife, commenting favorably on her having entertained at the White House the wife and daughter of Oscar DePriest, the first black representative to serve in Congress since 1901—a courtesy that seems routine now but in 1929 caused a furor like the Theodore Roosevelt–Booker T. Washington dinner, with several state legislatures in the South passing resolutions " 'condemning certain social policies of the administration in entertaining Negroes in the

White House on a parity with white ladies.' '' The committee also was instructed by the National Assembly to compose a letter to a Local Spiritual Assembly, responding to questions on the origin of racial differences.[25]

The restricted scope of the committee in 1929–30 undoubtedly led to the National Assembly's decision to incorporate amity work into the sphere of the Teaching Committee, an idea which had been tested briefly in 1928–29. In 1930 Louis Gregory was appointed the committee's ''secretary for amity activities,'' and in the August 1930 issue of *Baha'i News* he published an inspirational letter that reported plans for the upcoming Green Acre conference. Otherwise, he implied, the new committee structure would provide essentially a clearinghouse for reports and suggestions. In March 1931, for example, a general report on teaching in *Baha'i News* reminded readers that ''inter-racial contacts should be especially stressed'' and suggested new methods, such as interracial and international dinners, which departed from the amity conference format established in 1921. ''Through them,'' the report continued, ''a more vital and effective type of racial amity work may gradually unfold, although there is still a distinct place for our present racial amity conferences.''[26]

Almost inadvertently, the National Teaching Committee helped to arrange a conference for interracial amity in New York that illustrated the potential that the conference format still held. Informal contacts between a Bahá'í visitor to New York and two officers of the Urban League (one of whom, Samuel A. Allen, when a student at Howard University in 1912, had attended 'Abdu'l-Bahá's talk) eventually led to several striking accomplishments: a joint meeting of the National Teaching Committee with representatives of the Urban League to discuss amity work; participation by those Urban League officers in the next Green Acre amity conference; and, finally, cosponsorship by the National Teaching Committee, the Urban League, and the Spiritual Assembly of the Bahá'ís of New York of a conference for interracial amity on 2, 8, and 9 November 1930, with two sessions at the Bahá'í Center and one at the Urban League Auditorium. The speakers included representatives of the Urban League, the N.A.A.C.P., and the Bahá'í Faith. The conference was subsequently the subject of an article with photographs in the *Chicago Defender*. It also led to a second conference in March 1931 with Samuel Allen as one of the speakers. The National Teaching Committee made a full report in *Baha'i News* about the "sequence of events" that led to such notable cooperation, not only because the incidents held inherent interest but because they exemplified the results that follow sincere efforts to further the aims of the Faith—efforts applicable to any field of endeavor.[27]

Indeed, the attempt, implicit in the new committee structure, to incorporate interracial activities into the mainstream of teaching on the local level seems to have had considerable success. Louis Gregory's extensive travels that year set the standard, as always. A trip through the South included two weeks in the Washington, D.C.–Baltimore area and a return to Charleston. He lectured twice at a white college in Bricks, North Carolina, and gave an address on comparative religion at a college in Lynchburg, Virginia. In the North he traveled widely in Illinois, Wisconsin, Ohio, New York, and New England. At a state normal school in Wisconsin he spoke directly on the Bahá'í teachings to two hundred students. He was also invited to return to the University of Illinois to talk on race relations in the sociology department.[28]

The annual report of the "amity secretary" for 1930–31 mentions a number of interesting activities during the year. Among them were a Christmas dinner party to which several hundred black children were invited by the Bahá'í youth of New York, an interracial amity dinner for 120 persons in Pasadena, and an interracial discussion group organized by individual Bahá'ís in Washington, D.C., the only group of its kind in the capital. All of the activities reflected growing enthusiasm for and participation in innovative interracial events from coast to coast. Before the 1931 convention yet another remarkable effort had been made: a race amity conference on 19 April in Atlantic City overcame severe obstacles ("it had but one active Bahá'í worker on the field and was opposed by the orthodox among the clergy, an attitude which unfavorably affected the press") to bring into collaboration twelve local organizations and organize a meeting attended by four hundred people. Thus, when the new National Spiritual Assembly for 1931–32 decided to reappoint an Inter-racial Amity Committee, the move was not an effort to reactivate the work; rather, it seems to have reflected a recognition that interracial amity was too large and fertile a field to be subsumed under the general category of teaching.[29]

The decision was vindicated by a series of successful activities in 1931–32 which moved Louis Gregory to state in the committee's annual report in the spring of 1932 that "the past year has been the banner year in this particular line of activity during the period since it was started." The committee attributed much of the success to "the stimulus, encouragement, protection and mighty confirmation that have come to us from and through our beloved Guardian," because "with his powerful arm of assistance every difficulty has been met and successfully overcome."[30] Among the highlights of the year were two amity conferences in New York City and one in Pittsburgh, where the local branch of the Urban League assisted the city's small Bahá'í community. The Green Acre conference attracted more "people of capacity" than ever before to hear, among others, William Leo Hansberry of Howard University discuss scientific evidence of the "Negro Civilizations in Ancient Africa." Small-scale activities flourished in homes in Oakland and Berkeley, California. Following the lead of the Pasadena Bahá'ís, a number of communities organized interracial dinners. In Washington, D.C., about eighty influential people attended a banquet in November 1931 in honor of Martha Root, who had recently returned from a round-the-world teaching trip. At a dinner and program in Los Angeles in February, American Indians, Chinese, and Japanese were represented, along with white and black Americans. In Detroit in March seventy-two people attended "an informal family dinner"—open to members of "The Human Family," the invitation read, in order "to discuss progress toward World Peace through inter-racial friendship and understanding." Additional food was made available to the indigent, whose numbers, particularly among blacks, were swollen by the terrible hardships of the Depression.[31]

An unprecedented effort to take racial amity activities south of Washington, D.C., was also initiated in 1931. Inspired by a request of Shoghi Effendi that two Bahá'ís—a white and a black—should make a teaching trip together to the South, and heartened by the encouragement of Dr. Will W. Alexander of the Southern Inter-racial Commission, two interracial teams were

formed. First, Philip A. Marangella, a white, and Chauncey Northern, a black musician, presented a program that combined poetry
and music at a number of schools and colleges, both white and
black, in Washington, D.C.; Richmond and Hampton, Virginia;
Enfield, North Carolina; Orangeburg and Columbia, South Carolina. Wherever they went, they found not only a favorable response to themselves but to the Faith they represented. They regretted having free only two weeks rather than two months to devote to
the effort. [32]

In December 1931 Louis Gregory and Willard McKay, who had
taught for some time at the University of Texas, formed the second
team. They joined forces in Atlanta, where they established a
Bahá'í study class. Then they proceeded to tour the states of
Alabama, Tennessee, and Ohio. "They spent eighteen days together," a report in *Bahá'í News* observed,

> traveling by motor busses, eating together and most of the time
> sharing the same room, in their social relations thus running
> counter to all the traditions of their environment, yet without a
> single unpleasant incident to mar the harmony and usefulness of
> their trip, at each stage of their journey feeling under divine guid-
> ance and protection. They were treated with signal courtesy by
> people of all races, classes, colors and creeds, being astonished
> by what they saw and heard of the warmth, friendliness and hos-
> pitality of the South. [33]

Nonetheless, they "caused a sensation," Louis Gregory wrote,
and sparked interest in their shared beliefs, which bound them together in such demonstrable unity. One black college student told
Willard McKay "that the greatest news he could take back home to
his father was that a white man had slept in a Negro dormitory!" [34]

On their journey they concentrated mainly upon colleges and
universities. At Tuskegee Institute they spoke seven times in three
days. Their largest audience was a gathering of eighteen hundred at
the regular Sunday evening meeting. Robert R. Moton, Booker T.
Washington's successor as head of Tuskegee, reportedly stated
that "he wanted his students to hear this message." Both George
Washington Carver and Booker Washington's son indicated to the
visitors that they held the Bahá'í teachings in great esteem. At Fisk
University five meetings were held; addresses were also given at

the State Normal School and at a Nashville high school. After a stop in Louisville Mr. McKay and Mr. Gregory went on to Cincinnati. A public meeting was arranged by the Bahá'ís there, and a sociology professor at the University of Cincinnati opened his classes to the travelers.[35]

Both men were impressed by signs of change in the South—such as interracial meetings where refreshments were served, breaking the once-undisputed rule that the races must not eat together—and by the improved social atmosphere that made the journey possible. They felt that the spirit of a new age had pervaded many religious leaders, educators, and members of interracial commissions in the South, creating a new, milder climate of opinion about race.

Finally, the unusual achievements of the year were crowned by an interracial banquet in New York on 27 February 1932. About 150 people attended the banquet, which was organized by the national amity committee to honor the N.A.A.C.P. and the Urban League. The Bahá'í co-chairmen for the evening were Loulie Mathews and Louis Gregory, the chairman and secretary of the amity committee. Mrs. Mathews was the motive force behind the event and, along with her husband, underwrote the expense. Several Bahá'ís—Hooper Harris, Mary Hanford Ford, and Horace Holley—spoke briefly, noting the praiseworthy achievements of the two organizations and placing them in the context of a dawning era of unity. Among the guests responding with short speeches were Dr. DuBois, who, according to the *Chicago Defender,* "remarked the unity of the N. A. A. C. P. and of the National Urban league sitting down together at a banquet table"; Arthur B. Spingarn of the N.A.A.C.P.; Dr. John Hope, president of Atlanta University; Walter F. White, secretary of the N.A.A.C.P., who welcomed "the Bahai movement as one of the great forces of human understanding"; James Hubert, secretary of the New York Urban League; and Mary White Ovington, a social worker from New York who had played a major role in the founding of the N.A.A.C.P. "The peace and amity and love of mankind as advocated by the philosophy of the followers of the great and good Abdul Bahai [sic]," the lengthy article in the 5 March edition of the *Defender* began, "were expressed by and impressed upon the select interracial group which attended the banquet in honor of the work of both the N. A. A. C. P. and the National Urban league, held at the Hotel Shelton. . . .''³⁶

Apparently, Dr. DuBois was among those who were impressed. ''I want to tell you how much I enjoyed the dinner Saturday night and how grateful I am to you for it,'' he wrote to Loulie Mathews a few days afterward. ''It must have represented a great deal of effort and some of it very discouraging. You have a right, however, to feel that it was all justified in the end, and that everyone present was under deep obligations for your thought and ideals and accomplishment!'' No wonder that the amity committee called the event ''perhaps the most noteworthy success of Amity since the first Convention, held in 1921.''³⁷ It was a fitting conclusion to five years of real progress by the American Bahá'ís in putting the oneness of mankind ''to the fore'' in their efforts to build a new social order.

18   Holding On

The successful amity activities carried out from April 1931 to April 1932 continued to bear fruit in the following years. An interracial benefit concert was organized by the West Englewood, New Jersey, Bahá'ís late in 1932 to raise funds to assist the unemployed. Another interracial team—Louis Gregory and an Australian Bahá'í, Charles A. Wragg—toured the South in 1933. The annual race amity conferences at Green Acre went on as before. Elsewhere, race amity conferences and meetings were organized, although seldom on as large a scale as in earlier years.

New York continued to be a hub of activity. In May 1933 the national amity committee gave its second annual reception in honor of the N.A.A.C.P. and the Urban League; two hundred people attended. Bahá'í-sponsored amity meetings in New York City regularly received either formal or informal support from the two organizations. Among them was an amity conference on 9–10 December 1932, held in cooperation with the Urban League and with Alain Locke, Samuel A. Allen, James H. Hubert, Dr. Genevieve Coy of Columbia University, and Louis Gregory as speakers.[1] Many smaller meetings were held at the New York Bahá'í Center over the years, often with the artistic stamp that characterized the activities to which Loulie Mathews, as an officer of both the local and national amity committees, lent her talents, financial support, and influence. During the lean years of the Depression Mrs. Mathews funded a prize for outstanding works of fiction by black authors. Her daughter and son-in-law, Oliver and Wanden LaFarge, were involved (along with W. E. B. DuBois) in the administration of the prize.[2] Their collective circle of acquaintances included a large number of the leading black artists and intellectuals of the period.

But outside of New York, from mid-1932 on, the character of the amity work began to change. This was partly the result of

194

economic necessity as, despite the Depression, the Bahá'ís pressed forward to construct the Temple. The national committee members in 1932–33 served mainly as stimulators of race amity activity in their own communities and regions. Loulie Mathews in New York, Mabelle L. Davis in Detroit, Zia Bagdadi and Shelley N. Parker in Chicago and Wilmette, Sara E. Witt in Los Angeles, Coralie F. Cook in Washington, D.C., and even Louis Gregory, during his brief periods at home in Portsmouth, New Hampshire, and Eliot, Maine—all served as focal points for locally organized events. The committee had been given a budget of only one hundred dollars, insufficient for "any public meetings or direct committee activities," with the suggestion by the National Spiritual Assembly that contact with non-Bahá'í individuals and groups be maintained "through correspondence and the use of Bahá'í literature."[3]

The assigned role of the committee, and the actual achievements of its members, also reflected a new stage in the development of the Bahá'í administrative institutions in America. The National Assembly stated in its annual report for 1932–33 that

> A distinctly new trend set in motion has been the assumption of fuller responsibility by Local Spiritual Assemblies for the promotion of all Bahá'í activities in their respective areas of jurisdiction. The day when local communities may passively await representatives of National Committees to initiate teaching, racial amity and other activities has passed. The result will be to stimulate each Local Assembly in development toward its final consummation as a Local House of Justice.[4]

The immediate result in the field of racial amity, however, was not so much to stimulate local efforts as to allow them to lag, except where a strong interest already existed. In Detroit, for example, Mrs. Davis (who was white) had for some time carried out amity activities virtually on her own initiative. When the Local Spiritual Assembly was directed to assume greater responsibility for amity work, no regular activity was planned, and the only interracial effort in which the Assembly engaged was the sponsorship of public talks by Louis Gregory when he was able to visit the city. Blacks apparently were not welcomed into community-wide meetings.

Asked by the Spiritual Assembly in December 1932 to arrange for study classes in her home "for the colored people you have interested in the Cause," Mrs. Davis felt that whatever progress she had made in proclaiming the Bahá'í teachings on race during the past two years was about to be undone. She turned both to the National Spiritual Assembly and to Louis Gregory for help with the situation. Horace Holley, as national secretary, responded that she had to try to work the problem out at the local level and that the National Assembly had no jurisdiction in the initial stages of such a problem.[5] Louis Gregory, in his capacity as secretary of the National Bahá'í Committee for Racial Amity, wrote the Detroit Assembly an extremely loving and gentle letter—typical of his approach to white Bahá'ís who had difficulty with race—in which he praised Mrs. Davis as "one of our most intelligent and active workers" for amity and also pointed out the dangers of even appearing to stand for segregation:

> The intelligentsia of the colored race, of which there are many, many fine representatives in Detroit, will welcome any cooperative, interracial efforts on the part of the Baha'is and other liberal movements. They will also welcome to their own organizations . . . Baha'i speakers of any race. But they will fight to the last ditch any organization that proposes to segregate them. Their two foremost welfare organizations, the N. A. A. C. P. and the National Urban League, are both biracial. . . . For the Cause of Baha'u'llah to be committed to a different stand will put it under fire both of the colored and liberal whites. An eastern city which tried that some years ago was openly denounced by the N. A. A. C. P. and it has taken only much love and sacrifice on the part of the Baha'is of that city to recover the lost ground. An interracial study class will do good. But a segregated study class is fore-doomed to failure, I fear.[6]

He went on to give his views on the personal challenge of Bahá'í amity work:

> The whole matter of racial adjustment is very difficult and requires a world of patience and effort. Among the friends are some who have no heart for such work. It is not my wish to embarrass them. On the other hand there are those who love such

work and seem to have special qualifications to make it go. What I would always like to see is for both sides to be free, without any attitude of superiority on the part of either. If the Baha'is who know the value of this service to humanity upon which the Master and the Guardian have laid so much emphasis will lend their presence and cooperation to a study class for all races in Mrs. Davis' home or elsewhere, it will be a blessed means of progress and spirituality to those who like it and will not harm others. Nor will others harm it.

In conclusion he emphasized that he could only advise the Spiritual Assembly and that he did so out of feelings of "friendliness and gratitude to all of the Baha'is of Detroit." He also implied that he was concerned over the counterproductiveness of disunity between Mrs. Davis and the Assembly: "Our effective workers are pathetically few, while the demand for their services is very large. For this reason let us hope that no spiritual energy be lost in friction among the friends themselves. . . ."[7]

The friction continued unabated, however. A few months later Mrs. Davis was deeply disturbed to find that the only black member of the Detroit Bahá'í community had been removed from the membership roster—although she considered herself a Bahá'í—because she had not been able to attend meetings regularly. The rift between Mrs. Davis and the Assembly continued to deepen, and shortly thereafter she was also deprived of membership for a time.[8] The disagreement undoubtedly escalated as it did because of the strong personalities involved on both sides of the issue and because of the undue influence of such personalities in a small, slowly growing organization, a condition that was in itself indicative of the prevailing immaturity of the American Bahá'ís at that time in their attitude toward their own administrative order. The conflict reflected a basic need, on the one hand, to subdue the domination of Assemblies by forceful, entrenched leaders (however sincere) and, on the other hand, to channel the desire for change into constructive behavior rather than patterns of accusation and alienation. But race was not simply incidental to the dispute. No other issue cut deeper or demanded fuller examination of a Bahá'í's, or a Bahá'í institution's, words and deeds. Many white Bahá'ís were reluctant to look into their own hearts as carefully as

Shoghi Effendi had asked them and as some of their fellow believers expected them to do.

Little occurred to promote a change of heart during the administrative year that began in the spring of 1933. An almost completely new and predominantly white national amity committee was appointed for 1933–34. Mrs. Parsons served once again as chairman of the committee until she was struck by a car and killed in January 1934, at the age of seventy-three.[9] The only members reappointed from the previous year were Mrs. Mathews and Mr. Gregory. The committee was charged by the National Assembly with the task of maintaining ''the series of public racial amity conferences established by 'Abdu'l-Bahá, by training local assemblies to hold such conferences under their own auspices from time to time.'' The reasons for this limited role, national secretary Horace Holley explained in a letter to the committee, were that 1) funds were lacking, and 2) the Local Assemblies needed to assume more responsibility.[10] But local efforts continued to diminish during the year.

At a time when racial amity was generally neglected, New York and Chicago remained in the forefront. With the exception of the annual race amity conference at Green Acre, New York organized the only such full-scale conference that was held anywhere that year. New national amity committee member Ludmila Bechtold, who had served with Mrs. Mathews on the New York amity committee, was largely responsible for the conference. In addition, two large interracial meetings were held at the New York Bahá'í Center; at the first both Loulie Mathews and Louis Gregory were featured speakers. The local amity committee in Chicago also carried out a successful program, holding four public meetings and systematically supporting the work of other interracial groups. Outside these two major centers amity activities were maintained in only a few communities with a long history of involvement. The Bahá'ís of Urbana carried out an amity program at the University of Illinois, for example, and the informal interracial discussion group in Washington, D.C., continued to meet.[11]

With these few exceptions the Bahá'ís seem to have failed to arise to the call of the national committee. In a letter published in the January 1934 issue of *Baha'i News* the committee implied that the commitment to racial amity had suffered a serious setback since its high points in 1927 and 1932:

> Considering the vital need of cementing the bond of unity and harmony between the white and colored in America as a means of enlightenment and security both within and without, we submit that racial amity activities and reports should have a prominent rather than incidental place in the agenda of the National Spiritual Assembly, the annual Convention and in the monthly and annual meetings of each Spiritual Assembly and community consultation. Spiritual Assemblies should ever endeavor so to inspire their respective committees and communities that amity work should not only be sporadic and occasional, but an accepted ideal and a means of illustrating in daily life as often as possible the greatest principle of Bahá'u'lláh, the oneness of the world of humanity.[12]

The committee went on to recommend that amity conferences be held in each community at least once a year and smaller meetings more often, with a concerted effort to bring those attracted by the Bahá'í stand on race to a full acceptance of the Faith in all its aspects. The committee also stressed the need to appoint capable and experienced blacks to local and national committees, to reach black leaders, and to remove all traces of prejudice from within the ranks of the Bahá'ís, white and black alike. The letter ended with a quotation from Shoghi Effendi about " 'this most important field of activity.' "[13]

Consultation at the 1934 convention similarly revealed deep concern on the part of some Bahá'ís over what Shoghi Effendi had called the "silent compromise" of a vital Bahá'í principle. After the Race Amity Committee's report, which dealt inevitably with the marked decrease in amity activities, "a most spirited period of consultation" caused the time allotted to the topic to be extended by the delegates. In his account of the twenty-sixth annual convention, Louis Gregory noted that the delegates responded by passing a recommendation that "the National Spiritual Assembly directly or through the Amity Committee, send a circular letter to the Assemblies on the magnitude of the amity work, preferably substantiating their references from the teachings." Philip Sprague of

New York expressed the opinion that "some of the friends felt that their stand in this matter should reflect public opinion rather than the Divine Teachings." "Mr. [Alfred] Lunt," the report continued, "said that the friends should never adopt a policy of *'Safety First!'* Had the Persian believers in the early days adopted such a policy the Cause would never have spread." The consultation on race included a brief address by Robert S. Abbott, editor of the *Chicago Defender,* who had recently become a Bahá'í after years of friendship toward the Faith dating back to 'Abdu'l-Bahá's visit to America. " 'I hope to acquire more power, power to fight for the unity of humanity,' " he told the Convention. " 'I am identifying myself with this Cause and I go up with you or down with you. Anything for this Cause! Let it go out and remove the darkness everywhere. Save my people! Save America from herself!' " [14]

The convention recommendation with regard to a circular letter on race led the national amity committee to produce a document entitled "The Divine Call to Race Amity." The National Spiritual Assembly termed it a "remarkable statement" and published it in *Bahá'í News.* [15] Signed by Louis Gregory as chairman of the committee, the statement bears his indelible imprint: moderate and constructive in its tone, down-to-earth in its recommendations, so reasonable that no one could dispute it. After outlining the foundation of the concept of racial amity in Bahá'u'lláh's writings, the statement stressed the subsequent contributions by 'Abdu'l-Bahá and Shoghi Effendi:

> Those who were blessed in meeting 'Abdu'l-Bahá may well recall how He combined the courtliness, grace and strength of the lion with the loveliness, purity and gentleness of the dove when directing this service to America. His invigorating terms are found in many lessons and Tablets. Wherever He journeyed He sought to serve and teach the colored along with the white and both in public and private demonstrated His views in ways unmistakable. He brought the races into loving fellowship and showered His healing love upon all. Provincialism, prejudice and insularity of thought melted before His sublime wisdom and magnetic smile. On the streets and in the seats of the mighty, among the lowly and obscure and with those socially prominent He adhered to the great principles of Bahá'u'lláh. Moreover He promised the Confirmations of the Spirit to those who uphold

and apply the great principle of unity through love. Many and potent are His signs bearing upon this vital theme. In every city visited He attracted large audiences which hung upon His every word. People did not shrink from Him because His viewpoint enlarged theirs. Rather they seemed all the more happy to meet One who restored their souls. Ever more and more established becomes His vision of reality.

Turning to our Guardian, we find that he shows the same deep and practical interest in race amity as the Great Ones who preceded him. Who can read his persuasive and dynamic appeal . . . [of 12 April 1927] without having his soul stirred to the depths? This is a model worthy of the closest study and concentration. Pilgrims tell his interest. Others share his letters. But as we read his stirring, winged words, unmistakably intended for the body of the Cause, we are as it were in his presence and feel powerfully moved to action. The authority that here speaks is unquestionable; the standard set lacks nothing of perfection; the motivating power is the mystery of divine love. We are asked to sacrifice only the veils that separate, the superstitions that darken, the prejudices that foment strife—nothing that is real![16]

The statement proceeded to quote the supporting views on human oneness of a non-Bahá'í scholar. Then it outlined eleven suggestions toward furthering race amity: 1) that every Local Assembly appoint a local amity committee, over which the national committee would have no jurisdiction but which it could "joyfully" assist; 2) that "race amity conferences should be improved for 'intensive teaching' as well as bringing the races together"; 3) that more literature on the subject, by more authors, be published; 4) that an amity conference combined with a course on race relations be adopted by each Bahá'í summer school and large community; 5) that the national committee be called upon to help with this "undertaking"; 6) that better race relations be taught in word and action by the social life of the Bahá'ís; 7) that non-Bahá'í speakers at amity conferences be carefully chosen in order to avoid "any expressions that may through partisanship, politics or limited and destructive thoughts" reflect badly on the Faith; 8) that the Golden Rule taught by all the Messengers of God guide relations of whites with blacks and other minorities; 9) that discord be avoided and reliance put upon the force of reasonable arguments against prejudice based on sociology, religion, and practical experience; 10) that Bahá'í race amity workers join community organizations such as the N.A.A.C.P. and the Urban League and attend their meetings, thereby working toward a cooperative relationship between the Bahá'ís and other concerned groups; and 11) that all activities be carried out in a "prayerful and joyful attitude of service."[17]

The 1934 convention consultation and the publication of "The Divine Call to Race Amity" did not, however, cause any major upsurge in activities. Cincinnati's first race amity conference, held on 11–13 April 1935, was a noteworthy exception. The chairman of the first session was Dorothy Beecher Baker, a young Bahá'í descended from one of the great abolitionist families. She drew upon both her Bahá'í and abolitionist heritages to set the tone for the conference. The Cincinnati Assembly called the event their "crowning achievement of the year."[18] Nationally, several major black newspapers gave the Faith excellent publicity during the year. Washington, D.C., and Chicago reported on their recent programs at the 1935 convention. But, although the subject of race amity was placed prominently on the agenda of the convention, the committee's statement in *Baha'i News* had already said about all there was to say about present needs. The only recommendation made by the delegates as a result of the consultation was that a survey be made of the racial, religious, and ethnic backgrounds of the American Bahá'ís.[19]

Louis Gregory's remarks to the convention summed up the beleaguered mood of the hour: " 'The complexity of the racial situation in America makes the work of building race amity one of delicacy and difficulty that challenges constant efforts and the best resources of minds and hearts.' " Even among the Bahá'ís, he acknowledged, " 'tests are many and severe, making a constant demand for faith, fidelity, intelligence, broadmindedness, courage, love, patience, prayerfulness and Guidance.' "[20] Seven years of painstaking work toward the goal of racial unity had produced manifold "successes" and "confirmations," as Mr. Gregory himself often referred to them. Yet after seven years the demand for extraordinary effort remained constant. Nothing was so clear as the hard reality that prejudice is insidious and that no one was immune to its effects.

19   An Historical Record

The consultation on race at the 1935 national Bahá'í convention did nothing to reverse the gradual decline in race amity activity over the previous two years. Nonetheless the survey of racial, religious, and ethnic backgrounds that the delegates had recommended was soon carried out, yielding results of lasting value, as part of the first attempt at a "thorough and complete Bahá'í census" in America. In the summer of 1935 "Bahá'í Historical Records Cards" were distributed to Local Spiritual Assemblies, groups, and isolated believers with the goal of completing this "extensive undertaking" within a year. New Bahá'ís were to be asked to fill out the forms when they enrolled, and Local Assemblies were also requested to complete forms for deceased members of their communities "as far as possible."[1]

The records cards, which were collected over the next few years, finally reached a total of 1,813. According to Arthur Hampson's study of "The Growth and Spread of the Baha'i Faith," this figure represented about 60 percent of the Bahá'í population in the United States and Canada. Each individual was to complete his own card; however, the Local Assemblies were given the responsibility of seeing that "all enrolled members fill out and sign" the forms. The National Spiritual Assembly considered that this activity might well stimulate renewed contact between the Local Assemblies and those individuals who had not been attending community meetings.[2]

Each card was labeled "Bahá'í Historical Record." Nineteen items of personal information were requested: name, reporting Assembly, birthplace and birthdate, naturalization data, "National origin (whether of English or other stock)," "Race," "Color," sex, marital status and marriage date, children or dependents, "Religious origin (religion before becoming a Bahá'í)," date of becoming a Bahá'í, place where this occurred, date of membership in present community, general remarks, additional remarks (to be left blank), optional photograph, and signature.

Of the 1,813 individuals who completed the cards, ninety-nine—thirty-seven men and sixty-two women—identified themselves in some way as being black.[3] (Several managed to express their feelings about such distinctions, however, by stating that their "race" was "American," "Afro American," or "Oneness of Humanity.") The black respondents constitute 5½ percent of the total. They may well have been underrepresented to some degree. In at least some communities their participation was undoubtedly hindered by the dominance of whites, who tended to display conscious or unconscious attitudes of superiority and insensitivity toward minorities. Economic hardships, intensified by the general economic distress among blacks during these Depression years, also worked against full involvement. Educational disadvantages and negative feelings about the three separate questions focusing on "Race," "National origin," and "Color" may have added to reticence by blacks to fill out the forms. Moreover, there was a limited response from the South, where only five blacks—four from Nashville and one from Durham, North Carolina—filled out the cards. The project was coordinated by Local Spiritual Assemblies and active groups, few of which existed in the region. Thus the black Bahá'ís scattered through the Southern states (in Memphis and Atlanta, for example) were for the most part isolated and lacked motivation to participate in the survey.

Regardless of the limitations of the sample, the results are both interesting as statistics and valuable as a profile of a community of fellow believers. The black respondents to the survey came from all sections of the country and had entered the Faith at various times over a twenty-eight-year span. Louis Gregory was the first among them to accept the Faith, but a number of others had been Bahá'ís nearly as long as he. The most recent had enrolled in 1937. (See Table on page 205.)

The three long-time Bahá'ís had all enrolled in Washington, D.C. After Louis Gregory in 1909 came Alan A. Anderson in 1910. In the section of the card that asked for "General information you would like to have preserved in this historical record (about Bahá'í services, connection with the Cause in the early days, special talents, etc.)," Mr. Anderson wrote that in 1912

Table. Information about 99 black respondents among
1,813 Bahá'ís surveyed, 1935–c. 1937, from Bahá'í Historical Records Cards
in the National Bahá'í Archives, Wilmette, Illinois

| LOCATION OF ENROLLMENT | DATES, NUMBERS OF ENROLLMENTS IN BAHÁ'Í FAITH | | | | | NO DATE GIVEN | TOTAL |
	Up to 1912	1913–20	1921–26	1927–33	1934–37		
Chicago, IL		1 1918	2 1921 1 1925	2 1929 1 1930 7 1932	2 1934 1 1935		**17**
Evanston, IL				1 1929 1 1932			**2**
Washington, DC	1 1909 1 1910 1 1912	1 1913 1 1914 1 1918				1	**7**
San Francisco, CA		1 1915 1 1919					**2**
Boston, MA		2 1914 2 1916 +4*	1 1923	1 1930			**10**
Brookline, MA					1 1934		**1**
New York, NY		1 1917 2 1918	2 1921 1 1926				**6**
Los Angeles, CA					1 1935		**1**
Nashville, TN				1 1932	1 1934 2 1935		**4**
Teaneck, NJ					1 1935		**1**
Columbus, OH				1 1929			**1**
Cincinnati, OH				1 1929	2 1935		**3**
Cleveland, OH				2 1928 1 1932	1 1934		**4**
Philadelphia, PA			1 1924 1 1925				**2**
Pittsburgh, PA				2 1931		1	**3**
Portland, OR		1 1914	1 1925				**2**
Seattle, WA		1 1920	1 1921 1 1922 1 1923 1 1924	1 1931			**6**
Rochester, NY				2 1929 1 1932 1 1933			**4**
Geneva, NY				2 1933			**2**
Ann Arbor, MI				1 1932			**1**
Kansas City, MO				1 1929	1 1935		**2**
Durham, NC			1 1923				**1**
Minneapolis, MN		1 1920					**1**
Denver, CO					1 1935		**1**
Colorado (other)					2 1937		**2**
Visalia, CA			1 1925				**1**
Phoenix, AZ				2 1933			**2**
Racine, WI				2 1932			**2**
Muskegon, MI			1 1924				**1**
Dawson, Yukon Canada			1 1922				**1**
Atlantic City, NJ						1	**1**
Montclair, NJ		1 1920				1	**2**
Washington, PA				1 1930			**1**
Oakland, CA				2 1929			**2**
Totals	3	21	18	37	16	4	**99**

*children raised Bahá'í

'Abdu'l-Bahá had received him in Mrs. Parsons' home and had given a Persian name to his baby daughter. "I have no Special Bahai Talent," he added. "But I understand very well the Bahai Message and teachings." The third early believer from Washington was Leila Y. Payne, who attended her first Bahá'í meeting on the occasion of 'Abdu'l-Bahá's address to the Bethel Literary and Historical Association at the Metropolitan AME Church on 23 April 1912. The Master's talk, she recorded, "left its imprint on my memory for ever."

Twenty-one of the respondents had become Bahá'ís between 1913 and 1920. Among them were members of the Mapp and Oglesby families, who had studied the Faith with Harlan and Grace Ober in Boston. Mrs. Zylpha O. Mapp became a Bahá'í in 1916 and raised her two children, Benton and Zylpha, in the Faith. In 1930 her husband, Alexander, also enrolled. Mabry and Sadie Oglesby both stated that they had accepted the Faith in 1914; they reared their young daughter, Bertha Parvine, as a Bahá'í. Mrs. Oglesby and her daughter became the first black American women to make a pilgrimage to the Bahá'í World Center in the Holy Land. In Chicago Georgia M. DeBaptiste Faulkner entered the Faith in 1918 and, as a new member of the community, held weekly meetings in her home. Roy Williams and his sister Amy Williams both became Bahá'ís in New York City in 1918.

Eighteen others stated that they had enrolled between 1921 and 1926; thirty-seven between 1927 and 1933, during the heyday of racial amity activity; and fourteen in 1934 and 1935, the last years that seem to be well represented in the survey. (Four cards listed no date at all.) The years with the largest number of black respondents entering the Faith were 1932 (with fourteen), 1929 (with ten), 1935 (with nine), and 1921 (with six). Thus a large proportion of the active black Bahá'ís in the mid-1930s were recent entrants, from the era of emphasis on racial amity.

The survey does not show any consistent correlation between the holding of race amity conferences and an increase in black enrollments in the cities where the conferences were held. Philadelphia, Pittsburgh, and Cincinnati did gain some black members around the time of amity conferences they sponsored, but there is no evidence to suggest that the conferences led to the enrollments. One of those who became a Bahá'í in Cincinnati in 1935, the year of its first amity conference, was Elsie Austin, who was elected to the National Spiritual Assembly eleven years later.

The records indicate that Chicago experienced a significant growth in black membership beginning in 1932. Among the new Bahá'ís from that period was Ellsworth Blackwell, who enrolled in 1932 and became the fourth black elected to the National Spiritual Assembly. Chicago's amity committee was one of the most active in the nation at that time. The figures do not reveal, however, whether successful expansion efforts among blacks caused amity activities to flourish or whether the demonstration of principle led to increased enrollments. In either case Chicago rapidly became well-known as an interracial community.

The impact of the Bahá'í Faith on Chicago's black population and its reputation as an interracial movement are corroborated by a major study done in the 1930s and published under the title *Black Metropolis*. Based on research financed by the Works Projects Administration, the two-volume work mentions "Bahai" a number of times. In a section on the community's upper class an unnamed Bahá'í "who was reputed to have a white wife" was numbered among the thirty-one individuals who were unanimously agreed to be truly upper-class by their peers. Robert S. Abbott was described in another passage as having been a "key" man in the upper class; it is not clear whether his Bahá'í affiliation was known. [4] All of the other references to the Bahá'ís occur in a section on intermarriage. The Bahá'í Faith is described as one of two groups— the other being "left-wingers"—"which not only tolerate but, by their social philosophies, tend to encourage intermarriage." The story of an interracial Bahá'í couple is given in detail. Extending over five pages, the case of "Mr. and Mrs. Brown" is used to illustrate "how a mixed couple which begins as an ordinary middle-class family may be attracted to a group such as Bahai, to obtain social reassurance amid the vicissitudes of a world that can be rather rough on the intermarried." The Browns not only attended Bahá'í meetings regularly but socialized with other Bahá'ís—a majority of whom were white—in their leisure time. Their affiliation is described as being "the great stabilizing force in the lives of the Browns." [5] It is no wonder that black enrollments and amity activities abounded in Chicago, where interracial unity among the Bahá'ís was so evident.

In contrast to Chicago, New York did not have any respondents dating their enrollment from the period of outstanding amity work. Neither did Washington, D. C., after 1918. Of all the communities represented, Chicago led by a large margin with seventeen black respondents. Boston, where the Oglesbys and the Mapps were among the few entire black families in the United States to accept the Faith, followed with ten. Next came Washington with seven, all from the years when Louis Gregory resided there, and New York City with six. Seattle, which seems to have supported racial amity activity consistently, without ever sponsoring large-scale events, also had six black respondents, four dating from 1921–24, when Louis Gregory visited the Northwest and racial amity was first emphasized. Thus the figures suggest that amity activity did not necessarily lead directly to increases in black membership but that it probably contributed to the creation of a climate favorable to the spread of the Faith among blacks. The accomplishments of national and local amity committees are best measured by intangibles: increased goodwill, identification of the Bahá'í Faith with the cause of brotherhood, and moral support for the black believers.

The role of Louis Gregory is also suggested, if not easily measured, by the results of the survey. The years of his service on the National Spiritual Assembly, 1927–32, were not only the most active in amity activity but, according to the Historical Records Cards, also saw increased enrollments by blacks. Moreover, after 1932, at least four of the sixteen new black Bahá'ís can be attributed to his teaching work. Three were from Nashville, where he settled long enough to raise up an active new community. The fourth was his old friend Thomas C. Chapman, whose wife, Edith, had become a Bahá'í some years earlier. Yet Mr. Gregory's long years of effort in the South were not reflected in the survey. The Historical Records Cards do not reveal seeds sown, hearts touched, or commitments gained that could not be strengthened because years passed before Mr. Gregory or any other Bahá'í visited again. George Henderson and the other Bahá'ís in Memphis seem to have been drawn into the administrative order only in the 1940s, and Atlanta did not have a functioning Spiritual Assembly until the late 1930s. Louisville, Miami, Charleston—all of which had black members at one time—either did not have any longer or did not assure their participation in the survey.

BAHÁ'Í HISTORICAL RECORD

1. **Louis George Gregory**
   Name of individual believer

2. Reported through Spiritual Assembly **Eliot, Maine**
   City

3. Address **47** , **South** ,
   Number   *Street*

      Portsmouth,   **N. H.**
      City   *State*

4. Birthplace **Charleston S. C.**   Birthdate **6 June, 1874**

5. Naturalization (if foreign born)
        City and State   *Date*

6. National origin
   (Whether of English or other stock)   7. Race **Negro**

8. Color **Brown**   9. Sex **Male**   10. Married? **Yes**   **27 September, 1912**
                                                               Date

11. Children or dependents **None**   **None**
                                Minor   *Adult*

12. Religious origin (religion before becoming a Bahá'í) **Christian (Congregational Church)**

13. Date of acceptance of the Bahá'í Faith **On or about June, 1909.**

   A. As isolated believer   B. As member of Bahá'í group   C. As member of Bahá'í Community **Yes**

14. Place of acceptance of Bahá'í Faith **Washington, D. C.**

[SEE OVER]

15. Date of enrolment in present Bahá'í community (No. 2) .... ; ...... 4 August, 1935 ....

A. By transfer from previous community .... Yes ....; B. By enrollment as Bahá'í for first time ....

C. Subsequent transfers (leave blank) *In Boston Community Oct. 7, '36.*

16. General information you would like to have preserved in this historical record
(about Bahá'í services, connection with the Cause in early days, special talents, etc.)
Member, Bahá'í Temple Unity, 1912 to 1913
Member, National Spiritual Assembly, 1922 to 1924
and 1927 to 1932, 7 years in all.
Served as either secretary or chairman
Member, National Race Amity
Committee, 1927 to 1935. As travelling worker helped to
spread the Message in Canada and in nearly all of the United
States, especially the Southern states. Also served with
Race Amity Conferences in many cities. Pilgrimage to Akka
and Haifa in 1911, meeting 'Abdu'l Baha and Shoghi Effendi,
the latter a youth of fifteen, at Ramleh, Egypt. Here also
met Louise A. M. Mathew of England, whom I married a year
later by the advice and instructions of 'Abdu'l Baha.
(Additional notes may be attached to this card.)

17. Additional information (do not fill in)

Transmitted to Boston Community Oct. 7, '36.

19. Signature

Louis G. Gregory.

18. Photograph
(If possible, please attach photograph to
this record. Write name and date the picture was taken on back of photograph.)

Even among the ninety-nine respondents, Louis Gregory's influence would probably have been more clearly seen if more had filled out the section that asked for background information. Many left us with only the bare bones of dates and places. Others stated simply that they taught the Faith. Even those who chose to write something of themselves tended to reveal their humble devotion more than their origins or accomplishments. "The best that I can say, no special talents have I, but the Cause itself was a great inspiration for me to take new courage," Coranne Willis, who became a Bahá'í in Chicago in 1932, recorded. "In turn for my joy, I have given the message to many which is now terminating into good results." The most memorable statements are infused with the same spirit of joy. "In the name of God, I am more than happy to know of the Faith and Words of Baha'u'llah," Mount Oliver Roberts of Seattle wrote with touching sincerity. "Its sound like the tone of a bell in my mind at all times, and it make me very happy in this day."

Thus, if the Historical Records Cards tell only a small part of the story of black Americans in the Bahá'í community in the 1930s, they nonetheless provide some fascinating glimpses into Bahá'í history and a few sincere personal statements that speak volumes about the views of the black Bahá'ís at the time. Like Louis Gregory, they were fully aware that human unity was not a "side issue." It was the very core of a Faith that they had accepted with all their hearts. "I came in the Cause because I had a longing for the Oneness of Mankind," Lillian D. Manson, a New Yorker, stated simply. Another New York Bahá'í, Annie K. Lewis, who served on the national amity committee from 1932 to 1935, summarized the goals that motivated her efforts: "My only desire is to live to serve the Cause of Baha'u'llah. To work interracial till all mankind can live in peace, love and harmony and . . . to build the new world order."

20   A Cycle Ends

In the mid-1930s the longing for racial unity that animated the black Bahá'ís contrasted with the growing heedlessness of the American Bahá'í community as a whole. The slackening pace of amity activities between 1933 and 1936 betrayed a loss of enthusiasm for an endeavor that Louis Gregory had described as being demanding and challenging, fraught with tests that were " 'many and severe.' "[1] More than anything else, perhaps, his eloquence and magnetism kept the program alive while other concerns gained precedence. The Bahá'ís in Iran were enduring a wave of severe persecution; one of its consequences was the forced closing of the Tarbíyat School in Ṭihrán, the first educational institution for girls in the country, which had been established a quarter of a century earlier by an American Bahá'í, Dr. Susan Moody, and supported and staffed by American Bahá'ís over the years. In the Soviet Union the continued existence of a strong Bahá'í community in Turkistán, where the first Bahá'í Temple had been constructed early in the century, was seriously threatened. The world situation was equally bleak and unpredictable: the Depression continued to take its toll, and the fragile political order that had been established after the First World War began to crumble in Europe and Asia. Under the circumstances the dangers of racial injustice in America competed with an array of other problems for the attention of the American Bahá'ís.

Racial amity was further deemphasized in 1935, when the National Spiritual Assembly decided not to reappoint Louis Gregory to the amity committee. If he had any forebodings about the future of the program, they were at first outweighed by feelings of relief. "I am no longer on the Amity Committee," he wrote Edith Chapman, "and think the change is wise to prevent crystalization. Change is good in all such matters. I did not seek it but rather felt it was coming." Indeed, his exclusion from the committee wholly resolved an old dilemma. For years he had been uncomfortable with the role of spokesman for racial amity, "a colored man always clamoring for colored people's rights," and his presence on the committee had always made such leadership unavoidable. "I have always greatly enjoyed the work of this committee, which has been greatly confirmed," he confided. "But it has been embarrassing to be chairman." He preferred to support a committee led by white Bahá'ís.[2]

In fact, he did just this in 1935–36, while Loulie Mathews served as chairman. "Mr. Louis Gregory was asked to teach wherever opportunity offered," the committee's annual report observed; thus he experienced the satisfactions of traveling as a racial amity worker without the burdens of administrative duties. Many of the activities that year, according to the committee's report, were the result of a lecture tour he made in Ohio, Michigan, and Indiana. He spoke a number of times in Toledo and Ann Arbor, once to a class on race relations at the University of Toledo; in Lima to two black churches and a regularly scheduled weekly amity meeting sponsored by the Bahá'ís (one of very few in the country at that time); in Columbus and Cincinnati to four or five audiences each; in Dayton to groups at Wilberforce University five or six times and to the congregation of a Unitarian church; and in Cleveland to as many as five schools and clubs in one day ("indeed a very strenuous day"). Outside of New York City, which maintained a schedule of varied and frequent amity activities, the only other events reported for 1935–36 were an All Nations Conference held by the Milwaukee Assembly with the assistance of the N.A.A.C.P., the Urban League, and the Y.W.C.A., and the ninth annual race amity conference at Green Acre.[3]

The Green Acre conference was the culmination of a series of annual meetings going back to 1927, when Shoghi Effendi specifically urged that Green Acre be made a center for racial amity. Over the years many of the best known Bahá'í lecturers had spoken on race at Green Acre, as had a number of outstanding guests: scholars, theologians, representatives of the Urban League and the N.A.A.C.P.

The Green Acre conference was held that year on 17–18 August, following a week-long course on "Racial Likenesses and Differences: The Scientific Evidence and the Bahá'í Teachings" taught by Dr. Genevieve Coy, then principal of the Dalton School in New York. Dr. Coy also spoke at the conference, along with Dr. Glenn Shook of Wheaton College, Professor Stanwood Cobb, Alfred Lunt, and Dr. Samuel C. Mitchell, a Southern educator who had met 'Abdu'l-Bahá at the Lake Mohonk Peace Conference in 1912. Mr. Gregory reported that the event "attracted to Green Acre a varied and interesting company of friends representing many cities of America and some foreign lands."[4]

Louis Gregory's reports on race amity, many of which were published in *The Bahá'í World,* an international record of the development of the Faith, always emphasized the Green Acre conferences and described them in favorable terms. Often their success had to be measured by the interest and enthusiasm of those present rather than by the number attending. From the start Mr. Gregory had worried about attracting enough people—white and especially black—to Green Acre, particularly if the conference was scheduled in July, when attendance at the school tended to be low. The first year he had found it necessary to assign himself as chairman of one of the sessions, "so that the affair would not be too one-sided"; this apparently led to "a little under-current of bad feeling" among some of the Bahá'ís, an attitude which he found difficult to bear. But he did not allow either the undependability of support or the narrow criticism to dishearten him. He continued to be the mainstay of the conferences, and after the summer of 1933 he shared with Edith Chapman his obvious satisfaction over the success of Green Acre as a place of interracial fellowship: "Especially was it pleasing to see colored people of capacity coming during the entire season."[5] The lack of financial resources sometimes hindered the amity work at Green Acre. Nonetheless, Louis Gregory always devoted time and effort to it because Shoghi Effendi had encouraged it and because, regardless of the fluctuating fortunes of the national amity committee, the Green Acre conferences constituted one area of effort that was pursued with continuity year after year.

In 1935–36, when the fortunes of the amity committee were at a particularly low point, it sent out a questionnaire to all Spiritual Assemblies, inquiring about the ease or difficulty of "race adjustment" in the local community, the reasons for any difficulty, the effectiveness of the local amity committee, the relationship of the local committee with the Assembly under which it served, and the need for literature and speakers on the topic of racial amity. All the Assemblies responded. Most claimed that racial amity prevailed, and so many requested literature that the committee mailed to all *The Oneness of Mankind,* a compilation from the Bahá'í writings on race prepared by Mariam Haney and Louis Gregory.[6] Yet the responses, positive in tone as they were, also indicated some of the attitudes that workers for racial amity faced. The Assemblies did not seem to recognize that a problem existed, and, if they did, they tended to ignore or neglect it. Very few reported having delegated racial amity work to committees, with the result that, overburdened with other responsibilities, they seldom found time for its demands.

The San Francisco Spiritual Assembly's response to the questionnaire typified the paradoxical stand of many Bahá'ís at this time. Indeed, it so aptly expressed prevailing attitudes that the amity committee itself quoted it in its annual report, convinced that San Francisco's view was "worthy of holding as the right note for Amity in this Day": "the Bahá'í faith is not an inter-racial movement. It is a religious faith based on the oneness of humanity, one God and one universal world order through which mankind may progress. In this World Order, race is not recognized and therefore within the faith, there is no such thing as race, or race consciousness."[7]

Neither the San Francisco Bahá'ís nor the members of the national amity committee who shared this view seemed to realize its implications for a program that had been brought into existence by 'Abdu'l-Bahá, championed by Shoghi Effendi, and firmly grounded in the belief that differences were to be celebrated for their variety rather than ignored. In upholding this position as the keynote for the year, the committee unknowingly wrote its own epitaph. When new committee appointments were announced in July 1936, the following statement appeared under the familiar heading of "Race Amity": "The National Assembly has appointed no Race Amity Committee this year. Its view is that race amity activities have sometimes resulted in emphasizing race differences rather than their unity and reconciliation within the Cause. Local Assemblies are requested to provide for amity meetings and regard them as a direct part of teaching."[8]

The National Assembly's explanation posed a paradox of its

own: the national committee was discontinued because race amity activities had the negative effect of emphasizing "race differences," but Local Assemblies were requested "to provide for amity meetings." The statement, and the questions it left unresolved, shadowed the subject of race over the next three years.

In fact, most local communities had not been truly engaged in amity work since 1933. Before that their efforts had been stimulated by the national committee and by a general feeling that the work was important to the National Spiritual Assembly and above all to the Guardian. When the scope of the national committee was curtailed and the local communities were assigned responsibility for carrying on amity work in the mid-1930s, interest and commitment had declined markedly, contracting into a few large urban centers. From 1936 to 1939, after the national committee was disbanded, even these cities appear to have focused their energies on other projects.

Individuals who had been devoted to race amity did not suddenly abandon their concern, of course. At least a few communities probably carried on some kind of racial amity program. Chicago, with its large black membership, reported its well-publicized amity meetings in the March 1937 issue of *Baha'i News,* for example.[9] But elsewhere, if such activities existed, they were either not reported or little noticed. Even the annual race amity conferences at Green Acre were discontinued. The word *race* virtually disappeared from the pages of *Baha'i News.*

*Part 3/**A Middle Passage**

21 Crisis

For Louis Gregory, whose life work had been based on the conviction that among the Bahá'ís "inter-racial understanding" must be "to the fore," 1936 was undoubtedly a dark year. The discontinuation of the race amity committee was the climax of a series of events that could easily have been seen, even by so unassuming an individual, as a deliberate repudiation of all his efforts over the past twenty years. That he did not yield to feelings of rejection was largely the result of his having resolved a crisis that developed in 1932, when the National Spiritual Assembly, to which he had not been reelected for the first time in five years, voted to relieve him of his responsibilities as a full-time worker for the Faith.

Since 1917 he had not been financially independent. At the age of forty-three he had given up his livelihood in order to free himself to travel in the South and had sold his home to finance the effort, devoting himself wholly to his new calling. After his own funds were depleted, subsidization by the Bahá'í community had enabled him to continue. Gradually the arrangement that had been made in the early days of the Divine Plan had become formalized, assuring his uninterrupted services, and those of Albert Vail as well. The modest expenses of both were met by the National Bahá'í Fund.

Although some of the Bahá'ís were apparently uncomfortable about the practice, in view of the strictures against a paid clergy in the Bahá'í teachings, the general view seems to have been that the two men were not in fact salaried. Moreover, Shoghi Effendi, the authority on all such matters, had never ruled against the policy—according to Louis Gregory, not even when appealed to by a group of believers in 1923.[1] Thereafter, the subsidy had become a fixed item in the annual budget of the National Spiritual Assembly. In the year 1929–30, for example, $5,760 was budgeted for the "expenses of two teachers." The only other paid worker for the Faith at that time was the national secretary, who received two months' salary for a total of six hundred dollars.[2]

The investment in Louis Gregory's work enabled him to make unique contributions to the cause of racial unity and to the expansion of the Bahá'í Faith in this early period. For a decade he spent most of each year on the road, speaking of unity to thousands of people in diverse audiences all over the country. Doors to black organizations and schools, particularly in the South, seem always to have opened readily to him. The patterns of his service changed between 1922 and 1924, because of his membership in the National Spiritual Assembly, and again in 1927, when he was appointed executive secretary of the new amity committee and also reelected to the National Assembly. He regretted some aspects of his changed responsibilities, but he acquiesced. For him, the needs of the Faith had outweighed any personal considerations since 1917. He assumed that they always would.

There was no reason to doubt the continuation of Louis Gregory's position as a subsidized teacher until the end of 1931, when the policy was brought up for reconsideration by the National Spiritual Assembly on the eve of his first interracial teaching trip to the South. He was asked before he left to seek the views of the amity committee and of the National Teaching Committee, which was divided into eastern and western branches. The evaluation took place while he was engaged in a venture that proved to be not only an historic achievement but one of the crowning experiences of his life. The weeks he spent traveling with Willard McKay were a fulfillment of the dreams of equality that had been shattered in his Southern boyhood, a testament to the viability of the Bahá'í path to reconstruction, and a compensation for the manifold sacrifices, hardships, and lonely humiliations he had endured along the way. He returned north to find that the race amity committee and the eastern arm of the teaching committee had given highly favorable evaluations.

In January he forwarded these to Alfred Lunt, who was then secretary of the National Spiritual Assembly. As Louis Gregory and those of like views seemed to feel that itinerant teaching itself was in question, he added an impassioned defense of his chosen field of service. ''There is a mysterious connection between motion and life," he asserted. " 'Abdu'l Bahá makes one the test of the reality of the other. Yet is death so much easier than life and the discomforts, hardships and perils of travel are so far greater than the comforts of home, that it would be passing strange for anyone to prefer the former as a habit unless it be with a wish to please God rather than self."[3]

The National Assembly at its February meeting, in the absence of Louis Gregory, decided to drop the matter. It was brought up again a few months later, however, by the western branch of the National Teaching Committee, which stood alone among the committees concerned in its opposition to the subsidization of teachers. Its position, as the secretary of the committee, Charlotte Linfoot, explained it to the National Assembly, was that itinerant teaching was so vital that it should in no way be limited to a few paid individuals—as had been true in the past, the committee implied. Furthermore, the rise of a number of self-supporting teachers during the previous two years should not be curbed by limiting "the teaching to lecture campaigns on the part of supported, traveling teachers."[4] There is no indication that anyone was suggesting such a restriction (least of all Louis Gregory and Albert Vail themselves); indeed, the rise of self-supporting teachers to which the committee referred would seem to confirm that the existence of two subsidized teachers had not prevented the emergence of others. The letter did suggest one important point, however: the issue was not the value of itinerant teaching but the means by which it was to be accomplished.

The receipt of this letter just before the national convention reopened the subject at a time when it could not be resolved by that year's National Assembly. Thus Louis Gregory went to the convention in a state of some uncertainty. When he was not reelected to the National Spiritual Assembly, his position became even more insecure. His pride was not injured by the election results, but he had long since recognized that, in his case, there were forces at work behind the numbers of votes cast.

In 1922, for example, his election to the National Spiritual Assembly caused him to be subjected to an undercurrent of suspicion about his influence on the voting process. He confided to Alfred Lunt nearly a year later that, "toward the end" of the convention, after the election results were announced, he became aware of a negative reaction:

> I was greatly astonished to find a few people whom I love very dearly in a very critical and antagonistic attitude toward me. It was difficult to understand, but later a friend whispered to me that some persons whose expectations were disappointed in the election of the N. S. A. had spread the report that certain of them were defeated and my election secured by political juggling, to wit, that the Credentials Committee, on my influence had filled the vacancies in the list of delegates with people who would favor my aspirations for membership on the N. S. A. It appears that a few people actually believed this. It is hardly necesary to state its absurdity in point of fact.

Then he added, with his usual good humor: "It appears that among those who that day prayed that God would direct and guide the election of the N.S.A. were some who had little faith in their own prayers, especially as the result was in part, at least, contrary to their wishes."[5]

The gossip did not offend him personally. "I believe that false reports ever return, sooner or later, to those who utter them." Nor did he hold a grudge. "Certainly I have now no ill will toward those who circulated such a report. It was no doubt prompted by grievous disappointment. In the end, may all be healed." He was putting the incident in writing, he added, not because he had any doubts about Mr. Lunt's attitude toward him, but only because it was "barely possible" that he might "need an understanding of the facts."[6] Under the circumstances, Mr. Gregory's feeling that his period of membership on the national body was "almost ended" is understandable.[7] Nevertheless, he was reelected the following year and in 1927, after a two-year respite, began a long period of uninterrupted membership on the Assembly.

Although the election system was clarified and regulated under the Guardian so that there was no longer any possibility of juggling delegates (or of accusing anyone of such a flagrant assault on the underlying principles of Bahá'í administration), the partisan spirit did not immediately disappear. It focused once again on Louis Gregory before the 1932 convention. According to a statement that he later made to the National Spiritual Assembly, a letter from the National Teaching Committee to ''the various spiritual assemblies'' had implied that he ''should not be reelected to membership on the N. S. A. because of the necessary loss thereby to my teaching activities.'' Although the National Assembly had subsequently ''reproved'' the committee for violating the spirit of the Bahá'í election process, Mr. Gregory noted, the damage that had been done was irreversible and had in fact persisted in the convention itself: ''A number of very reliable people have told me that they were approached by people in the convention who asked them not to vote for me on the sole ground that I was a teacher.''[8]

He was disturbed both by the effort to wield such influence over the election and by its success. The issue, as he presented it, was one of justice rather than of personal loss or gain:

> Not being a member of the N. S. A. is no loss to me. I have no liking for administrative work. The sole value of my being there, if any, was the prestige it gave the amity work and the hope it spread among the darker peoples. This matter is mentioned, however, because I am wondering what your reactions would have been had politics . . . affected any other member of your body as it has me. . . . Can it be denied that politics in the cause is deplorable, contrary to the teachings, and may later recur to affect even you as it has me?[9]

Louis Gregory was the only member of the National Spiritual Assembly not reelected that year. The body met immediately after the Convention and voted to dispense with his services and those of Albert Vail. At that meeting Horace Holley was also elected secretary, replacing Alfred Lunt, who had served in that office for the past two years. Thus it was Mr. Holley who informed Louis Gregory on behalf of the Assembly that ''after most careful consideration it was felt that the institution of national teachers as maintained for many years has achieved its purpose in the construction of the Temple edifice.'' The teachers' expenses were to be paid through January 1933, the tenth month of the fiscal year, providing a period during which ''the Assembly believes that it will be possible for you to resume some professional work which will supply you with an economic foundation for your living in future.'' Their activities until January were to be left to their discretion, as ''the members thoroughly understand that during this time it will not be possible for you to give your full time to the teaching work.'' The Assembly expressed confidence ''that this change coincides not only with the immediate urgent needs of the Cause but with the profound spiritual principles controlling the life of every believer.'' The letter ended with expressions of ''heartfelt gratitude'' for Louis Gregory's ''noble and self-sacrificing services'' and ''loving best wishes'' for ''success in finding a position which will give full expression to your unusual gifts.''[10]

In view of the undercurrents before the convention, the National Assembly's decision could hardly have come as a surprise. Yet the apparent speed and coolness with which the two men were dispatched shocked Louis Gregory profoundly. He had weathered many storms in more than twenty years as a Bahá'í, beginning with his early confrontations over race in Washington, D.C. The passing of 'Abdu'l-Bahá had grieved but had not shaken him; his loyalty to Shoghi Effendi, unstinting from the announcement of the Master's chosen successor, had protected him from the excessive sense of loss that had weakened the faith of some of the older believers. With an attitude of patient optimism and a keen sense of humor he had met insensitivity, paternalism, hostility to his marriage, and patent prejudice among some of the Bahá'ís. ''If my work up to the present shows any signs of success,'' he later told the National Assembly, ''it has largely been by avoiding issues, depending upon the confirmations and continuing the effort under terms favorable or otherwise.''[11] In short, he had persevered.

But this test was unlike any other in his experience. His brief reply to the letter of dismissal revealed uncharacteristic bitterness: ''Please convey to the National Assembly my thanks for what the details of their action may imply of personal consideration and kindness.'' Having received the news as he was about to start on a tour of the northeastern states, he advised the National Spiritual Assembly that he might have more to say later on. ''It is barely possible,'' he wrote from Racine, Wisconsin, ''that later, when there is more time for reflection than these strenuous days afford, I shall write more fully.''[12]

His and Albert Vail's reflections were bound to return to one inescapable factor: the deficiency of the Bahá'í Fund. In March 1932, shortly after the issue of subsidization had come under consideration, Shoghi Effendi had written, "I grieve, beyond words, to learn of the scanty response of the friends to the Plan of Unified Action. . . ." The deepening Depression had adversely affected the next phase of Temple construction under the plan. The crisis lent a sense of urgency to the reexamination of every projected expenditure in the national Bahá'í budget. Although none of the committees had evaluated the subsidization in economic terms, the financial explanation became more prominent after the decision to dismiss the teachers had been made. The National Spiritual Assembly's letter of 5 May to Louis Gregory referred to "the immediate urgent needs of the Cause" and to the need "to effect a greater concentration of Baha'i activities throughout the coming year." Individual Bahá'ís seem also to have understood the decision to be fiscally based. Harlan Ober, for example, attributed the new policy to a general desire to cut expenses. "Undoubtedly the friends are anxious to save for the great effort ahead, at every turn," he wrote Alfred Lunt early in May. Later in the year Louis Gregory himself explained the move in similar terms. "The fund that supports Mr. Vail and myself," he wrote Edith Chapman, "is now needed for the Temple. . . ."[13]

From the point of view of the two traveling teachers, however, the economic rationale offered little comfort. With unemployment at its height, neither the ten-month-long reprieve nor the National Assembly's "best wishes" for success resolved their predicament. Both men had particular disadvantages as they faced the necessity to look for work. As a former clergyman, Albert Vail could hardly return to the profession for which he had been trained. Louis Gregory at fifty-eight had not practiced law for fifteen years. Although in more prosperous times he might have gone back to his profession (he had sought and gained admission to the bar in New Hampshire in 1930, possibly with the need for such an alternative in mind), the depths of the Great Depression made this course impossible.[14] Blacks had been even harder hit than other Americans, and prospects for black professionals in all fields were severely curtailed. Thus even a change of occupation—to teaching, for example—seemed unlikely to improve Mr. Gregory's position.

No matter how it was handled, the termination of Albert Vail's and Louis Gregory's status would have been trying for them personally, at their age and under such dismal social conditions. It would have required supreme objectivity for them to regard the end of their long years of service solely in terms of the "spiritual principles" that the National Assembly mentioned in passing. Given the tangle of views and actions that preceded the decision, other factors—such as personal motives—seemed at first to be both more pertinent and less "spiritual" than the official explanations.

At home in Portsmouth, New Hampshire, Louis Gregory finally composed a six-page letter to the National Spiritual Assembly. On 13 June he sent a draft to Alfred Lunt, seeking his advice. "With Louise away, there is no one here at present with whom I can consult about it. . . . Please read it over," he asked, "give me your suggestions and best judgment about it and then return it." He explained that he had decided to seek a review of the National Assembly's decision because of the manner in which it had been reached.[15] Indeed, the decision itself, although he disagreed with it, disturbed him far less than its timing and circumstances. As a loyal Bahá'í, he was bound to abide by the decisions of the Assembly, regardless of his personal views, for the sake of unity and in the assurance that any unwisdom would become obvious through compliance sooner than through subversion. In this case, however, the appearance of injustice impelled him to appeal.

At least in part, he saw the National Assembly's action, coupled with the recent election of Horace Holley as the body's chief executive officer, as evidence of Mr. Holley's increasing authority. In his first response to the news of his dismissal, he complimented the new secretary on his personal "victory" in achieving his aim after "efforts in this direction . . . oft and on over a period of nine years." His perception of Mr. Holley's persistent opposition and his knowledge of events during the previous months led him to conclude that the reversal of the Assembly's policy had not been the result of a disinterested review. As he told Alfred Lunt, "While I am quite confident that the plan to do away with Albert and myself was quite mature in the mind of Horace, yet my impression is that, from other things that occurred, there was not time to give the matter mature consultation at [the] Chicago meeting."[16]

He worried a bit about the tone that he had adopted in the letter, fearing in particular that Horace Holley might "take my banter so seriously as to become angry." "I am telling but the naked truth," he claimed, "that sometimes annoys people more than fiction. Of course I do not wish to do this with Horace." But Alfred Lunt had no objection to the letter's "humor and wit" and saw nothing in it to eliminate. Nor did he have any qualms about the issues Mr. Gregory raised. "It is just the sort of letter which the members should receive. . . . The spiritual implications of the letter are irrefutable and unerringly point to a condition which, to say the least, calls for very careful attention on the part of the members." He urged Mr. Gregory to "send the letter at once" and assured him that "in the long run it will do a great deal of good."[17]

Mr. Lunt's response suggested that he, too, was troubled by the circumstances surrounding Louis Gregory's changed status. He had already alluded, in an exchange of letters with Harlan Ober in May, to his regret about the election results. "It is most unfortunate," Mr. Lunt observed, "that no colored Bahai is on the Assembly." Although he did not refer to any attempt to influence the election directly, he linked the voting pattern to a periodic change of mood among the Bahá'ís, claiming that "every few years a reactionary trend seems to take possession." Both he and Harlan Ober were concerned about the impression that had been created by the National Assembly's decision to dismiss Louis Gregory immediately after the election. Mr. Ober remarked that "it is unfortunate that the old N.S.A. did not take this action, for the N.S.A. is changed in only one person."[18]

Louis Gregory followed Alfred Lunt's advice and completed the letter on 18 June, intending to send each member of the National Assembly a copy to read before their next meeting. When the meeting was postponed until 20 August, some sense of immediacy was undoubtedly lost, although the members were given two full months to reflect on Mr. Gregory's appeal.

He gave them much to consider. First, he called attention to the dubious appearance of the sequence of events that had resulted in the change in his status, beginning with the National Teaching Committee's "propaganda," which the National Assembly criticized but did not counteract, and ending with his summary dismissal after the convention. He clearly believed that the intention of manipulation was corroborated by these occurrences and that he had been the object of nothing less than a twofold rejection: "Thus am I doubly assured of your wish to dispense with my humble services."[19]

He questioned several aspects of the Assembly's decision, particularly in view of the explanation he had finally been given—that the teachers had worked themselves out of a job, in effect, by achieving their "purpose," which was "the construction of the Temple edifice." Louis Gregory had never understood this to be his purpose, and having been privy to the first round of consultation on the issue when he was still a member of the National Assembly, he found this rationale to be not only surprising but irrelevant—indeed, "indigestible."[20]

Rather than having worked themselves out of a job, he felt that the teachers had never seen greater opportunities for service. "The year ended was the most successful ever known in both amity and teaching fields," he claimed. "Corporations do not usually dismiss their workers when at the peak of success with the greatest demand coming from many directions for their services." The endorsement of continued subsidization of the two teachers that had been made by the amity committee and the eastern members of the National Teaching Committee several months earlier further confirmed his view that the system was working well and was more productive of visible results than ever before.[21]

Underlying these considerations, however, was Louis Gregory's conviction that his work had been initiated by 'Abdu'l-Bahá and had gained the implicit approval of Shoghi Effendi:

> Since the whole arrangement for these very humble activities of mine to be supported out of the Baha'i Funds, and this entirely without any solicitation on my part was made by 'Abdu'l Baha Himself and since that arrangement, brought to the attention of the Guardian, has been continued, would it not be better in an official, open and frank manner to consult the Guardian about it before arbitrarily ending it? I have been advised to appeal to the Guardian, but have declined, because I do not favor appeals except in very extraordinary matters and do not think the Guardian should be embarrassed by such matters as can be settled amicably by the friends themselves.[22]

With little reason to be convinced of the propriety of either the decision or the decision-making process, Louis Gregory could only conclude that politics and personality had triumphed over principle. Normally he would have minimized the personal elements of the problem. Over the years he had become a master at maintaining his dignity while cultivating a deeply ingrained habit of self-effacement. But, finally, this rejection was too much.

He was convinced that the rejection was the result of Horace Holley's ''dislike'' for Albert Vail and himself and of old rivalries going back to the days when the world unity program (in which Mr. Holley was deeply involved) vied with racial amity as the focus for public proclamations. Thus he questioned the motives behind Mr. Holley's persistent efforts to ''bring my teaching activities to a close.'' He also believed that Horace Holley exercised an undue influence over the National Assembly, a condition in which there was ''an element of danger, both for the cause and individual.'' In his distress over this deviation from the spirit of Bahá'í administration, he abandoned tact in favor of frankness:

> I yield to no one in my admiration for . . . [Horace's] abilities. Cleverness, industry, perseverence, efficiency, all have their great value in the cause. Organizations the world over are dominated by such qualities. The overwhelming influence and control which Horace exercises over the N. S. A. are always apparent. A spiritual body, however, does not of necessity register its highest value by these qualities, however valuable and indispensable. It must reflect divine Guidance. Such guidance may often appear through channels of very common clay.[23]

In fact, after years of looking only for good, he justified his bluntness by relating the dismissal to a fundamental social problem: ''In our American life issues between black and white, rich and poor, those who possess and those who lack influence end but one way and that way is obvious.'' Even among the Bahá'ís, he added, ''the same thing often happens that does in the world.'' Thus he spoke out, not only for himself, but for the ''common clay'' of humanity, and in doing so he took the risk of personalizing the crisis. ''Please pardon me, Horace especially,'' he asked, ''for what may be personal in parts of this letter. I want no issue with you or Horace. I want only facts looked in the eye and justice with kindliness.''[24]

As for Albert Vail, Mr. Gregory feared that there had been neither justice nor kindliness in the way that his colleague had been treated:

The report that he is now looking for a church has deep pathos. Think of him seeking shelter in the church which he abandoned to serve the Cause of God! Would an Oriental teacher be forced to ask a Mosque for aid? Will such knowledge if spread help this glorious cause? When the entire clergy of America were asleep, Albert was awake and went and put himself at the feet of the Master. Since then he left his church. Since then he has refused a salary of $7500 from another church because of his loyalty to this cause. Do you think that the one at whose feet he [knelt] is absent or out of the picture or will forget? I swear by the Greatest Name, upon which my hope depends for time and eternity, that if Albert Vail is now pierced by the sword of rancor, (which God forbid!) I would far rather be he than the wielder of that sword.[25]

In his impassioned defense of Albert Vail, as in the candor of the rest of the letter, he revealed much more of himself than he was accustomed to show. As a Bahá'í, he had learned since 1909 to give freely of the abundant qualities of his good nature: love, patience, optimism, strength, and joviality. During all these years probably no one had ever seen him discouraged or bitter, gripped by indignation, or wounded by rejection. There is no evidence from any of the people closest to him that he ever manifested any behavior more discomposed than the short-lived irritability that his wife had once attributed to exhaustion. The old hurts that his letter to the National Assembly reveals attest to his strength of character, which had enabled him to transcend the pain these trials had caused him and go on with his work.

His honesty with the National Assembly also constituted an act of trust. "In writing you thus fully I have shown you the depths of my own heart," he admitted. He asked the Assembly to consider the issue in the broad perspective of the need for teachers and the desires of 'Abdu'l-Bahá, with attention to the question of fairness in the decision-making process. But above all he challenged the Assembly to deal with the human element, with feelings of loss and sadness, humiliation, devotion to duty:

My first impulse was to accept the situation, to feel that my work was over and to retire from the field. But as I have prayed over the matter what has continually come to me is what I have written out for you. . . . Personally I am willing to be sacrificed, but the pleading souls that appear everywhere hold my attention and their abandonment, the thought of it, makes me inexpressibly sad. Personally I have always regretted the matter of being supported out of the funds. It has also its difficulties in making one the slave of every contributor. But what has held me has been this: 'Abdu'l Baha, in making the arrangement, told Harry Randall that my work for the cause would be such as would prevent me from earning a living. So under the instructions and stimulus that have flowed from Haifa during the past fifteen or more years I have continued. If the end is now to come I am glad that the responsibility is yours rather than mine.[26]

22 Resolution

Despite Louis Gregory's appeal of 18 June, the National Spiritual Assembly held to its decision to dismiss him and Albert Vail. The issue did not subside, however, for several years. Both men were loved and respected by Bahá'ís around the country; the value of their contributions was well known in virtually all the Bahá'í communities of North America. Countering the inevitable tide of concern for the two workers were the apparent implacability of the National Assembly and the austerity of the national budget. Under the circumstances strong feelings and opinions persisted on both sides of the issue.

The problem was also complicated by the long-term personal conflicts over style and approach that Louis Gregory's letter of appeal had revealed. Alfred Lunt had administered as a man of the people, accessible, warm-hearted, and responsive. The change in the secretaryship of the Assembly in 1932 signaled a shift away from these qualities and toward emphasis on clarity, proficiency, and administrative acumen, characteristics that Horace Holley exemplified. As secretary, Horace Holley was strong in these qualities. Probably no other American Bahá'í of that period understood as readily as he the general outline of Shoghi Effendi's vision. During these early years of the Guardianship the National Assembly was often guided by instinct more than by objective knowledge of principles and precedents. Horace Holley's administrative instincts were sound because he understood Shoghi Effendi's grand design.

In other areas Horace Holley's instincts were less reliable. Having served with him on the National Assembly for a number of years, Alfred Lunt and Louis Gregory perceived him to be autocratic and, therefore, often at odds with the spirit of the Bahá'í order. This perception apparently alienated them to some extent both from Mr. Holley and from his views on administration. Even his fondest admirers have acknowledged that he was difficult to know. The wife of the Guardian, Rúḥíyyih Khánum, who knew Horace Holley well for many years, has noted that ''his often caustic wit, his intense independence and individuality'' caused him to be easily misunderstood. [1] Those who found themselves the object of his wit or who bore the brunt of his independence and individuality—Alfred Lunt and Louis Gregory among them—had to judge for themselves the extent to which Mr. Holley's manner might have betrayed the nature of his heart.

By 1934 attitudes toward the two conflicting styles of administration represented by Alfred Lunt and Horace Holley threatened to polarize the American Bahá'ís. Outwardly, the controversy focused on such issues as the responsibility of the National Assembly members to the electorate, the right of the delegates and the community at large to affect policy, and confidentiality versus openness about the national decision-making process. The intrinsic issues, however, were related to the concern felt by some about the appearance of secrecy, aloofness, and unresponsiveness on the part of the Assembly and about the difficulty of assessing the effectiveness of the individual Assembly members when their positions on the issues were not made public. In his desire to confront these thorny questions Mr. Lunt put himself at risk of infringing on the Bahá'í principle of unified acceptance of any decision made by the majority of an Assembly—if, ''the Lord forbid'' (in 'Abdu'l-Bahá's words), unanimity could not be achieved. [2] Finally the National Assembly went so far as to consider administrative sanctions against Alfred Lunt.

At this point Shoghi Effendi intervened directly and forcefully. He cabled a ''passionate entreaty (and) grave warning'' to the American Bahá'ís, stressing that ''even [the] barest reference to [the] issues involved should be instantly dropped (and) forgotten.'' Although the Guardian took no sides, he reaffirmed the necessity of refraining from even the ''slightest criticism, expressed or implied, that must necessarily impair (the) undivided authority (of the) institution (of the) National Assembly.'' As for Alfred Lunt, Shoghi Effendi simply stated that his membership should be retained. Shoghi Effendi described the consequences of inattention to his instructions in terms that were unthinkable to any sincere Bahá'í: "Present controversy agitating American believers if unchecked will through its inevitable world-wide repercussions inflict irreparable injury (upon) Cause (of) Bahá'u'lláh."[3]

For Shoghi Effendi the overriding issue was unity. " 'If we Bahá'ís cannot attain to cordial unity among ourselves,' " he stated in another context, " 'then we fail to realize the main purpose for which the Báb, Bahá'u'lláh and the Beloved Master lived and suffered.' " And again: " 'Where there is want of harmony, there is lack of the true Bahá'í Spirit. Unless we can show this transformation in our lives, this new power, this mutual love and harmony, then the Bahá'í teachings are but a name to us.' "[4]

The community and the National Spiritual Assembly itself readily heeded the Guardian's plea. Less than a month later Shoghi Effendi wrote to the National Assembly in his own hand: "You have faced a critical situation with marvelous fidelity, high courage and unswerving loyalty. Nothing short of this spirit can enable you to weather the storms and overcome the obstacles that must confront you in the future."[5] In a real sense the Guardian's words were a tribute to both Alfred Lunt and Horace Holley, as well as to the institution they served. Mr. Holley worked tirelessly as a member of the National Spiritual Assembly until 1957 and at the Bahá'í World Center until his death in 1960. Mr. Lunt was returned to the National Assembly at the 1935 convention, when he was also elected chairman of the convention and Horace Holley secretary; he served again in 1936–37. When he died after a short illness in 1937, the Guardian cabled a message to America that praised him highly: "Shocked distressed premature passing esteemed well-beloved Lunt. Future generations will appraise his manifold outstanding contributions to rise and establishment Faith Bahá'u'lláh American continent. Community his bereaved co-workers could ill afford lose such critical period so fearless champion their Cause. . . . Convey Boston community assurance prayers deepest brotherly sympathy their cruel irreparable loss."

The Guardian directed the National Assembly itself to pay Alfred Lunt an unprecedented collective tribute: "Request entire body their National representatives assemble his grave pay tribute my behalf to him who so long and since inception acted as pillar institution they represent.'' Shoghi Effendi made it clear that Alfred Lunt's exceptional services were rooted in his admirable character. He was, as described by the Guardian, '' 'the living embodiment of such a rare combination of qualities as few can display and none can surpass.' ''[6]

The controversy that severely tested the loyalty and cohesiveness of the National Spiritual Assembly during the mid-1930s was paralleled in—and intersected with—the lives of Louis Gregory and Albert Vail. Indeed, the crosscurrents within the national community exacerbated the personal crisis for the two men by emphasizing the ambiguities of their situation. Yet as it gradually became apparent that the decision about their services would not be reversed, both men had no choice but to attempt to come to terms with the change in their lives. The immediate challenge was to overcome, on the one hand, natural feelings of disillusionment and personal rejection—feelings that could only estrange them from the National Assembly and from their fellow believers—and, on the other hand, discouragement about the future.

The hurt and anger that had at first filled Louis Gregory soon dissipated through conscious effort, and the rift between him and Horace Holley was bridged. ''For the sake of the cause and its glorious work we should try to dismiss at the earliest possible moment, all feelings of private griefs and irritation,'' he wrote Mr. Holley in October. In the same letter he sought to clear the air between them. His remarks were both frank and conciliatory:

> My impressions of your attitude toward me arose almost entirely from statements you from time to time made to me and in my hearing, not hearsay. It is conceivable that my view of these may have been exaggerated. There is always such a danger in the realm of the personal.
>
> 'Abdu'l Bahá once referred to one of the friends as having *''a sharp tongue but a kind heart,''* which may also perhaps apply to you. I am glad that you have no consciousness of harmful intent. . . .
>
> I thank you for your expressions of good will, which are reciprocated. I am not unmindful of the heaviness of the burdens of administration and wish for you strength and guidance and happiness therein.[7]

A month and a half later he wrote again to compliment Mr. Holley on his editorial on teaching in the current issue of *Baha'i News*. In a personal vein he added:

> I regret any grief that may have come to you or others from any comments of mine. The fact that my own feelings may have been wounded does not justify one, in the light of the teachings, of being hurtful to others. My shock-absorber has entirely removed my own griefs and may it do the same friendly turn for others. Just now I am very busy with preparation for work which I hope may be the means in future of financing my own Baha'i activities, God willing.[8]

Thus, within six months, he had effectively regained his equilibrium and had set aside his grievances.

Although his wounds were nearly healed, there was as yet no ready solution to the problem at hand: his future means of support. "I sometimes let myself drift into despondency," he confided to Edith Chapman, who was herself experiencing financial difficulties, "but am always ashamed of it. God has given us so much and has promised us so much more."[9]

Even in this difficult transition, however, he did not allow himself to become absorbed by his own worries. He could not forget that the Depression that limited his prospects had already caused widespread suffering, from which he had been spared. "So many people that I know are in serious difficulties that life itself would hardly seem justified," he admitted to Mrs. Chapman, "were I not absolutely assured that through the present depressing conditions the purposes of God are being fulfilled. . . ." In the same letter of 25 December 1932, the fourth he had written after receiving a "despondent" one from her concerning her own economic troubles, he observed that such tests were also useful to the individual by fostering "understanding of the sufferings of others." Although his own future remained uncertain, he enclosed a little money—five dollars—as a token of his concern for his old friends:

> Please accept with a brother's love the pittance that is enclosed. I am sending it not because . . . in itself it has much value, but sometimes by sending small sums to friends who are

distressed it has been the means of starting other things that have brought them prosperity. I hope and pray that it may be so in this case.

Obviously touched by the gesture, and realizing that even five dollars was a sacrifice at that time, Mrs. Chapman noted at the bottom of the letter the amount of money he had sent and that she had later returned six dollars to him.[10]

By the early fall of 1932 Louis Gregory had begun actively looking to the future. He considered going abroad, either to teach in Persia (following a suggestion of 'Abdu'l-Bahá in Egypt in 1911) or to join his wife, Louise, in Europe. If he were to remain in America, the prospect of becoming a paid professional lecturer seemed to hold some promise. On 25 September he wrote to Shoghi Effendi for advice, and, while waiting for an answer, he apparently concentrated on the latter possibility. "For some weeks past I have been trying to work out a plan to finance my own teaching work," he advised Mrs. Chapman on 4 November. "Some very noble friends have come to my aid with business instruction and training. Shoghi Effendi wants my work to continue and so I am hoping to earn enough to carry on. It looks now as if I shall have work which will keep me travelling."[11]

A few weeks later he shared news of his activities with Roy Wilhelm, a long-time colleague on the National Assembly. "I am boning up on such things as food and diet and color and withal how to run a circus," he joked. "As you have had rich experiences in that line I shall greatly appreciate any advice. Does it differ much from running an amity convention? You see I am trying to get ready to finance my own Baha'i activities."[12]

Although he did not explain his plans more fully, a subsequent letter to Mrs. Chapman made it clear that his "noble friends" were Orcella Rexford—a professional lecturer on topics such as color and diet, whose travels enabled her to make outstanding contributions to the Bahá'í teaching effort for more than two decades—and her husband, Dr. Gayne Gregory. "They are real friends and very wonderful souls," he wrote Mrs. Chapman in 1934. "They did so much for me at a time when I needed help. Helped in a way that challenges reverence."[13]

As his preparations for the coming year intensified, he seems to have gained a real appreciation of the respite that the National Assembly had allowed. On 17 November he thanked both Horace Holley and Roy Wilhelm, as members of the Assembly, for not having "applied the brakes too suddenly" but having given instead "a reasonable time for adjustment to the outside world."[14]

His reconciliation with Horace Holley and the National Assembly was simultaneously reinforced by the Guardian. In a letter dated 20 October 1932 and received between 17 and 21 November, Shoghi Effendi, writing through his secretary, encouraged Louis Gregory to maintain the positive attitude that he had already achieved and to look to the future:

> Shoghi Effendi wishes me to acknowledge the receipt of your letter dated September 25th 1932. He deeply sympathises with you in your difficulties and earnestly prays that God will guide you and enable you to take the right step at this cross-road of your life. He is sure that ultimately you will appreciate the wisdom of all this and will not be in the least sorry for what has transpired. What is however essential is that you have faith in the love and guidance of Baha'u'llah and be certain that He will not forsake a person like you who has for so many years spread his Cause so devotedly. It may be a period during which He will test your power of endurance and tenacity of faith, but with His help you shall win and see yourself victorious both spiritually and also in managing your material affairs.
>
> Shoghi Effendi knows that you can render inestimable service both if you go to Persia and also if you join Mrs. Gregory in Europe. . . . but Shoghi Effendi thinks that the place you are needed most is America. The Master asked you to work for the colored and among them and Shoghi Effendi would urge you to do the same. Your own people need you most and you have a duty towards them that you have to fulfil.
>
> Shoghi Effendi wishes you to take a kind of work like the one Mr. [Hyde] Dunn has taken in Australia, that would enable you to travel throughout the U. S. and both win your bread and serve the Cause. The kind of work Miss [Orcella] Rexford has [i.e., paid lecturing] Shoghi Effendi would not advise you for even though there is no harm in it, it may cause misunderstanding. The people may confuse what you say on the subject of the Cause with what you say in your other lectures. Keep also in

mind that the Faith cannot spare your services totally. You should take up a work that will give you ample time to teach among the colored.

In his moments of prayer at the Shrine Shoghi Effendi will pray for you and ask God to guide and assist you in this very critical period of your life.

At the bottom of the letter, as was his custom, Shoghi Effendi added a postscript in his own hand:

Dear and precious co-worker:
The spirit which you have demonstrated and which your welcome letter so powerfully reveals is indeed worthy of the praise and admiration of the Supreme Concourse. The place you occupy in my heart and the measure of admiration I cherish for the sublimity of your faith, I cannot describe. . . . I wish you to concentrate, within the limits which your changed material position imposes, on the teaching work in America and particularly among the colored inhabitants. My prayers will accompany you, wherever you may be. With a heart filled with love and gratitude,

Your true brother,
(Signed) Shoghi[15]

Although the letter put an end to Mr. Gregory's plans to follow Orcella Rexford's example and dispelled any lingering hopes for the reversal of the National Assembly's decision, he found great reassurance in Shoghi Effendi's counsels. "Since writing you, a letter has come to me from Haifa which graciously clarifies for me the past, present & future," he wrote Roy Wilhelm at the end of November. "I am not to do Orcella's work (no reflection upon her, of course) but other work which will give me ample time to travel and teach." The following day he exclaimed in another note to Mr. Wilhelm: "What a wonderful healer is S. E.! Before his letter came I was resigned to the inevitable. His word so clarifies the situation that I am happy over the change for myself."[16]

Louis Gregory's instantaneous response testifies to the strength of his faith and to his devotion to Shoghi Effendi. The tests that he had borne because of his race had given him countless opportunities over the years to follow 'Abdu'l-Bahá's example by responding constructively to even the most blatant injustices. He had always met hurts and reverses with the knowledge that 'Abdu'l-Bahá and Shoghi Effendi supported him. His problems as a result of his interracial marriage, his attempts to integrate the Bahá'ís of Washington, D.C., his role in racial amity work—all had been in the line of duty assigned to him by the Master and the Guardian. Since the 1932 convention, however, his attempt to accept "the inevitable" had been hindered by his conviction that his dismissal conflicted with the wishes of 'Abdu'l-Bahá and Shoghi Effendi. Thus his position had been ambiguous, awkward, even embarrassing, until Shoghi Effendi's letter "clarified" it. The Guardian's assurance that he would not only come to understand his changed status but would be glad about it relieved him—indeed, made him "happy." It also gave him strength: "Through the Powerful aid of the Guardian I am still able to carry on."[17] In the fall of 1933, a year after his earlier letter of encouragement, Shoghi Effendi praised Louis Gregory's achievement. "You have attained spiritual heights that few indeed can claim to have scaled," the Guardian wrote in his own hand. "You have displayed a spirit that few, if any, can equal."[18]

This spirit was both a great protection to him as an individual and to the American Bahá'ís. It served to moderate the impact on the community of Albert Vail's continuing distress and disaffection. After a year and a half Horace Holley wrote to the Guardian on behalf of the National Spiritual Assembly about the effects of the dismissal on Mr. Vail: "The transition from his status as a national teacher seems to have been extremely difficult, and unlike Mr. Gregory, he has not yet adjusted himself to the new situation." While the Assembly did not believe it could reverse its decision, Mr. Holley continued, it did feel "a very great responsibility in doing everything possible to retain Albert's loyalty and activity."[19]

Shoghi Effendi's response upheld the Assembly's decision on principle but expressed equal concern about Albert Vail and about the wider implications of the problem for the entire community: "The Guardian will pray that you may all be assisted and guided in your efforts to remedy a situation which has already caused such an uncertainty and coolness among some of the believers and which requires, therefore, your careful and effective intervention."[20]

Albert Vail, however, was never able to come to terms with his changed status, and neither the Guardian's nor the Assembly's concern for him succeeded in retaining his "loyalty and activity." As for the community in general, the feelings of "uncertainty and coolness among some of the believers" grew instead of being dispelled during the following year; they threatened for a time to divide even the National Assembly. When that body pulled back from the brink of self-destruction, it gained a real victory for the Covenant of Bahá'u'lláh. But the victory also belonged to Louis Gregory, whose example helped to mitigate the controversy.

Perhaps as much as any other factor, Mr. Gregory's continued involvement in the affairs of the Faith limited the divisive potential of the situation. Even those who disagreed most strongly with the timing or handling of his and Mr. Vail's dismissal, or with the substance of the decision itself, had to acknowledge that Louis Gregory had not been diminished by it. Instead, he had become more fully aware that the Faith to which he had devoted so many years of his life could not be conditioned by any individual's views or desires. "No one can have his own way in the cause of God," he advised Edith Chapman several years later. "The discipline of the administration, firmly tho' lovingly upheld will teach us this in all the experiences of life and service."[21]

23   New Directions

Dissuaded by Shoghi Effendi from becoming a lecturer like Orcella Rexford, Louis Gregory turned to other possibilities. He decided—"at least until I can land something which may be more effective"—to begin his travels again by demonstrating a mobile color organ developed by a Bahá'í, Glenn Shook.[1] He joined forces with Charles A. Wragg, an Australian, to combine business and Bahá'í work in another interracial tour of the South.

Their departure, however, was postponed until the fall of 1933. Louise Gregory returned home from Europe that summer for a four-month-long visit. In September she left once again for Eastern Europe; after remaining for a time with Marion Jack in Bulgaria, she proceeded to Belgrade, Yugoslavia, where she was the lone Bahá'í in a country in which the Faith was virtually unknown. After Louise's departure the two men set out for the South by car, spending most of their time in Virginia. Often they worked together to put on demonstration shows in churches, schools, and other public places. Sometimes Charles Wragg went alone to places where Louis Gregory would not have been welcome, making separate "appointments at the homes of white groups and . . . music clubs and literary societies." The color organ was presented as "a new artform," Mr. Wragg recalled, which "would in future help to establish by analogy harmonic relations between ethnic groups differing in skin-color and historic background."[2]

Years afterward Louis Gregory reminisced about his and his companion's escapades as "two inexperienced motorists." On their way south, having gotten lost in New Jersey, they were stopped by a policeman. Mr. Wragg had been driving and in confusion had reverted to the English practice of driving on the left. Even before the policeman discovered that only Mr. Gregory had a license, he threatened them with jail; when he discovered that the driver was

240

unlicensed, he went to consult a superior officer. Charles Wragg and Louis Gregory waited anxiously, their planned tour and their livelihoods hanging in the balance. "Thoughts of jail were not alluring," Mr. Gregory confessed. "As for the alternative of a heavy fine at such a time, shadows of bankruptcy and the poor-house loomed." But after hearing of their work and the trip they planned the officer relented, saying it was his birthday and he did not want to delay their journey.[3]

When Louise heard about their misadventures, she remonstrated with him:

> Don't you think in the overcrowded state of the roads from autos & careless drivers it would be better for you another time not to take your car? It is not worth risking your life in the chance of doing a little business & all the insurance in the world would not bring you back to life nor give you back the use of limbs if injured my sweet-boy & you see Baha'is are not immune & you cannot be spared either by your wife or the Cause & Shoghi Effendi needs you much. So next time if you escape this do please leave it behind.[4]

The travelers did in fact survive the trip without any mishap or racial incident. Yet the business aspects of the trip apparently were unsuccessful. Originally meant to last until spring, the tour was cut short; by November Mr. Gregory was in New York, where he devoted ten weeks to Bahá'í teaching. He continued to seek "more effective" work during the years ahead, at one time or another considering journalism, teaching, and a business venture in partnership with his friend George Henderson. None of these was ever adopted, however, and the details of his means of livelihood after 1932 remain obscure.

His recurrent concern over earning a living emerged in his correspondence with Louise, whose own small income seems to have stretched to support them both. His dependence did not disturb her; indeed, she constantly encouraged him not to be too worried about making money. Writing from Salzburg in 1934, acutely aware of the shadow of war over Europe (a war that would have profound effects on everyone's fortunes, she was convinced), she urged her husband to put his Bahá'í work ahead of any other consideration:

We have but the present time & there is *haste*. Do not just now concentrate or not chiefly on trying to earn money, but while you have the means to do it, my advice is concentrate on your own people getting the message & more of them becoming firm believers. There are many to teach the white people & few besides yourself to teach the colored.[5]

Shoghi Effendi, too, continued to stress Louis Gregory's important role in the South. In October 1933 the Guardian requested that he focus on a "few important centers in the South" and also that he "emphasize" among the Southern Bahá'ís the importance of "intensive teaching."[6] Mr. Gregory made immediate plans to leave in January with the intention of spending two months in Atlanta and one month in Nashville. From that effort evolved a new objective: to become the kind of teacher that Shoghi Effendi was soon to term a *pioneer*. As the National Teaching Committee reported in the spring of 1934: "Mr. Louis G. Gregory, in response to a new trend in our teaching work which the Guardian is encouraging, is settling in one of the larger cities of the south and concentrating on that city until a properly functioning Bahá'í Assembly is established."[7] The city he chose was Nashville, where his ties went back to his college days forty years earlier.

Shoghi Effendi described "intensive teaching" in terms that suggested an extension of the kind of effort that Louis Gregory had been making for years in the South:

"Your immediate objective, as you rightly state, should be to establish a small group of well-confirmed, devoted and active believers who will be able to carry on the work after your departure. The method of intensive teaching seems to be very effective and promising at present. The masses as a whole do not show much interest in religion. But there are always to be found some competent, sincere and eager souls to whom the Message has a profound appeal. It is for the Bahá'í teacher to look for them, and to try to deepen and sustain their interest and thus enable them eventually to embrace the Cause."[8]

The results Louis Gregory achieved in this new phase of intensive teaching were striking. Thelma Allison, one of the "competent, sincere and eager souls'' he found in Nashville, has recalled that she met him through her husband, a good friend of Mr. Gregory. A fireside meeting for inquirers was soon arranged. All of those who attended were black women, and they formed the nucleus of a study group. As Mrs. Allison put it, all fell in love with his presentation of the Faith; rather than giving his own views, he quoted extensively from the Bahá'í writings, and his listeners ''knew that those words were different.'' The effect was heightened by his ''beautiful, most lovely, most persuasive voice.'' By April six to eight black women had become Bahá'ís, augmenting the small community that had existed before Mr. Gregory's arrival —''a tiny group of believers,'' as he described it, ''six southern whites and one colored.'' Together they formed Nashville's first Local Spiritual Assembly. [9]

Louis Gregory wrote optimistically of the prospects for unity between the white and black Bahá'ís there, noting that ''two of the differ[e]nt white families have en[ter]tained a colored worker in their homes and another has opened her home for regular meetings weekly which both races attend.'' From the point of view of his years of experience with the white Bahá'ís, particularly in the South, such gestures seemed to him to be ''powerful confirmations.'' For Thelma Allison, however, integration in Nashville seemed to proceed slowly. She was a new Bahá'í, as impatient for change as he had been in 1909 when, immediately after his enrollment, he had sought to confront segregation in the Washington Bahá'í community. Mrs. Allison was impressed more by the difficulty of interracial adjustment than by any early signs of harmony. She remembered that, before Louis Gregory moved on, he tried to get the whites and the blacks to meet together, a step that the whites resisted. But one white woman of Jewish background led the way, and as the community united, it became one of the focal points for Bahá'í expansion in the South. [10] Both through the efforts of the white Bahá'ís, who gradually left the confines of their prejudiced environment, and of the blacks, whose patience was infinite, a solid foundation for the community was established.

After his pioneering stay in Nashville, Mr. Gregory resumed his travels. During the winter of 1935–36 he spent three months in New York and traveled extensively in Ohio and Indiana, par-

ticipating in many amity activities although he was no longer a
member of the national committee. "Have had opportunity to address 36 teaching meetings in about 30 days," he wrote Mrs. Chapman from Cincinnati. "Sub-zero weather most of the time. . . ."[11]
At the same time he was part of a teaching circuit—that is, an in-
terchange of speakers among the cities of a region. In this way he
resumed for a time his old roles as traveling Bahá'í lecturer and
itinerant racial amity worker.

Any illusion that amity activities might once again flourish was
soon dispelled by the 1936 decision to abolish a national amity
committee. Once again Louis Gregory was faced with a serious
test of his loyalty, as the work to which he had devoted so many
years fell under a cloud and the National Assembly claimed that
race amity activities "have sometimes resulted in emphasizing
race differences rather than their unity and reconciliation." If he
had not already survived the experience of dismissal in 1932, he
might have seen the National Assembly's position on race amity in
1936 as the final blow, an overwhelming rejection of his life work
by the body that he had always sought to serve.

But this time he was on sure ground, secure in both 'Abdu'l-
Bahá's and Shoghi Effendi's approval of racial amity work and
certain that it would prevail. In September 1936 he wrote to Shoghi
Effendi, touching on the subject, and on 11 November the Guardian's secretary replied, in part: "Concerning the racial amity
conferences; the Guardian firmly believes that they constitute a
vital & inseparable part of the teaching campaign now being carried on by the American believers. It is the duty of every loyal
Bahá'í to do all that he possibly can to promote this phase of Bahá'í
activity, without which no campaign of teaching can bear lasting
results." At the bottom of the letter Shoghi Effendi penned a brief
note:

> The teaching campaign, now in full swing in the United
> States and Canada, should, under no circumstances affect the
> progress, or detract from the importance & urgency of the racial
> amity work that challenges & confronts the believers in that
> continent. I hope & pray that in both fields you may be enabled
> to render magnificent services. I feel truly proud of your past
> achievements & cherish the brightest hopes for your future con-
> tributions to this noble & twofold task.[12]

Although Shoghi Effendi's statement cast considerable doubt on the National Assembly's policy of deemphasizing amity activities by doing away with the national committee, Louis Gregory simply forwarded to the national secretary a copy of the letter, along with a brief, mild comment: ''Enclosed is the copy of a letter received by me from the Guardian and which is sent you for the consideration of the National Spiritual Assembly as having a bearing upon the national campaign of teaching. It reconciles for me two conflicting viewpoints with regard to the racial amity work and is a further demonstration of the marvellous wisdom of the Guardian in dealing with complex problems.''[13] Then he put behind him a development that others might have taken as a personal defeat. Even as he wrote the National Spiritual Assembly, he was preparing to embark on a new, international pioneering venture.

24 Haiti

In the latter half of 1936 Louise Gregory returned to the United States after three years in Europe. Considering the length of their separation and their advanced years, the Gregorys might have been expected to retire to their little home in New England. Instead, within a few months, they were on their way to the Caribbean.

In going to Haiti the Gregorys once again responded to a new phase of the Divine Plan at its very beginning. In a 1 May cable to the 1936 convention Shoghi Effendi had stressed the importance of establishing at least one permanent center of the Faith in "every State within American Republic and every Republic in American continent" by the end of the first Bahá'í century in 1944. "Humanity entering outer fringes most perilous stage its existence," the Guardian warned. "Opportunities (of) present hour unimaginably precious." Later in the month he cabled another brief message calling for international teachers to volunteer their services: "Convention plea addressed to American believers cannot achieve its purpose unless dauntless pioneers promptly arise and, forsaking (their) homeland, permanently reside (in) countries where light of [the] Faith (has) not yet penetrated."[1]

An Inter-America Committee was immediately established by the National Assembly " 'to make careful research, and to advise and assist the N. S. A. in all activities related to the promotion of the Faith in Mexico, Central America, South America and the Islands of the Caribbean area.' " Ten Regional Teaching Committees were also formed in the United States and Canada. Thus a program of expansion and a committee structure to carry it out had already been created by June 1936, when the National Assembly received a letter from the Guardian calling for just such a "systematic, carefully conceived, and well-established plan." At that time he also directed the gradual extension of the plan to Europe, with par-

Louis Gregory as a young man

*Louis Gregory (center) with friends
at Green Acre Bahá'í School in 1928*

Louis G. Gregory (top row, center) at Green Acre,
which he helped develop as a center of interracial fellowship

Louis G. Gregory with delegates to the 1927 National Bahá'í Convention, Montreal, Canada, where historic consultations increased commitment to race amity

Louis G. Gregory with friends in Montreal, Canada, 1927

Louis Gregory
a photograph taken while he and Louise were living
in Haiti in 1937

Louis G. Gregory (top row, center) with friends,
Carmel by the Sea, California, 1926

ticular concentration on " 'those countries, such as the Baltic States, Poland, Greece, Spain and Portugal, were no avowed believer has established definite residence.' "[2]

Later in the year the Guardian restated his appeal in highly personal terms, by which Bahá'ís such as Louis and Louise Gregory, who had been closely attached to 'Abdu'l-Bahá and had always sought to fulfill His instructions, were inevitably inspired:

> The American believers, if they wish to carry out, in the spirit and the letter, the parting wishes of their beloved Master, must intensify their teaching work a thousand fold and extend its ramifications beyond the confines of their native land and as far as the most distant outposts of their far-flung Faith. . . . The present opportunity is unutterably precious. It may not recur again. Undaunted by the perils and the uncertainties of the present hour, the American believers must press on and prosecute in its entirety the task which now confronts them. I pray for their success from the depths of my heart.[3]

Soon after this appeal was published in the October 1946 issue of *Baha'i News,* the Gregorys left for Haiti.

Loulie Mathews, as a member of the Inter-America Committee, had apparently proposed the trip to the National Assembly and had offered to help subsidize it. The National Spiritual Assembly readily approved the idea of the Gregorys' "journey to Haiti, and if possible to adjoining islands." For their part the couple stated that they were "grateful for the opportunity." The venture promised to make good use of Louise's knowledge of French and her experience abroad and also to fulfill Louis' commitment to bring the Bahá'í teachings to members of his race. For the first time in their twenty-four years of marriage, their separate paths as Bahá'í teachers converged in a common effort of major importance. "May I add that Mrs. Gregory and I are happy," he wrote the National Assembly, "that thru this opportunity we can continue to be together in service."[4]

They sailed from New York on 14 January 1937, bearing letters of introduction to some influential Haitians, and were soon settled in Petion Ville, a suburb of Port au Prince. The polite welcome they received was promising. Mr. Gregory reported that

"Mr. Oswald Garrison Villard, a champion of Haitian freedom, received me with great courtesy as well as the director of the Haitian Hospital and a number of his assistants. Among those who are listening to the Message and studying the books are two men who have held the rank of statesmen, though now out of power, a happy circumstance that gives them the leisure to look more deeply into the Bahá'í Faith. A distinguished physician, two members of the present Haitian Cabinet, several members of the Senate and Chamber of Deputies, heads of schools, the American Consul and two sons of the late Episcopal Bishop of Haiti are among those who have availed themselves of this opportunity to study the Bahá'í Principles."[5]

In a letter to the National Assembly Mr. Gregory revealed—to a greater extent than in his formal reports—his impressions and feelings about Haiti and the task they had undertaken there:

After a month here we have some perspective of possibilities for service and think them excellent. A detailed report of the work so far is being sent Mrs. Loulie Mathews and this need not be duplicated. But suffice it to state that we are almost continually contacting people of high culture and capacity and rarely receive any rebuffs, but on the contrary, a courteous and inquiring attitude. We are also well advertized and our purpose here is well known. A few of the most influential people show a disposition to study deeply into the teachings. Also the young intelligentsia seem interested. Of course this may in part be set down to the French practice which prefers dissembling to rudeness. On the other hand we are among progressive people, and altho' few of the men are deeply interested in the old order of religion, altho' normally connected with various religious establishments, something that is virile and effective, scientific and reasonable cannot fail to reveal its power, if there is time.

We hold our meetings twice weekly whether or not any one comes. That attitude will in time prove effective. We know that a great many seeds must be sown before anything in the way of organization can be attempted.[6]

Although the Gregorys concentrated much of their attention on the educated elite at the beginning of their stay, they were well aware that the vast majority of the population, poor and uneducated, had to be reached as well. "We are also taking some steps toward contacting the most primitive people, the burden-bearers, the poor whom Baha'u'llah especially wishes to help and bless in His Day,'' Mr. Gregory reported. Their conditions of life shocked him profoundly. He had experienced poverty and hunger as a child, and in his travels as an adult had visited many poor black communities from Northern ghettoes to the rural South. But nothing had prepared him for Haiti:

> We find on the one hand wealth, culture, progress, on the other, never before such extremes of poverty and distress. Louise says that in the Balkans it is not unusual to see people literally in rags. But such I have never seen anywhere in the U.S., altho' at various times I have passed through all of them save the Dakotas.[7]

The challenge of reaching the poor peasantry was increased by ''their almost entire lack of education and their Creole dialect.'' However, the Gregorys made friends with ''a youth who can neither read nor write, but who can make himself understood in four languages,'' and gradually they discovered greater receptivity to the Bahá'í teachings among the common people than among the educated upper class. A study class was formed among a ''group of humble but very sincere souls.''[8]

Soon it became apparent that their projected stay of three months would barely enable them to begin work toward their aim of establishing the Bahá'í Faith in Haiti. ''There will be very much to be done that can not in all probability be accomplished before the time set for our return, toward the end of April,'' he wrote after a month on the island.

> Whether we should then return to the States, renewing our efforts here next autumn or winter, or since we are here and active, remain for a year at least or an indefinite time, are details still to be decided. . . . By retreating a few miles higher into the mountains, a popular place for the Haitians of rank in Summer, it will be possible to withstand the Tropical heat with no break in the continuity of service. . . . On the other hand, if we leave and return, we shall perhaps be better prepared for some of the adjustments needed in living in the Tropics for the first time, changes that involve health and the reasonable comforts of living.[9]

Coupled with a growing understanding of the scope of their task was a nagging uncertainty about the government's attitude toward them and the Faith they represented and a corresponding sense of urgency in moving toward their goal:

> Soon after their work had started, . . . they were told by a fellow American visitor that their every movement was watched, this due to the fact that a high ecclesiastical authority had warned the country that strangers would come to them, ostensibly to teach religion, but secretly to spread radical propaganda, with a view to sedition and revolution. Although the latter is remote from any Bahá'í practice or intention, yet not knowing, in the state of the official mind, how long they would be permitted to remain, these workers felt they should put whatever time there was to the best and immediate use.[10]

During the second month of their stay, the Gregorys' doubts about the government's position were suddenly removed. Attempting to step up their teaching efforts, they decided to hold a series of "publicly advertized Bahá'i meetings in Port au Prince similar to those held in various American cities," a plan that "met with an enthusiastic reaction among all the attracted friends to whom it was shown." But an official observed that police permission would be needed. When this was sought, the police chief in turn referred the matter to the Department of the Interior. There the proposal was firmly rejected. The Interior Secretary advised the Gregorys that authorization to hold public meetings was denied because the Department was formally opposed to the spread of the Bahá'í Faith in Haiti.[11]

Official opposition served to quicken the interest of several friends, and the Gregorys were confident, after the initial "shock and disappointment," that the ban would be not only temporary but ultimately beneficial to the establishment of the Faith there. As Louis Gregory told the National Assembly, "obstacles to the spread of truth almost invariably increase its vogue in future."[12]

Although they had been prepared to spend the summer months in the mountains of Haiti, the ban on their proposed activities convinced them to return to the United States as scheduled in April. The unaccustomed heat and Louise's health made travel to other parts of the Caribbean impractical at that time of year. Under the circumstances Louis Gregory concluded that "it seems from every angle wisest and best for us to return for the Summer and resume our Island activities in the Autumn." They left on 21 April, still hoping that it would be possible for them to return to Haiti and establish a center there. In three months they had attracted " 'one teacher of rare ability' " and three others who would assist with teaching, a nucleus, they hoped, that might be nurtured to Assembly status. They were convinced that an Assembly would in time be established—if not with the assistance of foreign pioneers, then by the interested Haitians themselves. [13]

25   The Seven Year Plan

The Gregorys returned to the United States at the end of April 1937, too late to attend the annual convention. It was the first that Louis Gregory had missed since 1911. "But as we grow older," he observed with good humor in a letter to Horace Holley, "a valuable lesson to learn is the vast number of things that can get on well without us."[1] Nonetheless, the teaching work badly needed their services. During the convention the Guardian announced the Seven Year Plan, the dual purpose of which was to continue the teaching plan already begun and to complete the exterior ornamentation of the Temple.

The Gregorys set aside the prospect of settling in the Caribbean in favor of the continued, pressing needs in Europe and the South, their special fields of service since the early years of the Divine Plan. Although they never returned to Haiti, their brief stay had not been futile. Three years later Ruth and Ellsworth Blackwell, another interracial couple, settled there to take up the work that the Gregorys had begun. The first Spiritual Assembly in Haiti was formed in Port au Prince on 21 April 1942.[2]

As the Seven Year Plan was put into motion, Louise returned to Belgrade for a time, and Louis went to the South. "In sixteen States of the South," Marion Holley reported on behalf of the Teaching Committee in *The Bahá'í World,* "there existed only eight Assemblies, two Groups, and forty-six isolated believers in 1936, while six of the States possessed no Bahá'ís at all." Much work needed to be done to meet the goals of the Plan in the South. During a seven-month-long sojourn Mr. Gregory combined both of the methods that he had already used in the region: itinerant teaching, to "renew contacts formerly made, and carry on follow-up teaching work in centers where he previously taught," as the National Teaching Committee put it; and short-term pioneering, to focus on a single locality until a community could be established.

His travels took him to Atlanta, where so many contacts had been made over a period of more than twenty years, and to twenty-six other "cities or communities." He chose to focus for a longer time, four months, on Tuskegee, Alabama; it was an ideal location, as Nashville had been, because of his many visits there since the days of Booker T. Washington and because Alabama was one of the six states were no Bahá'ís resided.[3]

Having arrived at Tuskegee on 1 December 1937, Mr. Gregory had established within a few months two regular weekly Bahá'í meetings. The National Teaching Committee quoted from his letters in its February 1938 report on the progress of the plan:

> Louis Gregory is now at Tuskegee Institute, Alabama, where many doors are opening for the spread and establishment of the Faith. A few extracts from recent reports will convey the manner in which the work is going forward. "The President of Tuskegee has twice invited me to his home, the second time for a dinner conference which lasted two hours. At the close he warmly shook hands and said it was a very helpful message." "The chief assistant to the Chaplain, a Baptist clergyman, has done wonders to help, even leaving me in charge of his pulpit while away, with freedom to give the Message." "During the meetings, the Y.M.C.A. Secretary, who has the Esslemont Book [*Bahá'u'lláh and the New Era*] and accepts the message, prayed a most eloquent prayer of thankfulness for 'the New Star of Bethlehem that has arisen.'" "Passing by a home one day I was called by a lady student who had heard a Bahá'í lecture in one of the classes. 'Come in and meet my husband, Prof. Otis, who is head of the Agricultural Department.' This led to an impromptu meeting; and also led to a lecture today before the Agricultural Department. *Now we have started two regular weekly meetings and are hoping for another.* There appears to be a considerable number who are more than superficially interested."[4]

The 1937–38 annual report of the Regional Teaching Committee for Alabama and Florida, published in April 1938, added that a meeting place had been "donated by the Institute and good cooperation is being given by teachers and prominent citizens of Tuskegee." Finally, the report noted that several of Louis Gregory's students were about to become enrolled as Bahá'ís.[5]

Although Mr. Gregory was assisted by the leadership in Tuskegee, a personal letter that he wrote in April made it clear that he did not link his teaching success to the participation of prominent people. Indeed, prominence did not confer any particular receptivity to the Bahá'í teachings. On the contrary, he felt that he had succeeded despite the atmosphere of privilege at Tuskegee: "It has been quite difficult as this is a prosperous community and somewhat 'high brow.' But more than twenty have already signed a humble letter to Shoghi Effendi and seven applications for membership. We hope to get some sort of an organization before I start north. . . ." [6]

Tuskegee's special prominence in the cultural life of black Americans, which Louis Gregory saw as something of an obstacle to immediate success in establishing the Bahá'í Faith there, served to extend the influence of his endeavors beyond the confines of the campus. In June the National Teaching Committee reported that his work was becoming known nationally through the Institute's publications. Moreover, Tuskegee proved to be a focal point from which the Faith spread to other centers. Within a few months one of the new Tuskegee members had moved to Montgomery, Alabama, becoming the first Bahá'í in that city. [7]

During the following year, 1938–39, the second year of the Seven Year Plan, the Gregorys spent the summer at Green Acre, then in October established their winter residence in Cambridge, Massachusetts. But Louis Gregory intended to travel, as he had each winter for so many years. "I am hoping to go South," he wrote Edith Chapman from Green Acre, "or wherever blown by the Breezes of Divine Bounty this Autumn and Winter. It does not seem wise to make plans." [8] As it turned out, the National Teaching Committee decided to send him to Arkansas, another state which had no Bahá'ís at the beginning of the Plan.

Lydia Martin—whose parents, Alexander and Mary Martin, had first been attracted to the Faith by a talk given by Louis Gregory in Cleveland in 1913—had recently been appointed Dean of Women at the state teachers college in Pine Bluff, and she opened the way for Mr. Gregory to be invited there in January 1939 to conduct the Religious Emphasis Week program. He was so warmly received that his stay at the college was extended another week. He remained in the town of Pine Bluff for an additional two weeks.

His schedule during the month-long visit was crowded with talks and study classes:

> Mr. Gregory spoke each Sunday at vespers, each noon at chapel, and maintained conference hours. In addition, he has addressed such groups as the Parent-Teachers Association, a conference on High School Education, a college class in government on the Bahá'í Administration, the Colored Ministers' Alliance, the Catholic School, City High School and various grade schools, and five joint sessions of the college Y.M.C.A. and Y.W.C.A. He has also conducted a study class of about eighteen students, and was invited to tell some thirty faculty members of the Faith, including the President and Dean. [9]

After he left Pine Bluff, Miss Martin maintained study classes for a time, attended by those who had become interested in the Faith as a result of his visit. On 11 June she wrote to Shoghi Effendi of the teaching work and soon received an extremely encouraging response:

> the Guardian's heart [was] immeasurably gladdened at the report of the outstanding teaching achievements which you and Mr. Gregory have been able to accomplish in Pine Bluff during this past year. His heart goes out in deepest gratitude to you both for all the sacrifice, determination & resourceful energy you have displayed all through your teaching work in that center, & he feels indescribably happy & encouraged to know that as a result the entire Negro population of Pine Bluff has heard of the Cause, that one of the college students . . . has already declared herself a believer, & that several others are on the point of becoming fully confirmed. . . .
> In view of these remarkable results you have accomplished in Pine Bluff, particularly among the student body in the Arkansas State College, & notwithstanding any opposition, veiled or open, which may be directed against you from certain quarters, the Guardian would strongly urge you to remain in that center, & to confidently persist in your efforts until you succeed in establishing a strong & united group of confirmed believers, capable of developing eventually into a local assembly. He wishes you, in particular, to concentrate on teaching the Negro inhabitants of Pine Bluff, & thus bring into the Cause this hitherto neg-

lected, though highly promising & spiritually receptive, element of the population in the Southern States.[10]

No immediate results, however, were seen in Pine Bluff. Despite Mr. Gregory's warm welcome and Miss Martin's best efforts, continued interest in the Bahá'í teachings was stifled by "opposition" and conservatism. She has recalled that "at that time people in the South were so fearful of criticism if they seemed to be different in any way" that few dared to discuss the Faith with her openly. In such a climate of fear it took many years for the seeds sown by Louis Gregory and tended by Lydia Martin to grow into a Bahá'í community in Pine Bluff.[11]

Shoghi Effendi's observation that blacks in the South had been "hitherto neglected" revealed his deep concern about the American Bahá'ís' commitment to attaining real diversity within their ranks. Obviously Louis Gregory's many trips to the South did not constitute neglect on his part. Yet he had been for many years virtually the sole intermediary between the blacks he taught in the South and the rest of the American Bahá'ís. He could no longer be expected to enroll and confirm new adherents singlehandedly. The national community itself had to become truly involved in the effort and enthused about the prospect of bringing in ever larger numbers of blacks, especially in the South. The Seven Year Plan marked a beginning in the long process of rectifying their neglect.

26 Chasm

The retreat from active concern for racial amity in the national Bahá'í community from 1936 to 1939 coincided with the beginning of a new stage in the development of the Faith that would ultimately bring greatly increased diversity. Indeed, the two trends were not entirely unrelated. From the time of Shoghi Effendi's 1936 convention message, and particularly after the launching of the Seven Year Plan in 1937, the American Bahá'ís were overwhelmingly preoccupied with a challenging set of goals: to establish the Faith in every state and in every country in North and South America, and to complete the exterior ornamentation of the Wilmette Temple by May 1944, the centenary of the founding of the Faith. The urgency of the need to spread Bahá'u'lláh's message of world unity and peace was further underlined by current events. In August 1937 Shoghi Effendi warned that the world was "perilously near cataclysmic convulsions" and called America the Faith's "one chief remaining citadel." Already the Bahá'í community in Germany had been dissolved by the Nazis, the American National Assembly reported, and "our International Teacher, the revered Martha L. Root, is in Shanghai, surrounded by the flame and smoke of war."[1] Worsening world conditions left practically no one but the Americans free to further the expansion of the Bahá'í order.

This expansion in itself was bound to challenge and finally to transform the community. Internationally, the Seven Year Plan, by firmly establishing the Faith throughout Central and South America and the Caribbean, was the first major advance toward increased racial and cultural diversity since the teachings spread from the Near East to the United States and Western Europe in the 1890s. Nationally, the Plan permanently altered the distribution of Bahá'ís in the United States. Diversity had been limited in part by the concentration of the Faith east of the Mississippi, north of the

Mason-Dixon line, and along the Pacific Coast. Seven states had no Bahá'ís; twenty-one had neither groups nor Assemblies, but only isolated individuals. A map showing the spread of the Bahá'í Faith in the United States reveals vast tracts where few, if any, Bahá'ís resided in 1937. Yet in all but one of the regions designated by 'Abdu'l-Bahá in the Divine Plan there was at least one concentration of Bahá'ís in Assemblies and groups. That exception was the South, which had no major Bahá'í population centers from which strength could flow to weaker areas.[2]

As increased attention was focused on the South, the problems of integration that Washington, D.C., and Nashville had experienced were repeated many times and in varying degrees. Such challenges were largely inevitable as the Bahá'í Faith began to make inroads into a society in which the races were separated by custom and by law. The ambivalence of the national community toward the active promotion of race unity from 1936 to 1939 was a handicap in meeting these challenges. In a sense the problems that faced the Bahá'ís served to reinforce the prevalent feeling that race was a subject better to avoid than to confront.

A case in point was an unprecedented incident of public criticism of Bahá'í racial policy, stemming from a series of meetings in Nashville in 1937. The National Spiritual Assembly had decided in 1936 to inaugurate a system of holding its meetings "in different parts of the country" to "provide occasions for Regional Conferences with the friends, as well as public meetings for promoting the Faith."[3] The first such meeting was held in San Francisco in November 1936 and the second in Nashville in January 1937.

Months beforehand the National Assembly had written to the Guardian concerning the advisability of holding public meetings in the city. He had replied through his secretary that he approved the plan to go to Nashville, "as it would greatly encourage the believers in that center." He also urged the holding of meetings—which, he implied, would be interracial—for the general public:

> The holding of public meetings in that city should be avoided only in case it would lead to grave and very serious results. Slight local criticisms and unpopularity should not act as deterrant [sic]. The issue should be met squarely and courageously, and an effort should be made to attract at first the most

cultured element among the colored, and through them establish contact with the white and the masses. Such individuals and groups, whether white or colored, who are relatively free from racial prejudice, should be approached, separately if necessary, and an endeavor should be made to bring them together eventually, not only on formal occasions and for specific purposes, but in intimate social gatherings, in private homes as well as in formally recognized Bahá'í centers. [4]

The meetings were carried out with apparent success. Three public meetings were held, one at Fisk, and two at a large hotel, and two gatherings took place in private homes. The teaching schedule was arranged by a white Nashville Bahá'í from the Regional Teaching Committee and a white visitor. No mention of race appeared in a subsequent report in *Baha'i News,* although "the special teaching problem existing in the South" was mentioned euphemistically as a subject of consultation that the National Assembly hoped to address after its firsthand experience there. [5]

In fact, the meetings in Nashville achieved something of a victory for the Faith in the South. A new community with a large percentage of black Bahá'ís was assisted by an influx of highly capable teachers, by a series of large meetings, and by unprecedented local publicity. Moreover, the public meetings at the racially exclusive Hotel Hermitage, although they were intended primarily for whites, were in fact attended by some blacks, whose welcome had been assured by the hotel management before the room was reserved. This was an unexampled concession to the Bahá'ís. Although the management gave the permission on condition that there would not be "too many" blacks present, according to Albert James, a member of the Nashville Bahá'í community at that time, the approval "was at least a foot in the door" of segregation. [6]

After their visit to Nashville, and in the light of their experiences there, the National Assembly decided to approve holding separate public meetings and study classes for blacks and whites in the South, in order to make the Bahá'í teachings accessible to both races, and asked the Guardian for his approval. On 22 March 1937 he condoned the new policy, with its goal of furthering teaching efforts in a region with few Bahá'ís, as a means of reaching "the two races in the south without the slightest discrimination." Thus whites would not necessarily be faced immediately with the prospect of attending integrated gatherings, nor would black inquirers be subjected to uncomfortable situations. Among declared Bahá'ís, however, there was to be no racial segregation. This separate but equal policy was to be strictly limited to those who were not yet "truly confirmed believers." The Guardian explained that

> the two races should ultimately be brought together, and be urged to associate with the utmost unity and fellowship, and be given full and equal opportunity to participate in the conduct of the teachings as well as administrative activities of the Faith. Nothing short of such an ultimate fusion of the two races can insure the faithful application of that cornerstone principle of the Cause regarding the oneness of mankind.[7]

The subject of the Nashville meetings was raised at the annual convention in April during a period of consultation on teaching in the South. At that time the delegates "voted to request the National Assembly to publish in *Bahá'í News* a statement explaining the meaning of separate meetings in the South."[8] This recommendation seems to have been met by publication of Shoghi Effendi's March 1937 letter. Clearly a majority of the delegates was concerned that the policy not be misunderstood or misrepresented.

The appropriateness of their concern was demonstrated six months later when a column by W. E. B. DuBois in the *Pittsburgh Courier* seized upon the issue and headlined "the Fall of the Baha'i." DuBois recalled meeting 'Abdu'l-Bahá personally in 1912 in New York and also hearing Him in Chicago. 'Abdu'l-Bahá's teachings, DuBois asserted, "seemed even then too fine a vision to be true of any ethic with an American following; and it was." All other religions that had begun with thoughts of brotherhood had ended up in compromise, he stated. "Only the Baha'i were left, and last year at their meeting in Nashville they succumbed. For the first time they held a public meeting in the Hermitage Hotel to which no Negroes, not even members, were invited," he claimed, inaccurately, "and they voted for color segregation at future meetings." Dr. DuBois went on to quote—with virtually complete accuracy—Shoghi Effendi's approval of the policy but not his reminder that the goal must be "ultimate fusion of the two races" once the individuals became Bahá'ís.[9]

Horace Holley promptly wrote a lengthy rebuttal on behalf of the National Spiritual Assembly that appeared in a subsequent issue of the *Courier*. He stated that blacks had attended all the meetings and that the hotel's policy had been adjusted for the Bahá'ís. He went on to outline the principle of oneness, stressed the equal participation of blacks in the administrative order and nondiscrimination in accommodations at Bahá'í summer schools, defended the policy of separate meetings for students of the Faith in the South, and placed all within the context of a spiritual rather than a social movement. But his letter, because of its length, was run only in the Southern states edition, and the Bahá'ís of Pittsburgh, who had originally called the column to the attention of the National Assembly, suggested that the matter be dropped, particularly since Dr. DuBois' views were not necessarily shared by a majority of blacks.[10]

Since 1934 DuBois had indeed lost much of his influence; increasingly caught up in his program for Negro separatism, he had broken with the N.A.A.C.P. and taken an academic position at Atlanta University. As his biographer, Francis L. Broderick, writes regarding DuBois' loss of leadership between 1934 and 1944, when he returned to the N.A.A.C.P.: "Few were listening, for his ideas failed to mesh with his era. He had broken with the fighters for integration and with his own great past just as the struggle for integration was about to register real gains."[11]

It is ironic that, at a time when his advocacy of "nondiscriminatory segregation" was isolating him from the mainstream of black thought in America, he should attack the Bahá'ís for a limited and provisional acceptance of segregation, applied to nonmembers, that was much less drastic than the separation he himself proposed. The events in Nashville and the revised Bahá'í policy may have been unpalatable to him because he perceived them to have been imposed by the white majority. In fact, however, the racially mixed Nashville Spiritual Assembly had approved of the way in which the meetings there were carried out, if only because they seemed to be the best means of dealing with a difficult situation. Moreover, by failing to verify all the details of his story, Dr.

DuBois overlooked the real success of the Bahá'ís in overcoming the color bar—even to a limited extent—at the Hermitage Hotel.

The force of DuBois' attack, after more than twenty-five years of amiable association with the Bahá'ís, tends to support the assumption that his outburst was motivated as much by personal concerns as by principle. His wife's recent affiliation with the Faith (which he did not mention) can hardly have been unrelated to his reaction. Marion Little, who knew him and had also helped to arrange the Nashville meetings, corresponded with him about his charges, pointing out the facts of the situation as she saw them.[12] He was also approached by Louis Gregory. DuBois remained immovable, however, and he took it upon himself to write a letter that severed his wife's connection with the Bahá'í Faith.

Louis Gregory referred to this letter in a lengthy reply he addressed to Dr. DuBois from New Orleans several years later. He reiterated the National Assembly's "regret . . . that a plan carried out in the best of faith should have been by you so greatly misunderstood." Then he went on to discuss his own perceptions of the events in Nashville and of the Bahá'í position on race:

> At the time of the Nashville incident, on the basis of information which reached me, like your own, from a place remote from the scene, I was also of the opinion that the National body had fallen into error. But after visiting Nashville, hearing from the colored Baha'is there and considering the Teachings and Instructions for a third of a century, I know well that no error was committed. This I once tried to tell you.
>
> The general & specific instructions of the Faith on race relations are summarized by Shoghi Effendi in *"The Advent of Divine Justice"* which you doubtless have read. Both 'Abdu'l Bahá in his administration and Shoghi Effendi more recently, have permitted the friends in various Southern cities to *start* the races in separate study classes when deemed wise and necessary. This is on the principle of not expecting a person to have a college education when he enters college. But when a person accepts the Faith he must abandon all prejudices. Certainly he must know what it all means before making so radical a change. Were the Baha'i Faith merely a cult with a human origin, it could attract only people who shared its views. Its mysterious Power is indicated by its ability to transform people whose views are diametrically opposed to its ideals and to give them

new minds and new hearts. This it has been my privilege to observe North and South over a long period of years. It is now making progress South, North and all around the world. It is here in the South uniting the races as nothing else has ever done or can do. It is creating the bond that is permanent, not the ephemeral bond of the old order. Neither the ideals of the Faith nor its wisdom of taking people where and as they are and teaching them, has been altered and they are not inconsistent and they are achieving victory.[13]

Mr. Gregory added that he was "writing this letter especially for Mrs. DuBois with whom I trust you will share it," in hopes that she would realize that "no misunderstanding should prevent her from joining the ranks" of believers. As for DuBois himself, Louis Gregory stated frankly that he saw little likelihood of a reversal of his attitude toward the Bahá'í Faith: "That you will see its value in time I have no doubt, but your recognition of this supreme source of guidance, illumination and unity will come too late, I fear, for you to do anything about it in this world! This however is a matter between yourself and your Creator."[14]

Whatever damage had been done to the reputation of the Faith by DuBois' attack, it seems clear that the charges were unfounded. They might never have been made, however, if the general climate of opinion on race among the American Bahá'ís had been different in 1936–37. The actions of the National Assembly might not have been subject to misinterpretation, for example, if the body had included even one black member or if there had been a visible emphasis on racial amity during the period. Shoghi Effendi had stressed ten years earlier that black representation was necessary "to express . . . [their] viewpoint, that you might understand . . . [their] position, that we might reach across this chasm."[15] Moreover, the decision not to appoint a race amity committee in 1936 had done nothing to dispel an aura of uncertainty over national Bahá'í racial policy that may have contributed to DuBois' attack.

The new approach to Southern teaching reflected a concerted effort to influence whites as well as blacks. Because white prejudice and white power ruled the region, any movement for change had to involve both races. But it also had to be carefully balanced to prevent the assumption of white superiority. Unfortunately, the formation of white study groups and even white Bahá'í communities in the South from 1936 to 1939 did not occur within the context of a strong national program to educate both members and nonmembers in the concept of human oneness—a program that Shoghi Effendi had declared in 1936 to be "a vital & inseparable" factor "without which no campaign of teaching can bear lasting results."[16] No interracial teaching teams toured the South, as they had in the early 1930s, and virtually no mention of race appeared in the issues of *Baha'i News* that new Southern believers received. The closest approach to a race unity program during this period was a request by the National Assembly that public meetings during January 1939 be devoted to the theme of the oneness of mankind. The determination of the American Bahá'ís to implement their vision of unity was clearly subject to question. Once again Shoghi Effendi would forcibly recall them to the realization that, like it or not, race amity must always be to the fore.

Part 4/*The Era of Racial Unity*

27 Advent

The Advent of Divine Justice, written by Shoghi Effendi in December 1938 and published a few months later, struck the American Bahá'ís with the force of a tidal wave. It began immediately to transform their consciousness and is still a potent factor in their development. The work assesses America's destiny as an international force for peace and expands on the role of its seemingly insignificant Bahá'í community in bringing about a new world order. The Guardian dealt unflinchingly with race prejudice as an issue "which the American believers are still far from having satisfactorily resolved." Indeed, he called it "the most vital and challenging issue confronting the Bahá'í community at the present stage of its evolution." The "urgency and importance" of coming to terms with race were linked, along with other "spiritual prerequisites of success," to the achievement of the goals of the Seven Year Plan and of the Divine Plan itself:

> A long and thorny road, beset with pitfalls, still remains untraveled, both by the white and the negro exponents of the redeeming Faith of Bahá'u'lláh. On the distance they cover, and the manner in which they travel that road, must depend, to an extent which few among them can imagine, the operation of those intangible influences which are indispensable to the spiritual triumph of the American believers and the material success of their newly-launched enterprise [the Seven Year Plan]. [1]

Shoghi Effendi elaborated on the Bahá'í attitude toward racial minorities, calling discrimination against any group "a flagrant violation of the spirit" of the Faith. The only discrimination to be allowed is discrimination "in favor of the minority, be it racial or otherwise," for "every organized community, enlisted under the banner of Bahá'u'lláh should feel it to be its first and inescapable obligation to nurture, encourage, and safeguard every minority belonging to any faith, race, class, or nation within it.'' In fact, preference should be given to the representative of a minority group in any voting tie or in any election where individuals being considered are equally qualified; and ''Bahá'í representative institutions, be they Assemblies, conventions, conferences, or committees'' should include as many diverse elements as possible.[2]

''Freedom from racial prejudice, in any of its forms, should, at such a time as this when an increasingly large section of the human race is falling victim to its devastating ferocity, be adopted as the watchword of the entire body of the American believers,'' Shoghi Effendi declared, ''in whichever state they reside, in whatever circles they move, whatever their age, traditions, tastes, and habits.'' Freedom from prejudice should be demonstrated on the level of social interaction among the Bahá'ís, on that of community activities, and on the national level: ''It should, above all else, become the keynote of the policy of that august body which, in its capacity as the national representative, and the director and coordinator of the affairs of the community, must set the example, and facilitate the application of such a vital principle to the lives and activities of those whose interests it safeguards and represents.''[3]

Shoghi Effendi recalled the example of 'Abdu'l-Bahá, quoted the words of Bahá'u'lláh and 'Abdu'l-Bahá in support of his argument, and ended with the Master's warning that the racial situation in America, if it remained unchanged, would create increasing '' 'enmity' '' and '' 'bloodshed.' '' The means of effecting change, Shoghi Effendi claimed, lay within the scope of each individual Bahá'í, black or white:

> Let the white make a supreme effort in their resolve to contribute their share to the solution of this problem, to abandon once for all their usually inherent and at times subconscious sense of superiority, to correct their tendency towards revealing a patronizing attitude towards the members of the other race, to persuade them through their intimate, spontaneous and informal association with them of the genuineness of their friendship and the sincerity of their intentions, and to master their impatience of any lack of responsiveness on the part of a people who have received, for so long a period, such grievous and slow-healing wounds. Let the negroes, through a corresponding effort on

their part, show by every means in their power the warmth of their response, their readiness to forget the past, and their ability to wipe out every trace of suspicion that may still linger in their hearts and minds. Let neither think that the solution of so vast a problem is a matter that exclusively concerns the other. Let neither think that such a problem can either easily or immediately be resolved. Let neither think that they can wait confidently for the solution of this problem until the initiative has been taken, and the favorable circumstances created, by agencies that stand outside the orbit of their Faith. Let neither think that anything short of genuine love, extreme patience, true humility, consummate tact, sound initiative, mature wisdom, and deliberate, persistent, and prayerful effort, can succeed in blotting out the stain which this patent evil has left on the fair name of their common country. Let them rather believe, and be firmly convinced, that on their mutual understanding, their amity, and sustained cooperation, must depend, more than on any other force or organization operating outside the circle of their Faith, the deflection of that dangerous course so greatly feared by 'Abdu'l-Bahá, and the materialization of the hopes He cherished for their joint contribution to the fulfillment of that country's glorious destiny.[4]

In April, shortly after the Guardian's message was disseminated to the American Bahá'ís, the National Spiritual Assembly published a forthright policy statement on "The Oneness of Mankind." "The Guardian, in 'The Advent of Divine Justice,' has created a new and higher standard of loyalty to the principle of the Oneness of Mankind on the part of the American Bahá'í Community, and has specifically declared that this standard must become the keynote of the policy of the National Spiritual Assembly," the statement began, reiterating several of the points stressed by Shoghi Effendi. "The National Spiritual Assembly must set the example and facilitate the application of this vital principle to the lives and activities of those whose interests it safeguards and represents."[5]

The Assembly's immediate response to *The Advent of Divine Justice* showed its willingness to assume a more active role in the struggle against prejudice, as Shoghi Effendi had directed, rather than simply to reflect the mixed values of the community. The statement went on to paraphrase the Guardian's remarks about minorities and about their protection and encouragement by, and involvement in, the Bahá'í order—including their representation in "Assemblies, Conventions, Conferences, and Committees."

The Assembly had decided to act in "accordance with the spirit" of Shoghi Effendi's message by publishing compilations of the Master's words on race and on "the reconciliation of Christians, Jews, and Muhammedans" and by incorporating such topics in the program of a conference to follow the 1939 national convention. "It is for the believers to realize each for himself the extreme desirability of fostering the minority elements in the Cause and contributing to the safeguarding of human life in America as a vital spiritual privilege and responsibility in the light of the Guardian's urgent appeal," the message concluded.

> The horizon of our Bahá'í love is to be extended, and our understanding of the true nature of Bahá'í unity is to be deepened and demonstrated in action. The ideal is so to develop the Bahá'í Community that it will become the haven of refuge for the grief-stricken and oppressed of all religions, races and classes in the land.
> The National Assembly is confident that the believers will take the Guardian's counsel to heart, and pray for wisdom in their effort to apply it to every aspect of their individual and collective Bahá'í life. The American Bahá'í Community must needs take a great step forward toward the goal of the World Order of Bahá'u'lláh.[6]

The effect of Shoghi Effendi's message on the American Bahá'ís was impressive. The spirit of *The Advent of Divine Justice* imbued the 1939 convention. "Early in the meeting it was voted to precede consultation on each subject with a reading from appropriate passages in 'The Advent of Divine Justice,' the power and majesty of which sustained the consciousness of the believers on a high level," the convention report in *Baha'i News* observed. "A description of the sessions written afterward, even a verbatim report of all discussion and remarks, would fail utterly to re-create the quality of the radiant and soaring spirit which so firmly united the delegates and visiting friends." In a letter to the Guardian written shortly after the convention, Harlan Ober remarked on the unifying effect of Shoghi Effendi's "soul stirring, challenging letter." "The Convention this year was undoubtedly the best we have ever held," he maintained. "It was unified and more mature, and there was really not one discordant note."[7]

The issue of race reportedly figured prominently in the consultation at the convention:

> The Guardian's vital statement on the Bahá'í responsibility for the application of the principle of the oneness of mankind had impressed the friends deeply before the Convention opened, and the passages in "The Advent of Divine Justice" bearing upon this urgent matter were pondered and discussed at length. A resolution calling upon the National Assembly to constitute Bahá'í Amity activities was the fruit of this consultation, which brought forth the sincere views of white and colored friends.[8]

One of the recommendations of the delegates was that "the living conditions of delegates during the Convention period" be free from segregation. The location of the Temple in a white, upper-class suburb had created problems for visiting black Bahá'ís over the years. In 1936 Louis Gregory had suggested that during the annual convention Edith Chapman and her husband might stay with a couple he knew in Evanston: "Their home is usually filled with Baha'is both colored and white. . . . I have often stayed with them. . . ." But once a room had been obtained, there was still the problem of meals. "Evanston, I regret to say, is very prejudiced against colored. The cafes in Wilmette serve everybody, however. Usually those who stay at the Fishers get breakfast & room there on very reasonable terms & take other meals at Wilmette." To obtain a hotel room was more difficult. Harlan Ober is said to have often taken a hotel room with the intention of sharing it with Mr. Gregory, since no black would have been allowed to register. Racist attitudes were so deeply entrenched that even in 1950 the National Spiritual Assembly was still working, with support from liberal leaders in the area, to ensure that the delegates and visitors to the convention were able to obtain hotel accommodations without being subjected to racial discrimination.[9]

Louis Gregory was once again elected to the Assembly that year—not surprisingly, considering not only Shoghi Effendi's impact on the convention but also the National Assembly's own comments prior to the convention about the election of members of minority groups. He served uninterruptedly from 1939 to 1946, more consecutive years than any of his earlier periods of membership. From 1939 to 1945 he was also an officer of the Assembly, serving as its first recording secretary.

If either ill feelings or uncomfortable memories were stirred by Mr. Gregory's return to the body that had dismissed him as a subsidized teacher seven years earlier, they seem to have been transcended by the message of *The Advent of Divine Justice*. Some of the members may have continued to think of Louis Gregory as being better suited to teaching than to administration. Indeed, Leroy Ioas (who had played a role in the 1932 crisis as a member of both the National Spiritual Assembly and the western branch of the National Teaching Committee) said as much in a letter to Harlan Ober shortly after the convention. Noting that "we all gladly accept the vote of the NSA," he nonetheless made it clear that he would have preferred to see someone else elected recording secretary. "Louis is more essential as a teaching expert, or in active public work; than to be burdened with recording work, which I really don't think he enjoys in any event," he asserted. "Perhaps that will work out in time."[10] And in time it did: for six years Louis Gregory was elected recording secretary of the Assembly by majority vote of his colleagues.

In this role he helped to advance the efficiency and smooth functioning of the National Assembly. According to Harlan Ober, who was himself a member at that time, the decision to create the office of recording secretary was the result of many months of consultation about the need to improve the minutes in order to produce a clear record of the proceedings of the National Assembly meetings. "This entire action," he reported to Shoghi Effendi, "has been taken in a desire and endeavor to place the responsibility for all actions of the N.S.A. in the body itself, at the time it is acting, rather than following the plan that has negligently been permitted to grow up, of having the Secretary assume the responsibility of making what he considered necessary changes afterward."[11]

The confidence in Louis Gregory's administrative abilities that was repeatedly expressed by his fellow Assembly members who elected him to office was shared by the delegates to the annual conventions. Several times during this period he received either the highest or the second highest number of votes cast.

Attitudes toward minority representation on the National Spiritual Assembly seem to have changed permanently in 1939. Since that time, with the exception of three years in the mid-1950s, at least one black has served annually; other minorities have been represented as well. During much of the period two or three blacks have been members simultaneously, thus constituting 20 to 30 percent of the nine-member body; since 1968 this high percentage has been maintained steadily. A total of ten capable and highly respected blacks have served on the Assembly from its inception to mid-1981. They constitute about 16 percent of the total number of individuals ever elected to that body.

The professional backgrounds of this distinguished group range over the fields of education, law, and journalism. Matthew Bullock, for example, was one of the outstanding black leaders of his generation. A graduate of Dartmouth (where he achieved fame as a football star in the early years of the century) and of Harvard Law School, he served on the front lines in Europe during World War I as an educational secretary of the Y.M.C.A., established a record of public service in Boston, and near the end of his long life received honorary degrees from Harvard in 1970 and from Dartmouth in 1971, where his efforts as a Bahá'í were specifically cited and, at the age of ninety, he received a standing ovation from an audience of five thousand. [12]

Several of the black representatives on the National Assembly have also achieved international recognition as Bahá'ís. Former Assembly member Amoz Gibson has served as a member of The Universal House of Justice, the supreme administrative body in the Bahá'í world, since 1963, the year of its inception. Two of the ten, Sarah Pereira and William Maxwell, have also been named to the Continental Boards of Counselors, the highest appointive institutions in the period since the founding of The Universal House of Justice. Five have pioneered outside of the United States, with two—Elsie Austin and Matthew Bullock—becoming Knights of Bahá'u'lláh, a designation given by Shoghi Effendi to those who filled special goals in a major international plan for expansion, the Ten Year Crusade, from 1953 to 1963. Along with Louis Gregory,

William Maxwell, and Ellsworth Blackwell, they helped to found Bahá'í communities in the Caribbean, Africa, the Far East, and the Pacific.

Two of the black National Assembly members have followed in Louis Gregory's footsteps by participating in the secretarial functions of the Assembly. Glenford E. Mitchell, who was first elected to membership in 1968, has been secretary of the National Spiritual Assembly and its chief spokesman to both the American Bahá'ís and the public since that time; his tenure of office as secretary has thus been longer than any except Horace Holley's. The ninth black elected to the Assembly, Magdalene Carney, has also served as its assistant secretary. The tenth, Wilma Brady, has represented the American Bahá'í community at the United Nations.

Louis Gregory's return to the National Spiritual Assembly in 1939 was thus a step forward for minority representation on the national level and a major advance along the "long and thorny road" toward racial unity that Shoghi Effendi in *The Advent of Divine Justice* had urged the American Bahá'ís to follow. His election firmly established a pattern of elevating blacks to positions of leadership that few racially mixed religious organizations in America—indeed, few organizations of any kind—have equalled.

28 Banner Years

After the 1939 convention the newly elected National Spiritual Assembly quickly reinstituted a special committee to promote the oneness of mankind. In keeping with Shoghi Effendi's strong language in *The Advent of Divine Justice* and with the heightened awareness he had created, the term *race unity* subsumed *race amity* as the stated aim of the American Bahá'ís. The five-member Race Unity Committee included Louis Gregory and Dorothy Beecher Baker, the vice-chairman of the National Assembly and a member since 1937, who became the committee's chairman.

Dorothy Baker was a major force on the committee until 1944. In a sense she took on the role that had originally been Agnes Parsons'. But the two were in many ways dissimilar. Mrs. Parsons had become active in promoting race amity at the direction of 'Abdu'l-Bahá, when she was nearly sixty; Dorothy Baker, in her early forties, came to the work through her own strong conviction. The social backgrounds of the women differed widely. Mrs. Baker's Northern liberalism, in the tradition of her famous forebears Henry Ward Beecher and Harriet Beecher Stowe, contrasted with the elitism and conservatism in which Agnes Parsons had been reared. Yet both were strong personalities, capable of inspiring genuine admiration, and inwardly illumined, as others described them, and both had been profoundly devoted to the Bahá'í Faith since the days of 'Abdu'l-Bahá. Their leadership could not be easily dismissed by those white coreligionists who preferred to ignore or deemphasize the racial issue. And, as Louis Gregory had once observed, the motives of such leaders could not be questioned—at least not as readily as those of even the most tactful and distinguished black. Louis Gregory happily watched Dorothy Baker emerge as a leading advocate of increased efforts for racial justice and understanding. He had admired her for years, and his respect continued to grow. "I regard her as the foremost Baha'i of the western world," he wrote in 1950.[1]

The first Race Unity Committee represented not only blacks, but other groups, including Chinese and Jewish. Henceforth the concept of race unity systematically encompassed various racial and religious minorities, a policy specifically approved by Shoghi Effendi. Indeed, in 1945 he asked that the committee focus attention on particular minority groups in those places where prejudice against them was most virulent (he cited the feelings against Japanese-Americans in the West, where antagonism had been exacerbated by the war with Japan, and against blacks in the South) in order "to counteract it by showing publicly the Bahá'í example of loving tolerance and brotherly association."[2]

One of the aims set by the committee was the education of the Bahá'ís themselves. Accordingly, beginning in January 1940, a series of articles appeared in *Bahá'í News* both to inform the Bahá'ís and to instill positive attitudes about the diversity of racial and ethnic groups in America. The first article quoted extensively from *The Advent of Divine Justice* and stressed the committee's concern "to help all Bahá'ís overcome our prejudices, for we all have prejudices in one degree or another." The second, "Books on Race Relations," dealt specifically with blacks in America. A similar article a few months later highlighted books on the Jews. A fourth dealt with the Eskimos, a group with which the Bahá'ís had not as yet made contact. This type of educational effort continued in subsequent years. In 1942 the Race Unity Committee published a bibliography on several minorities—Eskimo, Negro, Jewish, and Indian—and a list of references from the Bahá'í writings to the various aspects of racial unity. The committee also helped to prepare for publication a book called *Race and Man,* which combined Bahá'í and other references on race and was used extensively for many years.[3]

The committee's educational endeavors also took it into a newly defined area: college teaching projects. "The southern college project," Dorothy Baker explained, "came out of keen awareness of the problem that exists between the two great races of that area and the conviction that such a problem, spiritual in its nature, could be solved by the healing agencies of the Message of Bahá'u'lláh to a stricken world.''[4] Louis Gregory's practice of seeking open minds in Southern colleges and universities thus became the stated policy of the committee. Mr. Gregory was not an officer of the committee and—according to Margaret Kunz Ruhe, a fellow member—was unable to attend regular meetings when the committee was centered in the Midwest, where Dorothy Baker resided.[5] Nonetheless, he was one of the most active speakers on the college circuit.

Late in 1940 the Race Unity Committee engaged in a teaching project in the South, focusing particularly on black clubs, schools, and colleges. Initially, the goal of the lecture program was to present the Bahá'í views on the creation of a unified world society, with the issue of the oneness of mankind featured as a part of that program, rather than the central theme. Both Louis Gregory and Dorothy Baker participated as speakers, combining their efforts as committee members with the interests of the National Assembly, which met in Atlanta in November. Louis Gregory spoke in Georgia and the Carolinas, while Dorothy Baker followed the long path he had trod alone for so many years. From Fisk in Nashville she journeyed to the Henderson Business College in Memphis, to Tuskegee Institute, and to the state of Florida, visiting a total of thirty colleges.[6]

In 1941–42, under the committee's auspices, Dorothy Baker lectured in nearly fifty colleges—white, black, and Indian. Louis Gregory's circuit in March and April 1942 took him through West Virginia, Virginia, and the Carolinas; he also visited Ohio, Michigan, Minnesota, and Washington, D.C.[7]

In 1942–43 a separate College Foundation Committee (later known as the Bahá'í College Speakers Bureau) was appointed. Working closely with the Race Unity Committee, it utilized the speaking talents of Dorothy Baker, Louis Gregory, Joy Hill Earl, and others. Mrs. Baker concentrated on the Southwest, touring six states and lecturing in twenty-seven schools. That winter and the next Louis Gregory traveled through Ohio, Michigan, Tennessee, Kansas, Oklahoma, Texas, Mississippi, Alabama, Louisiana, West Virginia, Virginia, and North Carolina. Following a committee directive approved by the National Assembly, he spoke directly on the Faith in black colleges and in white schools presented the Bahá'í teachings on race relations. ''The friendly reactions of the white Schools, in the light of existing prejudices, are of deep interest to us,'' Dorothy Baker reported in *Bahá'í News*.

> Salem College, of West Virginia, writes: "The students were well pleased, and invited him to return. I want to thank you for sending him to us." In the heart of Mississippi, where race feeling runs so high as to make such a subject well-nigh impossible, the students waited in long rows in the hall, to shake his hand and wish him well. It was their first adventure in receiving a colored speaker, and only their second experience with the Faith of Bahá'u'lláh.[8]

Educational endeavors were also directed to the permanent Bahá'í summer schools. In 1940 both Green Acre and Geyserville Bahá'í Schools offered courses on race, with Louis Gregory and Curtis Kelsey teaching ''Race Unity'' at Green Acre. In 1941 the annual race unity conference at Green Acre was reinstituted. Held over a three-day period in August, the conference featured talks by a variety of speakers, including Louis Gregory; Roy Wilkins of the N.A.A.C.P., then editor of *The Crisis;* Matthew Bullock; and Dorothy Baker. The Green Acre committee reported it to be ''the high point'' of that summer's program.[9]

In 1942 the Green Acre conference had a similar format, combining open forum sessions with speeches by a number of noted Bahá'ís. One of the talks featured the work of two influential black poets, Phillis Wheatley and James Weldon Johnson. The following year the conference, which again took place over a three-day weekend, attracted the largest attendance of the 1943 season to hear talks by Harlan Ober, Louis Gregory, and other long-time proponents of racial amity.[10]

In 1944 the event drew upon the talents of Dr. Genevieve Coy, Mildred Mottahedeh (a noted businesswoman who later served for many years as a Bahá'í representative to the United Nations), Harlan Ober, Louis Gregory, Lydia J. Martin, her sister Dr. Sarah Martin (Pereira), and Matthew Bullock. A report of the conference in *Bahá'í News* stated that Mr. Bullock ''described in graphic terms the poignant disappointment of those like himself, who went abroad during the former world war, inspired by the hope that so great an upheaval would bring justice and peace to mankind." After the war, instead of "the promised relief," they found that "class tyranny was strengthened and prejudices were increased." Disillusionment over the apparent failure of the established religions had been replaced for him, however, by the "great joy" of discovering that a plan for world order existed and was being implemented by the Bahá'ís. The 1945 conference, with Dr. Pereira as one of its organizers, attracted as many as ninety-one people to one of its five sessions, and in 1946 the conference was preceded by a week's study course on "The Negro in American Life."[11]

The Race Unity Committee helped to reinstate other activities, in addition to the annual race unity conferences at Green Acre, that had been successful in previous years: banquets, socials, meetings of all kinds. Louis Gregory participated in these events, large or small, whenever possible. In Peoria, for example, he and Dorothy Baker spoke to about a hundred people in January 1940. In Cincinnati they shared the platform at an interracial dinner in March 1941. Wherever they traveled, the lecturers availed themselves of opportunities to address various groups. "As the doors would open," Albert James has recalled, Louis Gregory ". . . would be there to go in the door."[12]

In 1942 the Race Unity Committee helped the Chicago Assembly to hold its annual race unity banquet. Scheduled immediately before the National Convention and sponsored by the National Spiritual Assembly, it drew about 275 people, representing the diverse population of the city and Bahá'ís from all sections of the United States and Canada. Chicago remained in the vanguard of interracial activity, as it had for so many years. The reports published by the Race Unity Committee indicated that Chicago was a valued source of ideas and inspiration. During the summer of 1940, for example, the Bahá'ís there mounted a display at the National Negro Exposition celebrating the seventy-fifth anniversary of Emancipation. About 12,500 Bahá'í pamphlets were distributed, and a Bahá'í meeting during the Exposition drew a crowd of six hundred.[13]

Among the other efforts noted by the Race Unity Committee in *Bahá'í News* was the establishment of a local race unity committee by the Miami Bahá'ís. It was probably the first in the South. The committee sponsored bimonthly meetings in both white and black neighborhoods and general interracial meetings of the community. In March 1946 Joy Earl addressed a well-attended "race unity lecture" there. On the opposite side of the continent the Bahá'ís of Seattle held annually a race amity tea; in 1945 the event combined a musical program and a discussion on "Illusion of Separateness" with the distinguished artist Mark Tobey as a panelist. [14]

The Race Unity Committee's columns in *Bahá'í News* focused increasingly on the Indians. The Bahá'ís of Milwaukee reported that they had entertained fifty people from the Indian Councils of their city during a city-wide celebration of interracial friendship. On another occasion the first Indian Bahá'í of South America met the first enrolled North American Indian at a Milwaukee Bahá'í feast. A large group of Oneida Indians from Wisconsin visited the 1941 convention and were introduced on the floor. The enrollment of the first Eskimo Bahá'í, a resident of the Southwest, was also noted in *Bahá'í News* in 1943. [15]

Twice during this period the committee published a survey of community reports on local race unity work. The reports indicated inactivity—"we haven't done anything yet, but we hope to" or "we don't have a race unity problem in our Bahá'í community" —and modest efforts such as placing Bahá'í books in a black library. More active communities participated in a black community center, presented a radio broadcast on race, and assisted an interracial USO headed by a black Bahá'í. By calling for reports the committee not only compiled examples and suggestions for activity but provoked some response even from those communities that were not active in interracial work. On one occasion, seeking to reach the grass roots, the committee urged each community to make race unity the topic for consultation at a Nineteen Day Feast. [16]

At the national convention the Race Unity Committee's reports also provided opportunities to consult with the Bahá'ís and to inspire and encourage them toward increased action. Indian teaching took a prominent place in the race unity consultation at the 1940 and 1941 conventions; Southern teaching was the central topic in 1942 and college circuits in 1943. Eskimo teaching was discussed for the first time at the historic 1944 convention, which coincided with the first Bahá'í centennial celebration. Although no convention report was published for 1945, and the 1946 report did not mention race unity, it seems that the subject remained a major focus of attention. One of the recommendations approved by the delegates to the 1946 convention was ''that the American Bahá'ís should make clear to the world what the teachings of Bahá'u'lláh are on the subject of race unity; that a demonstration be made, comparable to that of the peace teachings in San Francisco [on the occasion of the founding of the United Nations]. '' The National Assembly approved the recommendation and referred it to the Race Unity Committee, although the idea seems to have foundered there.[17]

As convention reporter from 1940 through 1944, Louis Gregory helped to shape the American Bahá'í community's general consciousness of its annual conventions. Race unity was never short-changed in his accounts; indeed, he sometimes used the opportunity for a bit of gentle editorializing. In 1942, for example, he reiterated remarks by the Guardian on Southern teaching which seemed to have been generally forgotten:

> The first definite instructions of the Guardian about the work in the South, to wit, that teachers in that region should consult with the minority group, find out from them who are the liberals among the majority, and then proceed with teaching, is fraught with divine wisdom and if followed would greatly facilitate the progress of the cause. The world is now in a state of rapid change and those who are just and are genuinely interested in human welfare are obviously the most likely to be attracted by the Great Message.[18]

And in 1944 he expressed a note of slight disappointment:

> Perhaps more time might have been spent upon a theme so inseparably connected with the nation's destiny. But in reflection, the Convention itself was the greatest demonstration of race unity that history records, with so many traditionally discordant elements melted into oneness by the attracting power of the love of God. It was also the sign of the unity of religions and none the less, an index of world unity.[19]

In other words, if the Bahá'ís were still somewhat reluctant to talk frankly about race unity, they seemed to Louis Gregory to be getting better at living it.

Louis Gregory was also able, as a member of the National Assembly after 1939, to consult on race at the highest administrative level and thereby to influence the response to the most challenging issue in those critical years. From the beginning, some notable advances were achieved. In November 1940, for example, the National Spiritual Assembly traveled to Atlanta for its first meeting in the Deep South. Mr. Gregory's participation assured that the issue of race would neither be ignored nor handled with insensitivity.

At that time the predominantly white Bahá'í community in Atlanta was far from enthusiastic about putting racial unity into practice. All of the members of the newly elected Local Spiritual Assembly were white, and a group of new Bahá'ís who had been attracted through the efforts of Orcella Rexford hardly knew that the black Bahá'ís existed. In fact, race had been a source of deep disagreement within the community for months. When Louis Gregory, the first National Assembly member to arrive, went to a meeting that had been arranged for the evening of his arrival, he found that only a handful of people—the pro-integration faction—had come. The next day, according to a history written for the Spiritual Assembly of the Bahá'ís of Atlanta, when Dorothy Baker requested a meeting with her and Mr. Gregory, everyone came. "Mrs. Baker announced at this gathering in her own humorous way that she is the great granddaughter of Henry Ward Beecher, one of the outstanding preachers who advocated the emancipation of the Negro in the pre-Civil War days," the account continued.

> At this time Mrs. Baker also demonstrated the great Baha'i principle of consultation. Every single individual was given an opportunity to express himself. The fact that Mrs. Essie Robertson [a black] had been waiting to be accepted into the Faith, was brought to the attention of everyone present. Mrs. Baker made it clear that the Baha'i Community could never restrict anyone because of color. . . .
>
> At the next meeting of the Local Spiritual Assembly Mrs. Essie Robertson was accepted as a believer. Some of the white members . . . ceased attenting [*sic*] Baha'i Assembly and Feast

meetings, but there were other Baha'is living in the city who could take their places, when the new Assembly was elected.

The Atlanta Assembly itself soon began to reflect the interracial character of the community; Mrs. Robertson, who had been taught by Thelma Allison of Nashville, became its first black member.[20] During the National Spiritual Assembly's visit, public as well as Bahá'í-only meetings were open to both races. A public meeting at the Biltmore Hotel featured white speakers, but a large portion of the audience was black (which distressed some of the local white Bahá'ís but greatly encouraged the blacks). A teaching conference drew twenty-seven people, black and white, from six Southern states: residents of Atlanta and nearby communities and representatives of all the Southern regional teaching committees. Ways and means of reaching the white majority and the black and Jewish minorities were discussed. The participants concluded that the necessity of reaching whites—"who to a very great extent set the pattern of life, establish customs, and are responsible for the enactment of laws"—could not "be overestimated," even though whites were found to be generally unreceptive to the Bahá'í teachings.[21]

By meeting in Atlanta the National Spiritual Assembly helped to reinforce the movement toward racial unity among the Bahá'ís there. The whites were put on notice, even at the risk of their withdrawal from the Faith, that they had to come to terms with the principle of oneness in both their Bahá'í community life and in their approach to the public. It was no small thing to ask of them, requiring as it did courage to challenge the mores of a divided society and to expose oneself to hostility. That courage was often tested—when Olga Finke was asked by her landlord to move after Louis Gregory's visit, for example, or when in 1947 "the Ku Klux Klan broke up an interracial Bahá'í meeting in Atlanta."[22] But a firm stand assured that the Faith would grow in Atlanta and throughout the South, if not at first among the white population, which was not yet ready to accept change, then among the blacks, for whom change was grievously overdue.

Thus the National Spiritual Assembly's visit to Atlanta set a standard of uncompromising forthrightness on race of which Louis

Gregory could be proud. His and Dorothy Baker's influence helped to make the event a milestone in Bahá'í history in the South. Several months later Shoghi Effendi commended the National Assembly's efforts in Atlanta:

> The Guardian is very pleased to learn of the success that has attended the sessions at Atlanta and the removal of the disagreement within the community of that city and the work achieved by the regional conference and the public meeting open to both races. A special effort, he feels, should now be made to lay a foundation of unity between the white and colored Bahá'ís and weld the groups [in the region] into communities capable of forming Assemblies representative of both races.[23]

A second major achievement for race unity occurred in the fall of 1943, when the National Spiritual Assembly made it the theme for nationwide proclamation for two months during the final year of the Seven Year Plan. In a letter announcing the effort the Assembly stressed not only the inherent importance of the principle of oneness but also its "relation to the ominous manifestations of inter-racial bitterness which at present suggest the approach of a crucial stage in the ordered life of the nation." Then the Assembly proceeded to remind the American Bahá'ís of the connection between the struggle for race unity and the cause of international peace:

> As was pointed out during the course of the Bahá'í Race Unity Conference held at Green Acre this summer, the matter of race relations in America has become a world issue. The peoples look to North America for proofs of justice, esteem and spiritual fellowship among the races. When such proofs are forthcoming, the peoples will have a basis for hope in the development of true peace. Therefore our Bahá'í understanding and energetic effort in the promotion of the principle of the oneness of mankind represents a direct and indirect contribution to world justice and peace possessing incalculable possibility.[24]

The National Assembly's statement was set against a background of increasing racial strife in the United States. As had occurred during World War I, black soldiers were frequently subjected to abuse and discrimination, an ironic recompense for those who were fighting for their democratic government. Black Americans in general were affronted by such policies as that of the Red Cross in segregating ''white'' and ''Negro'' blood banks. Among the civilian population the migration of large numbers of blacks to cities with industrial jobs created predictable tensions, which were easily exploited by bigots and demagogues. In June 1943 a fight between a black and a white in Detroit led to the worst race riot of the war years; thirty-four people were killed and hundreds of thousands of dollars worth of property destroyed, with the black population bearing the major losses.[25]

Even as racial disturbances increased, however, Mr. Gregory kept his eye on the future and maintained a confident attitude. ''Rest assured that everywhere there are encouraging signs,'' he wrote Edith Chapman. Lydia Martin and Sarah Martin Pereira have recalled that ''once when he was visiting with us in Cleveland, when in the forties it began to appear that racism southern style was invading the North, Mr. Gregory responded to my question about whether things were getting worse for the Negro, by saying, 'No, indeed, conditions are getting better. For when these injustices are brought to light and discussed openly, that is the beginning of the end of prejudice.' ''[26] In fact, the war years, difficult as they seemed at the time, did much to change the legal and economic status of blacks in American life and to prepare the way for more dramatic changes in the next two decades.

The National Spiritual Assembly's unprecedented level of action in 1943–44 made it, in Louis Gregory's words, ''the banner year'' in race unity work. ''The past year has recorded the most progress in race unity since this movement began,'' he stated in his report on ''The Historic Thirty-Sixth Convention.'' Race unity meetings had been held in at least fifty-seven centers in response to the National Assembly's call to action. Among the most notable was a symposium on ''Racial Foundations for World Order'' at the Palace Hotel in San Francisco, distinguished by the participation of Leroy Ioas as chairman; Dr. Charles S. Johnson, a black social worker; Rabbi Rudolph I. Coffee; Dorothy Baker; and Robert W. Kenny, the attorney general of California. The event attracted about seven hundred and fifty people. Talks by Alain Locke and others in New York and by Louis Gregory in Flint, Michigan; Kenosha and Milwaukee, Wisconsin; and Cleveland, Ohio, also achieved noteworthy results during the year.[27]

While the Bahá'ís intensified their activities, the violence began to subside nationwide. After Detroit, John Hope Franklin has observed, "many communities were able to avert riots by making intelligent and careful approaches to the solution of the problems that created riots."[28] To the extent that the Bahá'ís, individually and collectively, became more active in race unity work, they contributed to easing the climate of confrontation.

The National Assembly made another major effort a few months later when it addressed a letter on race unity to President Franklin D. Roosevelt. In 1941, under pressure from A. Philip Randolph and other black leaders and seeking to avert a threatened march on Washington to demand equal employment for blacks in defense industries, Roosevelt had issued Executive Order 8802, which prohibited discrimination in defense industries and government service. The order aroused a storm of protest in the South and was only partially effective, but it was a significant achievement in the struggle for equal rights. The National Assembly referred to President Roosevelt's stand on equal employment in its letter of 4 January 1944, urging him not only to maintain but to extend his actions in behalf of blacks:

Dear Mr. President:

Your firm and powerful support of the principle of justice in race relations in connection with labor policy at this time, and your attitude of understanding and sympathy toward the economic and social hardships sustained by our Negro citizens, have been noted with grateful appreciation by all American Bahá'ís. It is our confident hope that through your authority and influence this gravest problem of civilization in America may at last be lifted up out of the darkness and distortion of prejudice and realized, by people and government alike, to be the fundamental ethical challenge laid by destiny upon our nation. How can we exercise the concentration of material and spiritual power in America for world peace if we continue to abuse that power in dealing with our own most helpless minority?

Therefore, because the Bahá'ís have for many years been conscious and aware of the vital importance of race unity as a foundation for world order, and have established race unity spiritually and socially in their own community, they now deem it a high privilege to express to their President these few words of sincere gratitude, and their heartfelt best wishes for full success in the noble effort to apply the divine law of human fellowship to political and social fields which have claimed exemption from the power of truth until the whole of humanity has become submerged in the sea of violence and strife.

Recently the Bahá'ís have issued a book entitled "Race and Man" in which are gathered together the most enlightened views of the time on aspects of this matter of race unity.

A copy of the book is being sent, and we trust that it will be accepted as a presentation for the Library of the White House.

Among the statements on race unity found in the Bahá'ís' Sacred Writings, the text of an address delivered by 'Abdu'l-Bahá at Howard University on April 13, 1912, seems particularly appropriate:

"In the estimation of God there is no distinction of color; all are one in the color and beauty of servitude to Him. . . . Therefore strive earnestly and put forth your greatest endeavor toward the accomplishment of this fellowship and the cementing of this bond of brotherhood between you. Such an attainment is not possible without will and effort on the part of each; from one, expressions of gratitude and appreciation; from the other kindliness and recognition of equality. Each one should endeavor to develop and assist the other (race) toward mutual advancement. This is possible only by conjoining of effort and inclination. Love and unity will be fostered between you, thereby bringing about the oneness of mankind. For the accomplishment of unity between the colored and whites will be an assurance of the world's peace."

"Then racial prejudice," 'Abdu'l-Bahá continued, "national prejudice, limited patriotism and religious bias will pass away and remain no longer."

In these fateful days when ethical foundations alone will support the structures of an enduring society, the question of race unity in America, we dare to hope, will receive the priority of effort and spiritual intention needed to create full assurance "of the world's peace" and security for mankind.

Respectfully,
National Spiritual Assembly of the Bahá'ís
of the United States and Canada
By: Horace Holley
Secretary[29]

The National Assembly's straightforward stand and broad vision, linking racial justice in America with the cause of peace in a world torn apart by war, was a tribute to Louis Gregory's long years of patient effort. For him there could have been no more fitting climax to the first Bahá'í century.

NATIONAL SPIRITUAL ASSEMBLY OF THE BAHÁ'ÍS OF THE UNITED STATES AND CANADA, 1941

Front row, left to right: George O. Latimer, Amelia E. Collins, Louis G. Gregory, Dorothy B. Baker, Siegfried Schopflocher

Back row, left to right: Horace Holley, Roy C. Wilhelm, Leroy Ioas, Allen B. McDaniel

LOUIS G. GREGORY BAHÁ'Í INSTITUTE
near Hemingway, South Carolina,
dedicated in 1972 in honor of Louis G. Gregory

LOUIS GREGORY CHILDREN'S SCHOOL
a part of Green Acre Bahá'í School, Eliot, Maine,
dedicated in 1970 in honor of Louis G. Gregory

29   Deferred Victories

The cycle of the Race Unity Committee closely paralleled that of the amity committee a decade before. In both 1927 and 1939 Shoghi Effendi had addressed major messages on race to the American Bahá'ís, thereby lending a great impetus to efforts toward the eradication of prejudice. National committees were established in both years, during a time of heightened awareness of the need for change. They and the activities they encouraged—from large public meetings, to the annual conference at Green Acre, to small local get-togethers—flourished, despite the onset of a major societal upheaval two years after each committee was formed: the Great Depression in 1929 and America's entry into the Second World War in 1941. The fifth year of each committee's life, 1931–32 and 1943–44, saw intense activity and unprecedented victories; it was, in each case, a banner year.

After 1944 the parallel continued, with only slight variations. This time Louis Gregory remained on the National Spiritual Assembly for two more years. The committee survived for three years after its peak (compared with four, from 1932 to 1936, in the earlier period); but during the last year no reports of its activities appeared in *Bahá'í News,* and the committee seems to have been already contemplating its demise.

In September 1946 the National Assembly called for a special national consultation on "race unity teaching," the purpose of which was to "intensify the influence of the entire Bahá'í community as an instrument for the removal of prejudice and separation between the races on this continent." The Race Unity Committee was invited to meet with the National Assembly, and "a general consultation" with representatives of the National Teaching Committee, the Regional Teaching Committees, and the Assemblies of the Southern and border states was also to be held. At first a major interracial banquet in Chicago was planned for the evening before the conference; this was later cancelled in favor of a special workshop session "to provide for more intensive consideration of the teaching policies involved in the best promotion of the Faith in the Southern areas."[1]

The results of the consultation, however, were never reported in *Bahá'í News*. At the 1947 convention the Race Unity Committee— of which Louis Gregory had been a member, although ill health limited his participation—itself recommended that it be discontinued. The delegates concurred in the recommendation, and the new National Spiritual Assembly decided "for the sake of better coordination" to incorporate the race unity responsibilities in the duties of the National Teaching Committee.[2] Although the decision seems to have stemmed from a desire to make the oneness of mankind an integral part of every facet of Bahá'í activity, rather than to compartmentalize it, the outcome followed the pattern of previous years. Once again, after a period of concerted activity, the view that specific race unity activities emphasize differences more than unity seems to have predominated. Yet, as before, without a special committee the most challenging issue was allowed to slip from the place of prominence that Shoghi Effendi and 'Abdu'l-Bahá had given it.

An incident at the 1947 convention illustrates the extent to which freedom from prejudice as "the watchword of the entire body of the American believers" was hampered by prevailing social attitudes. During a consultation on youth, a white delegate from Illinois "urged discretion" on young Bahá'ís, citing a case in Los Angeles where an interracial group was "stopped by squad cars" and "detained." The comment revealed a persistent tendency toward extreme caution among some Bahá'ís, whose "fear of unpopularity" and "dread of censure" led them toward "silent compromise" fully twenty years after Shoghi Effendi had warned that such attitudes were detrimental to the interests of the Faith. He had stated specifically in 1927 that the eyes of the Master and of the world were upon even the Bahá'í children, in their playgrounds, classrooms, and clubs—to measure the extent of their adherence to the Bahá'í standard, not their "discretion." Matthew Bullock, a delegate from Massachusetts that year, rose to his feet protesting, to applause from the assemblage, that "walking together is not indiscreet."[3] But the applause could not erase this signal of the need for constant education and vigilance among the Bahá'ís themselves.

Progress in the South remained slow. In a 1942 letter to an individual Bahá'í, Shoghi Effendi alluded to some of the thorny problems that hindered expansion there:

Regarding the whole manner of teaching the Faith in the South: the Guardian feels that, although the greatest consideration should be shown the feelings of white people in the South whom we are teaching, under no circumstances should we discriminate in their favor, consider them more valuable to the Cause than their Negro fellow-southerners, or single them out to be taught the Message first. To pursue such a policy, however necessary and even desirable it may superficially seem, would be to compromise the true spirit of our Faith, which permits us to make no such distinctions in offering its tenets to the world. The Negro and white races should be offered, simultaneously, on a basis of equality, the Message of Bahá'u'lláh. Rich or poor, known or unknown, should be permitted to hear of this Holy Faith in this, humanity's greatest hour of need.

This does not mean that we should go against the laws of the state, pursue a radical course which will stir up trouble, and cause misunderstanding. On the contrary, the Guardian feels that, where no other course is open, the two races should be taught separately until they are fully conscious of the implications of being a Bahá'í, and then be confirmed and admitted to voting membership. Once, however, this has happened, they cannot shun each other's company, and feel the Cause to be like other Faiths in the South, with separate white and black compartments. . . .

'Abdu'l-Bahá Himself set the perfect example to the American believers in this matter—as in every other. He was tactful, but the essence of courage, and showed no favoritism to the white people as opposed to their dark-skinned compatriots. No matter how sincere and devoted the white believers in the South may be, there is no reason why they should be the ones to decide when and how the Negro Southerner shall hear of the Cause of God; both must be taught by whoever rises to spread the Message in those parts.[4]

In 1950 the teaching committee for the Southeastern states reported that very few people were entering the Faith in the South, although teaching continued. At that time 69 percent of the Bahá'ís in the region were white and 31 percent black. The committee reported a small but perceptible move toward changed attitudes and relaxed segregation, observing that "even a faint light is bright in utter darkness."[5] But Shoghi Effendi's point had always been that the Bahá'ís should not wait for the light of the new age to dawn; rather, they should bring light through ceaseless effort in spreading Bahá'u'lláh's message of unity and brotherhood.

Once again it took Shoghi Effendi's direct intervention to bring the American Bahá'ís back to a more direct and aggressive stance with regard to race. In 1953 Dorothy Baker addressed the Bahá'ís gathered in Chicago for an All-America Conference celebrating an historic occasion of threefold importance: the centenary of Bahá'u'lláh's revelation, the dedication of the completed Wilmette Temple, and the launching of the Ten Year World Crusade. She shared with the audience of over two thousand Bahá'ís a theme that Shoghi Effendi had reiterated during her recent pilgrimage. "He said one driving thing over and over—that if we did not meet the challenging requirement of raising to a vast number the believers of the Negro race, disasters would result. And second," she continued, "that it was now for us to arise and reach the Indians of this country. In fact he went so far as to say on two occasions that this dual task is the most important teaching work on American shores today."[6]

The problem of achieving racial unity, as both Shoghi Effendi and 'Abdu'l-Bahá had always intimated, was not simply national in scope. As Dorothy Baker reported it, it was clearly related to a general shift in the balance of power from the old colonial regimes to their former subjects:

> Now the dark-skinned people, he said, would have an upsurge that is both spiritual and social. The spiritual upsurge will rapidly bring them great gifts because this is an act of God, and it is so intended. And all the world's prejudiced forces will not hold it back one hair's breadth. The Bahá'ís will glorify it and understand it. The social repercussions of race suppressions around the world will increase at the same time, and, frightened, the world's forces will see that the dark-skinned peoples are really rising to the top—a cream that has latent gifts only to be brought out by divine bounties.

Where do the Bahá'ís stand in this? Again and again he pointed out that the Bahá'ís must be in the vanguard of finding them and giving them the Faith. For the social repercussions will at times become dreadful if we do not, and we shall be judged by God.

I thought that I was rather a fanatic on the race question—at least a strong liberal. But I sat there judged by my Guardian, and I knew it. My sights were lifted immeasurably. . . .

God forbid that even in this coming year we fail in this. And the first solution is offered us by the Guardian. He wishes the appointment of two important national committees immediately. One is to reach the Negro minority of America with this great truth in vast numbers. Not just little publicity stunts either, but to make them believers. The second committee is to reach the Indian tribes of this continent. And some of us, to draw out further light on the subject, even questioned a great deal about the kind of psychology that might ensue if you had a committee just to reach the Negroes. But he rather scoffed at it, in a precious, twinkling kind of way, and firmly reiterated that without such special attention we simply had not done it—and that the important thing is to *do* it.[7]

With the appointment of an Interracial Teaching Committee, as it was called after 1953, the level of activity greatly increased once again. In February 1957, for example, Bahá'ís in thirty-five states held public meetings in conjunction with Negro History Week.[8] Yet ingrained racial attitudes persisted, hindering the spread of the Faith among blacks and among both races in the South. Thirty years after his first major message to the Americans on race, and just a few months before his death, the Guardian addressed a forceful letter to the Interracial Teaching Committee, stressing his view that a completely new emphasis must be given to the teaching work, particularly in the South:

White American Bahá'ís, he feels, although they have very much less prejudice than the American people, are nevertheless tainted to some extent with this national evil, perhaps wholly unconsciously so. Therefore, it behooves every believer of white extraction to carefully study his own attitude, and to see whether he is condescending in his relations with his fellow-Bahá'ís of negro extraction. . . .

The attitude toward teaching the Faith in the southern states of the United States should be entirely changed. For years, in the hope of attracting the white people, in order to "go easy" with them and not offend their sensibilities, a compromise has been made in the teaching work throughout the South. The results have been practically nil. The white people have not responded worth mentioning, to the Faith, and the colored people have been hurt and also have not responded.

He feels it is time that the Bahá'ís stopped worrying entirely about the white element in a community, and that they should concentrate on showing the negro element that this is a Faith which produces full equality and which loves and wants minorities. The Bahá'ís should welcome the negroes to their homes, make every effort to teach them, associate with them, even marry them if they want to. We must remember that 'Abdu'l-Bahá Himself united in Bahá'í marriage a colored and a white believer. He could not do more.

Also . . . the Faith must be representative of the population. In a great many places in the South, the majority of the population is still negro. This should be reflected in the Bahá'í Community, fearlessly. Both the white Bahá'ís and the colored Bahá'ís must steadily work to attain this objective of bringing the Faith to the colored people, and of confirming many of them in it. Both sides have prejudices to overcome; one, the prejudice which is built up in the minds of a people who have conquered and imposed their will, and the other the reactionary prejudice of those who have been conquered and sorely put upon.

Your committee should devote the major part of its effort towards attaining these goals in the South, and it should also as part of its work, urge the Bahá'ís, wherever they may be, to devote more attention to the minorities.[9]

Neither Shoghi Effendi's nor 'Abdu'l-Bahá's urgings—nor Louis Gregory's long, and for many years virtually single-handed, efforts—achieved unequivocal success during their lifetimes. For every victory for the oneness of mankind, there was a setback; for every demonstration of unclouded vision by the American Bahá'ís, there was an opposing element of insensibility. Gradually, however, notable changes appeared both among the Bahá'ís and in the American nation. On the one hand, though still wracked by prejudice, the United States began to make real strides toward assuring equal civil rights for blacks. On the other, the Bahá'í Faith began to enroll blacks and other minorities at an increasing rate. By the late 1960s and early 1970s the Faith was growing rapidly in the South, far more rapidly than anywhere else in the nation, and almost exclusively among blacks. In 1972 a Bahá'í teaching institute to promote further expansion was established in South Carolina; it was dedicated to the memory of Louis Gregory, whose name it bears.

It is unfortunate that Louis Gregory's last years—from 1947 to 1951—coincided with one of the twilight periods of Bahá'í activity for racial unity in America. Undoubtedly, he would have been happy in his retirement to see the work to which he had devoted so much effort maintain its momentum. But his concerns had been vindicated by Shoghi Effendi before, and his confidence that they would prevail was unshakable.

Meanwhile, he tried to encourage other black Bahá'ís troubled by the attitudes of some of their white fellow believers. In 1950, for example, he urged Edith Chapman to remain optimistic after she had become frustrated with some of the Missouri Bahá'ís. "We must give people credit for their sincerity, however their views may clash with ours," he wrote from long experience. "The Faith if adhered to will inevitably train people out of their prejudices and insularities of thought. Oftimes those most prejudiced go farthest to the other extreme when they discover the Spirit of Baha'u'llah." Even if some whites wished to hold separate meetings for inquirers, there was no reason to become distressed:

> Meetings where the races meet together have a very powerful confirmation since such gatherings have assurance of divine favor. However if any prefer to start their friends who are prejudiced in a private so called fireside meeting, I see no harm in it, since some people who were very strongly prejudiced have often made very fine Baha'is. . . .[10]

He wondered, however, whether such a cautious attitude among some of the whites might be the result of their not being "informed of the progress in such matters among progressive groups in the outside world," which was "simply amazing and . . . confined to no one section." Yet, if they insisted on holding separate firesides, he would not try to discourage them: "It may be wise to let those who think otherwise . . . try out their beliefs, and perhaps demonstrate their failure."[11]

The discouragement felt by Edith Chapman affected even Sadie Oglesby, a veteran believer, the first black woman to make a Bahá'í pilgrimage, who expressed her feelings in a letter to Shoghi Effendi. His answer, written in February 1942, detailed the kind of attitude that black Bahá'ís in America required for their own emotional and spiritual well-being and for the ultimate triumph of their vision of unity:

> He [the Guardian] is well aware that the conditions within the ranks of the believers in respect to race prejudice is [*sic*] far from being as it should be. However he feels very strongly that it presents a challenge to both white and coloured believers.
>
> As we neither feel nor acknowledge any distinction between the duties and privileges of a Bahá'í, whoever he may be, it is incumbent upon the negro believers to rise above this great test which the attitude of some of their white brethren may present. They must prove their innate equality not by words but by deeds. They must accept the Cause of Bahá'u'lláh for the sake of the *Cause*, love it, and cling to it, and teach it, and fight for it as *their* own Cause, forgetful of the shortcomings of others. Any other attitude is unworthy of their faith.
>
> Proud and happy in the praises which even Bahá'u'lláh Himself has bestowed upon them, they must feel He revealed Himself for them and every other down-trodden race, loves them, and will help them to attain their destiny.
>
> The whole race question in America is a national one and of great importance. But the negro friends must not waste their precious opportunity to serve the Faith, in these momentous days, by dwelling on the admitted short comings of the white friends. They must arise and serve and teach, confident of the future they are building, a future in which we know these barriers will have once and for all been overcome![12]

So fully did Louis Gregory exemplify this attitude—so completely, yet mildly, did he disregard conventional barriers—that, in a sense, he already existed in that future. He was its best advertisement in a painfully divided age.

30 Fulfillment

Louis Gregory stood as a symbol of racial equality to both the black and the white Bahá'ís of America, yet the range of his activities and interests showed that he was never circumscribed by any single preoccupation. In fact, his last years of membership on the National Spiritual Assembly, from 1939 to 1946, at a stage of life when most people would have retired or at least slowed down, were among the most active in all of the diverse areas of his life.

It was for him a period of intensive administrative activity. In all but one of those years he served as recording secretary of the National Assembly. He was also appointed—along with Dorothy Baker, Amelia Collins, and later Philip Sprague and Allen Mc-Daniel—to a Committee on Assembly Development. From 1942 to 1946 this committee, composed entirely of National Assembly members, assisted Local Assemblies, especially new Assemblies and those that were not growing in strength, to more effective functioning or to resolution of problems preventing their growth. In addition to correspondence, the committee emphasized personal visits by its members to a number of Assemblies annually. Mr. Gregory combined this work with his travels for the Race Unity Committee, to and from National Assembly meetings, and in connection with his teaching circuits. He was secretary of the committee for two years and a member for the duration of its existence. [1]

He was also a member of the Green Acre school committee for several years during the 1940s. Green Acre remained one of the constant sources of pleasure in his life. He lectured and taught there often, as he had for so many summers. On behalf of the Race Unity Committee he helped to organize the annual conferences at Green Acre, and one year he gave a course on race unity. But he taught other subjects as well: "The Laws of Bahá'u'lláh," for example, and "The Kitáb-i-Íqán" (Bahá'u'lláh's "Book of Certitude").

One year he handled local publicity for the school, which always attracted some residents and summer visitors to its public programs. In general, however, the people of Eliot seem to have kept aloof from Green Acre, even after half a century of its existence. A Bahá'í from Eliot, Emanuel Reimer, has recalled that he once asked Louis Gregory why, in his view, the local populace was not more aware of Green Acre and more interested in the principles for which it stood. Mr. Gregory replied that Green Acre was like a lighthouse; its beacon could be seen from far away, although, at its base, Eliot glimpsed little of its light. But someday, Mr. Gregory believed, the people of the area would realize Green Acre's importance.[2]

Another year he took charge of children's classes. He always loved children, and they in turn were charmed by his attentiveness to them. Margaret Kunz Ruhe, whose parents often entertained Mr. Gregory when he visited Urbana, remembers him as "an important part" of her childhood. Almost every morning of his stay she and her sister would enter the dining room to find their father and Mr. Gregory deep in discussion. Invariably Louis Gregory would make them feel as if their entrance were a joy to him, rather than an interruption; he would turn to them with a "chuckle" and "a most heavenly smile." Catharine Nourse, who grew up in Washington, D.C., and Atlantic City, has described him in similar terms. He was, for her, "a bit of Heaven." At Green Acre the Louis Gregory Children's School, dedicated in 1970, stands as a symbol of the special relationship between him and the young visitors to the campus. He spent much of his time with them, obviously enjoying an opportunity that his adult life had seldom provided. Once, when Louis Gregory must have been more than seventy, Emanuel Reimer saw him join a group of youngsters playing on the lawn, take the hands of two little ones, and start to play "ring-around-the-rosie"—"and going quite fast, I was surprised to see," Mr. Reimer remembers. "When they all tumbled down, as the story goes, Louis just dropped right down to the ground, *hard*." Mr. Reimer went over to him, protesting, " 'Louis, goodness gracious, you're going to hurt yourself. You shouldn't fall like that.'" But Mr. Gregory brushed aside the concern, saying that he wouldn't get hurt, that he was just having fun.[3] Even in play he gave the children his whole-hearted attention.

Such were the compensations that Green Acre always seems to have offered him. In 1945 he wrote to Mrs. Chapman, "Green Acre has had the most wonderful season in its history, save that of 1912 when His Holiness 'Abdu'l-Bahá Himself taught here."[4] In addition to the rest and steady diet and companionship with Louise that his Maine summers afforded, he drew upon Green Acre's special gifts: the tranquillity of its pastoral setting, the fellowship of the students, and the spiritual refreshment of concentrated study of the Bahá'í teachings.

Despite his hectic schedule throughout most of each year, he continued in the 1940s to make significant contributions as a Bahá'í writer. He served on *The Bahá'í World* editorial committee as editor for race unity activities and also wrote articles for two volumes: "Faith and the Man," the story of George Henderson, and "Accelerated Progress in Race Relations," an account of the 1943 and 1944 race unity conferences at Green Acre. His articles appeared as well in *World Order* magazine: "Bahá'í to Jew" in 1942, "Dr. Carver's Tribute" in 1943, and "Robert Turner" in 1946.[5] A member of the editorial committee for *Bahá'í News* for a time, he continued in the familiar role of convention reporter, which he had often filled since the days of the Temple Unity conventions. His last report covered the 1944 convention, which coincided with the hundredth anniversary of the Faith and of 'Abdu'l-Bahá's birth and the fiftieth since the Faith's establishment in the United States. He had helped to plan the convention as a member of the Centennial Committee, and, for those unable to attend and for posterity, no one was better suited to record it than he. His writing style, although often old-fashioned, was warm and inspirational. He had the gift of investing the annual convention, an administrative meeting, with spiritual significance:

All Bahá'í Conventions have inestimable value. They provide ways and means for wide consultation and more closely relate to each other the various activities and institutions of the Cause. They engage eager interest with news of progress. They pool spiritual values and increase harmony. They enable friends scattered over wide areas to know each other. They concentrate minds, hearts, means and labors over ever widening fields of service marked out by the Guardian. They delight the eye, brighten the mind and gladden the heart by the inspiring beauty of the Temple. . . . They are definite periods in the evolution of the Faith and furnish the most attractive means of teaching.[6]

His account of the 1944 convention was triumphant. In addition to honorary delegates from twenty-one South and Central American nations, fully a third of all the registered Bahá'ís in the United States and Canada attended—a remarkable number considering the difficulties of wartime travel. It was the largest and most diverse gathering of Louis Gregory's lifetime and the most important historically since 1919, when the Divine Plan was revealed, and 1912, when the annual convention was attended by 'Abdu'l-Bahá Himself. Louis Gregory savored every bit of its significance. At the end of his report he acknowledged the presence of the spirits of "the Dawn-Breakers of the East and the Trail-Blazers of the West, whose deeds and traces laid an imperishable foundation for this monumental triumph."[7]

Yet probably no living person present had blazed more trails than he or gained greater victories. Throughout his last years of active national participation he continued to follow the trails he had blazed in the early days, beginning with his first teaching trip in 1910. In October 1939 a National Assembly meeting in San Francisco enabled him to speak in the Bay Area; Southern California; Denver; Kansas City; Evansville, Indiana; West Virginia; and Philadelphia. He also visited Wilmington, Delaware, "where he addressed the National Association for the Advancement of Colored People, and spoke for three firesides." On his way to and from National Assembly meetings in Chicago, he visited many communities. In the spring of 1940, for example, he traveled west through New York state and on his return east made numerous stops; he spoke at a race unity dinner and gave a radio talk in Peoria, "was featured in two lectures and a radio talk on May 11th, at 'The Seventy-Five Years of Progress Exposition' arranged by the colored citizens of Detroit," and visited Lima, Ohio, Dorothy

Baker's home community. In 1942–43 he made his way through New York, Michigan, Ohio, and six Southern states.[8]

In his seventieth year, 1943–44, Louis Gregory journeyed from New England to Texas, stopping in Kentucky, Indiana, Ohio, Michigan, Wisconsin, Illinois, Missouri, Oklahoma, and Kansas. A report in *Bahá'í News* described his "highly successful" visit to Houston:

> Besides a series of advertised public meetings attended by 75 to 150 people of both races there were several fireside meetings and dinner parties. . . . The secretary of the Houston Assembly wrote that she had never witnessed such a clamoring for Bahá'í literature and for opportunity to hear a Bahá'í speaker. The people were "attending every meeting, bringing friends, and," in reality, "sitting at the feet of Louis Gregory." Many public meeting places were found where there was no segregation of races, and meetings were held in the Negro districts, with no objections whatsoever on the part of white inquirers.
>
> Very fine broad-minded business and professional men, both Negro and white, came to the meetings, also lieutenants and sergeants from Ellington Field.[9]

In 1944 and early 1945 Mr. Gregory traveled widely once again, visiting Missouri, Oklahoma, West Virginia, the Carolinas, Georgia, Tennessee, Illinois, Pennsylvania, New Jersey, and New York state. As in previous years Louise Gregory engaged in teaching work of her own while he was away; she spent the winter months in Brattleboro, Vermont, helping to establish a Bahá'í community there.[10] The activities of both of the Gregorys belied their years. Louise was in her late seventies; Louis was following as extensive an itinerary as he had in the early days of the Divine Plan, thirty years before.

After his last visit to Oklahoma City, a Bahá'í there reported that "this is the first opportunity many of us had to meet Mr. Gregory personally and we are deeply grateful for the privilege of association with this saintly soul."[11] These words aptly summarize the effect that Louis Gregory had upon his contemporaries. Active Bahá'í teacher, administrator, lecturer, writer, and amity worker that he was, his greatest achievement was perhaps his personal impact on those around him. At the full maturity of his powers as the first Bahá'í century ended and a new period of development began, Louis Gregory commanded love and respect won over nearly forty years of humanitarian service.

Part 5/*Culminations*

31   A Rounding Out of Life

Love and respect continued to surround Louis Gregory during the last five years of his life. Although he was ill for a time in 1946 and again a few years later, for most of this time he claimed that he felt as well and strong as ever. Louise was over eighty, however, and increasingly frail and dependent. Thus he was more or less confined after 1946 to the environs of Green Acre, where they had settled in a simple cottage.

At first he seems to have been a bit uncomfortable about his retirement from travel and active national involvement. Late in 1947 Shoghi Effendi, writing through his secretary, assured him that his services were still valuable:

> He [the Guardian] feels your loving association with the believers you are able to contact in Green Acre, and in the near-by towns, and the memories of the Master which you can share with them, as well as general Bahá'í instruction, of which you and your dear wife have such a store, and which you can impart to others—are the best ways you can serve the Cause at present.

Moreover, the difficulties of these years would soon pass: "In this world age and health and material conditions limit the soul. But in the next world it is free."[1]

Meanwhile the Gregorys were comfortable in Eliot. Both Mr. Gregory's race and their interracial marriage seem to have been accepted in the community with little or no comment. Emanuel Reimer has recalled seeing them walking together down the main street of the town, stopping to greet and talk to friends, an elderly couple like any other in the town. Eliot was peaceful and friendly; the Gregorys' door was never locked. In their garden they grew fresh vegetables, which pleased them because they shared an interest in diet and natural foods. During the long, quiet evenings, when

Mr. Gregory would stay up late working at his desk, Mr. Reimer often joined him there to talk awhile.[2]

Louis Gregory's only major trip during this time occurred in October 1948, when he flew to Kansas City to assist at the funeral of his old friend, Dr. Thomas C. Chapman, fulfilling a promise he had once made. A visiting Bahá'í enabled him to go by staying with Louise during his absence; and he wrote Edith Chapman later, "Louise, my dear wife, is glad that I took the trip." As always he seems to have enjoyed traveling, and the solemn occasion did not dampen his pleasure in serving and in visiting distant friends. "Bahá'í funerals are different from others," he observed to Mrs. Chapman, "in that there is always the assurance that life is continuous when one leaves this elemental plane." The trip itself was a pleasure, too; it was "quite wonderful," he exclaimed, "the first long one that I have ever made by air."[3] Its speed and comfort contrasted vividly with the long hours and days he had spent in Jim Crow cars, fighting a losing battle against grime and coal dust.

In December, only two months after his trip to Kansas City, he suffered a stroke. At first the doctor told Philip Sprague, who was visiting Eliot, that Mr. Gregory probably would live only a few days; if he survived, "he would not be mentally right." But within a few days he was so much improved that the doctor said he might be able to go home soon. By early January he was not only at home but catching up on his correspondence. In a letter to Mrs. Chapman he enclosed some material that he asked her to forward to a mutual friend; he had forgotten the man's name, he wrote, because "recently having had a slight stroke, followed by eighteen days of hospitalization, my memory is only gradually being restored." He continued, his handwriting somewhat weak and slanting across the page: "Gaining strength with pulse and temperature normal and a whale of an appetite. Quite worth while was it to be ill, with so many prayers ascending from many friends and the very best service, both hospital and now at home with my devoted wife and a Bahá'í friend who shares our home."[4]

By the summer of 1949 he seems to have been much recovered, his handwriting strong, when he wrote in longhand, the content of his typed letters as vigorous as ever, his outlook on his personal affairs more than ordinarily cheerful. "Louise and I are happy and grateful for countless favors, both material and spiritual," he wrote Mrs. Chapman in June. "Not only are we free from debt, but the long years of privation to serve the Cause have now brought to us increasing prosperity and new capacities to serve the beloved Faith."[5]

Since he was no longer traveling, he had much more time to write. He remained in contact with many of his friends through correspondence. "A letter of Mr. Gregory's was a precious and beautiful gift," Sarah Pereira and Lydia Martin have recalled. "His style was much like that of Abdu'l-Baha and one found herself reading his writing over and over for sustenance. He had friends whom he wrote in all age groups and students in every colored college and university in the Land. He always answered every letter. . . ."[6]

In addition to letters to friends, he corresponded in 1950 with a United States District Judge in Charleston, South Carolina, who had made some liberal rulings on race and had suffered ostracism by his community as a result. At Mr. Gregory's suggestion the National Spiritual Assembly itself wrote some words of encouragement to the judge.[7] Several writing projects also took up much of his time. He devoted himself to finishing a manuscript called "Racial Unity," a work that combined personal background and anecdotes, sketches of black leaders, and essays on various aspects of the Bahá'í principle of oneness. He was hopeful for a time that the book might be accepted by a commercial publisher and might add to his and Louise's income. He had no success with the venture, however, nor with trying to sell several articles that he completed during this time.

Nonetheless, the Gregorys' relative prosperity seems to have continued. They took it in stride, as they had accepted deprivation before. "Poverty was one of the best qualifications for effectiveness in my long years of travel teaching," he observed to Edith Chapman. "Now that wealth is needed for the upbuilding of Green Acre, Baha'u'llah has given me a Midas touch. Louise and I now have a large and growing income in an incredibly short time. It is now our effort to teach as long as we can and to aid others in the most confirmed of activities, especially those who have struggled and sacrificed so long for the Faith."[8] Because he never seems to have gone into detail in discussing his financial affairs, neither his friends nor his niece, Lauretta Noisette Moore (who became a

Bahá'í after moving from Charleston to New York, when she was young), know of any steady sources of income except for Louise's inheritance, which was held in trust in Europe.[9] This, however, seems to have grown through investments after the Second World War.

With a comfortable income, Mr. Gregory decided to buy a car, even though he was well over seventy and had not driven for many years. According to Emanuel Reimer, he received a perfect score on his written test, passed his road test as well, and was granted his license. Then he proceeded to purchase an old car, in which he took great pride. His days as a driver were numbered, however. One day, heading home from the library at Green Acre, he ran off the roadway, striking a large maple tree that still bears the scars of the accident. He was fortunate to be unhurt except for a bump on the head.[10] Afterward, even if he had wished to continue driving, Louise, who had worried about his driving years before, would no doubt have vetoed the idea.

During the summers of 1949 and 1950 Green Acre was closed as part of an austerity move, directed by Shoghi Effendi, in order to divert funds to complete the Wilmette Temple. Thus Eliot suddenly became remote from the mainstream of Bahá'í activity, far as it was from the large communities of the Northeast. As a result domestic concerns figured more prominently than usual in Louis Gregory's letters to Edith Chapman. In September 1949 he wrote:

What with details of house cleaning, grass cutting & planting, reaping, business and teaching, also cooking, my days are usually filled to overflowing. It seems good to be able to concentrate upon my own affairs, a far better rounding out of life, which must be balanced between matters material and spiritual, to reap the best results. Louise, my good wife, of course shares my efforts, with a strong will and an unusual range of accomplishment, but quite noticeably lessening strength.[11]

Shoghi Effendi continued to reassure them about their enforced retirement from more demanding fields of service. "Recently Louise and I were gladdened by a letter from our noble Guardian," Mr. Gregory wrote Edith Chapman in January 1950. "We had intimated in our letter to him, that although still trying to be active, yet there was a lessening in view of old age. But he assures us that our spirits are twenty years younger than our bodies, and that it is the spirit that counts. And so we shall have to continue to jog along."[12]

Louis Gregory faced old age with the same keen sense of humor that had helped to lighten the burdens of his younger years. Marzieh Gail has recalled one of the anecdotes with which he would "illustrate" his talks: "One of his stories was about a Persian who went to a doctor & recited a list of his symptoms. As he brought up each symptom, the doctor said: 'That is due to old age.' Finally he blew up, had a tantrum & upbraided the doctor. When he finished the doctor said, 'Your bad temper is also due to old age.' "[13]

Fortunately his own good health lasted well into 1950. "I have been doing eye exercises as well as [calisthenics] for many years," he wrote just a year before his death, "am very well indeed. . . ." Louise, however, continued to grow weaker. "My delay in writing has been caused by a very unusual pressure of work," he explained to Mrs. Chapman in May 1950. "My devoted wife is strong in will and spirit, but now quite frail in body, and so a great variety of tasks devolve upon me."[14]

Loving Green Acre as he did, its closing was undoubtedly difficult for him. The summer activities there had helped to ease the transition from the fast pace of his public life—travel, lecturing, and administrative work—to his final years of simply "jog[ging] along." The sessions had also helped to balance the routine of domestic responsibilities. "With Green Acre closed," he wrote in September 1949, "we miss the usual flow of summer visitors; although the local friends have been active. But yesterday four out of town visitors came, among them a Bishop of the African Orthodox Church. He drank in the message as eagerly as the others."[15]

The firesides and study classes that the Gregorys held in their home during those last years, extending to the very end of Louis Gregory's life, obviously helped to keep up his spirits. Teaching was the one activity without which he could not have survived. In turn, being in his home was a special experience for the visitor; Louis Gregory's presence was as magnetic in that plain setting as it had ever been in great lecture halls. As Marzieh Gail has described him, "Louis was living in a small, simple Green Acre house when we last met, and I remember contrasting that house with what I was sure would be a great mansion awaiting him in Heaven."[16]

Green Acre reopened in the summer of 1951. Louis Gregory mentioned it on 13 June in a letter to Alice Simmons Cox of Peoria, Illinois. He obviously looked forward to the influx of visitors during the season. Louise was "frail," he wrote, but, as for himself, "at 77, I am grateful for health and strength for service." On 30 July 1951 Louis Gregory passed away. Writing in tribute to his "dearly loved, universally respected" friend, Harlan Ober looked back on Mr. Gregory's last days:

> Although he had been frail in body for many months, the luminous spirit and great heart were so apparent, so overwhelming, that none anticipated his sudden departure.
> Only a week before, he had arranged and carried out a meeting in his home in Eliot, Maine, where he discussed the prophecies in the Bible, with their import for these perilous times. The dozen or more who gathered there will forever treasure this meeting which proved to be his last. Seated at his desk, his warm and radiant smile welcoming everyone, with his indescribable spiritual dignity, a manifest evidence of the world in which he lived, he carried on the meeting with joy and radiance. [17]

On 1 August 1951 a memorial service was held at Green Acre, the room overflowing. A few days later, on 6 August, a cablegram from Shoghi Effendi made clear the spiritual station that Mr. Gregory's friends had glimpsed decades earlier:

> Profoundly deplore grievous loss of dearly beloved, noble-minded, golden-hearted Louis Gregory, pride and example to the Negro adherents of the Faith. Keenly feel loss of one so loved, admired and trusted by 'Abdu'l-Bahá. Deserves rank of first Hand of the Cause of his race. Rising Bahá'í generation in African continent will glory in his memory and emulate his example. Advise hold memorial gathering in Temple in token recognition of his unique position, outstanding services. [18]

The station of Hand of the Cause had been instituted by Bahá'-u'lláh, Who appointed four Hands to assist Him. 'Abdu'l-Bahá and Shoghi Effendi had both conferred the rank posthumously. At the time of Louis Gregory's death Shoghi Effendi had named only six people Hand of the Cause after their passing, and only three were Westerners: Dr. J. E. Esslemont, author of *Bahá'u'lláh and the*

New Era, a basic text on the Bahá'í Faith that is still widely used throughout the world, and an assistant to Shoghi Effendi during the first difficult years of his Guardianship; Keith Ransom-Kehler, a noted American teacher who died of smallpox while on a mission for Shoghi Effendi in Iran; and Martha Root. It was only after Mr. Gregory died that the numbers of Hands were increased; in addition to two others appointed posthumously, thirty-two living Hands were named in several contingents between December 1951 and October 1957, shortly before the Guardian's passing. A number of them had been Louis Gregory's colleagues in teaching and administrative work; among them were Dorothy Baker, Horace Holley, Leroy Ioas, and Amelia Collins. Shoghi Effendi gave the living Hands duties and responsibilities based on instructions in the writings of 'Abdu'l-Bahá. But those who were appointed posthumously had risen to their station solely through their own efforts, without ever having been called to it directly.

Shoghi Effendi's cablegram also linked Louis Gregory with Africa, a connection that seems, on first thought, to be based solely on skin color. Louis Gregory had, after all, seen nothing of Africa except for a brief visit to Egypt, and his Bahá'í work had been confined to North America and Haiti. But Shoghi Effendi was not categorizing Louis Gregory by race or relegating him to a position of importance only in the Pan-African sphere. Since the time of 'Abdu'l-Bahá, the Bahá'í teachings had always linked racial unity in America to the cause of world peace. Indeed, as Dorothy Baker's 1953 speech at the All-America Conference demonstrated, the Guardian felt strongly that the development of the Faith among blacks in America was part of a general spiritual "upsurge" of the nonwhite peoples of the world prerequisite to the establishment of world order. He placed particular importance on the African continent. A year before Louis Gregory's death Shoghi Effendi had called upon the American Bahá'ís—and particularly upon blacks—to help establish the Faith in Africa, and just a few months after Mr. Gregory's death Shoghi Effendi cabled: "Rejoice at departure of first pioneer to Africa. . . . Time is short, tasks ahead manifold, pressing, momentous." [19] Thus Louis Gregory's effort to unite the races—the task given to him by 'Abdu'l-Bahá—was lifted to the global level, and his lifetime of service was given international significance on his passing.

In November 1951 the national memorial service called for by Shoghi Effendi was held at the Wilmette Temple. Louise Gregory was able to attend and read a prayer for the departed. Harlan Ober spoke of Mr. Gregory's early life, Joy Earl of his personal mission, and Dorothy Baker of his administrative achievements. Tributes from Bahá'ís were read—from Britain, India, Egypt, Tanganyika, and Ethiopia. The service, attended by Bahá'ís and friends from all parts of the country, was, according to *Bahá'í News,* "an occasion of great inspiration and spiritual re-dedication."[20]

Yet the occasion also marked a "grievous loss," as Shoghi Effendi had called it—the loss by humankind of one who saw beyond the barriers and lived for its wholeness and interdependence. The confinement of his last years had not dimmed his vision. "Light is everywhere breaking for the oppressed peoples of earth," he wrote in the concluding chapter of "Racial Unity":

Deep shadows prove the intensity of the light. The interests of no groups or classes will be overlooked or forgotten. The wish of the underprivileged to be treated as fairly as are other Americans in every avenue of human advancement is both proper and reasonable. Untenable is the attitude of those who would withhold it because of complexion or other superficial reasons. The friends of the oppressed show rapid increase in numbers and powers. Assuming that the victims of injustice will continue their struggle, no human might can long debar them from the long sought goal. Earth and air, fire and water, the stars in their courses, the high tide of destiny, and the Will of divine Providence are all arrayed against the forces of oppression.[21]

LOUIS and LOUISE GREGORY
pictured in front of their home in Eliot, Maine

The Hand of the Cause of God
Louis G. Gregory
6 June 1874–30 July 1951
"He is like unto pure gold. This is why he is acceptable in any market
and is current in every country." –'Abdu'l-Bahá

32   Pure Gold

In 'Akká in 1909 'Abdu'l-Bahá told Juliet Thompson that pilgrims responded in varying degrees to their experience there:

> "Some souls come here and return unaltered. It is precisely like one who comes to a fountain and, not being thirsty, returns exactly as he came. Or, like a blind man who goes into a rose-garden—he perceives not and, being questioned as to what he has seen in the rose-garden, answers, 'Nothing'.
> "But some souls who come here are resuscitated. They come dead; they return alive. They come frail or ill in body; they return healed. They come athirst; they return satisfied. They come sorrowing; they return joyous. They come deprived; they return having partaken of a share. . . .
> "These souls have in reality done justice to their Visit."[1]

Louis Gregory was indeed one of the thirsty ones, who did justice to his visit to the Holy Land and to his meeting with 'Abdu'l-Bahá. The pilgrimage integrated the different aspects of his life, all the varied strands of experience and personal development, and gave purpose to the whole. "He had become a new creation," 'Abdu'l-Bahá affirmed. "This man shall progress."[2] The opportunity to be with 'Abdu'l-Bahá again in America in 1912 accelerated that progress, providing more opportunities for Louis Gregory to drink in the lessons of the spirit that the Master constantly taught.

In the years that followed, growth was achieved through unceasing efforts and countless tests. The extent of Mr. Gregory's achievement was indicated by 'Abdu'l-Bahá Himself. "Do thou consider what a bounty God hath bestowed upon thee," He wrote Louise Gregory, "in giving thee a husband such as Mr. Gregory who is the essence of the love of God and is a symbol of guidance! How luminous is the face of this person! His character is (like unto) a rose-garden.'' In 1920, writing to a woman who had met Mr. Gregory in Texas, 'Abdu'l-Bahá paid him a remarkable tribute: ''That pure soul has a heart like unto transparent water. He is like unto pure gold. This is why he is acceptable in any market and is current in every country.''[3]

The ''pure gold'' of his nature inspired the kind of praise from his contemporaries that is usually voiced only after one's death. As a fellow Bahá'í observed in a 1930 letter to Alfred Lunt,

> I wish Mr. Gregory could hear what my nephew in Denver said about him—the impression that he made. I do not think we should wait until people are gone to tell all these nice things. I suppose I might as well tell you. He said some teachers, like Mr. Vail, for instance—their faces would light up at times as if they were catching a glimpse of the Spiritual Realms, but Mr. Gregory had that look all the time, as if he lived, moved and breathed in the atmosphere of the Spirit. Wasn't that a wonderful testimony of the purity and evanescence of this rare soul?[4]

Fifty years later a personal account by Elaine Snider Eilers, who recalled Louis Gregory's visits to Urbana during her childhood, was informed by the memory of his radiance:

> All the Baha'is had gathered for the Nineteen Day Feast. It was being held some eight or nine blocks from our house. Apparently, after the Feast a Local Spiritual Assembly meeting had been called. Mr. Gregory was our guest at the time, so rather than keep him there I was asked by my mother to guide him to our home. I was no more than eight years old and accepted the responsibility with great dignity. The night was dark and so was Mr. Gregory. I remember to this day one glance in which I looked up at him. My gaze was held for a moment on the beauty and peace of his face, but most of all, it was the shimmering radiance that was so remarkable, that seemed to be part of him. I was so amazed that in such darkness and also in the darkness of his coloring that there could be so much light. I was unable to take my eyes off of his face.[5]

Louis Gregory's bright spirit was never tarnished by attention or by praise. Self-importance had no place in his nature. He attributed the light that others perceived in him to the powerful force of unity.

Those who worked for brotherhood and peace, he truly believed, could illumine the world. He asserted at the first amity convention in Washington that, if we align ourselves with the forces of unity and love, God

> will give to us that inward peace which shall leave its bright traces in all the realm[s] of existence. It will make us true men and women; it will make us the torch-bearers of the light of God and will enable us to transmit a radiance by which the peace and pleasure and happiness of the whole world of existence will be adorned. And there is nothing more glorious for man than to realize this bright destiny.[6]

Thus, by stressing the potential of any human being to become illumined, Louis Gregory deflected personal praise. He felt that no one could take credit for the results of a spiritual law of causation. Illumination did not belong to him. Rather, he regarded it as an impersonal force that could even be tapped and utilized. In 1920, for example, he described for Joseph Hannen an experience he had in Corpus Christi, Texas, when the lights went out for "perhaps twenty to thirty minutes" while he was lecturing at a congregational church. Instead of stopping he "tried to make the inner light bright," he wrote, "and they listened with intense interest in the dark, so that there was no interruption."[7]

His attitude toward spiritual development helped him to balance words of praise against his own feelings of unworthiness; it enabled him to view a compliment as nothing more than encouragement in his efforts to become a "torch-bearer of the light of God." The tributes that 'Abdu'l-Bahá and Shoghi Effendi paid him meant the most. But, after theirs, no one's high regard could have meant more than that of Joseph Hannen, his teacher and close friend. Just a month before he was killed, Mr. Hannen wrote:

> Let me say that you can never ask anything of me that I shall not gladly grant. For you have done much for me, if I may have been privileged to be of some little importance in your life. Often, when I wonder what I have done in the Bahai work that is worth while, my thoughts go to you and your splendid work, and I feel that it is quite worth living for, to have helped to guide such a noble soul to the Kingdom.[8]

It was a letter to treasure, particularly after Joseph Hannen's untimely death, as indeed Louis Gregory did; the letter is one of very few from the early years that he retained in his papers to the end of his life.

A remarkably large number of his fellow Bahá'ís seem to have been aware not only of his unusual qualities, but of his station, not as a figurehead—the first black Bahá'í to do this or achieve that—but as one of the spiritual giants of his era. By the 1920s he had already come to be regarded by some as an historic figure. "It becomes increasingly evident in this country," May Maxwell told the 1929 convention on behalf of the National Teaching Committee, "that our beloved brother, Mr. Louis Gregory, is a unique instrument in the binding together of the white and coloured races. . . ." In 1925 Horace Holley added a penned note of unusual warmth to a letter regarding Mr. Gregory's recent teaching efforts in Florida: "The conditions of danger and sacrifice under which you are teaching, seem to me to approximate more closely the early days of the Revelation in Persia than can be found anywhere else in the West at this time. God bless you!"[9] The heroic terms in which Mr. Holley described Louis Gregory's work suggest one of the bases for the resilience of their relationship in later years.

In 1927 Charles Reed Bishop, a Bahá'í from the West Coast who later pioneered with his wife in Europe, had a dream about Louis Gregory while staying at the Geyserville Bahá'í School in California. The dream was so vivid that he told his wife, Helen, about it the next morning; she in turn immediately recounted it to Mr. Gregory. After thanking him for a recent letter and sending regards to Louise, she wrote: "Dear Louis—I know your sweet humility, but I wish to share with you an interesting dream which Charles had last night—and which brought him a marvelous wave of elation and joy." She explained that, as she was looking after a child from San Francisco for the week, Mr. Bishop had given up his bed and gone to sleep alone in another cabin, where he felt "an appalling loneliness" but finally, after praying, managed to go to sleep. "Just before he awakened in the morning," she continued,

> he was amazed to see you walking through the air, high in the clouds, with a banner which now unfurled to the breeze. He cried out to you in sheer astonishment, "Louis, you are walking in

the air!'', but you were wholly unconscious of your lofty height and went serenely on oblivious of the fact that you were in this unique station.

Then he observed that you had come out of the west to the east; you were turned to attention and then faced the South and continued your course with the banner high and shining.

Then he observed that there was a ''fleet'' of airships in the North, hundreds of them filling the sky.

Dear Louis—you can interpret this as it appears to you, but the reality which came to Charles through (and in) the dream was this: you had transcended all earthly limitations, had attained an ethereal consciousness and *alone* (this impressed him) with an unfaltering purpose and a steady pace would in time of crisis carry the banner of Bahá'u'lláh to spiritual victory. [10]

To these early Bahá'ís, who had been taught by the Master Himself that dreams are a proof of the existence of the soul and that they may have deep significance, such a dream seemed to be, as Helen Bishop described it, ''a true dream-vision.'' The Bishops discussed the dream with John and Louise Bosch, the founders of Geyserville, and a few other ''firm believers,'' and all agreed that it was meaningful—'' 'a bounty from 'Abdu'l-Bahá.' '' Its imagery calls to mind the words that Shoghi Effendi wrote six years later, when Louis Gregory had remained steadfast through a personal crisis that might well have shaken his Faith: ''You have attained spiritual heights that few indeed can claim to have scaled. You have displayed a spirit that few, if any, can equal.'' [11]

A tribute from Martha Root, the leading international teacher of the Faith, suggests the spiritual comradeship that bound together these early heroes of the Bahá'í Faith. ''Please give my love to Louis,'' she wrote to Louise in 1926. ''I never forget our happy times altogether, and I always feel he is one of the greatest disciples of this new day. Perhaps in the other world we shall all be working together.'' As Martha Root had lauded him, Louis Gregory in turn praised her achievements. ''Martha Root is now on the Pacific Coast,'' he wrote in 1931, ''and will probably be at the convention. What a wonderful service has been performed by this frail little woman!'' [12] These disciples of 'Abdu'l-Bahá, magnetized by His power and by the Faith for which He stood, had all given up the comforts and prospects of their conventional lives;

their recompense was their conviction that the work they were doing was far more important, and more beneficial to humanity, than anything else they might have done.

Louis Gregory faced numerous slights and indignities in carrying out his work, but he did not allow himself to be wounded by them. When he visited Dr. Ugo Giachery and his wife Angeline in New York, for example, he had to take the service elevator to their apartment. The insult undoubtedly bothered Dr. Giachery more than it did his guest, who was used to the color bar in its most extreme forms.[13] In 1973, forty years after their travels in the South, Charles Wragg described the way that Mr. Gregory dealt with hostility, whether it came from whites or from blacks:

> we sometimes received abrasive reactions such as he encountered with the well-known showman called Bojangles. It was on such occasions that his facial expressions were most illuminative, changing quickly from one of great anguish to a completely passive inward-look, as though searching his innermost being and beyond for a solution to a change in the relationship. This was his invariable reaction to difficulties and problems. I never saw him show anger, impatience or resentment, always it seemed to be an expression of earnest self-searching and seeking for guidance from beyond self-identity. I imagine that this was a reason why Abdul Baha said of him: ''He is pure gold''![14]

But his mildness clearly did not mask weakness. When he judged that the occasion warranted it, he could be formidable in defending principle. Among the stories told about him, which have passed from one generation of Bahá'ís to the next, are tributes to his courage and firmness in the face of prejudice. Although mostly unverifiable, such accounts indicate the kinds of problems that he experienced regularly but seldom recorded. According to one anecdote, attributed to Roy Wilhelm, Mr. Gregory was once jailed after a skirmish with the Jim Crow laws. Headed South from Chicago and not feeling well, he had purchased a Pullman ticket in order to rest during the trip. Instead of being allowed to occupy the accommodations for which he had paid, however, he was asked to move to the Jim Crow car as the train approached the Ohio-Kentucky border. When he protested, a policeman was called to take him off the train. After a night in a Kentucky jail, spent in discussing the Bahá'í teachings with the jailer and one of his fellow inmates, he was taken before a judge, who dismissed the case. Roy Wilhelm later wrote a letter of appreciation to the judge, which he showed to Walter Blakely, who has in turn told the story of the incident.[15]

In another story, told to Mr. Blakely by his aunt, Hebe Struven, Louis Gregory gained through patience a victory over an unexpected humiliation. A college in Pittsburgh had heard that a Mr. Gregory of Washington, D.C., was an outstanding speaker and had telephoned him with an invitation to lecture. He accepted, but when he arrived in Pittsburgh the group of students sent to meet him at the station had obviously not expected to have to provide hospitality for a black man. They excused themselves and left Mr. Gregory, who spent the night in the waiting room. The next day he kept his appointment, nonetheless, and at the end of his speech he received a standing ovation. "An apology was offered for the shabby treatment," Mr. Blakely recounts, "and he was invited to return and speak any time he could."[16]

The powerful impression that Louis Gregory made, so strong that it could bring a white audience to its feet, is still apparent in recollections shared almost thirty years after his passing by those who knew him. They describe him graphically, as if he had just left the room. He was tall, they tell us, perhaps only about six feet but appearing taller because of his unusually erect carriage. When he spoke, he looked people in the eye, his contemporaries say; and his beautiful, deep voice held their attention. In public lectures he quoted and paraphrased extensively from the Bahá'í writings, so that if his listeners closed their eyes they might have thought the words were 'Abdu'l-Bahá's own. The effect of Mr. Gregory's stately bearing was enhanced by his immaculate grooming and his great courtesy. He was, indeed, courtly in manner, but with no affectation. At the same time he was invariably humble, without any trace of an excessive modesty that calls attention to itself. In personal conversation his eyes sparkled, and his smile was always ready—"a most heavenly smile that will remain with me always," in Margaret Ruhe's words. Roy Williams, whose memories were especially vivid, has added other details to the portrait: Louis Gregory's delicate bone structure, his loose-jointed and agile movements, his sensitive, long-fingered hands; the black umbrella that he always kept on his arm, and the clean starched shirt that he managed to have ready to wear each morning; his dignity transcending his surroundings, as he spread a piece of newspaper for a prayer rug on a hotel room floor. [17]

Yet all the tributes paid to Louis Gregory, even during his lifetime, and all the reminiscences about his life and extraordinary character depict him with no more immediacy than his own voice— preserved in letters, articles, manuscripts, and transcripts of talks. Marzieh Gail recalls, "I once asked him how we know that Bahá'-u'lláh is the Báb's Promised One, and he replied: 'Bahá'u'lláh is His own proof.' Then, if memory serves, he went on to say that the sun does not need a sign on it for identification." [18] Borrowing his argument, we may suggest that Louis Gregory was his own proof. His spiritual station was apparent even in the lines of a face that would not harbor anger or resentment. When he wrote—and particularly when he spoke—he needed no labels. No words can say more about him than his own.

"Just a few months ago I was in far away Florida," he told an audience gathered to hear him give a public address on "The Oneness of Mankind" during the 1926 National Bahá'í Convention in San Francisco.

I was invited to join a group of workers going out to visit a country school. We had to pass along an unfrequented road, a distance of about eighteen miles. We had a Ford car which carried the party of four or five people. After we were well started on our journey it began to rain, which made the already difficult road, extremely difficult, but we continued on our way and finally reached our goal. It continued to rain all the time. We served the children as best we could and started on our way back. After we had gone two-thirds of the distance we got stuck in the mire. There were two men and two women in the party, and a small boy, and the entire party went to work and for an hour and a half, in the rain, we toiled and struggled to dislodge that machine. Our efforts were entirely fruitless. By-and-by we heard a noise in the distance, which grew greater and greater, and finally there came into sight an automobile truck driven by two white working men. Not knowing what would happen, we called upon them for assistance. I may say, parenthetically, that the working men of the world, whether black or white, have a community interest, and although not having seen that interest borne out in human experience, we called on them for assistance, not knowing what would happen, but gallantly they responded. They came to our aid and the four men, two white and two black, made a tremendous effort, but we were still unsuccessful. . . . They were prevailed upon to make another effort and this time the ladies and the small boy joined us, so the entire party, composed of youth and age, black and white, men and women, all made an effort and this time we were victorious. The automobile was dislodged and we went back a distance to a haven of safety much relieved by the removal of this embarrassing situation. We shook hands, across the color line, and our friends bade us good-bye. . . . [after some minutes spent fixing the car] We started once more on our way. The most interesting part of the story is this, it seems to me: We had not gone a distance of more than what would be covered by two or three of your city blocks before we came upon our two white friends and this time they were stuck in the mire. (Laughter) We were very happy, not because they were in difficulties, of course, but because we had the opportunity to return their kindness.

So, among all the different races and groups and classes of people in the world, the ideal of today is co-operation, mutuality, service. If one wants to distinguish himself let him become distinguished as a servant of humanity. (Applause) Let him stand upon this exalted principle of the oneness of God and the oneness of the entire human race. Who-ever stands upon this exalted principle will never be shaken by the shifting sands of time; who-ever stands upon this exalted principle, like the lever of Archimedes, will move the world.[19]

Notes

Notes

Part 1 / Foundations

Chapter 1 / Standard-Bearer

1. Shoghi Effendi, *The Advent of Divine Justice,* 3d rev. ed. (Wilmette, Ill.: Bahá'í Publishing Trust, 1969), p. 28.

2. Louis G. Gregory, ''A Heavenly Vista: Some Impressions of Abdu'l Baha During a Pilgrimage to Ramleh and the Holy City in 1911,'' TS, p. 1, Louis G. Gregory Papers, National Bahá'í Archives, Wilmette, Ill. The story of his pilgrimage was also published in a somewhat different form as *A Heavenly Vista: The Pilgrimage of Louis G. Gregory* (Washington: n.p., n.d.).

3. Louis G. Gregory, ''Some Recollections of the Early Days of the Bahai Faith in Washington, D.C.,'' TS, pp. 2–3, Louis G. Gregory Papers.

4. Gregory, ''Heavenly Vista,'' p. 1; Gregory, ''Some Recollections,'' p.

5. Gregory, ''Some Recollections,'' p. 5.

6. Louis Gregory to Joseph and Pauline Hannen, 7 June 1909, Hannen-Knobloch Family Papers, National Bahá'í Archives, Wilmette, Ill.

7. Gregory, ''Some Recollections,'' p. 5.

8. Louis Gregory to Hannens, 23 July 1909, Hannen-Knobloch Family Papers.

9. 'Abdu'l-Bahá to Louis Gregory, trans. 17 November 1909, Tablets of 'Abdu'l-Bahá, National Bahá'í Archives, Wilmette, Ill. (An approved translation of this tablet does not yet exist; consequently, this translation cannot be considered authentic. —ED.)

Chapter 2 / Pain and Promise

1. Kenneth M. Stampp, *The Era of Reconstruction, 1865–1877* (New York: Knopf, 1965), p. 172.

2. C. Vann Woodward, *The Strange Career of Jim Crow,* 2d rev. ed. (New York: Oxford Univ. Press, 1966), p. 32.

3. Ibid., p. 33.

4. August Meier and Elliott M. Rudwick, *From Plantation to Ghetto: An Interpretive History of American Negroes* (New York: Hill and Wang, 1966), p. 156.

5. Woodward, *Strange Career of Jim Crow,* p. 69.

6. Louis G. Gregory, "Racial Unity," Chap. 3: "Why Love the South?", TS, n. pag., Louis G. Gregory Papers, National Bahá'í Archives, Wilmette, Ill.; ibid., Chap. 1: "A Salient of Racial Understanding."

7. Ibid., Chap. 3: "Why Love the South?"

8. Ibid.

9. Dargan to Louis Gregory, 8 February 1949, Louis G. Gregory Papers.

10. Dargan to Louis Gregory, 26 February 1949, Louis G. Gregory Papers.

11. Gregory, "Racial Unity," Chap. 3: "Why Love the South?"

12. Ibid.

13. Ibid.

14. Horace Mann Bond, "The Negro Scholar and Professional in America," in *The American Negro Reference Book,* ed. John Preston Davis (Englewood Cliffs, N.J.: Prentice-Hall, 1966), p. 580.

15. Harlan F. Ober, "Louis G. Gregory," in *The Bahá'í World: A Biennial International Record, Volume XII, 1950–1954,* comp. National Spiritual Assembly of the Bahá'ís of the United States (Wilmette, Ill.: Bahá'í Publishing Trust, 1956), p. 667.

16. Gregory, "Racial Unity," Chap. 3: "Why Love the South?"

17. Ibid., Chap. 2: "Why Love the North?"

18. Woodward, *Strange Career of Jim Crow,* pp. 49–50, 67–68.

19. Meier and Rudwick, *From Plantation to Ghetto,* p. 145.

20. Gregory, "Racial Unity," Chap. 3: "Why Love the South?"

21. Ibid.

22. Ibid., Chap. 2: "Why Love the North?"

23. Meier and Rudwick, *From Plantation to Ghetto,* p. 147; Ober, "Louis G. Gregory," p. 667.

24. Karl E. Taeuber and Alma F. Taeuber, "The Black Population in the United States," in *The Black American Reference Book,* ed. Mabel M. Smythe (Englewood Cliffs, N.J.: Prentice-Hall, 1976), p. 169 (total black population in 1910 is given as 9,827,763); John Hope Franklin, *From Slavery to Freedom: A History of Negro Americans,* 3d ed. (New York: Knopf, 1967), p. 389.

Chapter 3 | The Path to Reconstruction

1. Horace Mann Bond, "The Negro Scholar and Professional in America," in *The American Negro Reference Book,* ed. John Preston Davis (Englewood Cliffs, N.J.: Prentice-Hall, 1966), p. 582.

2. James A. Cobb, quoted in Harlan F. Ober, "Louis G. Gregory," in *The*

Bahá'í World: A Biennial International Record, Volume XII, 1950–1954, comp. National Spiritual Assembly of the Bahá'ís of the United States (Wilmette, Ill.: Bahá'í Publishing Trust, 1956), p. 667.

3. Louis G. Gregory, "Some Recollections of the Early Days of the Bahai Faith in Washington, D.C.," TS, p. 1, Louis G. Gregory Papers, National Bahá'í Archives, Wilmette, Ill.; Louis G. Gregory, "Racial Unity," Chap. 18: "Reminiscent," TS, n. pag., Louis G. Gregory Papers.

4. Gregory, "Some Recollections," p. 1.

5. Joy Hill Earl to Dorothy Baker, 26 September 1951, Harlan F. Ober Papers, National Bahá'í Archives, Wilmette, Ill.

6. John Hope Franklin, *From Slavery to Freedom: A History of Negro Americans*, 3d ed. (New York: Knopf, 1967), pp. 439–40, 443.

7. Booker T. Washington, *Up From Slavery: An Autobiography* (New York: Doubleday, 1963), p. 160.

8. Gregory, "Racial Unity," Chap. 21: "Monuments."

9. Franklin, *From Slavery to Freedom*, p. 442.

10. W. E. Burghardt DuBois, *The Souls of Black Folk: Essays and Sketches* (Greenwich, Conn.: Crest-Fawcett Publications, 1961), pp. 42–43, 47.

11. Ibid., pp. 43, 48, 49, 53.

12. Franklin, *From Slavery to Freedom*, pp. 445–46.

13. "Niagara's Declaration of Principles, 1905," in *A Documentary History of the Negro People in the United States*, ed. Herbert Aptheker (New York: The Citadel Press, 1964), II, 903.

14. "Niagara Address of 1906," in ibid., p. 908.

15. Gregory, "Racial Unity," Chap. 18: "Reminiscent."

16. DuBois, *Souls of Black Folk*, pp. 50–51; Kelly Miller, quoted in Franklin, *From Slavery to Freedom*, p. 445.

17. Franklin, *From Slavery to Freedom*, p. 447.

18. Louis G. Gregory, "A Gift to Race Enlightenment," *World Order*, 2, no. 1 (Apr. 1936), 36–39; Gregory, "Some Recollections," p. 1.

19. Gregory, "Racial Unity," Chap. 18: "Reminiscent."

20. Gregory, "Some Recollections," pp. 1–2.

21. Ibid., p. 2.

22. W. E. B. DuBois, quoted in Gregory, "Gift to Race Enlightenment," p. p. 37. A slightly different version of the DuBois quotation appears in Francis L. Broderick, *W.E.B. DuBois: Negro Leader in a Time of Crisis* (Stanford: Stanford Univ. Press, 1959), p. 80.

23. Gregory, "Gift to Race Enlightenment," p. 37.

24. Louis Gregory to Holley [National Spiritual Assembly], 21 February 1937, Inter-America Committee Files, National Spiritual Assembly of the Bahá'ís of the United States and Canada Records, National Bahá'í Archives, Wilmette, Ill.

25. Spiritual Assembly of the Bahá'ís of Chicago, Julia Sobel, secy., to National Spiritual Assembly, Horace Holley, secy., 14 June 1934, Office of the Secretary, National Spiritual Assembly of the Bahá'ís of the United States and Canada Records.

26. Alain Locke, "Unity Through Diversity: A Bahá'í Principle," in *The Bahá'í World: A Biennial International Record, Volume IV, 1930–1932*, comp. National Spiritual Assembly of the Bahá'ís of the United States and Canada (New York: Bahá'í Publishing Committee, 1933), pp. 372, 374.

27. Gregory, "A Gift to Race Enlightenment," p. 39.

Chapter 4 / Agent of Change

1. Louis G. Gregory, "Some Recollections of the Early Days of the Bahai Faith in Washington, D.C.," TS, p. 3, Louis G. Gregory Papers, National Bahá'í Archives, Wilmette, Ill.

2. Anna Watson, Extract from a letter of 18 October 1904, TS, Thornton Chase Papers, National Bahá'í Archives, Wilmette, Ill.

3. Jos. H. Hannen, "Washington, D. C.," *Bahai News, 1*, no. 1 (21 Mar. 1910), 18–19.

4. Ibid., no. 2 (9 Apr. 1910), 13; Joseph H. Hannen, "Washington, D. C.," *Bahai News,* 1, no. 3 (28 Apr. 1910), 18.

5. Jos. H. Hannen, "Washington, D. C.," *Bahai News,* 1, no. 1 (21 Mar. 1910), 18–19; Joseph H. Hannen, "Washington, D. C.," *Bahai News,* 1, no. 3 (28 Apr. 1910), 19.

6. Joseph H. Hannen, "Washington, D.C.," *Bahai News,* 1, no. 7 (13 July 1910), 15; ibid., no. 6 (24 June 1910), 16; ibid., no. 9 (20 Aug. 1910), 14–15; ibid., no. 14 (23 Nov. 1910), 6; ibid., no. 16 (31 Dec. 1910), 6.

7. Gregory, "Some Recollections," pp. 4–5.

8. Louis Gregory to Chapman, 18 September 1935, Edith M. Chapman Papers, National Bahá'í Archives, Wilmette, Ill.

9. Louis Gregory to Hannens, 12 November 1910, Hannen-Knobloch Family Papers, National Bahá'í Archives, Wilmette, Ill.; "News Notes," *Bahai News,* 1, no. 18 (7 Feb. 1911), 9; Gregory, "Some Recollections," p. 6.

10. Louis Gregory to Joseph Hannen, 6 February 1911, Hannen-Knobloch Family Papers.

11. Albert H. Hall and Bernard M. Jacobsen, "Record of the Fourth Annual Convention of Bahai Temple Unity, Chicago, April 27th–May 1st, 1912," *Star of the West,* 3, no. 5 (5 June 1912), 6.

12. Lunt to Louis Gregory, 5 March 1923, Alfred E. Lunt Papers, National Bahá'í Archives, Wilmette, Ill.

13. Joseph H. Hannen, "The Public Meetings of the Fourth Annual Convention of Bahai Temple Unity, Chicago, April 27th–May 2d, 1912," *Star of the*

West, 3, no. 4 (17 May 1912), 4–5, 32; Roy Williams, memories of Louis Gregory, tape recorded 1975, National Bahá'í Archives, Wilmette, Ill.

14. Joseph H. Hannen, "Public Meetings of the Fifth Annual Convention of Bahai Temple Unity, New York City, April 26–29, 1913," *Star of the West,* 4 (5 June 1913), 85.

15. Alfred E. Lunt, "Sixth Annual Convention of Bahai Temple Unity, Chicago, April 25–28, 1914," *Star of the West,* 5 (5 June 1914), 70.

16. Joseph H. Hannen, "The Opening Session," *Star of the West,* 7 (13 July 1916), 53; Louis G. Gregory, "The First Session of the Convention and the Third Session of the Congress," *Star of the West,* 7 (13 July 1916), 53–56; "Mashrak-el-Azkar Convention and Bahai Congress," *Star of the West,* 8 (20 Aug. 1917), 105; Louis G. Gregory, "Centennial Celebration of the Birth of Baha'o'llah," *Star of the West,* 8 (23 Nov. 1917), 199; "The Feast of El-Rizwan and the Bahai Congress," *Star of the West,* 9 (17 May 1918), 43, 44; Louis G. Gregory, "The Power of the Holy Spirit," *Star of the West,* 10 (5 June 1919), 84–87, 90–91.

17. Louis G. Gregory, "Racial Amity," in *Bahá'í Year Book, Volume One, 1925–1926,* comp. National Spiritual Assembly of the Bahá'ís of the United States and Canada (New York: Bahá'í Publishing Committee, 1926), pp. 165–67, 169.

18. Ives to Louis Gregory, 27 September 1935, Louis G. Gregory Papers.

Chapter 5 / Pilgrimage

1. 'Abdu'l-Bahá to Gregory, in Louis G. Gregory, *A Heavenly Vista: The Pilgrimage of Louis G. Gregory* (Washington: n.p., n.d.), p. 29.

2. Louis G. Gregory, "A Heavenly Vista: Some Impressions of Abdu'l Baha during a Pilgrimage to Ramleh and the Holy City in 1911," TS, p. 5, Louis G. Gregory Papers, National Bahá'í Archives, Wilmette, Ill.

3. Joseph H. Hannen, "Washington, D. C.," in "News from the Occident," *Star of the West,* 2, no. 3 (28 Apr. 1911), 9.

4. Louis G. Gregory, "Racial Unity," Chap. 4: "Why Love the Negro?" TS, n. pag., Louis G. Gregory Papers.

5. 'Abdu'l-Bahá to Margaret Döring, trans. 15 August 1911, Tablets of 'Abdu'l-Bahá, National Bahá'í Archives, Wilmette, Ill. (An approved translation of this tablet does not yet exist; consequently, this translation cannot be considered authentic.—ED.) Also published with revisions in "Progress of the Cause in Germany," *Star of the West,* 2, no. 17 (19 Jan. 1912), 6.

6. Louis G. Gregory, "Some Recollections of the Early Days of the Bahai Faith in Washington, D.C.," TS, p. 6, Louis G. Gregory Papers.

7. Gregory, "Racial Unity," Chap. 18: "Reminiscent."

8. Ibid.

9. Gregory, *Heavenly Vista,* p. 10.

10. Ibid., pp. 12–13.

11. Ibid., pp. 13, 15.

12. Ibid., p. 15.

13. 'Abdu'l-Bahá to [Charles Mason Remey], in Gregory, *Heavenly Vista,* p. 31 (also excerpted with revisions in "The Removal of Race Prejudice," *Star of the West,* 12 [5 June 1921], 107); Gregory, "Heavenly Vista," p. 27.

14. Gregory, "Heavenly Vista," p. 28.

15. Shoghi Effendi, *The Promised Day Is Come,* 2d rev. ed. (Wilmette, Ill.: Bahá'í Publishing Trust, 1980), p. 113. Shoghi Effendi states: "The chief idols in the desecrated temple of mankind are none other than the triple gods of Nationalism, Racialism and Communism, at whose altars governments and peoples, whether democratic or totalitarian, at peace or at war, of the East or of the West, Christian or Islamic, are, in various forms and in different degrees, now worshiping."

16. 'Abdu'l-Bahá to Döring, trans. 15 August 1911, Tablets of 'Abdu'l-Bahá. (An approved translation of this tablet does not yet exist; consequently, this translation cannot be considered authentic.—ED.)

17. Frederich Schweizer, "News Notes," in "Progress of the Cause in Germany," *Star of the West,* 2, no. 17 (19 Jan. 1912), 8.

18. 'Abdu'l-Bahá to Döring, trans. 15 August 1911, Tablets of 'Abdu'l-Bahá. (An approved translation of this tablet does not yet exist; consequently, this translation cannot be considered authentic.—ED.)

19. 'Abdu'l-Bahá to Mary Ellen Hooper, trans. 15 July 1911, Tablets of 'Abdu'l-Bahá. (An approved translation of this tablet does not yet exist; consequently, this translation cannot be considered authentic.—ED.)

20. 'Abdu'l-Bahá, quoted in Harlan F. Ober, "Louis G. Gregory," in *The Bahá'í World: A Biennial International Record, Volume XII, 1950–1954,* comp. National Spiritual Assembly of the Bahá'ís of the United States (Wilmette, Ill.: Bahá'í Publishing Trust, 1956), p. 668.

Chapter 6 / *'Abdu'l-Bahá in America*

1. Joseph H. Hannen, "Persian-American Educational Society," *Star of the West,* 2, nos. 7 and 8 (1 Aug. 1911), 3; "Ghodsia Ashraf Khanum," *Star of the West,* 2, nos. 7 and 8 (1 Aug. 1911), 8.

2. Joseph H. Hannen, "Washington, D. C.," in "News Items," *Star of the West,* 2, nos. 7 and 8 (1 Aug. 1911), 15.

3. Louis G. Gregory, "Impressions of Abdul-Baha While at Ramleh," *Star of the West,* 2, no. 10 (8 Sept. 1911), 6.

4. H. M. Balyuzi, *'Abdu'l-Bahá: The Centre of the Covenant of Bahá'u'lláh* (London: George Ronald, 1971), pp. 171–72.

5. 'Abdu'l-Bahá, quoted in Howard MacNutt, Introd., *The Promulgation of Universal Peace: Discourses by Abdul Baha during His Visit to the United States in 1912,* by 'Abdu'l-Bahá, rpt. in 1 vol. (Wilmette, Ill.: Bahai Publishing Committee, 1943), p. i.

6. 'Abdu'l-Bahá, *Promulgation,* pp. 1, 2, 1.

7. "Abdul Baha on Religious Unity," *Washington Bee,* 27 Apr. 1912, p. 1, col. 5.

8. 'Abdu'l-Bahá, *Promulgation,* pp. 41–43. A new and substantially different translation of 'Abdu'l-Bahá's address at Howard University will appear in the forthcoming new edition of *The Promulgation of Universal Peace,* to be published in 1982. We have used the older translation as it is the one that would have been familiar to the Bahá'ís of this period.

9. Ibid., pp. 46, 48–49.

10. Louis G. Gregory, "Some Recollections of the Early Days of the Bahai Faith in Washington, D.C.," TS, p. 8, Louis G. Gregory Papers, National Bahá'í Archives, Wilmette, Ill.

11. Harlan F. Ober, "Louis G. Gregory," in *The Bahá'í World: A Biennial International Record, Volume XII, 1950–1954,* comp. National Spiritual Assembly of the Bahá'ís of the United States (Wilmette, Ill.: Bahá'í Publishing Trust, 1956), p. 668.

12. Diary of Juliet Thompson, "Abdul Baha in America," TS, p. 18, entry for 7 May 1912, National Bahá'í Archives, Wilmette, Ill.; Gregory, "Some Recollections," p. 8.

13. Allan L. Ward, *239 Days: 'Abdu'l-Bahá's Journey in America* (Wilmette, Ill.: Bahá'í Publishing Trust, 1979), pp. 40–41.

14. Diary of Juliet Thompson, "Abdul Baha in America," p. 19, entry for 7 May 1912.

15. 'Abdu'l-Bahá, *Promulgation,* pp. 53–54.

16. Ibid., p. 63.

17. Ibid., p. 65.

18. "The Fourth Annual Conference of the National Association for the Advancement of Colored People," *The Crisis,* 4 (June 1912), 80.

19. Ibid., p. 88. The version of this talk printed in *The Promulgation of Universal Peace* reads: "Man is not man simply because of bodily attributes. The standard of divine measure and judgment is his intelligence and spirit" (p. 67).

20. "History of the Washington, D.C. Bahá'í Community, 1900–1933," TS, p. 5, National Bahá'í Archives, Wilmette, Ill.

21. 'Abdu'l-Bahá, *Promulgation,* p. 415.

22. Ibid., pp. 420, 422, 421, 423.

23. Louis Gregory to Joseph Hannen, 30 September 1919, Hannen-Knobloch Family Papers, National Bahá'í Archives, Wilmette, Ill.

24. 'Abdu'l-Bahá, *Promulgation,* pp. 42–43, 49.

25. Louis G. Gregory, "Racial Amity," in *Bahá' í Year Book, Volume One, 1925–1926,* comp. National Spiritual Assembly of the Bahá'ís of the United States and Canada (New York: Bahá'í Publishing Committee, 1926), p. 165.

26. In 1956 Margaret Just Butcher, writing from notes left by Alain Locke, echoed this theme in *The Negro in American Culture,* rev. ed. (New York: New American Library, 1971), pp. 12–13: "The slow, consistently steady rise of the Negro's status since emancipation in 1863 has served as a base-level fulcrum for new freedom and wider foundations for American democracy. The Negro's progression from chattel to freedman, to legal citizenship, to increasing equality of rights and opportunities, to accepted neighbor and compatriot represents a dramatic testament to democracy's positive and dynamic character."

27. 'Abdu'l-Bahá, quoted in Louis G. Gregory, "Racial Amity in America: An Historical Review," in *The Bahá' í World: A Biennial International Record, Volume VII, 1936–1938,* comp. National Spiritual Assembly of the Bahá'ís of the United States and Canada (New York: Bahá'í Publishing Committee, 1939), pp. 653–54.

28. 'Abdu'l-Bahá to Antoinette Crump Cone, published in "The Removal of Race Prejudice—Continued: A Compilation of the Words of Abdul-Baha," *Star of the West,* 12 (24 June 1921), 121.

29. 'Abdu'l-Bahá to Williams, 2 August 1921, Tablets of 'Abdu'l-Bahá, National Bahá'í Archives, Wilmette, Ill. (An approved translation of this tablet does not yet exist; consequently, this translation cannot be considered authentic.—ED.)

30. 'Abdu'l-Bahá, quoted in Zia M. Bagdadi, " 'Now is the time for the Americans to unite both the white and colored races:' Words of Abdul-Baha to Dr. Zia M. Bagdadi," *Star of the West,* 12 (24 June 1921), 120–21.

31. Shoghi Effendi, *Citadel of Faith: Messages to America, 1947–1957* (Wilmette, Ill.: Bahá'í Publishing Trust, 1965), p. 126.

32. Gregory, "Racial Amity in America," p. 653.

33. 'Abdu'l-Bahá, *Promulgation,* p. 43.

34. Gregory, "Racial Amity," p. 167.

35. Louis Gregory to Joseph Hannen, 30 September 1919, Hannen-Knobloch Family Papers.

36. Gregory, "Racial Amity in America," p. 653.

Chapter 7 / Marriage

1. Louise Gregory to Parsons, 18 January 1921, Agnes S. Parsons Papers, National Bahá'í Archives, Wilmette, Ill.

2. Ibid.

3. Joy Hill Earl, "Louisa Mathew Gregory, 1866–1956," in *The Bahá'í World: An International Record, Volume XIII, 1954–1963,* comp. The Universal House of Justice (Haifa: The Universal House of Justice, 1970), pp. 876, 878.

4. Louise Gregory to Parsons, 18 January 1921, Parsons Papers; Louis Gregory to Pauline Hannen, 19 September 1912, Hannen-Knobloch Family Papers, National Bahá'í Archives, Wilmette, Ill.

5. 'Abdu'l-Bahá to [Charles Mason Remey], in Louis G. Gregory, *A Heavenly Vista: The Pilgrimage of Louis G. Gregory* (Washington: n.p., n.d.), p. 31.

6. Lunt to Parsons, 4 April 1914, Parsons Papers.

7. Louis Gregory to Chapman, 20 February 1935, Edith M. Chapman Papers, National Bahá'í Archives, Wilmette, Ill.

8. Louise Gregory to Parsons, 18 January 1921, Parsons Papers.

9. Louis Gregory to Pauline Hannen, 19 September 1912, Hannen-Knobloch Family Papers.

10. Shoghi Effendi (through his secy.), "Letter from the Guardian," *Bahá'í News,* no. 133 (Feb. 1940), p. 2.

11. Louis Gregory to Pauline Hannen, 30 September 1912, Hannen-Knobloch Family Papers.

12. Ibid.

13. Louise Gregory to Parsons, 18 January 1921, Parsons Papers.

14. Earl, "Louisa Mathew Gregory," p. 876.

15. Louis Gregory to Chapman, 20 February 1935, Chapman Papers.

16. Ibid.

17. Parsons to Randall, 26 September 1916, Parsons Papers.

18. Louise Gregory to Parsons, 5 February 1925, Parsons Papers.

19. Louis Gregory to Chapman, 27 September 1933 and 9 May 1950, Chapman Papers.

20. 'Abdu'l-Bahá to Gregorys, trans. 14 March 1914, Tablets of 'Abdu'l-Bahá, National Bahá'í Archives, Wilmette, Ill. (An approved translation of this tablet does not yet exist; consequently, this translation cannot be considered authentic.—ED.)

Chapter 8 / A Divided Community

1. Louise Gregory to Parsons, 21 December 1914, Agnes S. Parsons Papers, National Bahá'í Archives, Wilmette, Ill.

2. Louis G. Gregory, "Some Recollections of the Early Days of the Bahai Faith in Washington, D.C.," TS, p. 5, Louis G. Gregory Papers, National Bahá'í Archives, Wilmette, Ill.

3. Edna Belmont to Parsons, 2 March 1914, Parsons Papers.

4. Boyle to Parsons, 18 February 1914, Parsons Papers.

5. Ibid.

6. Ibid.

7. 'Abdu'l-Bahá to Edna Belmont, received 1 May 1914, Parsons Papers. (An approved translation of this tablet does not yet exist; consequently, this translation cannot be considered authentic.—ED.)

8. Louise Gregory to Parsons, 21 December 1914, Parsons Papers.

9. Minutes of a meeting held at Mrs. deLagnel's apartment, 1 Oct. 1914, Parsons Papers; A. W. Belmont and Marzieh Moss, general letter, 26 October 1914, Parsons Papers.

10. Louise Gregory to Parsons, 21 December 1914, Parsons Papers.

11. Parsons to "the Washington Friends," 13 October 1915, Parsons Papers.

12. E. C. Getsinger to Parsons, 29 May 1916, Parsons Papers.

13. "A Trumpet Call to Action," Editorial, *Star of the West,* 7 (8 Sept. 1916), 86.

14. Gregory, "Some Recollections," p. 6.

15. Shoghi Effendi, *The World Order of Bahá'u'lláh,* 2d rev. ed. (Wilmette, Ill.: Bahá'í Publishing Trust, 1974), p. 86.

Chapter 9 / A New Calling

1. Joseph H. Hannen, "Persian-American Educational Society," *Star of the West,* 4 (4 Nov. 1913), 221; Louis Gregory to Joseph Hannen, 5 February 1917, Hannen-Knobloch Family Papers, National Bahá'í Archives, Wilmette, Ill.; Louise Gregory to Joseph Hannen, 5 March 1916, Hannen-Knobloch Family Papers.

2. 'Abdu'l-Bahá to Gregorys, trans. 14 March 1914, Tablets of 'Abdu'l-Bahá, National Bahá'í Archives, Wilmette, Ill. (An approved translation of this tablet does not yet exist; consequently, this translation cannot be considered authentic.—ED.)

3. Spiritual Assembly of the Bahá'ís of Atlanta, Georgia, Inc., "Early Bahá'í History of Atlanta, Georgia," TS, p. 8, National Bahá'í Archives, Wilmette, Ill.

4. Ibid., p. 9.

5. 'Abdu'l-Bahá, *Tablets of the Divine Plan: Revealed by 'Abdu'l-Bahá to the North American Bahá'ís,* rev. ed. (Wilmette, Ill.: Bahá'í Publishing Trust, 1977), pp. 11–12.

6. Randall to Parsons, 2 October 1916, Agnes S. Parsons Papers, National Bahá'í Archives, Wilmette, Ill.

7. Louis Gregory to Joseph Hannen, 31 October 1916, Hannen-Knobloch Family Papers.

8. Louis G. Gregory, "The Teaching Campaign—News from the South:

'Fifteen thousand were reached directly,' " *Star of the West,* 7 (19 Jan. 1917), 170.

9. Louis Gregory to [Joseph Hannen], quoted in "News from the 'soldiers' at the front," *Star of the West,* 7 (31 Dec. 1916), 158.

10. Gregory, "Teaching Campaign," p. 170.

11. Joy Hill Earl to Dorothy Baker, 26 September 1951, Harlan F. Ober Papers, National Bahá'í Archives, Wilmette, Ill.; Louis Gregory to Lunt, 23 September 1917, Alfred E. Lunt Papers, National Bahá'í Archives, Wilmette, Ill.

12. 'Abdu'l-Bahá, *Tablets of the Divine Plan,* p. 66.

13. Pauline A. Hannen, "News from Washington, D. C.," *Star of the West,* 8 (16 Oct. 1917), 153.

14. Louis Gregory to Joseph Hannen, 4 August 1919, Hannen-Knobloch Family Papers.

15. Louis Gregory to Joseph Hannen, 24 November 1919, Hannen-Knobloch Family Papers.

16. Louis Gregory to Joseph Hannen, 4 August 1919, Hannen-Knobloch Family Papers.

17. Louis Gregory, quoted in Teaching Committee of Nineteen, *Teaching Bulletin,* no. 3 (19 Aug. 1920), p. 7, Lunt Papers.

18. Louis G. Gregory, "The Equality of Men and Women: Resume of Address by Mr. Louis G. Gregory at Boston," *Star of the West,* 8 (20 Aug. 1917), 120.

19. Louis Gregory to Louise Gregory, 5 November 1917, Louise Gregory Papers, National Bahá'í Archives, Wilmette, Ill.

20. Louis Gregory to Chapman, 4 November 1932 and 27 September 1933, Edith M. Chapman Papers, National Bahá'í Archives, Wilmette, Ill.

21. Louise Gregory to Parsons, 18 January 1921, Parsons Papers; Louis Gregory to Horace Holley [National Spiritual Assembly], 31 December 1936, Inter-America Committee Files, National Spiritual Assembly of the Bahá'ís of the United States and Canada Records, National Bahá'í Archives, Wilmette, Ill.

22. Louise Gregory to Louis Gregory, 4 March 1934, Louis G. Gregory Papers, National Bahá'í Archives, Wilmette, Ill.

23. Louise Gregory to Parsons, 18 January 1921, Parsons Papers.

24. Ibid.

25. Louis Gregory to Chapman, 17 June 1930, Chapman Papers.

26. 'Abdu'l-Bahá, *Tablets of the Divine Plan,* p. 12.

27. Louis Gregory to Ober, 9 September 1919, Ober Papers.

28. Ibid.; Louis Gregory to Joseph Hannen, 15 January 1920, Hannen-Knobloch Family Papers.

29. 'Abdu'l-Bahá, *Tablets of the Divine Plan,* p. 51.

30. Louis Gregory to Ober, 9 September 1919, Ober Papers.

31. Ibid.

32. Louis Gregory to National Spiritual Assembly of the Bahá'ís of the United States and Canada (copy), 18 June 1932, Lunt Papers.

33. Louis Gregory to Joseph Hannen, 15 January 1920, Hannen-Knobloch Family Papers; Blakely to Roger Dahl, 19 February 1980, Walter H. Blakely Papers, National Bahá'í Archives, Wilmette, Ill.

34. Blakely to Dahl, 19 February 1980, Blakely Papers; Roy Williams, memories of Louis Gregory, tape recorded 1975, National Bahá'í Archives, Wilmette, Ill.; Louis Gregory to Joseph Hannen, 20 December 1919, Hannen-Knobloch Family Papers.

35. Louis Gregory to Ober, 9 September 1919, Ober Papers; Louis Gregory to Chapman, [date illegible] June 1927, Chapman Papers.

36. Albert H. Hall, "Bahai Temple Unity Convention Held at Hotel Brunswick, Boston, Massachusetts, April 30th–May 2nd, 1917," *Star of the West,* 8 (8 Sept. 1917), 129; Harlan Foster Ober, "Report of the Tenth Annual Convention of the Bahai Temple Unity Held at the Auditorium Hotel, Chicago, April 27th to 30th, 1918," *Star of the West,* 9 (17 May 1918), 53; Ober, "Report of the Tenth Annual Convention [continued]," *Star of the West,* 9 (5 June 1918), 72.

37. Louis Gregory to Chapman, 15 April 1940 and 14 July 1949, Chapman Papers.

38. 'Abdu'l-Bahá, *Tablets of the Divine Plan,* p. 42.

Chapter 10 / The Divine Plan

1. Lunt to Louis Gregory, 18 September 1917, Alfred E. Lunt Papers, National Bahá'í Archives, Wilmette, Ill.

2. "News from the 'soldiers' at the front," *Star of the West,* 7 (31 Dec. 1916), 158; Friends of the Harlem Branch to the Bahai Assembly in Convention in Chicago, n.d. [1918], Harlan F. Ober Papers, National Bahá'í Archives, Wilmette, Ill.

3. "Allah-o-Abha!," Editorial, *Star of the West,* 10 (17 May 1919), 52.

4. 'Abdu'l-Bahá, *Tablets of the Divine Plan: Revealed by 'Abdu'l-Bahá to the North American Bahá'ís,* rev. ed. (Wilmette, Ill.: Bahá'í Publishing Trust, 1977), p. 38.

5. Ibid., pp. 66–67.

6. Ibid., pp. 67–68.

7. Joseph H. Hannen, "The Convention of Abdul-Baha," *Star of the West,* 10 (17 May 1919), 54; Louis G. Gregory, "Opening of the Convention and Congress—The Feast of El-Rizwan," *Star of the West,* 10 (17 May 1919), 57.

8. Hannen, "Convention of Abdul-Baha," p. 55.

9. Ibid., p. 56.

10. Martha Root, "A Bahai Pilgrimage to South America: Compiled from letters written by Miss Martha Root while enroute," *Star of the West*, 11 (13 July 1920), 107.

11. 'Abdu'l-Bahá, *Tablets of the Divine Plan*, p. 49.

Chapter 11 / The Sowing of Seeds

1. 'Abdu'l-Bahá, *Tablets of the Divine Plan: Revealed by 'Abdu'l-Bahá to the North American Bahá'ís*, rev. ed. (Wilmette, Ill.: Bahá'í Publishing Trust, 1977), p. 67.

2. Joseph H. Hannen, "Editorial—The Southern States contribute a General Outline," *Star of the West*, 10 (5 June 1919), 88–89; Joseph H. Hannen, "News and Notes from the Southern Field," *Star of the West*, 10 (5 June 1919), 89–90.

3. Louis Gregory to Ober, 9 September 1919, Harlan F. Ober Papers, National Bahá'í Archives, Wilmette, Ill.

4. Hannen, "News and Notes," p. 89.

5. Louis Gregory to Joseph Hannen, 15 January 1920 and 9 January 1920, Hannen-Knobloch Family Papers, National Bahá'í Archives, Wilmette, Ill.

6. Louis Gregory to Joseph Hannen, 9 January 1920 and 6 December 1919, Hannen-Knobloch Family Papers.

7. Roy Williams, memories of Louis Gregory, tape recorded 1975, National Bahá'í Archives, Wilmette, Ill.; 'Abdu'l-Bahá to Louis Gregory, trans. 24 July 1919, in *Star of the West*, 11 (5 June 1920), 92; Spiritual Assembly of the Bahá'ís of Atlanta, Georgia, Inc., "Early Bahá'í History of Atlanta, Georgia," TS, p. 10, National Bahá'í Archives, Wilmette, Ill.

8. Louis Gregory to Joseph Hannen, 9 January 1920, Hannen-Knobloch Family Papers.

9. Ibid.

10. Teaching Committee of Nineteen, *Teaching Bulletin*, no. 1 (19 Nov. 1919), n. pag., Alfred E. Lunt Papers, National Bahá'í Archives, Wilmette, Ill.

11. Louis Gregory to Joseph Hannen, 15 January 1920, Hannen-Knobloch Family Papers.

12. 'Abdu'l-Bahá, *Tablets of the Divine Plan*, p. 12.

13. Louis Gregory, quoted in Mariam Haney, "Activities in the American Field: Extracts from Bulletin No. 2, issued July 19, 1920, by the Teaching Committee of the United States and Canada . . . ," *Star of the West*, 11 (20 Aug. 1920), 148; Louis Gregory to Lunt, 23 September 1917, Lunt Papers; Louis Gregory to Joseph Hannen, 22 October 1919, Hannen-Knobloch Family Papers; Louis G. Gregory, "Faith and the Man: The Remarkable Story of Henderson Business College, a Bahá'í Enterprise," in *The Bahá'í World: A Biennial Inter-*

national Record, Volume VIII, 1938–1940, comp. National Spiritual Assembly of the Bahá'ís of the United States and Canada (Wilmette, Ill.: Bahá'í Publishing Committee, 1942), p. 901.

14. Louis Gregory to Chapman, 21 June 1929, Edith M. Chapman Papers, National Bahá'í Archives, Wilmette, Ill.; "Teaching Work of Mr. Gregory," *Bahai News Letter,* no. 38 (Feb. 1930), p. 8.

15. Gregory, "Faith and the Man," p. 901.

16. "Spiritual Assembly of the Bahá'ís of Memphis, Tennessee, newly established April 21, 1941," photograph, *Bahá'í News,* no. 147 (Oct. 1941), p. 9; Louis G. Gregory, "George W. Henderson," in *The Bahá'í World: A Biennial International Record, Volume X, 1944–1946,* comp. National Spiritual Assembly of the Bahá'ís of the United States and Canada (Wilmette, Ill.: Bahá'í Publishing Committee, 1949), pp. 538–39.

17. Louis Gregory, in Haney, "Activities in the American Field," pp. 148–49.

18. Teaching Committee of Nineteen, *Teaching Bulletin,* no. 3 (19 Aug. 1920), p. 7, Lunt Papers.

19. Beecher to Lunt, 23 March 1921, Lunt Papers.

20. Teaching Committee of Nineteen, *Teaching Bulletin,* no. 3 (19 Aug. 1920), pp. 7–8, Lunt Papers.

21. Beecher to Lunt, 7 April 1921, Lunt Papers.

22. Louis G. Gregory, "Dr. Moses L. Murphy," *Star of the West,* 12 (2 Mar. 1922), 312.

23. "Bahá'í Community of Louisville, Ky., who established a Spiritual Assembly April 21, 1943," photograph, *Bahá'í News,* no. 166 (Nov. 1943), p. 5.

24. Louis Gregory, quoted in Haney, "Activities in the American Field," p. 148.

25. Spiritual Assembly of Atlanta, "Early Bahá'í History." p. 9.

26. Louis Gregory to Joseph Hannen, 16 May 1917, Hannen-Knobloch Family Papers; Spiritual Assembly of Atlanta, "Early Bahá'í History," p. 3.

27. Finke to Louis Gregory, 15 April 1951, Louis G. Gregory Papers, National Bahá'í Archives, Wilmette, Ill.

28. Louis Gregory to Joseph Hannen, 9 January 1920, Hannen-Knobloch Family Papers.

29. Charles Mason Remey, "Joseph H. Hannen," *Star of the West,* 10 (2 Mar. 1920), 345–46; Louis Gregory to Joseph Hannen, 3 February 1920, Hannen-Knobloch Family Papers.

30. Louis Gregory to Joseph Hannen, 31 October 1916, Hannen-Knobloch Family Papers.

31. Remey, "Joseph H. Hannen," p. 346.

32. Louis Gregory to Pauline Hannen, "Sunday Morning" [n.d.], Hannen-Knobloch Family Papers.

33. Remey, "Joseph H. Hannen," p. 346.

34. Louis Gregory to Pauline Hannen, 18 February 1920, Hannen-Knobloch Family Papers.

35. Haney, "Activities in the American Field," p. 148.

36. Louis Gregory to Lunt, 18 March 1922, Lunt Papers; Haney, "Activities in the American Field," p. 148.

Chapter 12 / Time of Transition

1. Greatest Holy Leaf to Wilhelmite, cablegram, 28 November 1921, facsimile printed in *Star of the West,* 12 (12 Dec. 1921), 245; Greatest Holy Leaf to Wilhelmite, cablegram, 16 January 1922, copy printed in *Star of the West,* 12 (19 Jan. 1922), 258; Shoghi Effendi, "Cablegram from Shoghi Rabbani to American Bahais," *Star of the West,* 12 (7 Feb. 1922), 273; Shoghi Effendi, "Now, in this world of being . . . ," *Star of the West,* 13 (21 Mar. 1922), 17–18.

2. Louis Gregory to Lunt, 18 March 1922, Alfred E. Lunt Papers, National Bahá'í Archives, Wilmette, Ill.

3. National Teaching Committee, *Teaching Bulletin,* 31 Mar. 1922, pp. 3–4, Lunt Papers.

4. Ugo Giachery, *Shoghi Effendi: Recollections* (Oxford: George Ronald, 1973), p. 5.

5. National Teaching Committee, *Teaching Bulletin,* 31 Mar. 1922, p. 3, Lunt Papers.

6. Ibid.

7. Louis Gregory to Lunt, 18 June 1924, Lunt Papers.

8. "Proceedings of the Annual Meeting of the Bahai Temple Unity, Auditorium Hotel, Chicago, Illinois, April 24–26, 1922," p. 111, Temple Unity Records, National Bahá'í Archives, Wilmette, Ill.

9. Louis Gregory to Chapman, 14 July 1949, Edith M. Chapman Papers, National Bahá'í Archives, Wilmette, Ill.; National Teaching Committee, *Teaching Bulletin,* 10 Dec. 1921, p. 2, Lunt Papers.

10. National Teaching Committee, *Teaching Bulletin,* 10 Dec. 1921, pp. 2–3, Lunt Papers.

11. Ibid., pp. 3–4.

12. National Teaching Committee, *Teaching Bulletin,* 31 Mar. 1922, p. 3, Lunt Papers.

13. Ibid., p. 4.

14. Ibid.

15. Ibid., p. 5.

16. Ibid., pp. 6–7.

17. Ibid., p. 7.

18. Ibid., pp. 8–9.

19. Ibid., p.10.

20. Ibid., pp. 10–11.

21. Ibid., p. 12.

22. Louis Gregory to Chapman, 14 July 1949, Chapman Papers.

23. National Teaching Committee, *Teaching Bulletin,* 31 Mar. 1922, p. 11, Lunt Papers.

24. National Teaching Committee, *Teaching Bulletin,* 19 June 1922, pp. 3–4, Lunt Papers; National Teaching Committee, *Teaching Bulletin,* 16 Oct. 1922, p. 8, Lunt Papers.

25. "News of the Cause," *Bahai News Letter,* no. 4 (Apr. 1925), p. 4; Louis Gregory to Parsons, 27 March 1925, Agnes S. Parsons Papers, National Bahá'í Archives, Wilmette, Ill.; Francis L. Broderick, *W. E. B. DuBois: Negro Leader in a Time of Crisis* (Stanford: Stanford Univ. Press, 1959), p. 163.

26. "17th Annual Baha'i Convention, Green Acre, Eliot, Maine [1925]," TS, pp. 60–61, National Bahá'í Archives, Wilmette, Ill.; Louis Gregory, quoted in Mariam Haney, "Activities in the American Field: Extracts from Bulletin No. 2, issued July 19, 1920, by the Teaching Committee of the United States and Canada . . . ," *Star of the West,* 11 (20 Aug. 1920), 148; 'Abdu'l-Bahá, *Tablets of the Divine Plan: Revealed by 'Abdu'l-Bahá to the North American Bahá'ís,* rev. ed. (Wilmette, Ill.: Bahá'í Publishing Trust, 1977), p. 67.

27. "17th Annual Convention," pp. 61–62.

28. "News of the Cause," *Baha'i News Letter,* no. 10 (Feb. 1926), p. 6; Louis G. Gregory, "Eighteenth Annual Convention of the Baha'is of the United States and Canada," *Baha'i News Letter,* no. 12 (June-July 1926), p. 4.

29. Louis G. Gregory, "Eighteenth Annual Convention," pp. 2–3; National Spiritual Assembly of the Bahá'ís of the United States and Canada to the Spiritual Assemblies of the United States and Canada, 18 February 1926, Lunt Papers.

30. Boyle (Southern Regional Teaching Committee) to El Fleda Spaulding (National Teaching Committee), 15 April 1926, Parsons Papers.

Part 2 / The Era of Racial Amity

Chapter 13 / A Program for Racial Amity

1. 'Abdu'l-Bahá to Antoinette Crump Cone, published in "The Removal of Race Prejudice—Continued: A Compilation of the Words of Abdul-Baha," *Star of the West,* 12 (24 June 1921), 121.

2. John Hope Franklin, *From Slavery to Freedom: A History of Negro Americans,* 3d ed. (New York: Knopf, 1967), p. 480.

3. Ibid., pp. 480–81, 484.

4. Executive Board of Bahai Temple Unity, Minutes, 13 Aug. 1919, Bahá'í

Temple Unity Records, National Bahá'í Archives, Wilmette, Ill.; Bahai Temple Unity, Proceedings of the Annual Meeting, 24–26 Apr. 1922, pp. 311–13, Bahá'í Temple Unity Records.

5. Executive Board of Bahai Temple Unity, Minutes, 13 Aug. 1919, Bahá'í Temple Unity Records. The members of the Executive Board in 1919–20 were Harlan Ober, Harry Randall, Corinne True, Alfred Lunt, Roy Wilhelm, Zia Bagdadi, Mason Remey, May Maxwell, and Frederick D'Evelyn.

6. Louis Gregory to Chapman, 3 October 1919, Edith M. Chapman Papers, National Bahá'í Archives, Wilmette, Ill.

7. Teaching Committee of Nineteen, *Teaching Bulletin,* no. 1 (19 Nov. 1919), n. pag., Alfred E. Lunt Papers, National Bahá'í Archives, Wilmette, Ill.

8. Executive Board of Bahai Temple Unity, Minutes, 11 Sept. 1919, Bahá'í Temple Unity Records.

9. Louis Gregory to Ober, 9 September 1919, Harlan F. Ober Papers, National Bahá'í Archives, Wilmette, Ill.

10. Louis G. Gregory, "Racial Amity in America: An Historical Review," in *The Bahá'í World: A Biennial International Record, Volume VII, 1936–1938,* comp. National Spiritual Assembly of the Bahá'ís of the United States and Canada (New York: Bahá'í Publishing Committee, 1939), p. 655.

11. Franklin, *From Slavery to Freedom,* p. 481; quoted in ibid., p. 489.

12. Ibid., p. 490.

13. Louis G. Gregory, "Racial Amity," in *Bahá'í Year Book, Volume One, 1925–1926,* comp. National Spiritual Assembly of the Bahá'ís of the United States and Canada (New York: Bahá'í Publishing Committee, 1926), p. 165.

14. Shoghi Effendi, *God Passes By,* rev. ed. (Wilmette, Ill.: Bahá'í Publishing Trust, 1974), p. 217.

15. Louis Gregory to Joseph Hannen, 16 October 1919, Hannen-Knobloch Family Papers, National Bahá'í Archives, Wilmette, Ill.

16. Louis Gregory to Chapman, 18 September 1935, Chapman Papers.

17. Mariam Haney, "Mrs. Agnes Parsons," in *The Bahá'í World: A Biennial International Record, Volume V, 1932–1934,* comp. National Spiritual Assembly of the Bahá'ís of the United States and Canada (New York: Bahá'í Publishing Committee, 1936), pp. 410, 412–13.

18. Bahai Temple Unity, Proceedings of the Annual Meeting, 1922, p. 308, Bahá'í Temple Unity Records.

19. Louis G. Gregory, "Racial Amity at Green Acre," in *The Bahá'í World (Formerly: Bahá'í Year Book): A Biennial International Record, Volume III, 1928–1930,* comp. National Spiritual Assembly of the Bahá'ís of the United States and Canada (New York: Bahá'í Publishing Committee, 1930), p. 181.

20. Bahai Temple Unity, Proceedings of the Annual Meeting, 1922, p. 309, Bahá'í Temple Unity Records.

21. Louis Gregory to Parsons, 16 December 1920, Agnes S. Parsons Papers,

National Bahá'í Archives, Wilmette, Ill.

22. Ibid.; 'Abdu'l-Bahá, quoted in Zia M. Bagdadi, " 'Now is the time for the Americans to unite both the white and colored races': Words of Abdul-Baha to Dr. Zia M. Bagdadi," *Star of the West,* 12 (24 June 1921), 121.

23. Gregory, "Racial Amity in America," p. 655; Haney, "Mrs. Agnes Parsons," p. 413; Louis Gregory, "Inter-racial Amity," in *The Bahá'í World (Formerly: Bahá'í Year Book): A Biennial International Record, Volume II, 1926–1928,* comp. National Spiritual Assembly of the Bahá'ís of the United States and Canada (New York: Bahá'í Publishing Committee, 1928), p. 281.

24. Gregory, "Racial Amity in America," p. 655; Gregory, "Inter-racial Amity," p. 281; Gregory, "Racial Amity in America," p. 655.

25. Reproduced in Horace Holley, "Survey of Current Bahá'í Activities in the East and West," in *The Bahá'í World (Formerly: Bahá'í Year Book): A Biennial International Record, Volume II, 1926–1928,* comp. National Spiritual Assembly of the Bahá'ís of the United States and Canada (New York: Bahá'í Publishing Committee, 1928), pp. 22–23.

26. Bahai Temple Unity, Proceedings of the Annual Meeting, 1922, pp. 309–10, Bahá'í Temple Unity Records.

27. Ibid., p. 310.

28. John Hope Franklin, *An Illustrated History of Black Americans* (New York: Time-Life Books, 1970), p. 120; Franklin, *From Slavery to Freedom,* p. 511.

29. 'Abdu'l-Bahá, quoted by Mountfort Mills, in Gregory, "Racial Amity in America," p. 656.

30. Louis Gregory to Parsons, 16 December 1920, Parsons Papers.

31. Gregory, "Racial Amity in America," p. 656.

32. 'Abdu'l-Bahá to Parsons, 29 April 1921, 27 September 1921, and 29 April 1921, Tablets of 'Abdu'l-Bahá, National Bahá'í Archives, Wilmette, Ill. (Approved translations of these tablets do not yet exist; consequently, these translations cannot be considered authentic.—Ed.)

33. 'Abdu'l-Bahá to Parsons, 26 July 1921 and 7 October 1921, Tablets of 'Abdu'l-Bahá. (Approved translations of these tablets do not yet exist; consequently, these translations cannot be considered authentic.—Ed.)

34. 'Abdu'l-Bahá to Parsons, 26 July 1921 and 27 September 1921, Tablets of 'Abdu'l-Bahá. (Approved translations of these tablets do not yet exist; consequently, these translations cannot be considered authentic.—Ed.)

Chapter 14 / The Work Continues

1. Bahai Temple Unity, Proceedings of the Annual Meeting, 24–26 Apr. 1922, pp. 324–25, Bahá'í Temple Unity Records, National Bahá'í Archives, Wilmette, Ill.

2. 'Abdu'l-Bahá to Parsons, 27 September 1921 and 7 October 1921, Tablets of 'Abdu'l-Bahá, National Bahá'í Archives, Wilmette, Ill.

3. Roy Williams, "Convention for Amity Between the White and Colored Races, Springfield, Massachusetts, December 5 and 6, 1921," *Star of the West,* 13 (28 Apr. 1922), 51.

4. Bahai Temple Unity, Proceedings of the Annual Meeting, 1922, p. 329, Bahá'í Temple Unity Records.

5. Ibid.

6. Ugo Giachery, *Shoghi Effendi: Recollections* (Oxford: George Ronald, 1973), pp. 5–6.

7. Louis Gregory, "Inter-racial Amity," in *The Bahá'í World (Formerly: Bahá'í Year Book): A Biennial International Record, Volume II, 1926–1928,* comp. National Spiritual Assembly of the Bahá'ís of the United States and Canada (New York: Bahá'í Publishing Committee, 1928), pp. 282–83; Louis G. Gregory, "Racial Amity in America: An Historical Review," in *The Bahá'í World: A Biennial International Record, Volume VII, 1936–1938,* comp. National Spiritual Assembly of the Bahá'ís of the United States and Canada (New York: Bahá'í Publishing Committee, 1939), p. 657.

8. Gregory, "Racial Amity in America," p. 657.

9. National Spiritual Assembly of the Bahá'ís of the United States and Canada, Horace Holley, secy., to all Local Spiritual Assemblies, 19 May 1924, Agnes S. Parsons Papers, National Bahá'í Archives, Wilmette, Ill.

10. Spiritual Assembly of the Bahá'ís of Philadelphia, Jessie E. Revell, secy., general letter to "the Baha'is throughout the world," 29 October 1924, Parsons Papers.

11. Ibid.

12. Philadelphia Convention for Amity program, Parsons Papers; Spiritual Assembly of the Bahá'ís of Philadelphia, Revell, secy., to "The Clergy," 9 October 1924, Parsons Papers; Spiritual Assembly of the Bahá'ís of Philadelphia to the Bahá'ís of the world, 29 October 1924, Parsons Papers.

13. Spiritual Assembly of the Bahá'ís of Philadelphia to the Bahá'ís of the world, 29 October 1924, Parsons Papers.

14. Gregory, "Racial Amity in America," p. 657.

15. C. Vann Woodward, *The Strange Career of Jim Crow,* 2d rev. ed. (New York: Oxford Univ. Press, 1966), pp. 123–24.

16. Ibid., pp. 124–26.

17. Bessye Bearden, "New York Society," *Chicago Defender,* 5 Mar. 1932, part 2, p. 1, col. 1–2.

18. Woodward, *Strange Career of Jim Crow,* p. 125; "News of the Cause," *Baha'i News Letter,* no. 10 (Feb. 1926), p. 6; Alaine [*sic*] Locke, "Impressions of Haifa," in *The Bahá'í World (Formerly: Bahá'í Year Book): A Biennial International Record, Volume II, 1926–1928,* comp. National Spiritual Assembly of

the Bahá'ís of the United States and Canada (New York: Bahá'í Publishing Committee, 1928), pp. 125, 127. (Also published in *The Bahá'í World [Formerly: Bahá'í Year Book]: A Biennial International Record, Volume III, 1928–1930,* comp. National Spiritual Assembly of the Bahá'ís of the United States and Canada [New York: Bahá'í Publishing Committee, 1930], pp. 280, 282.) For a perspective on the Bahá'í influence on Locke's thinking, see Ernest D. Mason, "Alain Locke's Social Philosophy," *World Order,* 13, no. 2 (Winter 1978–79), 25–34.

Chapter 15 / Setback

1. Louis Gregory to Horace Holley [National Spiritual Assembly], 19 November 1924, Interracial Committee Correspondence, Office of the Secretary, National Spiritual Assembly of the Bahá'ís of the United States and Canada Records, National Bahá'í Archives, Wilmette, Ill.

2. Louis G. Gregory, "An Inter-racial Committee: Its Great Need, and How It Can Serve Washington, the Nation, and the World," TS, p. 1, Interracial Committee Correspondence, Office of the Secretary, National Spiritual Assembly of the Bahá'ís of the United States and Canada Records.

3. Ibid.; Louis Gregory to Holley [National Spiritual Assembly], 3 December 1924, Interracial Committee Correspondence, Office of the Secretary, National Spiritual Assembly of the Bahá'ís of the United States and Canada Records.

4. Louis Gregory to Parsons, 3 December 1924, Agnes S. Parsons Papers, National Bahá'í Archives, Wilmette, Ill.; Louise Gregory to Parsons, 5 February 1925, Parsons Papers; Louis Gregory to Parsons, 27 March 1925, Parsons Papers.

5. Louis Gregory to Parsons, 24 October 1925, Parsons Papers.

6. "Official Proceedings Twenty-Second Annual Convention of the Baha'is of the United States and Canada held at Foundation Hall—Baha'i Temple, Wilmette, Illinois, April 25–27, 1930," TS, p. 178, National Bahá'í Archives, Wilmette, Ill.

7. Louis Gregory to Lunt, 17 March 1923, Alfred E. Lunt Papers, National Bahá'í Archives, Wilmette, Ill.

8. Ibid.

9. Holley to Parsons, 28 February 1925, Parsons Papers.

10. "Work of National Committees," *Baha'i News Letter,* no. 10 (Feb. 1926), p. 2.

11. Shoghi Effendi, "Guardian Endorses 'Plan of Unified Action,' " *Baha'i News Letter,* no. 10 (Feb. 1926), p. 1; Shoghi Effendi, "Extracts of Letters Written by the Guardian to the Treasurer of the National Spiritual Assembly About the Plan of Unified Action," *Baha'i News Letter,* no. 21 (Jan. 1928), p. 3; Carl

Scheffler, ''Statement by the Treasurer about the Plan of Unified Action,'' *Baha'i News Letter*, no. 21 (Jan. 1928), p. 1.

12. ''The Mashriqu'l Adhkar,'' *Baha'i News Letter*, no. 3 (Mar. 1925), p. 3; Shoghi Effendi, ''Latest Words of the Guardian About the Plan of Unified Action,'' *Baha'i News Letter*, no. 22 (Mar. 1928), p. 1.

13. National Spiritual Assembly, Holley, secy., to the Bahá'ís of the United States and Canada, published in *Baha'i News Letter*, no. 10 (Feb. 1926), p. 1; ''Committees of the National Spiritual Assembly,'' *Baha'i News Letter*, no. 12 (June-July 1926), pp. 6–7.

14. ''News of the Cause,'' *Baha'i News Letter*, no. 13 (Sept. 1926), pp. 6–7; ''World Unity Conferences in Cleveland and Boston,'' *Baha'i News Letter*, no. 15 (Jan. 1927), p. 5; ''World Unity Conferences in January and February,'' *Baha'i News Letter*, no. 16 (Mar. 1927), pp. 4–5; ''The World Unity Conferences,'' *Baha'i News Letter*, no. 14 (Nov. 1926), p. 3.

15. ''The World Unity Conferences,'' *Baha'i News Letter*, no. 14 (Nov. 1926), p. 3.

16. Carl Scheffler, ''Annual Report of the Treasurer of the National Spiritual Assembly of the Bahá'ís of the United States and Canada for the Period from April 1, 1926 to March 31, 1927,'' *Baha'i News Letter*, no. 19 (Aug. 1927), p. 4; ''World Unity Conferences,'' *Baha'i News Letter*, no. 20 (Nov. 1927), p. 5.

17. Transcript of two talks at 1927 convention, attachment, Lunt to Louis Gregory, 4 August 1927, TS, p. 9, Lunt Papers.

18. Louis Gregory to Parsons, 4 February 1927, Parsons Papers.

19. Louis Gregory to Parsons, 21 January 1927, Parsons Papers.

20. Louis Gregory to Holley [National Spiritual Assembly], 28 December 1926, Interracial Committee Correspondence, Office of the Secretary, National Spiritual Assembly of the Bahá'ís of the United States and Canada Records.

21. Ibid.

Chapter 16 / The Challenge to Action

1. National Spiritual Assembly of the Bahá'ís of the United States and Canada, Horace Holley, secy., to Parsons et al., 13 November 1926, Agnes S. Parsons Papers, National Bahá'í Archives, Wilmette, Ill.

2. Louis Gregory to Holley [National Spiritual Assembly], 28 December 1926, Interracial Committee Correspondence, Office of the Secretary, National Spiritual Assembly of the Bahá'ís of the United States and Canada Records, National Bahá'í Archives, Wilmette, Ill.

3. Special Committee on Racial Amity to National Spiritual Assembly, 8 January 1927, Interracial Committee Correspondence, Office of the Secretary, National Spiritual Assembly of the Bahá'ís of the United States and Canada Records.

4. National Spiritual Assembly of the Bahá'ís of the United States and Canada, Holley, secy., to Parsons et al. [Race Amity Committee], 14 January 1927, Parsons Papers; "National Committee on Racial Amity Appointed," *Baha'i News Letter*, no. 16 (Mar. 1927), p. 5.

5. National Spiritual Assembly of the Bahá'ís of the United States and Canada, Holley, secy., to Parsons et al., 14 January 1927, Parsons Papers; Boyle to Holley, 1 February 1927, Interracial Committee Correspondence, Office of the Secretary, National Spiritual Assembly of the Bahá'ís of the United States and Canada Records.

6. Louis Gregory to Chapman, 18 September 1935, Edith M. Chapman Papers, National Bahá'í Archives, Wilmette, Ill.

7. National Spiritual Assembly, Holley, secy., to Louis Gregory, 4 March 1927, Interracial Committee Correspondence, Office of the Secretary, National Spiritual Assembly of the Bahá'ís of the United States and Canada Records.

8. Parsons to Holley, 2 February 1927, Interracial Committee Correspondence, Office of the Secretary, National Spiritual Assembly of the Bahá'ís of the United States and Canada Records.

9. Holley to Parsons, 8 February 1927, Interracial Committee Correspondence, Office of the Secretary, National Spiritual Assembly of the Bahá'ís of the United States and Canada Records.

10. Boyle to Holley, 1 February 1927, Interracial Committee Correspondence, Office of the Secretary, National Spiritual Assembly of the Bahá'ís of the United States and Canada Records.

11. Holley to Parsons, 9 August 1925, Parsons Papers.

12. Parsons to Holley (handwritten copy), 13 August 1925, Parsons Papers.

13. Holley to Parsons, 19 August 1925, Parsons Papers.

14. Parsons to Holley (copy), 21 August 1925, Parsons Papers; Holley to Parsons, 26 August 1925, Parsons Papers; Holley to Parsons, 21 September 1925, Parsons Papers.

15. Boyle to Holley, 1 February 1927, Interracial Committee Correspondence, Office of the Secretary, National Spiritual Assembly of the Bahá'ís of the United States and Canada Records.

16. Louis Gregory to Parsons, 5 February 1915 and 10 June 1915, Parsons Papers.

17. Louis Gregory to Parsons, 30 September 1925, Parsons Papers; Louis Gregory to Chapman, 18 September 1935, Chapman Papers; Louis Gregory to Parsons, 4 February 1927, Parsons Papers.

18. National Committee on Inter-racial Amity, Gregory, secy., to National Spiritual Assembly and all Local Spiritual Assemblies, 23 February 1927, Interracial Committee Correspondence, Office of the Secretary, National Spiritual Assembly of the Bahá'ís of the United States and Canada Records; Bahá'u'lláh and 'Abdu'l-Bahá, *The Oneness of Mankind: Teachings Compiled from the Utter-*

ances of Bahá'u'lláh and 'Abdu'l-Bahá, [comp. Mariam Haney and Louis G. Gregory] (New York: Bahá'í Publishing Committee, n.d.).

19. Louis G. Gregory, "Racial Amity in America: An Historical Review," in *The Bahá'í World: A Biennial International Record, Volume VII, 1936–1938*, comp. National Spiritual Assembly of the Bahá'ís of the United States and Canada (New York: Bahá'í Publishing Committee, 1939), p. 658.

20. Shoghi Effendi, *Bahá'í Administration: Selected Messages 1922–1932*, 7th rev. ed. (Wilmette, Ill.: Bahá'í Publishing Trust, 1974), p. 129; originally published in "Letters from Shoghi Effendi," *Baha'i News Letter*, no. 18 (June 1927), pp. 7–8.

21. Gregory, "Racial Amity in America," p. 658; Shoghi Effendi, *Bahá'í Administration*, p. 129.

22. Shoghi Effendi, *Bahá'í Administration*, pp. 129–30.

23. Ibid., pp. 130–31.

24. Ibid., pp. 131–32.

25. Ibid., p. 131.

26. National Inter-racial Amity Committee, Gregory, secy., to National Spiritual Assembly and all Local Spiritual Assemblies, 12 December 1927, excerpted in "Inter-racial Amity Conferences," *Baha'i News Letter*, no. 22 (Mar. 1928), p. 5.

27. Louis Gregory to Parsons, 23 January 1928, Parsons Papers; exchange of letters between Parsons and Holley, July 1929, Parsons Papers; Louis Gregory to Parsons, 7 April 1929, Parsons Papers.

28. Shoghi Effendi to Louis Gregory, 31 October 1928, Letters of Shoghi Effendi, National Bahá'í Archives, Wilmette, Ill.

Chapter 17 / Apogee

1. Transcript of two talks at 1927 convention, attachment, Lunt to Louis Gregory, 4 August 1927, TS, pp. 3, 2, Alfred E. Lunt Papers, National Bahá'í Archives, Wilmette, Ill.

2. Ibid., pp. 5, 7, 9–10.

3. Ibid., pp. 5, 7, 12, 7, 8.

4. Ibid., pp. 14, 8, 15.

5. Lucy Jane Marshall and Louis G. Gregory, "The Nineteenth Annual Convention," *Baha'i News Letter*, no. 18 (June 1927), pp. 4–5.

6. Ibid., pp. 3, 4.

7. Louis G. Gregory, "Racial Amity in America: An Historical Review," in *The Bahá'í World: A Biennial International Record, Volume VII, 1936–1938*, comp. National Spiritual Assembly of the Bahá'ís of the United States and Canada (New York: Bahá'í Publishing Committee, 1939), p. 658.

8. Louis Gregory, "Inter-racial Amity," in *The Bahá'í World (Formerly:*

Bahá'í Year Book): A Biennial International Record, Volume II, 1926–1928, comp. National Spiritual Assembly of the Bahá'ís of the United States and Canada (New York: Bahá'í Publishing Committee, 1928), p. 284.

9. Gregory, "Racial Amity in America," p. 661.

10. Gregory, "Inter-racial Amity," p. 285; Gregory, "Racial Amity in America," p. 656.

11. National Committee on Inter-racial Amity to National Spiritual Assembly and all Local Spiritual Assemblies, quoted in "Inter-Racial Amity Conferences," *Baha'i News Letter,* no. 22 (Mar. 1928), p. 5.

12. Louis Gregory to Parsons, 23 January and 5 February 1928, Agnes S. Parsons Papers, National Bahá'í Archives, Wilmette, Ill.

13. "World Unity Conferences," *Baha'i News Letter,* no. 20 (Nov. 1927), p. 5; "World Unity Conferences Obtain Legal Charter," *Baha'i News Letter,* no. 22 (Mar. 1928), p. 8.

14. Gregory, "Racial Amity in America," pp. 659–60; Louis Gregory to Parsons, 5 February 1928, Parsons Papers.

15. "Inter-Racial Amity Conferences," *Baha'i News Letter,* no. 22 (Mar. 1928), p. 5; "Official Proceedings Twenty-first Annual Convention Baha'is of the United States and Canada held at Baha'i Temple, Wilmette, Illinois, April 26 to 28 1929," TS, p. 90, National Bahá'í Archives, Wilmette, Ill.; "Western Assemblies Combine Material with Spiritual Hospitality," *Baha'i News Letter,* no. 23 (Apr. 1928), p. 3.

16. "Letter from Amity Committee," *Baha'i News Letter,* no. 30 (Mar. 1929), pp. 6–7.

17. Spiritual Assembly of the Bahá'ís of Rochester, N.Y., Report of interracial amity convention, 8 March 1929, Interracial Committee Correspondence, Office of the Secretary, National Spiritual Assembly of the Bahá'ís of the United States and Canada Records, National Bahá'í Archives, Wilmette, Ill.; Louis Gregory to Parsons, 7 April 1929, Parsons Papers.

18. Louis Gregory to Chapman, 13 December 1927, Edith M. Chapman Papers, National Bahá'í Archives, Wilmette, Ill.

19. "Mr. Louis Gregory's Teaching Activities," *Baha'i News Letter,* no. 30 (Mar. 1929), p. 8.

20. Ibid.

21. "Teaching Work of Mr. Gregory," *Baha'i News Letter,* no. 38 (Feb. 1930), pp. 7–8; Louis Gregory to Chapman, 21 June 1929, Chapman Papers.

22. "Teaching Work of Mr. Gregory," p. 8.

23. Louis Gregory to members of amity committee, 23 June 1929, Parsons Papers; National Spiritual Assembly, "To Complete the Temple Fund by January 1, 1930: A Message from the National Spiritual Assembly," *Baha'i News Letter,* no. 34 (Oct. 1929), p. 3; National Spiritual Assembly, "Temple Construction Fund Completed," *Baha'i News Letter,* no. 39 (Mar. 1930), p. 1.

24. "Interracial Amity Committee," *Baha'i News Letter*, no. 40 (Apr. 1930), pp. 10–12.

25. Ibid., p. 12; quoted in John Hope Franklin, *From Slavery to Freedom: A History of Negro Americans*, 3d ed. (New York: Knopf, 1967), p. 526.

26. Louis G. Gregory, "Inter-racial Amity," *Baha'i News*, no. 43 (Aug. 1930), pp. 5–6; R. C. Collison, "To the Members of the Interassembly Teaching Committees," in "Reports from Teaching Committee," *Baha'i News*, no. 49 (Mar. 1931), p. 6.

27. Doris McKay, "Reports from Teaching Committee," *Baha'i News*, no. 48 (Feb. 1931), pp. 3–4; "New York Amity Conference Reported in Leading Negro Paper," *Baha'i News*, no. 48 (Feb. 1931), p. 10.

28. National Teaching Committee, "Annual Committee Reports, 1930–1931: Teaching," published in *Baha'i News*, no. 51 (Apr. 1931), pp. 4, 2–3.

29. Louis G. Gregory, "Inter-racial Amity," *Baha'i News*, no. 51 (Apr. 1931), pp. 4–5; Gregory, "Racial Amity in America," p. 662; Louis G. Gregory, "The Annual Convention," *Baha'i News*, no. 52 (May 1931), p. 3. The members that year were Loulie Mathews, chairman, Louis Gregory, secretary, Zia M. Bagdadi, Mabelle L. Davis, Frances Fales, Sara L. Witt, Alain Locke, Shelley N. Parker, Annie K. Lewis. See "National Bahá'í Committees: 1931–1932," *Bahá'í News*, no. 53 (July 1931), p. 2.

30. "Annual Reports of the National Committee [*sic*] of the National Spiritual Assembly of the Bahá'ís of the United States and Canada—1931–1932: Report of Racial Amity Committee," *Bahá'í News*, no. 62 (May 1932), p. 7.

31. Louis G. Gregory, "Light on Basic Unity: Green Acre and the Bahá'í Ideal of International Amity," in *The Bahá'í World: A Biennial International Record, Volume IV, 1930–1932*, comp. National Spiritual Assembly of the Bahá'ís of the United States and Canada (New York: Bahá'í Publishing Committee, 1933), p. 486; "Annual Reports—1931–1932: Report of Racial Amity Committee," pp. 7–9.

32. Gregory, "Racial Amity in America," p. 664; "The Heart of Dixie: Teaching Amity in the South," *Bahá'í News*, no. 58 (Jan. 1932), p. 3.

33. Gregory, "Racial Amity in America," pp. 664–65; "Heart of Dixie," p. 3.

34. Gregory, "Racial Amity in America," p. 665; Horace Holley, "Survey of Current Bahá'í Activities in the East and West," in *The Bahá'í World: A Biennial International Record, Volume IV, 1930–1932*, comp. National Spiritual Assembly of the Bahá'ís of the United States and Canada (New York: Bahá'í Publishing Committee, 1933), p. 62.

35. "Heart of Dixie," p. 3.

36. "Annual Reports—1931–1932: Racial Amity Committee," *Bahá'í News*, no. 62 (May 1932), pp. 8–9; Bessye Bearden, "New York Society," *Chicago Defender*, 5 Mar. 1932, part 2, p. 1, col. 1–2.

37. DuBois to Mathews (copy), 1 March 1932, W. E. B. DuBois Papers (microfilm, reel 37), University of Massachusetts Library, Amherst, Mass. (The letter is quoted by permission of David DuBois; use of this material without the express consent of Mr. DuBois is forbidden.); "Annual Reports—1931–1932: Racial Amity Committee," p. 8.

Chapter 18 / Holding On

1. "Committee Reports: Committee on Inter-Racial Amity," *Baha'i News,* no. 74 (May 1933), p. 13; National Bahá'í Committee for Racial Amity, Gregory, secy., "Inter-Racial Amity Activities," *Baha'i News,* no. 72 (Apr. 1933), p. 6.

2. Correspondence between W. E. B. DuBois and Oliver and Wanden La Farge, 1932, W. E. B. DuBois Papers (microfilm, reel 37), University of Massachusetts Library, Amherst, Mass.

3. National Racial Amity Committee, Gregory, secy., "A Letter from the Inter-Racial Amity Committee," *Baha'i News,* no. 69 (Dec. 1932), pp. 2–3; National Spiritual Assembly, Horace Holley, secy., to Race Amity Committee, 21 June 1932, Interracial Committee Correspondence, Office of the Secretary, National Spiritual Assembly of the Bahá'ís of the United States and Canada Records, National Bahá'í Archives, Wilmette, Ill.

4. National Spiritual Assembly, Holley, secy., "Annual Report, National Spiritual Assembly of the Baha'is of the United States and Canada, 1932–1933," *Baha'i News,* no. 74 (May 1933), p. 3.

5. Detroit Spiritual Assembly, Helen Eggleston, secy., to Davis, 8 December 1932, Mabelle L. Davis Papers, National Bahá'í Archives, Wilmette, Ill.; Davis to Holley, 14 December 1932, Davis Papers; National Spiritual Assembly of the Bahá'ís of the United States and Canada, Holley, secy., to Davis, 20 December 1932, Davis Papers.

6. Louis Gregory to Detroit Spiritual Assembly (copy), 14 December 1932, Davis Papers.

7. Ibid.

8. Davis to Detroit Spiritual Assembly (copy), 15 February and 10 March 1933, Davis Papers; Davis to Alfred E. Lunt (copy), 13 May 1934, Davis Papers.

9. Mariam Haney, "Mrs. Agnes Parsons," in *The Bahá'í World: A Biennial International Record, Volume V, 1932–1934,* comp. National Spiritual Assembly of the Bahá'ís of the United States and Canada (New York: Bahá'í Publishing Committee, 1936), p. 410.

10. National Spiritual Assembly, Holley, secy., to Race Amity Committee, 11 October 1933, Interracial Committee Correspondence, Office of the Secretary, National Spiritual Assembly of the Bahá'ís of the United States and Canada Records.

11. "Annual Committee Reports, 1933–1934: 9. Race Amity," *Baha'i News,* no. 88 (Nov. 1934), pp. 9–10.

12. Racial Amity Committee, Gregory, secy., "Letter from Inter-racial Amity Committee," *Baha'i News,* no. 80 (Jan. 1934), pp. 6–7.

13. Ibid., p. 7.

14. Louis G. Gregory, "The Spirit of the Convention," *Baha'i News,* no. 84 (June 1934), p. 5.

15. "Second Report on 1934 Convention Resolutions," *Baha'i News,* no. 90 (Mar. 1935), p. 3; National Race Amity Committee, "The Divine Call to Race Amity," *Baha'i News,* no. 90 (Mar. 1935), pp. 4–7.

16. Race Amity Committee, "Divine Call," p. 5.

17. Ibid., pp. 6–7.

18. "News of the Cause," *Baha'i News,* no. 94 (Aug. 1935), p. 2; Louis G. Gregory, "Racial Amity in America: An Historical Review," in *The Bahá'í World: A Biennial International Record, Volume VII, 1936–1938,* comp. National Spiritual Assembly of the Bahá'ís of the United States and Canada (New York: Bahá'í Publishing Committee, 1939), pp. 663–64.

19. "The Twenty-Seventh Annual Convention: A Summary of the Proceedings," *Baha'i News,* no. 92 (June 1935), pp. 1–2.

20. Louis Gregory, quoted in Nellie S. French, "United States and Canada," in "Survey of Current Bahá'í Activities in the East and West," in *The Bahá'í World: A Biennial International Record, Volume VI, 1934–1936,* comp. National Spiritual Assembly of the Bahá'ís of the United States and Canada (New York: Bahá'í Publishing Committee, 1937), p. 118.

Chapter 19 / An Historical Record

1. "N.S.A. Action on Resolutions Adopted by the 1935 Convention," *Baha'i News,* no. 97 (Jan. 1936), pp. 5–6; National Spiritual Assembly, "A Baha'i Historical Record: Letter from the National Spiritual Assembly," *Baha'i News,* no. 93 (July 1935), p. 2; "Decisions of the National Spiritual Assembly," *Baha'i News,* no. 99 (Apr. 1936), p. 3.

2. Arthur Hampson, "The Growth and Spread of the Baha'i Faith" (Ph.D. diss., University of Hawaii, 1980), p. 263; National Spiritual Assembly, "Baha'i Historical Record," p. 2.

3. Bahá'í Historical Records Cards, National Bahá'í Archives, Wilmette, Ill. Analysis of the results of the survey is this author's. All personal statements from the cards quoted in this chapter may be located under the respondent's name in this collection.

4. St. Clair Drake and Horace R. Cayton, *Black Metropolis: A Study of Negro Life in a Northern City* (New York: Harper, 1962), II, 530.

5. Ibid., I, 139, 149–53.

Chapter 20 / A Cycle Ends

1. Louis Gregory, quoted in Nellie S. French, "United States and Canada," in "Survey of Current Bahá'í Activities in the East and West," in *The Bahá'í World: A Biennial International Record, Volume VI, 1934-1936,* comp. National Spiritual Assembly of the Bahá'ís of the United States and Canada (New York: Bahá'í Publishing Committee, 1937), p. 118.

2. Louis Gregory to Chapman, 18 September 1935, Edith M. Chapman Papers, National Bahá'í Archives, Wilmette, Ill.

3. "Annual Committee Reports, 1935-1936 (Concluded): Race Amity," *Baha'i News,* no. 100 (May 1936), p. 10.

4. Louis G. Gregory, "Racial Likenesses and Differences: The Scientific Evidence and the Bahá'í Teachings," in *The Bahá'í World: A Biennial International Record, Volume VI, 1934-1936,* comp. National Spiritual Assembly of the Bahá'ís of the United States and Canada (New York: Bahá'í Publishing Committee, 1937), pp. 659, 661-64.

5. Louis Gregory to Parsons, 13 July and 1 October 1927, Agnes S. Parsons Papers, National Bahá'í Archives, Wilmette, Ill.; Louis Gregory to Chapman, 27 September 1933, Chapman Papers.

6. "Annual Committee Reports, 1935-1936," pp. 9-10; Bahá'u'lláh and 'Abdu'l-Bahá, *The Oneness of Mankind: Teachings Compiled from the Utterances of Bahá'u'lláh and 'Abdu'l-Bahá,* [comp. Mariam Haney and Louis G. Gregory] (New York: Bahá'í Publishing Committee, n.d.).

7. "Annual Committee Reports, 1935-1936," p. 10.

Part 3 / A Middle Passage

Chapter 21 / Crisis

1. Louis Gregory to National Spiritual Assembly, 18 June 1932, Office of the Secretary, National Spiritual Assembly of the Bahá'ís of the United States and Canada Records, National Bahá'í Archives, Wilmette, Ill.

2. "National Assembly Budget—1929-1930," *Baha'i News Letter,* no. 33 (July 1929), p. 8.

3. Louis Gregory to National Spiritual Assembly, Alfred E. Lunt, secy., 20 January 1932, Office of the Secretary, National Spiritual Assembly of the Bahá'ís of the United States and Canada Records.

4. National Teaching Committee, Charlotte Linfoot, western secy., to National Spiritual Assembly, Lunt, secy., 8 April 1932, Office of the Secretary, National Spiritual Assembly of the Bahá'ís of the United States and Canada Records.

5. Louis Gregory to Lunt, 3 March 1923, Alfred E. Lunt Papers, National Bahá'í Archives, Wilmette, Ill.

6. Ibid.

7. Louis Gregory to Lunt, 17 March 1923, Lunt Papers.

8. Louis Gregory to National Spiritual Assembly, 18 June 1932, Office of the Secretary, National Spiritual Assembly of the Bahá'ís of the United States and Canada Records.

9. Ibid.

10. National Spiritual Assembly, Horace Holley, secy., to Louis Gregory (copy), 5 May 1932, Office of the Secretary, National Spiritual Assembly of the Bahá'ís of the United States and Canada Records.

11. Louis Gregory to National Spiritual Assembly, 18 June 1932, Office of the Secretary, National Spiritual Assembly of the Bahá'ís of the United States and Canada Records.

12. Louis Gregory to Holley, 21 May 1932, Office of the Secretary, National Spiritual Assembly of the Bahá'ís of the United States and Canada Records.

13. Shoghi Effendi, ''Recent Appeal of the Guardian to the National Spiritual Assembly, March 14, 1932,'' *Bahá'í News,* no. 61 (Apr. 1932), p. 1; National Spiritual Assembly, Holley, secy., to Louis Gregory (copy), 5 May 1932, Office of the Secretary, National Spiritual Assembly of the Bahá'ís of the United States and Canada Records; Ober to Lunt, 8 May 1932, Lunt Papers; Louis Gregory to Chapman, 4 November 1932, Edith M. Chapman Papers, National Bahá'í Archives, Wilmette, Ill.

14. State of New Hampshire, Certificate admitting Louis G. Gregory to the bar, 5 Nov. 1930, Louis G. Gregory Papers, Spiritual Assembly of the Bahá'ís of Eliot, Maine.

15. Louis Gregory to Lunt, 13 June 1932, Lunt Papers.

16. Louis Gregory to Holley, 21 May 1932, Office of the Secretary, National Spiritual Assembly of the Bahá'ís of the United States and Canada Records; Louis Gregory to Lunt, 13 June 1932, Lunt Papers.

17. Louis Gregory to Lunt, 13 June 1932, Lunt Papers; Lunt to Louis Gregory (copy), 15 June 1932, Lunt Papers.

18. Lunt to Ober (copy), 17 May 1932, Lunt Papers; Ober to Lunt, 8 May 1932, Lunt Papers.

19. Louis Gregory to National Spiritual Assembly, 18 June 1932, Office of the Secretary, National Spiritual Assembly of the Bahá'ís of the United States and Canada Records.

20. Ibid.

21. Ibid.

22. Ibid.

23. Ibid.

24. Ibid.
25. Ibid.
26. Ibid.

Chapter 22 / Resolution

1. Rúhíyyih Khánum, "Horace Hotchkiss Holley, April 7, 1887–July 12, 1960," in *The Bahá'í World: An International Record, Volume XIII, 1954–1963,* comp. The Universal House of Justice (Haifa: The Universal House of Justice, 1970), p. 856.

2. 'Abdu'l-Bahá, quoted in *Principles of Bahá'í Administration: A Compilation,* 4th ed. (London: Bahá'í Publishing Trust, 1976), p. 42.

3. Shoghi Effendi, "Cablegram from Shoghi Effendi," *Baha'i News,* no. 87 (Sept. 1934), p. 3.

4. Shoghi Effendi (through his secy.), quoted in *The Bahá'í Life: Excerpts from the Writings of the Guardian,* The Universal House of Justice, comp. (n.p.: National Spiritual Assembly of the Bahá'ís of Canada, 1974), pp. 3, 2.

5. Shoghi Effendi, "Communications from Shoghi Effendi," *Baha'i News,* no. 88 (Nov. 1934), p. 1.

6. Shoghi Effendi, quoted in "Well Beloved Lunt," *Baha'i News,* no. 110 (Sept. 1937), p. 3; quoted in Louis G. Gregory and Harlan Ober, "Alfred Eastman Lunt," in *The Bahá'í World: A Biennial International Record, Volume VII, 1936–1938,* comp. National Spiritual Assembly of the Bahá'ís of the United States and Canada (New York: Bahá'í Publishing Committee, 1939), p. 534.

7. Louis Gregory to Horace Holley, 5 October 1932, Office of the Secretary, National Spiritual Assembly of the Bahá'ís of the United States and Canada Records, National Bahá'í Archives, Wilmette, Ill.

8. Louis Gregory to Holley, 17 November 1932, Office of the Secretary, National Spiritual Assembly of the Baha'ís of the United States and Canada Records.

9. Louis Gregory to Chapman, 4 November 1932, Edith M. Chapman Papers, National Bahá'í Archives, Wilmette, Ill.

10. Louis Gregory to Chapman, 25 December 1932, Chapman Papers.

11. Louis Gregory to Chapman, 4 November 1932, Chapman Papers.

12. Louis Gregory to Wilhelm, 17 November 1932, Roy C. Wilhelm File, National Spiritual Assembly of the Bahá'ís of the United States and Canada Records.

13. Louis Gregory to Chapman, 8 February 1934, Chapman Papers.

14. Louis Gregory to Holley, 17 November 1932, Office of the Secretary, National Spiritual Assembly of the Bahá'ís of the United States and Canada Records.

15. Shoghi Effendi to Louis Gregory (copy), 20 October 1932, Louis G.

Gregory Papers, National Bahá'í Archives, Wilmette, Ill.

16. Louis Gregory to Wilhelm, 30 November and 1 December 1932, Roy C. Wilhelm File, National Spiritual Assembly of the Bahá'ís of the United States and Canada Records.

17. Louis Gregory to Chapman, 9 January 1934, Chapman Papers.

18. Shoghi Effendi to Louis Gregory, 24 October 1933, Letters of Shoghi Effendi, National Bahá'í Archives, Wilmette, Ill.

19. National Spiritual Assembly, Holley, secy., to Shoghi Effendi (copy), 9 November 1933, Office of the Secretary, National Spiritual Assembly of the Bahá'ís of the United States and Canada Records.

20. Shoghi Effendi (through his secy.) to National Spiritual Assembly, 14 December 1933, Office of the Secretary, National Spiritual Assembly of the Bahá'ís of the United States and Canada Records.

21. Louis Gregory to Chapman, 28 March 1939, Chapman Papers.

Chapter 23 | New Directions

1. Louis Gregory to Wilhelm, 30 November 1932, Roy C. Wilhelm File, National Spiritual Assembly of the Bahá'ís of the United States and Canada Records, National Bahá'í Archives, Wilmette, Ill.

2. Wragg to *World Order* Editorial Board, Betty J. Fisher, assoc. ed., 9 March 1973, File "Morrison—Louis Gregory correspondence," *World Order* Files, Wilmette, Ill.

3. Louis G. Gregory, "Progress in Racial Amity," TS, p. 2, Louis G. Gregory Papers, National Bahá'í Archives, Wilmette, Ill.

4. Louise Gregory to Louis Gregory, 8 February 1934, Louis G. Gregory Papers.

5. Louise Gregory to Louis Gregory, 4 September 1934, Louis G. Gregory Papers.

6. Shoghi Effendi (through his secy.) to Louis Gregory, 24 October 1933, Letters of Shoghi Effendi, National Bahá'í Archives, Wilmette, Ill.

7. Teaching Committee, "Annual Committee Reports, 1933–1934: 1. Teaching Committee," *Baha'i News,* no. 85 (July 1934), p. 8.

8. Shoghi Effendi, quoted in Bahá'í Teaching Committee, Charlotte Linfoot, secy., to Gregory, 26 March 1935, Louis G. Gregory Papers.

9. Telephone interview with Thelma Allison, 29 Oct. 1977; Louis Gregory to Chapman, 20 February 1935, Edith M. Chapman Papers, National Bahá'í Archives, Wilmette, Ill.

10. Louis Gregory to Chapman, 20 February 1935, Chapman Papers; telephone interview with Thelma Allison, 29 Oct. 1977.

11. Louis Gregory to Chapman, 2 March 1936, Chapman Papers.

12. Shoghi Effendi (through his secy.) to Louis Gregory, 11 November 1936, Letters of Shoghi Effendi.

13. Louis Gregory to Horace Holley [National Spiritual Assembly], 31 December 1936, Inter-America Committee Files, National Spiritual Assembly of the Bahá'ís of the United States and Canada Records.

Chapter 24 / Haiti

1. Shoghi Effendi, quoted in "America's Spiritual Mission: National Spiritual Assembly Announces Teaching Policy for 1936–1937," *Baha'i News,* no. 101 (June 1936), p. 1.

2. National Spiritual Assembly statement, quoted in ibid., p. 2; "Fresh Conquests and Unprecedented Triumphs," *Baha'i News,* no. 101 (June 1936), pp. 2–3; Shoghi Effendi, quoted in National Spiritual Assembly of the Bahá'ís of the United States and Canada, "Annual Report," *Baha'i News,* no. 108 (June 1937), p. 10.

3. Shoghi Effendi, "Intensify Teaching Work a Thousandfold," *Baha'i News,* no. 103 (Oct. 1936), p. 3.

4. National Spiritual Assembly, Horace Holley, secy., to Louis Gregory (copy), 4 January 1937, Inter-America Committee Files, National Spiritual Assembly of the Bahá'ís of the United States and Canada Records, National Bahá'í Archives, Wilmette, Ill.; Louis Gregory to Holley [National Spiritual Assembly], 31 December 1936, Inter-America Committee Files, National Spiritual Assembly of the Bahá'ís of the United States and Canada Records.

5. Louis Gregory, quoted in Inter-America Committee, "Annual Report," *Baha'i News,* no. 109 (July 1937), p. 3.

6. Louis Gregory to Holley [National Spiritual Assembly], 21 February 1937, Inter-America Committee Files, National Spiritual Assembly of the Bahá'ís of the United States and Canada Records.

7. Ibid.

8. Louis Gregory to Mathews, 6 April 1937, Inter-America Committee Files, National Spiritual Assembly of the Bahá'ís of the United States and Canada Records; Louis Gregory to Holley [National Spiritual Assembly], 22 April 1937, Inter-America Committee Files, National Spiritual Assembly of the Bahá'ís of the United States and Canada Records.

9. Louis Gregory to Holley [National Spiritual Assembly], 21 February 1937, Inter-America Committee Files, National Spiritual Assembly of the Bahá'ís of the United States and Canada Records.

10. Louis G. and Louise Gregory, "A Teaching Campaign in Haiti," TS, n. pag., Louis G. Gregory Papers, National Bahá'í Archives, Wilmette, Ill.

11. Louis Gregory to Holley [National Spiritual Assembly], 14 March 1937,

Inter-America Committee Files, National Spiritual Assembly of the Bahá'ís of the United States and Canada Records.

12. Ibid.

13. Louis Gregory to Holley [National Spiritual Assembly], 13 April 1937, Inter-America Committee Files, National Spiritual Assembly of the Bahá'ís of the United States and Canada Records; Inter-America Committee, "Annual Report," *Baha'i News,* no. 109 (July 1937), pp. 3–4.

Chapter 25 / The Seven Year Plan

1. Louis Gregory to Horace Holley [National Spiritual Assembly], 14 March 1937, Inter-America Committee Files, National Spiritual Assembly of the Bahá'ís of the United States and Canada Records, National Bahá'í Archives, Wilmette, Ill.

2. Photograph with caption published in *Bahá'í News,* no. 162 (Apr. 1943), p. 6.

3. Marion Holley, "Pioneer Teachers in the Seven Year Plan," in *The Bahá'í World: A Biennial International Record, Volume VIII, 1938–1940,* comp. National Spiritual Assembly of the Bahá'ís of the United States and Canada (Wilmette, Ill.: Bahá'í Publishing Committee, 1942), p. 57; National Teaching Committee, "Praying Further Success!," *Baha'i News,* no. 113 (Jan. 1938), p. 3; Louis Gregory to Love, 26 June 1938, R. D. Love Letter, National Bahá'í Archives, Wilmette, Ill.

4. National Teaching Committee, " 'It Must Go On; Continually Go On,' " *Baha'i News,* no. 114 (Feb. 1938), p. 3.

5. Regional Teaching Committee for Alabama and Florida, "Regional Teaching Committees: Alabama, Florida," in "Annual Committee Reports, 1937–1938," *Baha'i News,* no. 115 (Apr. 1938), p. 18.

6. Louis Gregory to Chapman, 10 April 1938, Edith M. Chapman Papers, National Bahá'í Archives, Wilmette, Ill.

7. National Teaching Committee, " 'Appreciate Ye the Value of This Time,' " *Baha'i News,* no. 116 (June 1938), p. 6.

8. Louis Gregory to Chapman, 30 August 1938, Chapman Papers.

9. National Teaching Committee, "Teaching Activity," *Baha'i News,* no. 124 (Apr. 1939), p. 3.

10. "National Committees: Teaching," in National Spiritual Assembly of the Bahá'ís of the United States and Canada, *Annual Reports: National Spiritual Assembly of the Baha'is of the United States and Canada; Trustees; and National Committees, 1938–1939* (West Englewood, N.J.: National Spiritual Assembly of the Bahá'ís of the United States and Canada, n.d.), p. 12; Holley, "Pioneer Teachers in the Seven Year Plan," p. 57; Shoghi Effendi to Martin, 20 July 1939,

Letters of Shoghi Effendi, National Bahá'í Archives, Wilmette, Ill.

11. Lydia J. Martin, "Early Years of the Baha'i Faith in Arkansas," TS, p. 2, attachment to Martin to *World Order* Editorial Board, Betty J. Fisher, assoc. ed., 12 December 1979, File "Morrison—Louis Gregory correspondence," *World Order* Files, Wilmette, Ill.

Chapter 26 / Chasm

1. Shoghi Effendi, " 'An Inescapable . . . Responsibility': Cablegram from the Guardian," *Baha'i News*, no. 110 (Sept. 1937), p. 2; National Spiritual Assembly, "Redirect with Added Force Nationwide Appeal to Entire Community," *Baha'i News*, no. 110 (Sept. 1937), p. 1.

2. Arthur Hampson, "The Growth and Spread of the Baha'i Faith" (Ph.D. diss., University of Hawaii, 1980), p. 268.

3. "Meetings of the N. S. A.," *Baha'i News*, no. 103 (Oct. 1936), p. 2.

4. Shoghi Effendi (through his secy.), "Letters from the Guardian," *Baha'i News*, no. 103 (Oct. 1936), p. 1.

5. "Public Meetings in Nashville," *Baha'i News*, no. 105 (Feb. 1937), p. 2.

6. National Spiritual Assembly, Horace Holley, secy., to Shoghi Effendi (copy), 23 January 1937, Office of the Secretary, National Spiritual Assembly of the Bahá'ís of the United States and Canada Records, National Bahá'í Archives, Wilmette, Ill.; Albert James, memories of Louis Gregory tape, recorded 4 Jan. 1981, National Bahá'í Archives, Wilmette, Ill.

7. Shoghi Effendi (through his secy.), "Letters from the Guardian (to the National Spiritual Assembly)," *Baha'i News*, no. 108 (June 1937), pp. 1–2.

8. "Twenty-Ninth Annual Convention," *Baha'i News*, no. 108 (June 1937), p. 3.

9. W. E. B. DuBois, "Forum of Fact and Opinion," *Pittsburgh Courier*, 30 Oct. 1937, Clipping, Spiritual Assembly of the Bahá'ís of Pittsburgh File, National Spiritual Assembly of the Bahá'ís of the United States and Canada Records.

10. National Spiritual Assembly, Holley, secy., to Editor, *Pittsburgh Courier* (copy), 3 Nov. 1937, Spiritual Assembly of the Bahá'ís of Pittsburgh File, National Spiritual Assembly of the Bahá'ís of the United States and Canada Records; Alice N. Parker to Holley [National Spiritual Assembly], 12 December 1938, Spiritual Assembly of the Bahá'ís of Pittsburgh File, National Spiritual Assembly of the Bahá'ís of the United States and Canada Records.

11. Francis L. Broderick, *W. E. B. DuBois: Negro Leader in Time of Crisis* (Stanford: Stanford University Press, 1959), p. 190.

12. Little to Holley [National Spiritual Assembly], n.d., Regional Teaching Committee Files, National Spiritual Assembly of the Bahá'ís of the United States and Canada Records.

13. Louis Gregory to DuBois, 29 March 1943, W. E. B. DuBois Papers (microfilm, reel 55), University of Massachusetts Library, Amherst, Mass.

14. Ibid.

15. Transcript of two talks at 1927 convention, attachment, Lunt to Louis Gregory, 4 August 1927, TS, p. 8, Alfred E. Lunt Papers, National Bahá'í Archives, Wilmette, Ill..

16. Shoghi Effendi (through his secy.) to Louis Gregory, 11 November 1936, Letters of Shoghi Effendi, National Bahá'í Archives, Wilmette, Ill.

Part 4 / The Era of Racial Unity

Chapter 27 / Advent

1. Shoghi Effendi, *The Advent of Divine Justice,* 3d rev. ed. (Wilmette, Ill.: Bahá'í Publishing Trust, 1969), pp. 28, 18, 28–29.

2. Ibid., pp. 29–30.

3. Ibid., p. 30.

4. Ibid., pp. 33–34.

5. National Spiritual Assembly, "A Deepening of Spirit," *Baha'i News,* no. 123 (Mar. 1939), p. 3; National Spiritual Assembly, "The Oneness of Mankind," *Baha'i News,* no. 124 (Apr. 1939), p. 1.

6. National Spiritual Assembly, "Oneness of Mankind," pp. 1–2.

7. "The Thirty-First Annual Convention," *Baha'i News,* no. 125 (May 1939), p. 3; Ober to Shoghi Effendi (copy), 11 May 1939, Harlan F. Ober Papers, National Bahá'í Archives, Wilmette, Ill.

8. "Thirty-First Annual Convention," *Baha'i News,* no. 125 (May 1939), pp. 3–4.

9. Ibid., p. 4; Louis Gregory to Chapman, 11 April 1936, Edith M. Chapman Papers, National Bahá'í Archives, Wilmette, Ill.; Lydia J. Martin and Sarah Martin Pereira, 25 August 1979, "Answers to Questions Asked About The Life and Activities of Mr. Louis Gregory, Hand of the Cause of Baha'u'llah," TS, p. 2, File "Morrison—Louis Gregory correspondence," *World Order* Files, Wilmette, Ill.; Ernest F. Tittle to Horace Holley, 19 March 1948, reproduced in *Bahá'í News,* no. 227 (Jan. 1950), p. 10.

10. Ioas to Ober, 20 May 1939, Ober Papers.

11. Ober to Shoghi Effendi, 11 May 1939 (copy), Ober Papers.

12. H. Elsie Austin, "Matthew W. Bullock, 1881–1972, Knight of Bahá'u'lláh," in *The Bahá'í World: An International Record, Volume XV, 1968–1973,* comp. The Universal House of Justice (Haifa: Bahá'í World Centre, 1975), pp. 535–39.

Chapter 28 / Banner Years

1. Louis Gregory to Chapman, 9 May 1950, Edith M. Chapman Papers, National Bahá'í Archives, Wilmette, Ill.
2. Shoghi Effendi (through his secy.) to Dorothy Baker, February 1941, excerpted in "Letters to Believers," *Bahá'í News*, no. 152 (Apr. 1942), pp. 2–3; Shoghi Effendi (through his secy.) to Race Unity Committee, 30 December 1945, excerpted in "Object of Inter-Racial Work," *Bahá'í News*, no. 188 (Oct. 1946), pp. 3–4.
3. Race Unity Committee, "Race Unity," *Bahá'í News*, no. 132 (Jan. 1940), pp. 9–10; Race Unity Committee, "Books on Race Relations," *Bahá'í News*, no. 133 (Feb. 1940), pp. 10–11; Race Unity Committee, "Race Unity: A Reading List," *Bahá'í News*, no. 135 (Apr. 1940), p. 7; Race Unity Committee, "Race Unity," *Bahá'í News*, no. 137 (July 1940), pp. 7–8; Race Unity Committee, "Race Unity: An Up-to-Date Bibliography," *Bahá'í News*, no. 155 (Aug. 1942), pp. 7–8; Race Unity Committee, "Race Unity Committee," *Bahá'í News*, no. 157 (Nov. 1942), pp. 7–8; Maye Harvey Gift and Alice Simmons Cox, comp., *Race and Man: A Compilation* (Wilmette, Ill.: Bahá'í Publishing Committee, 1943).
4. Dorothy Baker, "The Bahá'í Faith in the Colleges," in *The Bahá'í World: A Biennial International Record, Volume IX, 1940–1944*, comp. National Spiritual Assembly of the Bahá'ís of the United States and Canada (Wilmette, Ill.: Bahá'í Publishing Committee, 1945), pp. 773–74.
5. Margaret Kunz Ruhe, "Some Recollections of Hand of the Cause Mr. Louis Gregory," TS, p. 2, attachment to Ruhe to Gayle Morrison, 14 May 1979.
6. "Race Unity," in National Spiritual Assembly of the Bahá'ís of the United States and Canada, *Annual Report, 1940–1941* (Wilmette, Ill.: National Spiritual Assembly of the Bahá'ís of the United States and Canada, n.d.), p. 32; Race Unity Committee, "The Race Unity College Project," *Bahá'í News*, no. 151 (Feb. 1942), p. 6; "Regional Teaching, 8: North Carolina, South Carolina, Southern Georgia," in *Annual Report, 1940–1941*, p. 19; "Progress in Teaching," *Bahá'í News*, no. 142 (Mar. 1941), p. 8; Louis G. Gregory, "The Thirty-third Convention: Race Unity," *Bahá'í News*, no. 144 (June 1941), p. 6.
7. Annual report of Race Unity Committee, excerpted in Horace Holley, "International Survey of Current Bahá'í Activities in the East and West," in *The Bahá'í World: A Biennial International Record, Volume IX, 1940–1944*, comp. National Spiritual Assembly of the Bahá'ís of the United States and Canada (Wilmette, Ill.: Bahá'í Publishing Committee, 1945), pp. 71, 73.
8. Ibid., pp. 73–76; Dorothy Baker, "Among the Colleges," *Bahá'í News*, no. 161 (Mar. 1943), pp. 5–6.
9. "Green Acre School" and "Geyserville School" in *Annual Report, 1940–1941*, pp. 34–36; Louis G. Gregory, Race Unity Committee, "Race Unity

at Green Acre,'' *Bahá'í News,* no. 147 (Oct. 1941), pp. 10–11; "Green Acre
School" in National Spiritual Assembly of the Bahá'ís of the United States and
Canada, *Annual Bahá'í Reports Presented to the Bahá'ís of the United States and
Canada for the Year 1941–1942* (Wilmette, Ill.: National Spiritual Assembly of
the Bahá'ís of the United States and Canada, n.d.), p. 52.

10. Race Unity Committee, "Race Unity Conference," *Bahá'í News,* no.
156 (Oct. 1942), pp. 4–5; Race Unity Committee, "Oneness of Humanity Keynote of Green Acre Conclave," *Bahá'í News,* no. 166 (Nov. 1943), pp. 4–5.

11. Race Unity Committee, "Race Unity at Green Acre," *Bahá'í News,* no.
171 (Nov. 1944), pp. 18–19; "Green Acre," in National Spiritual Assembly of
the Bahá'ís of the United States and Canada, *Annual Bahá'í Reports Presented to
the Bahá'ís of the United States and Canada for the Year 1945–1946: Communications from the Guardian, National Committees, Trustees* (Wilmette, Ill.: National Spiritual Assembly of the Bahá'ís of the United States and Canada, n.d.),
p. 54; Green Acre Race Unity Conference, Sarah Martin Pereira, chrmn., "Race
Unity Conference at Green Acre, 1945," *Bahá'í News,* no. 182 (Apr. 1946), pp.
4–5; "Green Acre School, 1946," *Bahá'í News,* no. 182 (Apr. 1946), pp. 3–4.

12. Race Unity Committee, "Race Unity," *Bahá'í News,* no. 138 (Sept.
1940), pp. 6–7; Race Unity Committee, "Race Unity," *Bahá'í News,* no. 146
(Sept. 1941), p. 8; Albert James, memories of Louis Gregory, tape recorded 4
Jan. 1981, National Bahá'í Archives, Wilmette, Ill.

13. Louis G. Gregory, "The Spirit of the Convention," *Bahá'í News,* no.
153 (June 1942), p. 2; Race Unity Committee, Mrs. Fred Mortensen, secy.,
"Race Unity Projects," *Bahá'í News,* no. 140 (Dec. 1940), p. 8.

14. "Race Unity in Miami," *Bahá'í News,* no. 183 (May 1946), p. 6; "Race
Unity Meetings," *Bahá'í News,* no. 176 (Aug. 1945), p. 12.

15. Race Unity Committee, "Race Unity Projects," pp. 7–8; Race Unity
Committee, "Race Unity," *Bahá'í News,* no. 166 (Nov. 1943), pp. 3–4; Race
Unity Committee, "Race Unity," *Bahá'í News,* no. 146 (Sept. 1941), p. 8; National Teaching Committee, "Notes from the Teaching Front," *Bahá'í News,* no.
166 (Nov. 1943), pp. 5–6.

16. Race Unity Committee, Dorothy Baker, chrmn., Sarah Walrath, secy.,
"Race Unity: Reports From the Assemblies," *Bahá'í News,* no. 158 (Dec.
1942), pp. 3–4; Race Unity Committee, Dorothy Baker, chrmn., "Race Unity:
Reports from the Assemblies (Continued)," *Bahá'í News,* no. 160 (Feb. 1943),
p. 3; Race Unity Committee, Mrs. Fred Mortensen, secy., "Race Unity," *Bahá'í
News,* no. 139 (Oct. 1940), p. 9.

17. National Spiritual Assembly, "Recommendations of the 1946 National
Convention," *Bahá'í News,* no. 191 (Jan. 1947), p. 4.

18. Gregory, "Spirit of the Convention," p. 4.

19. Louis G. Gregory, "The Historic Thirty-Sixth Convention," *Bahá'í
News,* no. 170 (Sept. 1944), p. 7.

20. Spiritual Assembly of the Baháʾís of Atlanta, Georgia, Inc., "Early Baháʾí History of Atlanta, Georgia," TS, pp. 24–25, National Baháʾí Archives, Wilmette, Ill.

21. Regional Teaching Committee [for] Kentucky, Middle and East Tennessee, Northern Georgia, and Alabama, Nellie J. Roche, secy., "Presenting the Baháʾí Faith in the South," *Baháʾí News*, no. 141 (Jan. 1941), p. 4.

22. Finke to Louis Gregory, 15 April 1951, Louis G. Gregory Papers, National Baháʾí Archives, Wilmette, Ill.; Marzieh Gail, "Wilmette Letter: 1947," *Baháʾí News*, no. 196 (June 1947), p. 9.

23. Shoghi Effendi (through his secy.), "Excerpts from Letter from the Guardian," *Baháʾí News*, no. 145 (July 1941), p. 3.

24. National Spiritual Assembly, "Letter from the National Spiritual Assembly," *Baháʾí News*, no. 165 (Sept. 1943), pp. 1–2.

25. John Hope Franklin, *From Slavery to Freedom: A History of Negro Americans*, 3d ed. (New York: Knopf, 1967), pp. 597–98.

26. Louis Gregory to Chapman, 18 April 1940, Chapman Papers; Lydia J. Martin and Sarah Martin Pereira, 25 August 1979, "Answers to Questions Asked About The Life and Activities of Mr. Louis Gregory, Hand of the Cause of Bahaʾ-uʾlláh," TS, p. 3, File "Morrison—Louis Gregory correspondence," *World Order* Files, Wilmette, Ill.

27. Gregory, "The Historic Thirty-Sixth Convention," p. 7; National Spiritual Assembly, "Letter from the National Spiritual Assembly," *Baháʾí News*, no. 166 (Nov. 1943), p. 2; Race Unity Committee, "Race Unity," *Baháʾí News*, no. 166 (Nov. 1943), p. 3; "Teaching the Oneness of Mankind" in National Spiritual Assembly of the Baháʾís of the United States and Canada, *Annual Baháʾí Reports Presented to the Baháʾís of the United States and Canada for the Year 1943–1944* (Wilmette, Ill.: National Spiritual Assembly of the Baháʾís of the United States and Canada, n.d.), pp. 21–24.

28. Franklin, *From Slavery to Freedom*, p. 598.

29. National Spiritual Assembly of the Baháʾís of the United States and Canada, Horace Holley, secy., to the President [Franklin D. Roosevelt], 4 January 1944, reproduced in "Letter to the President on Race Unity," *Baháʾí News*, no. 174 (Apr.-May 1945), p. 12.

Chapter 29 / Deferred Victories

1. National Spiritual Assembly, "National Consultation on Race Unity," *Baháʾí News*, no. 188 (Oct. 1946), p. 4; National Spiritual Assembly, "Race Unity Consultation: Change in Agenda," *Baháʾí News*, no. 189 (Nov. 1946), p. 5.

2. "Resolutions of the 1947 Convention," *Baháʾí News*, no. 199 (Sept. 1947), p. 13.

3. Marzieh Gail, "Wilmette Letter: 1947," *Bahá'í News,* no. 196 (June 1947), p. 6.

4. Shoghi Effendi (through his secy.) to Mabel Ives, 5 July 1942, excerpted in National Spiritual Assembly of the Bahá'ís of the United States and Canada, *Annual Bahá'í Reports Presented to the Bahá'ís of the United States and Canada for the Year 1942–1943* (Wilmette, Ill.: National Spiritual Assembly of the Bahá'ís of the United States and Canada, n.d.), p. 11.

5. "Annual Reports, 1949–1950," *Bahá'í News,* no. 230 (Apr. 1950), p. 22.

6. Dorothy Baker, address tape recorded at All-America Conference, Chicago, 3–6 May 1953, National Bahá'í Archives, Wilmette, Ill.

7. Ibid.

8. "Race Amity Meetings in 35 States Proclaim Bahá'í Teaching of the Oneness of Mankind," *Bahá'í News,* no. 314 (Apr. 1957), p. 6.

9. Shoghi Effendi (through his secy.) to Bahá'í Inter-racial Teaching Committee, Dorothy Frey, chrmn., 27 May 1957, Letters of Shoghi Effendi, National Bahá'í Archives, Wilmette, Ill.

10. Louis Gregory to Chapman, 13 May 1950 and 9 May 1950, Edith M. Chapman Papers, National Bahá'í Archives, Wilmette, Ill.

11. Louis Gregory to Chapman, 13 May 1950, Chapman Papers.

12. Shoghi Effendi (through his secy.) to Oglesby, 9 February 1942, Letters of Shoghi Effendi.

Chapter 30 / *Fulfillment*

1. "Assembly Development," in National Spiritual Assembly of the Bahá'ís of the United States and Canada, *Annual Bahá'í Reports Presented to the Bahá'ís of the United States and Canada for the Year 1942–1943* (Wilmette, Ill.: National Spiritual Assembly of the Bahá'ís of the United States and Canada, n.d.), p. 26; "Assembly Development," in National Spiritual Assembly of the Bahá'ís of the United States and Canada, *Annual Bahá'í Reports Presented to the Bahá'ís of the United States and Canada for the Year 1943–1944* (Wilmette, Ill.: National Spiritual Assembly of the Bahá'ís of the United States and Canada, n.d.), pp. 45–46; "Assembly Development," in National Spiritual Assembly of the Bahá'ís of the United States and Canada, *Annual Bahá'í Reports Presented to the Bahá'ís of the United States and Canada for the Year 1944–1945* (Wilmette, Ill.: National Spiritual Assembly of the Bahá'ís of the United States and Canada, n.d.), pp. 23–24; "Assembly Development," in National Spiritual Assembly of the Bahá'ís of the United States and Canada, *Annual Bahá'í Reports Presented to the Bahá'ís of the United States and Canada for the Year 1945–1946* (Wilmette, Ill.: National Spiritual Assembly of the Bahá'ís of the United States and Canada, n.d.), p. 27.

2. Emanuel Reimer, memories of Louis Gregory, tape recorded 12 Sept. 1979, National Bahá'í Archives, Wilmette, Ill.

3. Margaret Kunz Ruhe, "Some Recollections of Hand of the Cause Mr. Louis Gregory," TS, p. 1, attachment to Ruhe to Gayle Morrison, 14 May 1979; Catharine Nourse, tape recorded by Gary Morrison during October 1978; Emanuel Reimer, memories of Louis Gregory.

4. Louis Gregory to Chapman, 17 September 1945, Edith M. Chapman Papers, National Bahá'í Archives, Wilmette, Ill.

5. Louis G. Gregory, "Faith and the Man: The Remarkable Story of Henderson Business College, a Bahá'í Enterprise," in *The Bahá'í World: A Biennial International Record, Volume VIII, 1938–1940,* comp. National Spiritual Assembly of the Bahá'ís of the United States and Canada (Wilmette, Ill.: Bahá'í Publishing Committee, 1942), pp. 901–03; Louis G. Gregory, "Accelerated Progress in Race Relations," in *The Bahá'í World: A Biennial International Record, Volume IX, 1940–1944,* comp. National Spiritual Assembly of the Bahá'ís of the United States and Canada (Wilmette, Ill.: Bahá'í Publishing Committee, 1945), pp. 876–80; Louis G. Gregory, "Bahá'í to Jew," *World Order,* 8, no. 4 (July 1942), 119–22; Louis G. Gregory, "Dr. Carver's Tribute," *World Order,* 9, no. 6 (Sept. 1943), 202–05; Louis G. Gregory, "Robert Turner," *World Order,* 12, no. 1 (Apr. 1946), 28–29.

6. Louis G. Gregory, "The Historic Thirty-Sixth Convention," *Bahá'í News,* no. 170 (Sept. 1944), p. 1.

7. Ibid., pp. 1, 8.

8. National Teaching Committee, " 'A New Faith Rising . . .': Report of the National Teaching Committee," *Bahá'í News,* no. 133 (Feb. 1940), p. 7; National Teaching Committee, "Teaching Activities, North America," *Bahá'í News,* no. 139 (Oct. 1940), p. 7; Dorothy Baker, "Among the Colleges," *Bahá'í News,* no. 161 (Mar. 1943), p. 6; "National Committees: Teaching: Part II. Regional Teaching Committees," in National Spiritual Assembly of the Bahá'ís of the United States and Canada, *Annual Bahá'í Reports Presented to the Bahá'ís of the United States and Canada for the Year 1942–1943* (Wilmette, Ill.: National Spiritual Assembly of the Bahá'ís of the United States and Canada, n.d.), p. 20; "College Foundation," in ibid., p. 28.

9. "Teaching Committee," in National Spiritual Assembly of the Bahá'ís of the United States and Canada, *Annual Bahá'í Reports Presented to the Bahá'ís of the United States and Canada for the Year 1943–1944* (Wilmette, Ill.: National Spiritual Assembly of the Bahá'ís of the United States and Canada, n.d.), p. 30; "Regional Teaching," in ibid., pp. 39, 40; "Local Communities: Current Activities," *Bahá'í News,* no. 174 (Apr.-May 1945), p. 11.

10. "Local News Letters," *Bahá'í News,* no. 174 (Apr.-May 1945), pp. 16, 17–18; National Teaching Committee, "Teaching in North America: Part II: Regional Teaching," *Bahá'í News,* no. 174 (Apr.-May 1945), p. 7; "Annual

Committee Reports: Teaching,'' in National Spiritual Assembly of the Bahá'ís of the United States and Canada, *Annual Bahá'í Reports Presented to the Bahá'ís of the United States and Canada for the Year 1944–1945* (Wilmette, Ill.: National Spiritual Assembly of the Bahá'ís of the United States and Canada, n.d.), pp. 8, 12, 11.

11. "Local News Letters," pp. 17–18.

Part 5 / Culminations

Chapter 31 / A Rounding Out of Life

1. Shoghi Effendi (through his secy.) to Louis Gregory, 18 December 1947, Letters of Shoghi Effendi, National Bahá'í Archives, Wilmette, Ill.

2. Emanuel Reimer, memories of Louis Gregory, tape recorded 12 Sept. 1979, National Bahá'í Archives, Wilmette, Ill.

3. Louis Gregory to Chapman, 20 October 1948, Edith M. Chapman Papers, National Bahá'í Archives, Wilmette, Ill.

4. Sprague to National Spiritual Assembly, Horace Holley, secy., 29 December 1948, Office of the Secretary, National Spiritual Assembly of the Bahá'ís of the United States Records, National Bahá'í Archives, Wilmette, Ill.; Louis Gregory to Chapman, 12 January 1949, Chapman Papers.

5. Louis Gregory to Chapman, 30 June 1949, Chapman Papers.

6. Lydia J. Martin and Sarah Martin Pereira, 25 August 1979, "Answers to Questions Asked About The Life and Activities of Mr. Louis Gregory, Hand of the Cause of Baha'u'llah," TS, p. 3, File "Morrison—Louis Gregory correspondence, *World Order* Files, Wilmette, Ill.

7. (Judge) J. Waties Waring to Louis Gregory, 26 April 1950 and 20 November 1950, Louis G. Gregory Papers, National Bahá'í Archives, Wilmette, Ill.; National Spiritual Assembly of the Bahá'ís of the United States, Holley, secy., to Louis Gregory, 26 March 1951, Louis G. Gregory Papers; National Spiritual Assembly, Holley, secy., to Waring (copy), 26 March 1951, Louis G. Gregory Papers.

8. Louis Gregory to Chapman, 14 July 1949, Chapman Papers.

9. Telephone interview with Lauretta Noisette Moore, 8 Mar. 1981.

10. Emanuel Reimer, memories of Louis Gregory.

11. Louis Gregory to Chapman, 27 September 1949, Chapman Papers.

12. Louis Gregory to Chapman, 15 January 1950, Chapman Papers.

13. Gail to *World Order* Editorial Board, Betty J. Fisher, assoc. ed., 25 March 1978, File "Morrison—Louis Gregory correspondence," *World Order* Files.

14. Louis Gregory to Chapman, 16 July 1950 and 9 May 1950, Chapman Papers.

15. Louis Gregory to Chapman, 27 September 1949, Chapman Papers.
16. Gail to *World Order* Editorial Board, Fisher, assoc. ed., 25 March 1978, File "Morrison—Louis Gregory correspondence," *World Order* Files.
17. Louis Gregory to Cox, 13 June 1951, attachment to Cox to *World Order* Editorial Board, Betty J. Fisher, assoc. ed., 2 February 1980, File "Morrison—Louis Gregory correspondence," *World Order* Files; Harlan F. Ober, "Louis G. Gregory," in *The Bahá'í World: A Biennial International Record, Volume XII, 1950–1954,* comp. National Spiritual Assembly of the Bahá'ís of the United States (Wilmette, Ill.: Bahá'í Publishing Trust, 1956), p. 666.
18. Shoghi Effendi, *Citadel of Faith: Messages to America, 1947–1957* (Wilmette, Ill.: Bahá'í Publishing Trust, 1965), p. 163; also published in "Messages from the Guardian," *Bahá'í News,* no. 247 (Sept. 1951), p. 1.
19. Shoghi Effendi, *Citadel of Faith,* p. 98; also published in "Messages from the Guardian: 'Mighty Supplementary Task,' " *Bahá'í News,* no. 250 (Dec. 1951), p. 1.
20. "The Louis G. Gregory Memorial Service," *Bahá'í News,* no. 252 (Feb. 1952), pp. 15–16.
21. Louis G. Gregory, "Racial Unity," Chap. 28: "Conclusion," TS, n. pag., Louis G. Gregory Papers.

Chapter 32 / Pure Gold

1. Diary of Juliet Thompson, "Akka, Summer of 1909," TS, p. 32, entry for 7 July 1909, National Bahá'í Archives, Wilmette, Ill.
2. 'Abdu'l-Bahá to Margaret Döring, trans. 15 August 1911, Tablets of 'Abdu'l-Bahá, National Bahá'í Archives, Wilmette, Ill. (An approved translation of this tablet does not yet exist; consequently, this translation cannot be considered authentic.—Ed.) Also published with revisions in "Progress of the Cause in Germany," *Star of the West,* 2, no. 17 (19 Jan. 1912), 6.
3. 'Abdu'l-Bahá to Louise Gregory, 16 October 1920, Tablets of 'Abdu'l-Bahá; 'Abdu'l-Bahá to Anna Reinke, 16 October 1920, Tablets of 'Abdu'l-Bahá. (Approved translations of these tablets do not yet exist; consequently, these translations cannot be considered authentic.—Ed.)
4. Henrietta Wagner to Lunt, 8 July 1930, Alfred E. Lunt Papers, National Bahá'í Archives, Wilmette, Ill.
5. Elaine Snider Eilers, "Recollections of Hand of the Cause Mr. Louis Gregory," TS, part II, attachment to Margaret Kunz Ruhe to Gayle Morrison, 28 July 1979.
6. Louis G. Gregory, "Racial Amity," in *Bahá'í Year Book, Volume One, 1925–1926,* comp. National Spiritual Assembly of the Bahá'ís of the United States and Canada (New York: Bahá'í Publishing Committee, 1926), p. 169.

7. Louis Gregory to Joseph Hannen, 15 January 1920, Hannen-Knobloch Family Papers, National Bahá'í Archives, Wilmette, Ill.

8. Joseph Hannen to Louis Gregory, 10 December 1919, Louis G. Gregory Papers, National Bahá'í Archives, Wilmette, Ill.

9. "Official Proceedings Twenty-first Annual Convention Baha'is of the United States and Canada held at Baha'i Temple, Wilmette, Illinois, April 26 to 28, 1929," TS, p. 54, National Bahá'í Archives, Wilmette, Ill.; National Spiritual Assembly of the Bahá'ís of the United States, Horace Holley, secy., to Louis Gregory, 23 December 1925, Louis G. Gregory Papers.

10. Bishop to Louis Gregory, 16 August 1927, Louis G. Gregory Papers.

11. Ibid.; Shoghi Effendi to Louis Gregory, 24 October 1933, Letters of Shoghi Effendi, National Bahá'í Archives, Wilmette, Ill.

12. Root to Louise Gregory, 21 August 1926, Louise Gregory Papers, National Bahá'í Archives, Wilmette, Ill.; Louis Gregory to Chapman, 9 February 1931, Edith M. Chapman Papers, National Bahá'í Archives, Wilmette, Ill.

13. Personal interview with Dr. Ugo Giachery, Kauai, Hawaii, 7 Jan. 1981.

14. Wragg to *World Order* Editorial Board, Betty J. Fisher, assoc. ed., 9 March 1973, File "Morrison—Louis Gregory correspondence," *World Order* Files, Wilmette, Ill.

15. Blakely to Roger Dahl, 11 February 1980, Walter H. Blakely Papers, National Bahá'í Archives, Wilmette, Ill.

16. Ibid.

17. Margaret Kunz Ruhe, "Some Recollections of Hand of the Cause Mr. Louis Gregory," TS, p. 1, attachment to Ruhe to Gayle Morrison, 14 May 1979; Roy Williams, memories of Louis Gregory, tape recorded 1975, National Bahá'í Archives, Wilmette, Ill.

18. Gail to *World Order* Editorial Board, Betty J. Fisher, assoc. ed., 25 March 1978, File "Morrison—Louis Gregory correspondence," *World Order* Files.

19. "Eighteenth Annual Convention of the Bahá'ís of the United States and Canada, April 29,–May 2, 1926. Hotel Whitcomb Roof Garden, San Francisco," TS, pp. 393–95, National Bahá'í Archives, Wilmette, Ill.

Index

Index to Places

United States

Other Countries and Continents

General Index

Abbott, Robert S., 28, 150, 207
addresses 1934 Bahá'í convention, 200
'Abdu'l-Bahá
American journey of, in 1912, 27, 49–57
Bahá'í convention addressed during, 37, 55
purpose of, 50–51
death of, 114–15, 144–45, 146
descriptions of
by Juliet Thompson, 53–54
by Louis Gregory, 43–44
devotion of American Bahá'ís to, 30–31, 176
disciples of, bonded together by spiritual comradeship, 317–18
Divine Plan of, 79, 96–100
Gregorys go to Haiti in response to new phase of, 246–47
increased international responsibilities for America in, 97
outpouring of Bahá'í teachers called for by, 79–80, 84
Seven Year Plan extends America's international role, 246–47, 257
Tablets to the Southern states, 84 86, 98, 101–02
unveiled at Convention of Covenant, 97
dream of, about disharmony, 31
European journey of, 50
freed by Young Turks, 41
Louis Gregory and. See Gregory, Louis

race amity conventions initiated by, 132, 134, 136
first convention praised, 142–43
message to first convention, 141
Springfield convention approved, 144–45
race unity affirmed by, 3, 44–48, 51–62, 73, 74, 200–01, 291
demonstrated at society luncheon, 53–54
disastrous consequences of not achieving, 59–60, 129, 142, 180
Howard University speech, 51–52, 53, 139, 287
intermarriage encouraged, 45–46, 62, 63–64, 66–67, 69, 72
linked to world peace, 52, 54
N.A.A.C.P. Convention addressed, 55, 150
positive approach to, 57–58, 60
saddened by lack of race unity among Bahá'ís, 45, 75–76
speeches on, 51–57, 58
story of Isfandíyár, 56–57
writings on, 7, 45–46, 48, 59
separated from believers by World War I, 76, 79, 80–81, 96
Addams, Jane, 55, 150
speech at amity convention, 146
Africa. See Index to Places
Alexander, Will W., 190
Allen, Samuel A., 188, 189, 194
Allison, Thelma, 242–43, 283
American Indians, 276–77, 280
first Eskimo Bahá'í, 280

Gregory, Louis *(continued)*
  gave up profession to become
    itinerant teacher, 85
  income increases during retire-
    ment, 307–08
  means of livelihood after 1932,
    240–42
  sale of house provided funds for
    travel, 85–86
  Shoghi Effendi gives advice on
    work, 236–37
  views on poverty, 94–95, 307
Green Acre, 91, 117, 122, 123,
    184, 185, 186, 254, 278
  Gregory residence near, in Eliot,
    305–06, 308
  importance of, to Louis Gregory,
    49, 297–99, 309
  Louis Gregory Children's School
    dedicated in 1970, 298
Hand of Cause of God, posthu-
    mously appointed as, 310–11
Hannens and. *See* Hannen, Joseph
    and Pauline
health of, 305, 306, 309, 310
Historical Records Cards (Bahá'í
    census), 204
legal training and work
  LL.B. from Howard, 17–18
  partnership with Cobb, 18
  return to, impossible during
    Depression, 223
  turned from, to race amity work,
    7, 85–86
  U.S. Treasury Dept., 18–19, 24
Louis Gregory Children's School,
    298
Louis Gregory Institute, 295
marriage of, to Louisa Mathew,
    63–72, 82
  'Abdu'l-Bahá introduces Louisa,
    43, 46, 64
  accepted by citizens of Eliot, 305
  common interests and purposes
    bound them together, 66,
    71–72

description of ceremony of,
    67–68
difficulties in traveling and living
    together, 70
encouraged by 'Abdu'l-Bahá, 46,
    64, 66–67
first meetings, 43, 46, 64
importance of, 62, 65, 69, 72
negative attitude of many Bahá'ís
    toward, 64–66, 70–71
separations during, due to teach-
    ing trips, 70–71, 88–92, 186
summers together in New Eng-
    land, 91, 186, 254
teaching together in Haiti, 246–51
pilgrimage of, to Bahá'í holy places,
    41–49, 313
pioneering to Haiti, 246–51
  official opposition encountered,
    250
  sponsored by Inter-America
    Committee, 247
race amity conventions, 137–38,
    140, 148, 149, 183–84
  worries about cessation of,
    153–63, 165
race prejudice, 3
  confronted in Washington, D.C.,
    5–6, 30–34, 73, 78, 82
  exhibits patience and tact in deal-
    ing with those having difficulty
    with, 73, 82, 196, 318–19
  shared views on, with Executive
    Board of Bahai Temple Unity,
    130–31
race unity
  'Abdu'l-Bahá asks Louis to work
    for, 34–35, 44–46
  concludes blacks have made
    unique adaptation to America,
    42–43
  constant commitment to, 3–4, 7,
    32, 37–38, 41, 153–63, 177,
    218, 288, 311
  engaged in struggle for racial
    equality, 19, 24, 28–29, 32